Global Shakespeares

The Global Shakespeares series, edited by Alexa Alice Joubin, explores the global afterlife of Shakespearean drama, poetry and motifs in their literary, performative and digital forms of expression in the twentieth and twenty-first centuries. Disseminating big ideas and cutting-edge research in e-book and print formats, this series captures global Shakespeares as they evolve.

Jane Kingsley-Smith ·
W. Reginald Rampone Jr.
Editors

Shakespeare's Global Sonnets

Translation, Appropriation, Performance

Editors
Jane Kingsley-Smith
University of Roehampton
London, UK

W. Reginald Rampone Jr.
Orangeburg, SC, USA

ISSN 2947-8901   ISSN 2947-891X (electronic)
Global Shakespeares
ISBN 978-3-031-09471-2   ISBN 978-3-031-09472-9 (eBook)
https://doi.org/10.1007/978-3-031-09472-9

This Palgrave Macmillan imprint is published by the registered company Springer Nature
Switzerland AG
The registered company address is: Gewerbestrasse 11, 6330 Cham, Switzerland

CONTENTS

NOTES ON CONTRIBUTORS

Chiari Sophie is Professor of Early Modern Literature at Université Clermont, Auvergne, France. She specializes in Shakespeare studies and is the author of *Shakespeare's Representation of Weather, Climate and Environment: The Early Modern "Fated Sky"* (Edinburgh University Press, 2019) and *Shakespeare and the Environment: A Dictionary* (The Arden Shakespeare, Bloomsbury, 2022). She has edited or co-edited several collections of essays including *Spectacular Science, Technology and Superstition in the Age of Shakespeare* with Mickaël Popelard (Edinburgh University Press, 2017), *Freedom and Censorship in Early Modern English Literature* (Routledge, 2018), and *Performances at Court in the Age of Shakespeare* with John Mucciolo (Cambridge University Press, 2019).

Cohen Walter is Professor of English at the University of Michigan, and was previously Professor of Comparative Literature at Cornell University from 1980 to 2014. He is the author of *Drama of a Nation: Public Theater in Renaissance England and Spain* (Cornell UP, 1985) and of *A History of European Literature: The West and the World from Antiquity to the Present* (Oxford UP, 2017), as well as of about 40 articles on various topics. He is also an editor of *The Norton Shakespeare* (W.W. Norton, 1997, 2008, 2015). His current research centers on the literature of ecological catastrophe, with secondary interests in the histories of African and of Jewish literature.

x   NOTES ON CONTRIBUTORS

Cottegnies Line is Professor of Early Modern Literature at Sorbonne Université. She has published widely on seventeenth-century literature, Caroline poetry and early modern women. She has co-edited several collections of essays, for instance, *Women and Curiosity in Early Modern England and France* (Brill, 2016), with Sandrine Parageau. She also works on Elizabethan drama and has published *Henry V: A Critical Guide* (The Arden Shakespeare, Bloomsbury, 2018), with Karen Britland. Moreover, she has edited fifteen plays for Gallimard's bilingual complete works of Shakespeare (*Œuvres complètes*, Bibliothèque de la Pléiade, 2002–2019, 7 vol.) and one play, *2 Henry IV*, for *The Norton Shakespeare 3*. She has co-edited *Robert Garnier in Elizabethan England*, with Marie-Alice Belle (MHRA Tudor and Stuart Translation Series, 2017). Her most recent research interests have included the translation and circulation of texts between England and France. She is currently editing three of Behn's translations from French for the *Complete Works of Aphra Behn*, to be published with Cambridge. She has most recently published a critical anthology of French translations of the Sonnets in *Sonnets et autres poèmes* (*Œuvres complètes*, Gallimard, 2021, Vol. VIII).

de Scarpis Valerio has held the post of Associate Professor of English Literature at the Universities of Padua and then Venice, Italy, and is Fellow of the Venice Ca' Foscari International College. He has published on Elizabethan and Jacobean poetics and the epistemic background of the late Renaissance (including the Elizabethan cult of the Sovereign). He has devoted particular attention to the Sonnet, to the poetic theory and practice of Thomas Campion, and to the poetic and dramatic development of Shakespeare's art, starting from the enigma of the so-called "Lost Years".

Drozd David is Assistant Professor at the Department of Theatre Studies, Faculty of Arts, Masaryk University and at the Theatre Faculty of Janáček Academy of Performing Arts in Brno, Czech Republic. His main research and teaching interests are the theory of drama and theatre, the Prague structuralist school, modern and post-modern directing, and performance analysis. He co-ordinated two subsequent research projects, "Theory of Theatre: Czech Structural Thought on Theatre: Context and Potency" (2011–2015) and "Theatre as a Synthesis of the Arts: Otakar Zich in Context of Modern Science and Contemporary Potential of His Concepts" (2016–2018). He also works occasionally as a dramaturge and translator (with a focus on British drama): Liz Lochhead, Sarah Kane, David Harrower, Martin Crimp, Sue Glover, and David Greig.

Ellis Jim is Professor of English at the University of Calgary and director of the Calgary Institute for the Humanities. He has written books on Early Modern English poetry, including *Sexuality and Citizenship: Metamorphosis in Elizabethan Erotic Verse* (U. of Toronto P, 2003) and the forthcoming monograph, *The Poem, the Garden and the World: Poetry and Performativity in Elizabethan England* (Northwestern UP, 2022). He has also written on British cinema, most extensively on the artist, writer, and filmmaker Derek Jarman, including the book *Derek Jarman's Angelic Conversations* (Minnesota UP, 2009).

Ingham Mike is a former Professor of English Studies in the English Department at Lingnan University in Hong Kong and currently works as Adjunct professor with Chinese University of Hong Kong. His principal areas of research expertise are in theatre, film, and poetry-to-song adaptation, especially in the context of Shakespeare Studies. He is a founder member of *Theatre Action*, a company specializing in action research on dramatic texts. His research and publication fields explore the relationship between song and literary works, stage and screen drama, drama in education and documentary film. His article "'The true concord of well-tuned sounds': Musical adaptations of the sonnets" was published in *Shakespeare* (Taylor and Francis) in 2012, and his 2017 monograph for Routledge, *Stageplay and Screenplay: The Intermediality of Theatre and Cinema*, incorporated a number of Shakespeare case studies and theatre broadcasts. His latest monograph, in preparation, deals with literary intertextuality in Anglophone popular song.

Joubin Alexa Alice is Professor of English at George Washington University in Washington, D.C., where she co-founded the Digital Humanities Institute. Her latest books include *Shakespeare and East Asia* (Oxford University Press, 2021); *Race* (Routledge's New Critical Idiom, co-authored with Martin Orkin, 2019); *Local and Global Myths in Shakespearean Performance* (co-edited with Aneta Mancewicz, 2018); and *Shakespeare and the Ethics of Appropriation* (co-edited with Elizabeth Rivlin, 2014).

Keinänen Nely is Senior Lecturer in the Department of Languages at the University of Helsinki and has published widely on Shakespeare in Finland. In Finnish, she is the editor of a special issue of *Synteesi* ([Journal of the Finnish Semiotics Society], 2016) on Shakespeare in Finland, and *Shakespeare Suomessa* [Shakespeare in Finland] (WSOY, 2010), a collection of essays by translators, directors, and actors on doing Shakespeare in Finland. At present, with Per Sivefors (Linnaeus University, Sweden), she is editing a two-volume collection of essays on the early reception of Shakespeare in the Nordic countries, covering the 19th and early 20th centuries (Bloomsbury). She has published articles in *Shakespeare, Multicultural Shakespeare*, and *English Text Construction*, and in volumes with Oxford University Press and Routledge. She has also translated over thirty contemporary Finnish plays into English.

Khair Tabish is Associate Professor of English Literature at Aarhus University, Denmark, and author of multiple works of fiction and poetry, including a recent e-book of rewritings of Shakespeare's Sonnets (*Quarantined Sonnets: Sex, Money and Shakespeare*, Kitaab, 2020). He is also the author of studies including *Babu Fictions: Alienation in Indian English Novels* (Oxford UP, 2001), *The Gothic, Postcolonialism and Otherness* (Palgrave, 2009), and *The New Xenophobia* (Oxford UP, 2016). He is the winner of the All India Poetry Prize and other awards and fellowships. His fiction has also been shortlisted for more than 20 national and international awards and translated into seven languages.

Kingsley-Smith Jane is Professor of Shakespeare Studies at the University of Roehampton, London. She is the author of three monographs: *Shakespeare's Drama of Exile* (Palgrave, 2003), *Cupid in Early Modern Literature and Culture* (Cambridge, 2010), and the first book-length study of the Sonnets' reception, *The Afterlife of Shakespeare's Sonnets* (Cambridge, 2019). She has edited *Love's Labor's Lost* for the Norton 3 Shakespeare (2015) and *John Webster and John Ford: The Duchess of Malfi, The White Devil, The Broken Heart and 'Tis Pity She's a Whore* for Penguin (2014). She will shortly edit Shakespeare's Sonnets for the new *Cambridge Shakespeare Editions*.

Krajník Filip is Assistant Professor at the Department of English and American Studies, Faculty of Arts, Masaryk University in Brno, Czech Republic. His main areas of interest are late medieval English poetry, English Renaissance theatre and English theatre of the Restoration period. Recently, he has co-authored a chapter for Nicoleta Cinpoeş, Florence March and Paul Prescott's volume *Shakespeare on European Festival Stages* (Bloomsbury, 2022). He is currently editing a volume entitled *Restoration Reshaping: Shifting Forms, Genres and Conventions in English Theatre, 1660–1737* (Charles University Press, forthcoming). His translation of *Hamlet* into Czech premiered in South Bohemian Theatre in České Budějovice in 2022 (dir. Jakub Čermák).

Laghi Simona received her Ph.D. in English Literature, with Doctor Europaeus certification in 2018, from Roma Tre University with a thesis entitled "Dress and Law in Shakespeare's Plays". Her research interests lie in the field of law and literature with a focus on Shakespeare, equity, material culture, especially dress, intangible cultural heritage, and ELT. She is the author of "Utopias in *The Tempest*" (*Pólemos, Journal of Law, Literature and Culture*, 11 (1), 2017), "La rappresentazione della verità nel *Julius Caesar* di Shakespeare" ("Representing the Truth in Shakespeare's *Julius Caesar*") in the volume *Shakespeare e la Modernità*, 2018, and "Witchcraft, Demonic Possession and Exorcism: The Problem of Evidence in Two Shakespearean Plays" (*Journal of Early Modern Studies*, Vol. 10, 2021).

Lehtonen Jussi is Artistic Designer of the Finnish National Theatre's Touring Stage, where he also works as a director and an actor. The troupe takes theatre performances out on the road to places like health care institutions and prisons, and contributes community-oriented documentary theatre to the National Theatre's repertoire. His latest works as director are *Undocumented Love* (2020), *Other Home* (2017), and *Vapauden kauhu* [Fear of Freedom] (2015). Lehtonen defended his Theatre Arts Ph.D. on the actor's contact with audiences living in care facilities in 2015 at The Theatre Academy of The University of Arts, Helsinki. His writing credits include "Documentary Theatre as a Platform for Hope and Social Justice" in Eeva Anttila and Anniina Suominen (eds.) *Critical Articulations of Hope*, Routledge 2018; "Imagining What it is Like to be You: Challenges of a Hybrid Community" (Nordisk dramapedagogisk tidsskrift 2019) and *Samassa valossa: näyttelijäntyö hoitolaitoskiertueella* (Avain 2010) [Under the Same Lights: An Actor on Tour in Care Facilities]. He was given the Art Award of The Finnish Ministry of Culture in 2011 and the Helsinki City Artist Award in 2020.

Levi Melih is Assistant Professor in the Department of Western Languages and Literatures at Boğaziçi University in Istanbul. He studies English, Irish, and Turkish modern poetry, as well as connections between poetics in the modern period and the Renaissance.

Minier Márta is Associate Professor of Theatre and Media Drama at the University of South Wales, UK. Her research interests include Shakespeare reception, Translation Studies, Adaptation Studies, biopics and biographical drama. Her relevant publications include *Hamlet and Poetry*

(*New Readings* 2012, co-edited with Ruth J. Owen), *(Re)Translations: Diachronic and Synchronic Perspectives on Giving New Voice to Shakespeare* (*Multicultural Shakespeare* 2017, co-edited with Lily Kahn), and *Shakespeare and Tourism: Place, Memory, Participation* (co-edited with Maddalena Pennacchia, 2019). Márta is joint editor of the *Journal of Adaptation in Film & Performance*.

Oya Reiko is Professor of English at Keio University, Tokyo. She is the author of *Representing Shakespearean Tragedy: Garrick, the Kembles and Kean* (2007), and publishes extensively on Shakespeare's reception in the 18th through to the 20th century. Her work on the Sonnets includes "'Or was it Sh-p-re?': Shakespeare in the Manuscript of Virginia Woolf's *To the Lighthouse*", in Gordon McMullan, Lena Cowen Orlin, and Virginia Mason Vaughan, eds., *Women Making Shakespeare: Text, Reception, Performance* (2014); "Scar on the Face: Ted Hughes Reads Shakespeare's Sonnets", in Hannah Crawforth, Elizabeth Scott-Baumann, and Clare Whitehead, eds., *Sonnets: The State of Play* (2017); and "'Talk to Him': Wilde, his Friends and Shakespeare's Sonnets", in Paul Franssen and Paul Edmondson, eds., *Shakespeare and His Biographical Afterlives* (2020). She frequently contributes to *Shakespeare Survey*, where her most recent articles are "Authenticating the Inauthentic: Edmond Malone as Editor of the Apocryphal Shakespeare" (2016); and "The Comedy of Hamlet in Nazi-Occupied Warsaw: An Exploration of Lubitsch's *To Be or Not To Be* (1942)" (2019).

Pfister Manfred was Professor of English at the Freie Universität, Berlin, and Guest Professor at the universities of Vienna, Gdansk and Dartmouth College and is a member of the Berlin-Brandenburgische Akademie der Wissenschaften. He was co-editor of the *Shakespeare Jahrbuch* and *Poetica* and author of *Das Drama. Theorie und Analyse* (Munich, 1982; Engl.: CUP, 1988). Among his more recent book publications are *Laurence Sterne* (2001), *A History of English Laughter* (2002), *Performing National Identity: Anglo-Italian Transactions* (2008), *Shakespeare's Sonnets Global, A Quatercentenary Anthology* (2009, 2014), *Dialoge zwischen Wissenschaft, Kunst und Literatur in der Renaissance* (2011), *Heroen und Heroisierungen in der Renaissance* (2013) and editions of Bruce Chatwin's *In Patagonia* (2003), Samuel Butler's *Notebooks* (2005), Shelley's *Zastrozzi* (2009) and Sir Thomas Browne's *Urne Buriall and Selected Writings* (2014) and *Englische Lyrik des Fin de siècle* (2019). He is also a translator and, as such, one of the German voices of Robert Lowell (1982), Ezra Pound (*Die Cantos*, 2012), and John Clare (2021). Together with linguist Ekkehard König, he has written a book on *Literary Analysis and Linguistics* (2017). Since his retirement, he has spent half of his time in the Italian Maremma, where he pursues, among others, Anglo-Italian crossways.

Rampone Jr. W. Reginald is Associate Professor of English at South Carolina State University. He has published *Sexuality in the Age of Shakespeare* (ABC-Clio, 2010), and he has co-edited with Professor Barbara Solomon, Emerita, at Iona College *An African Quilt: 24 Modern African Stories* (Signet Classic, 2012). He has published many book reviews in *The Sixteenth-Century Journal.* He is currently working on a critical edition of Shackerley Marmion's *Hollands Leaguer.*

Refskou Anne Sophie is Research Assistant at Aarhus University, Denmark, where she teaches comparative literature. She has published on global and intercultural Shakespeare reception, including *Eating Shakespeare: Cultural Anthropophagy as Global Methodology*, co-edited with Vinicius Mariano de Carvalho and Marcel Alvaro de Amorim (Arden Shakespeare, Bloomsbury, 2019). She is currently completing a monograph on Shakespeare and compassion in early modern culture.

Salkeld Duncan is Professor Emeritus of Shakespeare and Renaissance Literature at the University of Chichester and Visiting Professor at the University of Roehampton. He is author of three monographs: *Madness and Drama in the Age of Shakespeare* (Manchester University Press, 1993), *Shakespeare Among the Courtesans: Prostitution, Literature and Drama 1500–1650* (Ashgate, 2012), and *Shakespeare and London* (Oxford University Press, 2018). He is currently co-editing a collection of essays on *Arden of Faversham.*

Schober Katalin is Junior Professor of Language Education at the University of Konstanz, Germany. She received her Ph.D. in English Literature and Culture from Humboldt University, Berlin, and worked as a teacher of English and French at grammar schools in Frankfurt (O.) and Potsdam. Her research interests focus on questions of literary and media literacies, intermediality, transculturality, and diversity. Her publications include a monograph on eighteenth-century travellers touring Greece and the Levant as well as articles about Language Education.

Steenson Allison L. received her Ph.D. Eu. from the University of Padua and is currently an MSCA researcher in British literature at the Centre for Medieval and Early Modern Studies, University of Sussex. Her work has focused on British Early Modern literature, Jacobean court literature, and on the meter and stylistic features of the sonnet form in English. More recently, she has been working on the Hawthornden manuscripts of William Fowler, the subject of her first monograph (Routledge 2021), and on Scoto-British Jacobean writers. She has contributed to research and museum projects focusing on archival and manuscript material, and on early printed books.

Szele Bálint graduated in 2001 as a teacher of English and completed his Ph.D. in 2006 defending his thesis about Hungarian translations of Shakespeare's plays. Since 2004 he has worked for Kodolányi János University as a lecturer and has been responsible for talent management at the university. His interests include language development, translation, intercultural communication, and literary history. His two books on Shakespeare are *"To converse with him that is wise"—11 Interviews with Hungarian Translators of Shakespeare* (2008, in Hungarian) and *Lőrinc Szabó's Shakespeare Translations* (2012, in Hungarian). In his free time, he plays the drums, goes hiking, or reads about astronomy.

Trissino Luca is a Ph.D. student and Assistant at the Institute of Italian Studies (ISI), University of Italian Switzerland, Lugano. He has earned a master's degree in Modern Philology at the University of Padua and is currently pursuing a second master's degree in Art History at the University of Trent. He has taught Italian language and literature at college level in Vicenza. His research interests include the poetic language of the twentieth century and its formal manifestations, modern Italian literature, and its relations to European literatures. He has recently published his first monograph (*Luigi Fallacara e gli ermetismi. Lingua, stile e metrica*, QuiEdit, 2020).

Weiss Stefan is Professor of historical musicology at the Hochschule für Musik, Theater und Medien Hannover (Hanover University of Music, Drama and Media), Germany. Since his graduation from the University of Cologne with the dissertation *Die Musik Philipp Jarnachs* (1997), he has published on a wide spectrum of 20th-century musical styles. Specializing in the field of Russian and Soviet music, his research is mainly devoted to the composer Dmitri Shostakovich on the one hand and musical relations between Russia and the West on the other. Recently he has edited a collection of essays *Deutsch-russische Musikbegegnungen 1917–1933* (2021). A German handbook on Shostakovich (co-edited with Dorothea Redepenning) is in preparation.

LIST OF FIGURES

LIST OF TABLES

CHAPTER 1

Shakespeare's Global Sonnets: An Introduction

W. Reginald Rampone Jr.

The sonnet and the sonnet sequence or cycle have long been a staple of the literary landscape in Britain. The English or Elizabethan sonnet had been very popular throughout the sixteenth century, when one of its most notable uses was as a means by which young men communicated their heartfelt affection for their beloveds. I recall being told as an undergraduate that some 300,000 sonnets had been composed during the English Renaissance. One could easily imagine a young man with aristocratic pretentions penning a sonnet to his lady love, but one must wonder how such a numerical determination could have been made by literary historians, but apparently it was. From Sir Philip Sidney's *Astrophil and Stella* to Edmund Spenser's *Amoretti* to Michael Drayton's *Idea* to Lady Mary Wroth's *Pamphilia to Amphilanthus*, the early modern period abounds with brilliant sonnet sequences.

W. R. Rampone Jr. (✉)
Richmond, VA, USA
e-mail: regrampone@yahoo.com

© The Author(s), under exclusive license to Springer Nature Switzerland AG 2023
J. Kingsley-Smith and W. R. Rampone Jr. (eds.), *Shakespeare's Global Sonnets*, Global Shakespeares, https://doi.org/10.1007/978-3-031-09472-9_1

1

While Shakespeare was the composer of some 154 sonnets, which comprised his sonnet sequence, he also included sonnets in his plays, where they are penned by love-sick young men. Paul Edmondson and Stanley Wells assert that "The most heavily sonnet-laden of all Shakespeare's plays is *Love's Labour's Lost*, written we believe around 1594–5, at the height of the fashion for sonnet writing" (2020, 11). The climax of the play arrives when the King of Navarre and the three courtiers overhear each other reciting sonnets that they have written to ladies whom they claim to love. Certainly, they are not the last male characters in a Shakespearean play to make such attempts at writing sonnets. Orlando in *As You Like It* is chastised by Jaques for attaching sonnets to trees in the Forest of Arden. Even Hamlet's attempt at writing a sonnet to Ophelia is criticized by Polonius for his use of the "vile" phrase, "beautified Ophelia." Benedick, in *Much Ado About Nothing*, is yet another inept composer of sonnets, who has finally admitted to himself that he loves Beatrice and laments his inability to express his love in verse: "Marry, I cannot show it in rhyme; I have tried; I can find out no rhyme to 'lady' but 'baby,' an innocent rhyme; for 'scorn,' 'horn,' a hard rhyme; for 'school,' 'fool,' a babbling rhyme; very ominous endings; no, I was not born under a rhyming planet, nor I cannot woo in festival terms" (5.2.33–39) (147). Yet, in the same play, as Edmondson and Wells point out, Claudio hangs an epitaph on Hero's funeral monument, "which has the rhyme scheme of a sonnet sestet (though it is written in trochaic tetrameters, not the usual iambic pentameters) which is followed by an additional couplet" (13). This is followed by lines that form a quatrain, and then another quatrain. Perhaps the most archetypal of all Shakespeare's couples is Romeo and Juliet, who express their love for each other via a sonnet when they initially meet at the Capulets' masked ball. Marjorie Garber describes this as a "most unusual sonnet, in that it is spoken by two people, and thus breaks the convention of the love sonnet of the adoring lover who writes of, and to, his beloved because he cannot reach her in person, whether she is married to someone else, or because she insists (like Rosaline) on remaining chaste" (2005, 194).

Shakespeare's sonnet sequence is highly unusual in the period for refusing to name its beloved(s), generating considerable interest in the real-life prototypes for these "characters." Alvin Kernan praises the sonnets as "the supreme love poems of the English language, and attention has long focused almost exclusively on their exquisite language and subtle feelings" (1995, 172), but he goes on to refer to the "older, socially inferior poet" and the "aristocratic young patron." John Kerrigan observes that, "When the Sonnets appeared in 1609 they were introduced by a dedication which included [the Earl of] Southampton's initials in reverse" (2006, 73), though he questions whether the initials, W. H., refer to Henry Wriothesley or to Shakespeare's future patron, William Herbert, third Earl of Pembroke, to an unidentified man, or a fictive personage (74). How we answer these questions will influence how we interpret the poems as a whole, but at the same time, "the answers will also be shaped by the experience of grappling with particular poems" (74).

The purported division between the first 126 sonnets, supposedly addressed to the young man, and the remaining 28 sonnets, addressed to the proverbial "dark lady," dates back to 1780 when Edmund Malone edited the Quarto (Kingsley-Smith 2019, 2). This bipartite division of the sonnet sequence has been a source of contention for many years. Writing the introduction for the Signet edition of the sonnets in 1964, W. H. Auden noted the seeming division within the sonnet sequence, but he also noticed that not all of the sonnets appeared to be in correct chronological order, as Sonnets 40 and 42 "must be more or less contemporary with 144 and 152" (xxi). Even if readers were to take the first 17 sonnets of this sonnet sequence as one thematic cluster, Sonnet 15 does not belong in this unit as it does not mention marriage (xxi). Literary scholars, however, are slowly changing their minds regarding this bipartite division within the sonnets, just as Auden did 58 years ago.

In *The Afterlife of Shakespeare's Sonnets,* Jane Kingsley-Smith suggests that "the reasons why we continue to perpetuate a bipartite division are varied but include the fact that 'it is easier to discuss these poems critically if one can determine to whom they refer and what story they tell.' It certainly makes them easier to teach" (3). Likewise, editors have seen fit through the ages to change whatever they considered necessary about the sonnets. For example, John Benson thought it was best in his 1640 edition of the sonnets to change "pronouns from male to female in Sonnet 101 and [he] replaced 'boy' with 'love' in Sonnet 108" (Kingsley-Smith 3), but Benson was not the last editor to change the gender of the male addressee. We will see in Line Cottegnie's essay, "The Rival Poet and the Literary Tradition: Translating Shakespeare's *Sonnets* in French" that Leon de Wailly "changed the gender of the addressee to female in two sonnets, even though he also argued that the sonnets to the dark lady were at least as immoral as the ones to the young man, if not more."

Edmondson and Wells have brilliantly cut the Gordian knot regarding the sexuality of the speaker in the sonnets by suggesting that he is actually bisexual: "Whilst some critics have focused on reading Shakespeare's Sonnets through a gay lens, relatively few have celebrated them as the seminal bisexual texts of literature in English" (31). They cite Marjorie Garber's bisexual reading of the sonnets and her challenge to critical orthodoxy: "Why avoid the obvious? *Because* it is the obvious? Or because a bisexual Shakespeare fits no one's erotic agenda?" (31).

Regardless of what controversy engages the world of Shakespearean studies, people from all over the globe will continue to read Shakespeare's sonnets in their own unique fashion, just as the speaker in Sonnet 18 states in the couplet, "So long as men can breathe, or eyes can see,/ So long lives this, and this gives life to thee." In keeping with the theme of the globality of these sonnets and their applicability to all nations and nationalities, Kingsley-Smith makes clear in her own essay, "'Mine is Another Voyage': Global Encounters with Shakespeare's Sonnets," how Shakespeare's sonnets have migrated from the British Isles to every region of the world. In many ways, this collection of essays demonstrates not only the on-going popularity of these sonnets throughout the globe, but also how powerfully they affect and influence those who read them or watch them performed in front of live actors. These essays are extraordinarily wide-ranging, taking readers from Helsinki to Hong Kong and from Italy to India. They are not simply interpretative analyses of the sonnets as printed texts, but consider the treatment of these sonnets in both the dramatic and cinematic spheres. In Nely Keinanen and Jussi Lehtonen's essay, "Institutions of Love and Death: Shakespeare's Sonnets in Elderly Care Facilities," Keinanen describes how Lehtonen poignantly performed these sonnets in convalescent homes for the entertainment of the sick and elderly, who responded very powerfully to the themes of love, loss, and death. Lehtonen reported that one nurse thought that his performance of the sonnets was "not suitable for old people's homes. 'Because the residents prefer very traditional art.'" It is hard for me to envision more "traditional art" than Shakespeare's sonnets, but, be that as it may, the residents in these convalescent homes were greatly moved by Lehtonen's performances. Obviously, not all of the essays in this volume pull upon one's heartstrings as this essay does, but this particular essay shows how the sonnets can be put to use in a therapeutic, salutary, and practical fashion and do not necessarily function as rarified, literary documents that bear little if any relation to the experiences of ordinary women and men.

In another example of an essay that renders the sonnets in an unexpectedly beautiful fashion, "Reclaiming the Sonnets in *The Angelic Conversation*: Derek Jarman's Queer Home Movies," Jim Ellis invites us into the extraordinary world of this gay, British independent filmmaker. Jarman created a truly magical, dramatic iteration of the sonnets in his film, *The Angelic Conversation*, which depicts a gay male relationship set in an Elizabethan manor while the actors wear the conventional attire of men in the 1980s. This was a truly ground-breaking cinematic rendition of two gay men interacting with each other, as veteran British actress, Judi Dench, read 14 of the 154 sonnets in such a way as to structure a relationship between the two men. This film, made in 1985, was especially apropos given the outbreak of AIDS in the gay community at this time. The two essays written by Keinanen and Lehtonen and Ellis serve as powerful examples of how the contributors to this collection have interpreted the various ways in which the sonnets have been taken out of the study and into the lives of ordinary men and women.

Global Translations: Defining the Nation, Refining Poetics

Line Cottegnie's essay, "The Rival Poet and the Literary Tradition: Translating Shakespeare's *Sonnets* in French," offers an extraordinary overview of the chronology of the various translators who have tackled these sonnets. As she states: "This chapter offers a comprehensive study of the translation history of Shakespeare's *Sonnets* over 200 years. Focusing on several key aspects of the cultural and literary history, it shows how translating Shakespeare's sonnets has often been a way of confronting the ultimately canonical 'rival poet,' but also of challenging the French literary tradition." She addresses the major concerns that have troubled translators over the centuries, specifically the "sonnets' autobiographical nature, the elusive identities of the addressees, and the enigmatic narrative thread," as well as the sonnets' perceived homosexuality. Nevertheless, Shakespeare's sonnets have been perceived as the "ultimate touchstone, a holy grail of poetry" by nineteenth and twentieth century French translators.

Just as Cottegnie is concerned with the history of the translation of Shakespeare's sonnets, so too are Allison L. Steenson and Luca Trissino in their essay, "A Stylistic Analysis of Montale's Version of Sonnet 33: Translation, Petrarchism and Innovation in Modern Italian Poetry." They

observe early on in the discussion that "The text of sonnet 33 as translated by Montale provides a clear illustration of one of the main aspects
of literary translation, i.e. its functioning as a site for cultural mediation and providing a space for the negotiation of cultural (linguistic,
ideological) constructs." As in Cottegnie's essay, Steenson and Trissino
emphasize how Shakespeare's poetry "inform[s] modern literary traditions in languages other than English." Montale uses a paradigm based
upon the "high style of the Italian tradition, while at the same time
treasuring Shakespeare's formal exhortations and adapting the idea of
faithfulness to the form of his own poetic score." The essay offers an
extremely fine close reading of Sonnet 33, which is virtuosic in its exacting
textual analysis.

Valerio de Scarpis's essay, "Addressing Complexity: Variants and the
Challenge of Rendering Shakespeare's Sonnet 138 into Italian," first
discusses the differences between the version of this sonnet that appeared
as the first poem in the 1599 *Passionate Pilgrim* miscellany and its later
inclusion in the 1609 Quarto collection as No. 138. What is most striking
about this essay, apart from the support it offers to the idea of Shakespeare as a reviser of his sonnets, is the wide range of rhetorical terms that
de Scarpis deploys, employing such terms as polyptoton, chiasmus, polysemy, and syntactic amphibology. He makes clear that the major division
within the poem concerns the (in)sincerity *vs* sexual (mis) behavior of the
speaker and his interlocutor, and explores the implications of the sonnet's
textual variants. Subsequent translators follow two precisely defined interpretations: "that of a straightforward, more candid reading, and that of a
probing, malicious reading, both substantially legitimized by the ambivalence of the text." De Scarpis examines three modern Italian translations
of Sonnet 138 in detail to demonstrate how divergent interpretations can
be.

Balint Szele, too, provides a wonderfully comprehensive overview of
the history of the translation of the sonnets in his country in "'Far
from Variation or Quick Change': Classical and New Translations of
Shakespeare's Sonnets in Hungary." In the first complete edition of
Shakespeare's works, the sonnets finally appeared in print thanks to
Karoly Szasz (1829–1905) and Vilmos Gyory (1838–1885). Although
their sonnets "follow[] the form and structure of the original," Szele
informs us that "the imagery is weak, the language is contorted, many
metaphors and puns are omitted, moods and feelings are not conveyed
adequately." It was Lorinc Szabo, who, in 1921, "translated all of the

sonnets into a contemporary, modern, clear Hungarian version." Since Szabo's translation, others have tried their hand, and Szele focuses on three contemporary poets—Tibor Csillag, Anna Szabo T., and Sandor Fazekas—all of whom demonstrate their appreciation of the sonnets' complexity.

Melih Levi's essay, "*Sonnets* in Turkish: Shakespeare's Syllables, Halman's Syllabics," focuses on Talat Sait Halman's translation of the sonnets in Turkish from a "comparative prosody angle." Halman chose "syllabic verse, one of two dominant metrical structures in Turkish poetry, the other being *aruz*, a quantitative scheme based on syllable length." Levi notes that both Shakespeare and Halman chose meters that "had claims of nationalism, nativity, and plainness attached to them." Once the modern Turkish Republic was founded, reforms in language were introduced, which solidified the movement for syllabic verse. Although Halman had his doubts about syllabics, he finally decided upon 14 syllable lines with a caesura in the middle: "Syllabics proves perfect for capturing this tension between experiential stability and variability, between sustained conviction and self-deception." Levi's essay sustains a cogent and compelling argument about the superiority of syllabics over *aruz* in the translation of Shakespeare's sonnets into Turkish and raises the question of whether Halman's translations influenced the syllabic renaissance of the 1990s. He concludes that "a comparative approach to debates concerning verse and poetic form in these divergent contexts [of Shakespeare and Halman] reveals conceptual engagements that are strikingly similar in nature: the association of syllabic verse with plainness, a native style, nationalism, and a desire toward epigrammatic rhetoric." Levi's essay provides his audience with a wonderfully comprehensive understanding of Turkish poetics regarding the sonnets that readers will appreciate for years to come.

In Tabish Khair and Anne Sophie Refskou's essay, "New Words: Language and Shakespeare's *Sonnets* in the Global South," we move even further south and east as the sonnets travel into India, the Caribbean, and Brazil. Khair and Refskou begin with the translation work of Rabindranath Tagore, who was greatly influenced by Shakespeare's sonnets and plays, and acknowledge also the Malayalam critic and writer, K. Satchidanandan, who has recently published verse and prose translations of the sonnets. Looking back to the 1930s, Khair and Refskou discuss Una Marson's "Caribbean engagements with the sonnets" in her *Tropic Reveries,* which "evoke a Shakespearean presence." Moving on to

Brazil, they consider the work of Geraldo Carneiro, who has translated the sonnets in *O Discurso do Amor Rasgado* (*Speeches of torn love*). Finally, in the global North of Canada, Sonnet L'Abbé, writing as a mixed-race Canadian woman, "draws on the poetics of erasure to rewrite the Sonnets, but she does so by rearranging each letter of the original Shakespearean sonnet into a new, and lengthier prose version which subsumes and overwrites the original." Khair and Refskou conclude that "this text-centered network ... is a diverse, global Shakespearean textuality," and most certainly, that is exactly what a "Global Shakespearean" community is.

Reiko Oya's essay, "The Pauper Prince Translates Shakespeare's Sonnets: Ken'ichi Yoshida and the Poetics/Politics of Post-war Japan," examines Yoshida's engagement with the Sonnets, "against the backdrop of the rapidly democratizing Japanese society of the late 1940s through the 60 s." Oya's essay takes us from Yoshida's initial interest in Shakespeare's poetry because of his fascination with line 4 of Sonnet 18 through to the rewriting of his book, *English Literature,* in a colloquial style. The translator of 50 full-length books, Yoshida was most well-known for his 1955 translation of 43 of the 154 sonnets. He uses two different second-person pronouns so that his perceptions of the young man and the Dark Lady are more clearly shown—his view of the Dark Lady being overtly misogynistic. Oya concludes her essay by arguing that Yoshida's translation of Shakespeare's sonnets "created a new language for contemporary Japanese society," as well as influencing contemporary poets and the language that they used to create their own art. Her overview of post-war politics and poetics in Japan is both engaging and edifying, an intellectual delight for anyone interested in the assimilation of Shakespeare's sonnets into Japanese literary culture.

Alexa Joubin's essay, "Translational Agency in Liang Shiqui's *Sonnets*," discusses the problematic process of translating Shakespeare's sonnets into a language that is not Anglo-European. Citing the scholarship of Stephen Ullmann, Joubin discusses the linguistic challenges of translating a European language into Chinese because it does not have the same "patterns of sound symbolism." Liang was the first literary scholar to translate all of Shakespeare's work into Chinese, driven by two commitments: to "the role of translation in extending the life of the canon" and to "enriching the Chinese vernacular, a new form he promotes through the translation of pre-modern English literature." Liang was very fortunate to have patronage from Hu Shi, an important philosopher, who encouraged

Liang in his translation of Shakespeare's plays and poetry, during his time in Taiwan, where he lived having fled China. Joubin argues that Liang and Hu's goal was to "elevate the status of the vernacular." His decision to use gender-neutral pronouns anticipates Paul Edmondson and Stanley Wells' claim that the "addressees in many sonnets cannot always be gendered because the context is fluid and ambiguous." Joubin concludes her essay by arguing that Liang's "concept of community" reflects that of the French philosopher, Jean-Luc Nancy, and that Liang "expand[s] the meanings of the Sonnets and the vernacular without subjugating one to the other." In many ways, this essay forces one to reflect upon the in-betweenness of translation, as both texts strive to provide as accurate a reflection of reality as their particular language is able to provide.

Sonnets in Performance: Theatre, Film, and Music

Filip Krajnik and David Drozd's essay, "Playing the Poems: Five Faces of Shakespeare's Sonnets on Czech Stages," once again takes us into the realm of the theatrical performance of the sonnets, represented here by five twenty-first century productions. In the program for the 2001 production *Sonety, panove, sonety! (Sonnets, Gentlemen, Sonnets!)*, the dramaturge, Zora Vondrackova, explains the play's feminocentric perspective: "In 28 pieces, addressed as the Dark lady is a woman mainly subjected to reproach for the suffering that she causes to the poet and his friend ... These sonnets are concerned with the fear of death, the changes of time that affects both the human soul and body, and other more general issues, and one can find consolation in the hope that, when writing this rich poetry, Shakespeare had women in mind as well." This production's *mise en scène* was a women's prison, a "world of men that dominates and objectifies women." The second production in question, written by Lucie Trmikova and directed by Jan Nebesky in 2013, was entitled *Kabaret Shakespeare (The Shakespeare Cabaret)*. Three principal characters appear: "the Poet, the fair Youth, the addressee of the first group, and the mysterious Dark Lady, the addressee of the second group," and the performance focused upon the sexuality of the relationships. In 2017, the producers of the Municipal Theatre of Mlada Boleslav (Central Bohemia) transformed the sonnets into a narrative of Every Man and Every Woman in a production entitled *Sonety (The Sonnets)*. Krajnik and Drozd juxtapose this production with one performed at the Viola

Theatre in Prague, entitled *Svatecni Shakespearova posta* (*Shakespeare's Festive Letters*), in which the poet and director, Milos Horansky, impersonates Shakespeare and meets Martin Hilsky, the most significant and well-known translator of Shakespeare's sonnets. The final production that they critique is a 2019 production in Dlouha Theatre in Prague, entitled *Sonety* (*Sonnets*). These spellbinding dramatic performances will forever change audiences' understanding of the sonnets.

Marta Minier's essay, "'Not for the Faint Hearted': Volcano Theatre's *L.O.V.E.* as a Physical Theatre Adaptation of Shakespeare's Sonnets" explores the play created and first performed by a Welsh experimental theatre company in 1987. This "narrative dramatization" of the sonnets was written for three actors, the Lovely Boy, the Poet, and the Dark Lady. Minier describes the controversy caused by *L.O.V.E.* on account of its inclusion of a male-male kiss and locates it within the context of Volcano's approach to physical theatre, in which the "'sexiness' of corporeality" is stressed "over the weight of erudition." The actors in this production of the sonnets interrogated "bourgeois theatre-going habits" by invasive interactions with the audience: kissing them, sitting in their laps, or through some other form of intimate interaction. By doing so, Volcano Theatre challenged the audience's notion of what constituted appropriate actor-audience behavior.

In moving from spoken word to music, Manfred Pfister's essay, "'Music to Hear...': From Shakespeare to Stravinsky," explores Sonnet 8 as adapted for musical performance. The first section explores the similarities and differences between two music-themed sonnets, 8 and 128. In Sonnet 128, the speaker "stages a living genre scene in which the lover watches his lady perform on a virginal," focusing on a particular object "close to erogenous parts of the beloved's body," while in Sonnet 8 the speaker implores the beautiful young man to marry. In his discussion of Igor Stravinsky's adaptation of Sonnet 8, Pfister notes how he changed the older male speaker's voice to that of a female, a mezzo-soprano. Stravinsky made this change in order to transform the young man's narcissism into the woman's voice as wooer. Pfister believes that Stravinsky is "working with, and against, Shakespeare's poem at the same time, marking historical distance and difference while attempting to bridge it in his subtle inter-art negotiations between Renaissance and present, between poetry and chamber music."

In "Shakespeare's Sonnets in Russian Music: Traditions-Genres-Forms," Stefan Weiss argues that to "set a sonnet to music is likely to lead to unusual interpretations of form based on a strophic conception." He provides two examples of this practice. First, in Sonnet 130, Weiss shows how Igor Novikov "shapes two musically identical strophes (A) from the first two quatrains," and then how Valery Golovko stresses the couplet as the point of climax. Having provided his readers with two demonstration models, Weiss divides the essay into two sections: Shakespeare Sonnets in Russian and Soviet Art Song Traditions (1900–1970) and Shakespeare Sonnets in Soviet Popular Music (1970–1990). Weiss notes that there was an increase in setting the sonnets to music during World War II when the Soviet alliance became engaged with the culture of their allies. By 1974, the sonnets had become so popular that Leonid Kharitonov's version of Dmitri Kabalevsky's Sonnet 30 was actually filmed as it was performed.

Mike Ingham's essay, "'Moody Food of Us That Trade in Love': Re-Mediations of Shakespeare's *Sonnets* in Popular Music," follows in the same vein as Weiss's essay concerning the incorporation of the sonnets into popular music. Ingham's essay "explores the intertextual and reme-dial relations between the respective singer-songwriters' settings and their hypotexts, as well as focusing on the intrinsic qualities that lend them-selves to musical adaptation found in the sources." Ingham cites the adaptations of Sonnets 20 and 29 and 18 and 138, produced by Rufus Wainwright and Paul Kelly, respectively, and how they interpret the sonnets' musical qualities such as melody and tempo. Ingham opines that "Wainwright's piano and vocal rendition of Sonnet 29 ('When in disgrace with fortune and men's eyes')" was truly "'a marriage of true minds', inaugurating what has proved an enduring relationship between Shakespeare's sonnets and Wainwright's songwriting and performance practices." Of Kelly's adaptation of Sonnet 18, he writes that "the song's characteristic interplay between major and minor harmony not only underscores the light and shade that is central to its meaning, but also informs its binary imagery." Ingham performs a virtuosic analysis of all four sonnets musically, but goes on to suggest that they might better suit the genre of hip hop, because rap is "closer to spoken-word delivery than most other genres."

GLOBAL ISSUES IN THE SONNETS

The final section of the collection examines contemporary issues that tran-scend national boundaries and are particularly likely to inform the work of the sonnets in the classroom. Sophie Chiari's essay, "'O'er-green my bad'

(Sonnet 112): Nature Writing in the *Sonnets*," argues that "the amorous ordeal of the poet is conveyed in terms of ecological crisis." Chiari divides her essay into three sections. In "Good Husbandry," she explores the association of the fair youth with the word "green," suggesting comparison with a plant which needs to be nurtured so that it does not wither away. At the same time, "the language of nature is intertwined with that of commerce." There is an innate antipathy "between nature and market," which is "challenged early on in the poems: natural beauties are undermined by self-interested relationships and monetary ambitions." In the second section, "Black Pastoralism," Chiari explores a shift in the sonnets' natural imagery to reflect feelings of "envy, despair, disgust, and helplessness." In the third section, "Nature's Agency," the speaker "de-centres the traditional anthropocentric perspective on which most early modern poets relied. Whereas they compared plants to humans, he compares humans to plants." In her conclusion, "Overgreening the Sonnets," Chiari argues that "Shakespeare's sonnets reveal a changing dynamic between the Elizabethans and their environment. We have seen that the natural habitat presented by the poet, marked by the advent of the Anthropocene, is in no way a space untouched by humans." This essay is an intense intellectual interrogation of how Shakespeare's sonnets engaged with the natural world.

Duncan Salkeld's essay, "Black Luce and Sonnets 127–54," suggests that "the connections between blackness and beauty" in these sonnets are informed by Shakespeare's familiarity with Black Luce, a celebrated prostitute who operated a brothel in Clerkenwell. Her name is listed among those who attended the Great Hall of Gray's Inn in December 1594, only eight days before Shakespeare's *Comedy of Errors* was to be performed there; a play in which "Dromio puns on the name of the kitchen-maid Luce, whom he describes as 'swart.'" Another "dark lady," Rosaline, appears in *Love's Labour's Lost* and occasions an impassioned defense of black beauty from Biron. Like Rosaline, the "dark lady" of the sonnets "allows us to see a power in the mistress's complexion: to dazzle, captivate, create wonder, and poetry." Perhaps the early modern English world's notion of beauty was as complex as that of the twenty-first century.

Simona Laghi's essay, "Shakespeare's Sonnets in the ELT Classroom: The Paradox of Early Modern Beauty and 21st Century Social Media," takes up the theme of beauty and colorism, examining how Sonnets 127–130, 131, and 132 "might be the starting point to reflect on the impact that unrealistic digital images disseminated via social media has on identity formation as well as on mental health, and how these images become the basis of discrimination." In the first short section, Laghi debunks the notion that these sonnets are necessarily divided into two clearly demarcated sections, Sonnets 1–126 and Sonnets 127–154, or that the sonnet sequence narrates a biography of Shakespeare's life. She argues that the "discourse of beauty and identity that circulated in the Renaissance appears to be embedded in Sonnets 127, 130, 131, and 132," but that it also resonates surprisingly with today's beauty standards. It goes without saying that having students close read Sonnets 127, 130, 131, and 132 could be extremely conducive in improving their analytical skills concerning early modern English poetry, but at the same time this exercise makes them acutely aware of how one's complexion influences the way one is perceived and judged.

Katalin Schober's essay, "Pop Sonnets: The Interplay Between Shakespeare's Sonnets and Popular Music in English Language Teaching," analyzes popular songs rewritten as sonnets by Erik Didriksen. Like the Shakespearean sonnet, these songs have three quatrains and a couplet, and are written for the most part in iambic pentameter. Schober demonstrates how Didriksen's versions of the Spin Doctors' "Two Princes," Van Morrison's "Brown-Eyed Girl," and Soft Cell's "Tainted Love" are very similar thematically to Sonnets 21, 116, and 147. Schober explores the pedagogical value of these sonnets in creating "multiliteracies," a term which "on the one hand ... comprises a sensitivity to different cultures entailing a sense of empathy, that is the capacity to imaginatively put oneself in one someone else's shoes in order to gain some understanding of his or her condition. On the other hand, the concept of multiliteracies refers to the ability to decode various modes of meaning making." Schober argues that these pop sonnets encourage students to ask questions about what they wish to do with their lives and what is of importance in friendships and romantic relationships. The tables with instructions that Schober provides are especially helpful for teaching the sonnets.

Encompassing some 20 essays by writers from 15 nations, this collection offers a multiplicity of topographies, chronologies, and critical approaches. When readers have completed their reading, they may be confronted with the question of how these essays change how they read, study, and teach Shakespeare's sonnets. Will they understand the sonnets in a radically new, transformative fashion? Will they perceive how film and theatre can transform these stunningly beautiful sonnets into extraordinary productions of sound, voice, color, and movement? Will their appreciation for the art of translation be enriched and expanded because of these fine essays? It is my hope that these essays will enable their readers to accomplish all of these goals. If anything, it is my hope that all those who read these essays will be more fully aware of the global reach of these sonnets' influence on individuals' lives and can even change their lives for the better, wherever they call home.

REFERENCES

Edmondson, Paul and Stanley Wells, (eds). 2020. *All the Sonnets of Shakespeare.* Cambridge: Cambridge University Press.

Garber, Marjorie. 2005. *Shakespeare After All.* New York: Anchor Books.

Kernan, Alvin. 1995. *Shakespeare, the King's Playwright: Theater in the Stuart Court, 1603–1613.* New Haven and London: Yale University Press.

Kerrigan, John. 2006. "Shakespeare's Poems". In *The Cambridge Companion to Shakespeare*, ed. Margreta de Grazia and Stanley Wells, 65–82. Cambridge: Cambridge University Press.

Kingsley-Smith, Jane. 2019. *The Afterlife of Shakespeare's Sonnets.* Cambridge: Cambridge University Press.

Shakespeare, William. 1924. *Much Ado About Nothing.* Ed. Grace R. Trenery. London: Methuen and Co.

Shakespeare, William. 1964. *The Sonnets and Narrative Poems: The Complete Non-Dramatic Poetry.* Introduction. W. H. Auden. New York: Penguin Group.

Shakespeare, William. 1997. *The Norton Shakespeare.* 1st ed. New York: Norton.

PART I

Global Translations: Defining the Nation, Refining Poetics

CHAPTER 2

"Mine Is Another Voyage": Global Encounters with Shakespeare's Sonnets

Jane Kingsley-Smith

In 2012, as part of London's Cultural Olympiad, thirty-seven of Shakespeare's plays were performed at Shakespeare's Globe, over a six-week period from 21 April to 9 June by theatre companies from across the world, in 37 different languages. The positioning of Shakespeare's Sonnets within this festival is revealing.[1] The performance—a reading of all 154 Sonnets by actors in twenty different languages—was scheduled for the Sunday and tickets were free, making it a "pre-Festival" event. If it was marginal, it was also supplemental in the sense that it included "over 20 different languages NOT represented in the Festival" (website, qtd

---

[1] The publicity eschewed the claim that this was all of Shakespeare's complete works, perhaps because there was no production of *The Two Noble Kinsmen*. Although the focus was on Shakespeare's dramatic work, the poems did make an appearance not only through the Sonnets, but the inclusion of *Venus and Adonis* as a play performed in, among other languages, Afrikaans, Swahili and English. *The Rape of Lucrece* was not included.

J. Kingsley-Smith (✉)
University of Roehampton, London, UK
e-mail: J.Kingsley-Smith@roehampton.ac.uk

© The Author(s), under exclusive license to Springer Nature
Switzerland AG 2023
J. Kingsley-Smith and W. R. Rampone Jr. (eds.), *Shakespeare's Global Sonnets*,
Global Shakespeares, https://doi.org/10.1007/978-3-031-09472-9_2

Silverstone 2013, 38). It was often forgotten in descriptions of the event, which the director, Tom Bird, summarised as "thirty-seven different plays plus *Venus and Adonis*" (2013, 13), and in the essay collection, *Shakespeare Beyond English: A Global Experiment* (2013) the Sonnets have no chapter and are only mentioned twice.[2] Hence, in a collection intended "not just to document the events in the order in which they appeared on the stage but also to trace the debates that developed over the Festival's six weeks" (Bennett and Carson 2013, 8), the Sonnets have no voice. In a recording on YouTube of the final performance of Sonnet 154, as spoken by the participants simultaneously on the Globe stage,[3] we find a cacophony of voices in which any identifying features of the Shakespearean sonnet, any sense of its rhyme, rhythm or subject matter, are lost in Babylonian confusion.

This treatment of the Sonnets as marginal and supplemental to Shakespeare's works will come as no surprise to anyone familiar with their critical reception in England from at least 1609 to 1780 (Kingsley-Smith 2019), and, for all that the Sonnets' canonicity within Western literature now seems secure, their inveterate liminality comes back into sight every time a group of editors decides to produce a Complete Works of Shakespeare (where to put the Sonnets?), and any time a theatre company desires to perform all of Shakespeare (how to act them?).[4] But the sense of the Sonnets as extraneous—both preliminary and leftover—apparent in the Globe-to-Globe festival also serves as a useful prologue to the current collection, because it reminds us of how peripheral the Sonnets remain to our conversations about Global Shakespeare. In the majority of critical monographs which have come to define this field, the Sonnets merit barely a mention,[5] and yet they have their own unique contribution to make to the history of Shakespeare's global reception, as the following

---

[2] They are also missing from *A Year of Shakespeare: Re-living the World Shakespeare Festival* (2013), apart from one reference to Sonnet 30 in a production of the play, *Forests*, adapted by Mark Rosich and Calixto Bieito, 250.

[3] See 'Finale of Sonnet Sunday', https://www.youtube.com/watch?v=rIZcKi8Mf6I.

[4] This has sometimes required them to change their form entirely and be translated into music, as in the 2006 RSC "Complete Works" season.

[5] They are omitted in some of the best work in this area, such as Massai (2005), Fotheringham et al. (2008) and Huang and Rivlin (2014), as well as various collections devoted to particular countries or regions.

essays make clear. This chapter will smooth our passage into that discussion by addressing two central questions, which have not been attended to before: first, how is the Sonnets' journey across the world different to that of Shakespeare's plays and why?[6] And second, how does an understanding of the Sonnets' global reception change how we think about "Global Shakespeare" and the Sonnets in their original language?

The following brief history of Shakespeare's global dissemination is inevitably reductive. It does not take into account the volatility of Shakespeare's reception in different parts of the Globe, as when Shakespeare performances were banned by Japan during the Second World War, or during the Cultural Revolution of the 1960s and 70 s in China. Nor does it attempt to distinguish different levels of cultural assimilation across vast territories such as India or South America. There is an increasing number of critical studies on these location-specific Shakespeares ("Asian Shakespeare", "Indian Shakespeare", "South African Shakespeare" and so on) that readers are encouraged to consult. Nevertheless, it is valuable to have a broad strokes account of the historical phases of Shakespeare's acculturation across the world so that we may compare the Sonnets' different transmission and assimilation.[7]

Shakespeare's plays first travelled into Europe during his lifetime, through the agency of English strolling players who journeyed through the Low Countries and into Germany, performing adapted versions of London plays with a chorus-like Clown, speaking in the local language. There is evidence of a version of *Romeo and Juliet* being performed at Nordlingen as early as 1604 (Williams 1990, 38); adaptations of *Twelfth Night* and *The Merchant of Venice* were performed at Graz in 1608 (Stríbrný 2000, 7); and in a record of the plays performed at Dresden in 1626, we find *Romeo and Juliet*, *Hamlet*, *Julius Caesar* and *King Lear* (Stríbrný 2000, 12–13). Although this early Shakespeare contact influenced local playing, producing fascinating hybrids such as the German tragedy, *Der Bestrafte Brudermord (Fratricide Punished)* (1710), which

---

[6] This chapter addresses the gap identified by Manfred Pfister and Jürgen Gutch in the most important, and only, extended global reception history the Sonnets have received. As Pfister notes: "a survey of the translations across the globe" is "still sadly lacking" (2009, 10).

[7] I am indebted here to over forty country-specific entries in Dobson and Wells (2001), as well as to Pfister and Gutch (2009).

may have been a response to the first Quarto of *Hamlet*, there was no unbroken transmission of Shakespeare's plays into the eighteenth century.

Shakespeare's rediscovery in continental Europe famously began with the French writer and philosopher, Voltaire, who became acquainted with Shakespeare during his exile in London from 1726–9. In Letter 18 of *Lettres écrites de Londres sur les Anglois* (*Letters on the English*, 1734), Voltaire opined that "*Shakespear* boasted a strong, fruitful Genius; he was natural and sublime, but had not so much as a single Spark of good Taste, or knew one rule of the Drama ..." (qtd Willens 2012, 9). Voltaire would later berate himself for all that he had done to encourage the French appreciation of Shakespeare: "I was the first who showed to the French a few pearls which I had found in his enormous dunghill" (Voltaire 1967, 175), but the damage was done. The French writer and translator Pierre-Antoine de La Place would go on to produce the first-ever translation of Shakespeare's plays (1745–6), and it was from these texts that Jean-François Ducis (who could not read English) produced the adaptations that would make Shakespeare popular in French theatres. The expanded translation of Shakespeare's plays by Pierre Le Tourneur (1776) would disseminate Shakespeare into Russia and Turkey, as well as into South America via Spain and Portugal. It was also the French language that brought Shakespeare to other art forms, such as ballet and opera (Bosman 2010, 286).

At a time when Germany was questioning its cultural standing, and the literary and poetic capacity of the German language, the rediscovery of Shakespeare was a transformative opportunity. Gotthold Ephraim Lessing published an essay in 1759 identifying Shakespeare's natural affinity with the Germanic taste for "the great, the terrible, the melancholic", in defiance of the French preference for "the pretty, the tender, the amorous" (Williams 1990, 9), and Shakespeare became a champion of the young writers of the *Sturm und Drang* movement. As Roger Paulin characterises this period,

> the reservations that had preoccupied most eighteenth-century criticism were brushed aside in an ecstatic embrace of the Bard as a commanding genius. For the first time we hear a native German voice addressing Shakespeare, not one adapting French or English positions ... With this goes an independence in critical intelligence, not invoked for specifically national purposes, but in the awareness of Shakespeare's universality and timelessness, his creativity not confined by cultural borders. (2012, 319)

The German translations at this time certainly enabled Shakespeare's border-crossing. The first translation of twenty-two plays in prose by Christoph Martin Wieland (1762–6) was expanded by Johann Joachim Eschenburg (1775–82), before Schlegel's collaboration with Ludwig Tieck produced an edition of Shakespeare's plays (1797–1832) that would become a classic of German literature in its own right, but would also prove influential across Eastern European and Arab countries.

If French and German were important vehicles for Shakespeare's dissemination across the world, the privileged status afforded to the English language as a consequence of British imperialism also played a crucial role. As James R. Brandon puts it, "'Doing Shakespeare' was an unquestioned, if unofficial thread in the fabric of British expatriate colonial life" (2010, 22). This was initially through the performance of Shakespeare's plays by English actors, as, for example, in the theatres of Calcutta in 1757 or Jamaica in 1781–2. The travels of Shakespeare's collected plays as private reading material also brought Shakespeare to the colonies: Sydney Parkinson carried a copy (perhaps Johnson's 1765 edition) onboard the Endeavour during James Cook's voyage to New Zealand and Australia in 1769 (Houlahan 2016, 796), and in North America in 1764, a British explorer, Thomas Morris, was disconcerted by a native American chief (in what would become Illinois), making him a gift of a "volume of Shakespear's plays" (Dobson 1992, 193). Shakespeare became part of the official curriculum in higher education colleges in India in 1817—even before he was taught in English universities. His plays featured heavily in the British colonialist enterprise to create "a class of persons Indian in blood and colour, but English in taste, in opinions, in morals and in intellect" (Macaulay 1835, qtd Trivedi 2011, 233).

The final major movement of Shakespeare across the Globe occurred in East Asia in the late nineteenth/early twentieth century. But unlike Hong Kong or Malaysia which were under colonial rule, when young students from Japan, China and Korea reached out to Shakespeare, it was not in response to British imperialism but part of a voluntary desire to embrace Western culture. Shakespeare was not only part of the university syllabus—a formative experience which produced the first Japanese translator of the complete works, Tsoubouchi Shôyô (1859–1935)—he was also disseminated more widely through Charles and Mary Lamb's *Tales of Shakespeare* (1807). This was a collection of twenty prose narratives based on the plays and marketed as moral tales for women and children. In 1903, an unknown translator translated ten of the stories into Chinese, and they became the basis for the first Chinese theatrical performances of Shakespeare (Zhengkun 2009, 105). In Japan, the *Tales* were translated and printed more than ninety times between 1877 and 1928, and also formed the basis of early Japanese productions (Joubin 2011, 76). Translations of the original English texts (a Japanese *Julius Caesar* in 1883; a Chinese *Hamlet* in 1922) would continue to extend the reach of Shakespeare alongside these hybrid dramatic forms. Today, it can be argued that the Asian continent is the leading force in the continued globalisation of Shakespeare (Trivedi et al. 2020, 1–2).

So much for the transmission of the plays—for that is what is primarily understood by the term "Shakespeare" in the brief history above. If we try to extricate the transmission of Shakespeare's Sonnets from this process, we find that their journey across the Globe takes a different route and looks decidedly late.[8] For example, if the first Shakespeare play is translated into French in 1731, the first few sonnets do not appear until 1821 in Amedée Pichot's translation, and the full 154 must wait for Francois-Victor Hugo in 1857. The first Russian Shakespeare play is *Hamlet* in 1748, but the Sonnets do not follow in printed translation until 1859 (with a complete edition in 1880). In India, Bengali translations of the plays began in the mid-nineteenth century, but the complete sonnets would not be translated into Bengali until the twentieth, most notably in the 1950s work of Manindranath Roy and Sudhanshu Ranjan Ghosh (Roy 2009, 349).

There are a number of reasons for this belatedness. If, as Anston Bosman suggests, we can trace the global dissemination of Shakespeare through three main networks—"a theatrical network, made up chiefly of performers and directors; a textual network, comprising writers, editors and translators; and a digital network employing a range of media and devices" (2010, 286–7)—we may begin to discern why the Sonnets took their time. As Bosman notes, "The globalization of Shakespeare began with actors. Years before literary translations of the plays appeared, foreign versions took shape on stage and in real time as an actor, or, rarely, a spectator, mediated between English and a local tongue" (287). However, the phenomenon of the famous actor performing Sonnets is a relatively modern one. When troupes of English actors travelled across the Continent and into the Caribbean in the seventeenth century, or into India

---

[8] This is a recurring theme in the Introductions to the global translations procured and published by Pfister and Gutsch.

and the Americas in the eighteenth, they did not take the Sonnets as part of their repertoire. This is hardly surprising given the lyrics' famous lack of narrative or plot, and the absence of any clearly defined characters. It is also worth noting that in most cases the Sonnets were translated as a handful of lyrics rather than a sequence, further hindering the discernment of any sustained narrative.

In terms of text, the Sonnets' global reception was impacted by their limited domestic reproduction, with only one edition of *Shake-speares Sonnets* produced in England in 1609, before a gap of 31 years when John Benson published his miscellany, *Poems: written by Will. Shakespeare, Gent* (1640). A copy of *Venus and Adonis* must have got abroad, since the first 810 lines were translated into Dutch in 1621 (Hoenselaars 2012b, 4), suggesting that it was either the Sonnets' lack of print copies (as compared with the inexhaustible reprinting of *Venus*) and/or their lack of audience appeal that prevented them from travelling abroad. The fact that the Sonnets were not included in the First Folio (1623) also had a lasting impact. One reason Stríbrný suggests for a fresh batch of Shakespeare plays in the repertoire of the English players at Dresden in 1626 was the publication of the Folio three years earlier, which "made Shakespeare's plays easily available to all companies" (13). Only in the eighteenth century did Shakespeare scholars in England begin to add the Sonnets to the Complete Works through additional volumes, most famously when Edmond Malone published the Quarto sequence in 1780 as a *Supplement* to the 1778 edition of the plays by Johnson and Steevens. But this pattern also pertained on the Continent. Eschenberg, who completed a German translation of all the plays in 1775–7, produced a single volume of 56 sonnets in 1778. Similarly, Ludwig Tieck published twenty-six of the Sonnets in 1826—printed under his name although translated by his daughter, Dorothea—but her complete translation (1823–4) remained unpublished until 1992. Part of this reluctance by editors and/or the book-buying public was the libidinal, adulterous and "homosexual" content of the Sonnets. It was this that prevented George Steevens from including the Sonnets in his 1793 edition, insisting that "the strongest act of parliament that could be framed would fail to compel readers into their service" (vii), and Tieck ran into similar opposition from the German Shakespeare scholars, Hermann Ulrici and Georg Gottfried Gervinus, over the Sonnets' same-sex desire (Paulin 2003, 473–474). Finally, we should note that the Lambs' *Tales of Shakespeare*, which had such an influence on the Japanese and Chinese reception of Shakespeare, did not, by definition, include the Sonnets.

If we turn to "the digital network employing a range of media and devices" as the third means by which Shakespeare went global, the Sonnets again have some disadvantages as lyric poems. Without the performance history that would freeze them into instantly recognisable and reproducible images, their iconography is less immediately striking and their position in a visual tradition of Shakespeare underwhelming. Not surprisingly, the Sonnets are almost entirely missing from Stuart Sillars' extensive work on Shakespeare and the visual tradition, including *The Illustrated Shakespeare, 1790-1875* (2008), *Shakespeare, Time and the Victorians* (2011) and *Shakespeare Seen* (2018). In a recent discussion of "post-textual Shakespeare", Douglas Lanier identifies the impulse to globalization as contributing towards Shakespeare's "post-textualisation": "images travel well and, in Shakespeare's case, visual media would seem more commensurate with his putative universality" (2011, 149). The Sonnets have certainly gained more visibility through stage production and film in the twentieth century, but it remains the case that their transmission is still largely textual and aural—through the recording of Sonnets as voiceover in films, as talking heads by famous actors and, most importantly, as adapted to music.

In the face of these disadvantages/distinctives, it becomes less surprising that the Sonnets should have taken time to find a global audience. Indeed, English readers only really started to pay attention to Shakespeare's Sonnets when lectured by a German critic, August Wilhelm von Schlegel:

> It gives away an extraordinary lack of critical acumen that among the many interpreters of Shakespeare we know it has come to no one's mind so far to use his sonnets for writing his biography. They depict quite evidently the poet's real situations and moods, they acquaint us with the passion of the man himself, yes, they even contain curious confessions of the confusions of his youth. (1815, 352)

This argument for reading the Sonnets would become a common justification for translating them. In 1857, Victor-Hugo's French translation was prefaced with the argument that "here it is no longer Shakespeare the writer we see, but Shakespeare the man: it is not the poet who speaks, but the friend, the lover ..." (qtd Schwartz-Gastine 2009, 229). In the first Bulgarian translation, published anonymously in 1886 and based on a Russian text, the preface asserts "There's hardly any doubt that Shakespeare's sonnets are not among his best works ... His sonnets, however, have another important aspect in that through them whoever ventures to read or study the immortal poet's works will get acquainted with the poet's inner life" (trans. Shurbanov 2009, 87). This biographical interpretation of the Sonnets has ever since promoted their inter-semiotic translation into novels and plays about Shakespeare (see the chapters here by Minier, Krajnik and Drozd).

There were (and remain) some significant impediments to translating the Sonnets, not least if one was ambitious to render them in verse. The compressing of Romance languages with multiple syllables into English decasyllables is one such difficulty, often requiring that the pentameter line be stretched into alexandrines or fourteen syllable lines. Sonnets such as 141 ("In faith, I do not love thee with mine eyes") lean particularly hard on monosyllables, of which there is a comparative dearth in French, Italian, Romanian, Turkish, etc. Pronouns translated from English into a gendered language will raise particular questions that do not trouble the plays, as Eva Spîsiaková remarks,

> ... poetry translation presents a very particular gendered dilemma, as the poetic form itself is frequently vague, fragmented, and lacking the contextual clues that are typical in prose writing. Shakespeare's Sonnets are largely constructed as a one-sided proclamation of an unspecified "I" for an equally unspecified "you" or "thou". When translated into a gendered language, like Czech or Slovak, this ambiguity compels the translators to make a choice. (2021, 52)

Cultural allusions have also proven a challenge. Sonnet 18 ("Shall I compare thee to a summer's day") turns out to be a favourite across the world, but the seasons which different nations experience as "summer" has meant that changes need to be made to capture that famous temperateness.

I would like to suggest that the global transmission of the Sonnets—as linguistically complex texts with no easy access point other than translation—has significantly shaped how they have been received across the world, and that their difficulty bestowed a particular literary prestige on the act of translation, which was often part of a nationalist poetics. As Lawrence Venuti observes: "Nationalist movements have frequently enlisted translation in the development of national languages and cultures, especially national literatures" (2005, 178). In the case of Shakespeare's Sonnets, this began in the nineteenth century, with the German rejection of French translations of Shakespeare, and extended particularly into Eastern Europe in the twentieth century, where Sonnet 66 ("Tired with all these, for restful death I cry") became "more popular in translation than it has ever been in English", for nations suffering under Soviet dictatorship and for writers struggling to express an "art made tongue-tied by authority" (Hoenselaars 2012a, 742).[9] The Sonnets' appeal to political prisoners and exiles in the twentieth century more broadly is the subject of a fascinating piece by Manfred Pfister (2013). The reason for the Sonnets' appeal in exile has little to do with their explicit content, although their promises to endure after death undoubtedly resonate. It seems rather to inhere in the Sonnets' complexity: one can beguile away "an otherwise unendurably sterile and painful time ... by searching one's own language for inflections of voice, verbal ambiguities, metaphorical clusters or rhymes equivalent to those in the original" (2013, 253). It is also a reflection of their physical restriction as sonnets and as a sequence of sonnets: "The spatial constraints of the prison cell or the internment camp" have a natural affinity with the "self-contained narrowness of [the sonnet's] shape built up of three strictly-bound quartets and culminating in a yet tighter couplet ... translating one quartet after another, one sonnet after another, fits in perfectly with the strictly parcelled-out time and space of the prison regime" (Pfister 2013, 254).

There are other kinds of ideological constraint against which the act of translating the Sonnets might perform a kind of resistance. Dorothea Tieck (1799–1841) was one of the first women to translate the sonnets in German, though her work was repeatedly ascribed to a young male friend by her father. Although she made no claims for women's creativity, and led a life of religious probity and chastity, her translations of the Sonnets allow for a surprisingly direct and assertive first-person voice, which often draws attention to its own speaking. As Olivia Landry has shown, Dorothea was able to co-opt the Sonnets' sexuality to create a "desiring subjectivity" of her own, within a broader context of political self-expression:

---

[9] See Pfister's ground-breaking essays on this sonnet, "Route 66: The Political Performance of Shakespeare's Sonnet 66 in Germany and Elsewhere" (2003) and "Route 66 and No End: Further Fortunes of Shakespeare's Sonnet 66" (2010).

Just as the German (male) romantics utilized their translations of Shakespeare as a means of consolidating their national identity and larger place in *Weltliteratur*, Tieck was perpetuating this for herself on a smaller scale. If the romantics could appropriate Shakespeare for Germany, then Tieck, both as translator and woman, could and did appropriate Shakespeare for herself. (Landry 2012, 18)

We should also acknowledge the ways in which the Sonnets' sexuality has enhanced their cultural visibility. In many of the essays included in this collection, it is clear that this sexuality—which is both adulterous and non-heterosexual—actively delayed the Sonnets' assimilation into the canon of Shakespeare's works in many countries across the world and remains an issue today. However, repressive regimes have also, paradoxically, *enabled* translations of the Sonnets' sexuality.

Spîsiaková has recently compared fifteen Czech and Slovak translations of the Sonnets in the period 1923–2010, i.e. those produced during the Soviet era, and those after the Velvet Revolution and the fall of Communism in 1989. Surprisingly, she finds that in the later period, when same-sex unions had gained more visibility and even legal acceptance, translations of the Sonnets tended to place less emphasis on the romantic and/or erotic relationship between the male speaker and the Fair Youth. By contrast, in the earlier period, when homosexuality was criminalised and treated as a taboo, the translators' work showed "no intention of altering, obscuring or removing the possibility of reading the Sonnets as a collection of emotionally charged poems about love from a man to another man" (2021, 98). This may be because the regime was unwilling to see the powerful male bonds explored in the Sonnets as sexualised, but nevertheless "it is probable that many non-heterosexual readers of the Sonnets in this time period recognised their own feelings in Shakespeare's text, and it is particularly intriguing to imagine that the apparent blindness of the regime to this issue enabled some readers to find the representation they could not find elsewhere" (2021, 100). Not only does this argument have an impact on Queer Translation Studies, which have tended to assume that repressive regimes inhibit the articulation of non-heteronormative desire, it leads into a discussion of what translation into foreign languages can do for the Sonnets. To put it another way, how do the Sonnets' global encounters change how we perceive them in their original language, and what might their inclusion add to our conversations about Global Shakespeare?

One of the features of Global Shakespeare about which most critics now agree is the value of its decentring perspective and its rejection of a universal Shakespeare. As the editors of *Asian Interventions in Global Shakespeare* (2020) observe,

> Universal Shakespeare was a construct of colonialism, part of the civilising impetus of the empire, fixed and unchanging, meaning the same for all. The critical difference of Global Shakespeare is that he is distinct in different parts of the Globe, speaking in different voices, responsive to different stimuli and manifesting himself in diverse, re-formed and renewed instantiations. In fact, the global has exposed the "constructed" nature of the "universal" as an accident of history and an imposition of political regimes. (Trivedi et al. 2020, 4)

The different transmission of the Sonnets reminds us not to slip into unthinking platitudes about Shakespeare's universality. Yet it is also the case that their colonial and postcolonial history remains largely unexamined. To give one example, the Sonnets have received almost no attention in discussions of the Shakespeare curriculum as a tool of empire in British India, but at least two of the teachers at Hindu College in Calcutta (founded in 1817) were engaged with Shakespeare's Sonnets as well as his plays. David Lester Richardson (1801–1865), an officer of the East India Company who later became a Professor of English Literature at Hindu College, published an essay on the Sonnets in his collection, *Literary Leaves, or Prose and Verse chiefly written in India*, first published in Calcutta in 1835. He quotes extensively from the poems and observes that "Those persons to whom I may have the good fortune to introduce Shakespeare as a sonnet-writer will feel no little surprise at the extreme eloquence and accuracy of his verse" (1836, 170). He may well be referring to the readers of his book, but it seems likely that this would also apply to his young Hindu students. The Indian-born poet, Henry Derozio (1809–31), who was assistant headmaster at the college, not only taught Shakespeare but published sonnets on Shakespearean themes.[10] There is also some evidence of the Sonnets being deployed in the service

---

[10] On Derozio's negotiation of his allegiances to the Western Romantic tradition and to Indian nationalism see Chander (2017). On the Shakespeare teaching at Hindu College more generally, see Dahiya (2018).

of Arabic poetry in late eighteenth century India. The first Indian newspaper, *Hicky's Bengal Gazette or the Original Calcutta Advertiser* no. IX, 17–24 March 1781, features an article by C. D. who includes a transcription of Sonnet 99 ("The forward violet thus did I chide") as an implied contrast with the lyric poetry of the fourteenth-century Iranian poet, Hafiz I-Shirazi, and this was a comparison that the famous Orientalist, William Jones, would also make. In the newspaper, it serves as evidence of English cultural superiority; but for Jones, it represents the richness of Persian poetry that it should resemble Shakespeare and also hints at a potential indebtedness: "This little song is not unlike a sonnet ascribed to Shakespeare, which deserves to be cited here, a proof that the Eastern imagery is not so different from the European as we are apt to imagine" (Jones 1807, 4.542).

As Anne Sophie Refskou and Tabish Khair contend in this collection, a greater attention to Shakespeare's Sonnets in translation not only exposes how they have been shaped by, and are implicated in, the colonial and postcolonial history of the Global South, it also offers an important challenge to current thinking about Global Shakespeare. To include the Sonnets as a case study "requires first and foremost an unavoidable literary focus on the poetics of texts and their languages"—something Refskou and Khair argue is largely missing from the field of Global Shakespeare, which is overwhelmingly focused on the plays and their inter-semiotic translation. As a consequence, scholars "unintentionally overlook the rich literary and linguistic traditions of the global cultures that have engaged with the Shakespearean canon and continue to recreate it", and they are also, paradoxically, in danger of reinforcing the assumption that the language of Shakespeare is English. I would argue that paying attention to the Sonnets in translation is particularly valuable to Anglophone scholars for what it exposes about the racial hierarchies embedded in the Sonnets (see Hall 2013). In the Western academy, we have belatedly admitted the reality of a Black woman behind Shakespeare's Dark Lady (see Salkeld in this volume), but non-Anglophone translators in the Global South have long co-opted the racialist language of the Sonnets for their own articulations of racial inequality or to insert Black voices into these historically white texts. Refskou and Khair note how the Brazilian poet and translator Geraldo Carneiro incorporates an intertextual allusion to popular culture in Sonnet 15, in a way that "destabilises the dichotomous fair youth/dark lady trope in the Sonnets by effectively writing a young black woman into the procreation sequence".

The question of what kinds of otherness inhere within the Sonnets also relates to questions about the inside/outside dynamics of Global Shakespeare. One recurring observation about the 2012 Globe to Globe festival is that it celebrated Shakespeare "coming home" to Britain (Purcell 2012). Although the languages chosen were intended to represent and incorporate those "on the periphery", this well-intentioned inclusivity arguably reinforced the outsider status of those same languages/peoples (Refskou 2019, 203). This is particularly the case with the Sonnets. On the one hand, their performance in, for example, Cornish, Scots and Te Maori, was historically appropriate, given that the Sonnets have had a long history of giving cultural visibility to minority languages. But on the other hand, the generic marginalisation of the Sonnets within a festival of plays potentially reinforced the subordinate status of, for example, Scotland or Cornwall in Britain. More attention to the Sonnets' reception *within* a diverse and multicultural United Kingdom could be an effective response to Refskou's call for a Global Shakespeare in which "some scholarship ... 'begin[s] at home' and address[es] perceptions of internal otherness in a sustained manner, reiterating that intercultural encounters do not always involve national border crossings or passports" (2019, 204).

It is certainly the case that Shakespeare's Sonnets are defamiliarised by the process of Global reading: whether that is through translation which illuminates some gendered or racialist assumption that the Anglophone reader need never confront; or through the articulation of colonial or postcolonial identities that the Sonnets have enabled; or simply because the multiple voices which speak the Sonnets in any Global reading illuminate the multiple voices that already inhere within *Shake-speares Sonnets*. As Sonia Massai has observed, "World-wide appropriations of Shakespeare stretch, challenge and modify our sense of what 'Shakespeare' is" (2005, 6). The implications of this for the Sonnets are only just beginning to be felt, but the current collection is an important start.

References

Bennett, Susan and Christie Carson. 2013. "Introduction: Shakespeare Beyond English". In *Shakespeare Beyond English: A Global Experiment*, ed. Christie Carson and Susan Bennett, 1–11. Cambridge: Cambridge University Press.

Bird, Tom. 2013. "The Globe to Globe Festival: An Introduction". In *Shakespeare Beyond English: A Global Experiment*, ed. Christie Carson and Susan Bennett, 13-18. Cambridge: Cambridge University Press.

Bosman, Anston. 2010. "Shakespeare and Globalization". In *The New Cambridge Companion to Shakespeare*, ed. Margreta de Grazia and Stanley Wells, 285–302. Cambridge: Cambridge University Press.

Brandon, James R. 2010. "Other Shakespeares in Asia: An Overview". In *Re-Playing Shakespeare in Asia*, ed. Poonam Trivedi and Minami Ryuta, 21–40. New York: Routledge.

Chander, Manu Samriti. 2017. *Brown Romantics: Poetry and Nationalism in the Global Nineteenth Century*. Lewisburg: Bucknell University Press.

Dahiya, Hema. 2018. *Essays on Shakespeare: Texts and Contexts*. Newcastle-upon-Tyne: Cambridge Scholars Publishing.

Dobson, Michael. 1992. "Fairly Brave New World: Shakespeare, the American Colonies, and the American Revolution". *Renaissance Drama* 23: 189–207.

Dobson, Michael and Stanley Wells (eds). 2001. *The Oxford Companion to Shakespeare*. Oxford: Oxford University Press.

Fotheringham, Richard, Christa Jansohn and R. S. White (eds). 2008. *Shakespeare's World/World Shakespeares: The Selected Proceedings of the International Shakespeare Association World Congress, Brisbane 2006*. Newark: University of Delaware Press.

Hall, Kim F. 2013. "'These Bastard Signs of Fair": Literary Whiteness in Shakespeare's Sonnets". In *Post-Colonial Shakespeares*, ed. Ania Loomba and Martin Orkin, 64–83. London and New York: Routledge.

Hoenselaars, Ton. 2012a. "Shakespeare and the World". In *The Oxford Handbook of Shakespeare*, ed. Arthur F. Kinney, 735–51. Oxford and New York: Oxford University Press.

Hoenselaars, Ton. 2012b. *Shakespeare and the Language of Translation*. London: Arden Shakespeare.

Houlahan, Mark. 2016. "Unsettling the Bard: Australasia and the Pacific". In *The Oxford Handbook of Shakespearean Tragedy*, ed. Michael Neill and David Schalkwyk, 795–810. Oxford: Oxford University Press.

Huang, Alexa and Elizabeth Rivlin (eds). 2014. *Shakespeare and the Ethics of Appropriation*. New York: Palgrave.

Jones, William. 1807. *Poeseos Asiaticae Commentariorum Libri* (1774). In *The Works of Sir William Jones*. London, 13 vols., vol. 4.

Joubin, Alexa Alice. 2011. "Shakespeare and Translation". In *The Edinburgh Companion to Shakespeare and the Arts*, ed. Mark Thornton Burnett, Adrian Streete, and Ramona Wray, 68–87. Edinburgh: Edinburgh University Press.

Kingsley-Smith, Jane. 2019. *The Afterlife of Shakespeare's Sonnets*. Cambridge: Cambridge University Press.

Landry, Olivia. 2012. "Verbal Performance in Dorothea Tieck's Translation of Shakespeare's Sonnets". *Women in German Yearbook* 28: 1–22.

Lanier, Douglas. 2011. "Post-Textual Shakespeare". *Shakespeare Survey* 64: 145–62.

Massai, Sonia. 2005. "Defining Local Shakespeares". In *World-Wide Shakespeare: Local Appropriations in Film and Performance*, ed. Sonia Massai. London: Routledge.

Paulin, Roger. 2003. *The Critical Response to Shakespeare in Germany, 1682–1914*. Hildesheim: George Ulms.

Paulin, Roger. 2012. "Shakespeare in Germany". In *Shakespeare in the Eighteenth Century*, ed. Fiona Ritchie and Peter Sabor, 314–330. Cambridge: Cambridge University Press.

Pfister, Manfred. 2010. "Route 66 and No End: Further Fortunes of Shakespeare's Sonnet 66". *Linguaculture* 2: 39–50.

Pfister, Manfred. 2013. "Shakespeare's Sonnets *de profundis*". In *Shakespeare and Conflict: A European Perspective*, ed. Carla Dente and Sara Soncini. Basingstoke and New York: Palgrave Macmillan.

Pfister, Manfred and Jürgen Gutch. 2009. *Shakespeare's Sonnets for the First Time Globally Reprinted: A Quatercentenary Anthology*. Edition SIGNAThUR: Dozwil TG, Switzerland.

Purcell, Stephen. 2012. "Circles, Centres and the Globe to Globe Festival", *Blogging Shakespeare*, https://bloggingshakespeare.com/reviewing-shakespeare/year-of-shakespeare-circles-centres-and-the-globe-to-globe-festival/ accessed 2/02/22.

Refskou, Anne Sophie. 2019. "'Not Where He Eats But Where He Is Eaten': Rethinking Otherness in (British) Global Shakespeare". In *Eating Shakespeare: Cultural Anthropophagy as Global Methodology*, ed. Anne Sophie Refskou, Marcel Alvaro de Amorim and Vinicius Mariano de Carvalho, 201–23. London and New York: Bloomsbury Arden Shakespeare.

Roy, Amitava. 2009. "Shakespeare's Sonnets 'by the Indian Ganges's Side'". In *Shakespeare's Sonnets for the First Time Globally Reprinted*, ed. Manfred Pfister and Jürgen Gutch, 345–58. Edition SIGNAThUR: Dozwil TG, Switzerland.

Schlegel, August Wilhelm von. 1815. *A Course of Lectures on Dramatic Art and Literature*. Trans. John Black. London, 2 vols.

Schwartz-Gastine, Isabelle. 2009. "The Sonnets in French: '*Translating Shakespeare's Sonnets! This Verges on the Absurd*'". In *Shakespeare's Sonnets for the First Time Globally Reprinted*, ed. Manfred Pfister and Jürgen Gutch, 227–41. Edition SIGNAThUR: Dozwil TG, Switzerland.

Shurbanov, Alexander. 2009. "Shakespeare's Sonnets in Bulgarian". In *Shakespeare's Sonnets for the First Time Globally Reprinted*, ed. Manfred Pfister and Jürgen Gutch, 87–98. Edition SIGNAThUR: Dozwil TG, Switzerland.

Silverstone, Catherine. 2013. "Festival Showcasing and Cultural Regeneration: Aotearoa New Zealand, Shakespeare's Globe and Ngakau Toa's *A Toroihi raua ko Kahiri (Troilus and Cressida)*". In *Shakespeare Beyond*

English: A Global Experiment, ed. Christie Carson and Susan Bennett, 35-47. Cambridge: Cambridge University Press.

Spîsiaková, Eva. 2021. *Queering Translation History: Shakespeare's Sonnets in Czech and Slovak Transformations.* London: Routledge.

Stríbrný, Zdenek, 2000. *Shakespeare and Eastern Europe.* Oxford: Oxford University Press.

Trivedi, Poonam, Paromita Chakravarti and Ted Motohashi (eds). 2020. *Asian Interventions in Global Shakespeare: "All the World's His Stage".* London: Routledge.

Trivedi, Poonam. 2011. '"You Taught Me Language": Shakespeare in India'. *Shakespeare Survey* 64: 231–9.

Venuti, Lawrence. 2005. "Local Contingencies: Translation and National Identities". In *Nation, Language, and the Ethics of Translation,* ed. Sandra Bermann and Michael Wood, 177–202. Princeton: Princeton University Press.

Voltaire. 1967. *Voltaire on Shakespeare.* Ed. Theodore Besterman. Genève: Droz.

Willens, Michèle. 2012. "Voltaire". In *Voltaire, Goethe, Schlegel, Coleridge: Great Shakespeareans: Volume III,* ed. Roger Paulin. London: Bloomsbury.

Williams, Simon. 1990. *Shakespeare on the German Stage. Vol. 1, 1586–1914.* Cambridge: Cambridge University Press.

Zhengkun, Gu. 2009. "Shakespeare's Sonnets in Mainland China". In *Shakespeare's Sonnets for the First Time Globally Reprinted,* ed. Manfred Pfister and Jürgen Gutch, 105–119. Edition SIGNAThUR: Dozwil TG, Switzerland.

CHAPTER 3

The Rival Poet and the Literary Tradition: Translating Shakespeare's *Sonnets* in French

Line Cottegnies

Although the first complete translation of Shakespeare's *Sonnets* was published in 1857 by Victor Hugo's son, François-Victor Hugo, it is Amédée Pichot, the translator of Byron, who must be credited with introducing them in France, exactly two hundred years ago. In 1821, Pichot published a meagre choice of six sonnets in prose in the first volume of Shakespeare's *Œuvres complètes* which he edited with François Guizot.[1] As is well-known, the reception of Shakespeare's dramatic works was delayed in France for reasons that were both cultural and political: his *oeuvre* was mostly ignored until Voltaire and the mid-eighteenth century, when Pierre-Antoine de La Place published a choice of ten plays in prose

---

[1] Shakespeare 1857; Shakespeare 1821. The Guizot-Pichot edition of Shakespeare's complete works is a revision of Le Tourneur's earlier translation in 20 volumes (Shakespeare 1776–1783). For a selective anthology and short presentations of the French translations, see Cottegnies 2021.

L. Cottegnies (✉)
Sorbonne Université, Paris, France
e-mail: line.cottegnies@sorbonne-universite.fr

J. Kingsley-Smith and W. R. Rampone Jr. (eds.), *Shakespeare's Global Sonnets*, Global Shakespeares, https://doi.org/10.1007/978-3-031-09472-9_3

(Shakespeare 1745–1746). But even in light of this delay, the even more belated reception of the *Sonnets* is intriguing. This chapter examines the reasons behind this deferred first encounter in comparison with the gradual integration of the dramatic works into mainstream culture. It is all the more surprising in light of the later success met by the *Sonnets* in French: over seventy different translations, selective or complete, have been published since Pichot's first attempt—and there is no sign of the craze abating. The published translations manifest an extraordinary range of choices that reflect each translator's "translating horizon", a complex notion into which are subsumed their conceptions of language and of translation, their own cultural "epistemes" and their investments into the national literary tradition (Berman 1995, 64-95). These translations can have different pragmatic functions and agendas. While some translators show an awareness of the patrimonial dimension of their texts, others see translation as a fruitful confrontation with an iconic text that is often considered as the ultimate poetic touchstone. Shakespeare's *Sonnets* thus seem to have functioned as a magnet to a number of French poets, and it is a remarkable feature of their history in French that about a third of their translators are themselves published poets. This chapter offers a comprehensive study of the translation history of Shakespeare's *Sonnets* over two hundred years. Focusing on several key aspects of this cultural and literary history, it shows how translating Shakespeare's *Sonnets* has often been seen as a way of confronting the ultimately canonical "rival poet", but also of challenging the French literary tradition.

The fraught reception of Shakespeare's works in the Restoration reminds us that "the Bard" was not always treated in England itself with the reverence that he was later to inspire (Dobson 1992; Dugas 2006, 6-68); moreover, the *Sonnets* were long marginalized in the Shakespearean canon (Kingsley-Smith 2019; Acker 2020). In Classical France, marked by little tolerance for the English language and its rejection of dramatic forms that ignored Aristotelian rules and decorum, Shakespeare was largely ignored, until Voltaire—in exile in London in the 1720s— expressed his ambivalent admiration for his works, tinged with irritation at what he saw as the juxtaposition of sublime flights of fancy with irregular and lowly traits. Voltaire, who ignored the poems, thus famously described *Hamlet* as produced by the imagination of a "drunken savage" (cited in Besterman 2008, 182).[2] It would take the Romantics to recognize the potential of Shakespeare's drama to challenge French classicism, in the early nineteenth century, when he appeared as an alternative to a sterile and ossified home-grown tradition. The first eighteenth-century translators of Shakespeare's plays, La Place and Le Tourneur, both postulated, however, that his works could not be staged in France for reasons of decorum, and they offered homogenized versions in prose, which were meant to be read rather than performed.[3]

While the French reception of the *Sonnets* is partly indebted to the reception of the drama, it also has a history of its own, which is inextricably linked with the national poetic tradition, the history of poetic forms, but also the *Sonnets'* reception history in England. While Milton's epic, first translated into French in 1729, went through a string of new translations in the course of the eighteenth century (Tournu 2017, 140–164), the minor genres of the sonnet and the epyllion fell out of favour. It is only with François-Victor Hugo's complete translation of Shakespeare from 1857 to 1866, and the 1862 *Oeuvres complètes* edited by François Guizot (alone this time, without Pichot) that they became available in French (Shakespeare 1862). The *Sonnets* had held a marginal status in the early editions of Shakespeare's works in England, and this was naturally also the case in France. The 1609 Thorpe and 1640 Benson editions were not reprinted in seventeenth-century England, and by the eighteenth century, the sonnets had become "something of an aesthetic and sexual embarrassment" (Roberts 2007, 260). Nicholas Rowe dismissed them as apocryphal, and did not include them in his 1709 edition, even though Charles Gildon published them in an additional volume the following year in the order of the Benson edition (Shakespeare 1709, 1710).[4] It was not until Malone's 1780 supplement to Steevens's edition that the *Sonnets* joined the plays and were integrated into the Shakespearean canon, in the order of the Thorpe edition, together with historical and lexical glosses expanding the autobiographical aspect of the sonnets (Shakespeare 1780; Kirwan 2021, 154).

---

[2] On Shakespeare's reception in France, see Willems 2007 and Cottegnies 2018.

[3] La Place's translation is actually more a transliteration than an actual translation.

[4] Bernard Lintott had in fact reprinted Shakespeare's *Sonnets* in volume II of *A Collection of Poems in Two Volumes*, but this seems to have gone largely unnoticed at the time (Lintott 1711). Edward Capell annotated a copy of Lintott while preparing an edition of the sonnets which remained in manuscript (See Jane Kingsley-Smith 2022).

Nineteenth-century editors and critics, like William Hazlitt, continued to express embarrassment towards the *Sonnets*, which can be attributed both to their dissatisfaction with the Petrarchan conventions and the alleged "immorality" of the sonnets (Hazlitt 1848, 343–345). It was their possible autobiographical subtext that caused unease, all the more so as it was compounded with a combination of obscurity, wryness and raunchiness, not to mention their homoeroticism. All these naturally constituted an obstacle to a straightforward integration into French culture, as the sonnets broke the sacrosanct rules of decorum on several grounds. Three entangled questions focused most of the French anxiety: the sonnets' possible autobiographical nature; the elusive identities of the addressees; and the enigmatic narrative thread tentatively emerging through a sequential reading. Pichot was the first to comment on their mixture of impropriety and beauty, remarking in a foreword that "several [sonnets] have a very dodgy meaning and a few offer enchanting poetry" (Shakespeare 1821, 147).[5] Author and translator Léon de Wailly, who published a critical essay together with rhymed versions of three sonnets in an 1833 issue of *La Revue des deux mondes*, exclaimed with ironic candour: "Good God, what do I see as I go through some of the first sonnets again? [...] [C]ould I have got this wrong? Can these sonnets be addressed to a man? Shakespeare! Great Shakespeare! Is it possible that you followed the example of Virgil?" (Wailly 1834, 688). He then turns to the conventions of Renaissance friendship to explain away the difficulty: Shakespeare's passion for his patron could only be "an ardent friendship and an intellectual adoration" (691). De Wailly was the first translator thus explicitly to confront the question of homoeroticism in the sonnets; in spite of his light-heartedness, he changed the gender of the addressee to female in two sonnets, even though he also argued that the sonnets to the dark lady were at least as immoral as the ones to the young man, if not more. The Catholic translator Ernest Lafond, who, one year before François-Victor Hugo's complete translation appeared, offered a choice of forty-eight sonnets in verse, was less amused. In his preface, he described the sonnets as the intimate and occasionally shameful portrait of the man Shakespeare, "like pages fallen out of a diary" (Shakespeare 1856, xiv). His version is much more censorious, and he reassigns forty sonnets of the fair youth section to an idealized lady, even turning her into an angel

---

[5] All translations from the French are mine.

of domesticity in Sonnet 109 (where the poet's breast is described as "the home of love"). Other passionate sonnets to the youth become lukewarm poems of "tender friendship", like Sonnet 29.

For many early translators, the homoerotic subtext, like the gender of the addressee, was clearly an issue—and this was still the case until quite recently. To resolve the breach of decorum, some translators thought they could solve the dilemma of the sequence's organization by altering the sonnets' order. As early as 1857, François-Victor Hugo, who was well-informed about the critical debates in England, decided to "restore" their underlying logic, which he thought had been obscured to protect the identities of the parties involved. Denying the legitimacy of the Thorpe order,[6] he created new sections that focused on the relationship between the speaker and his female lover, turning the interaction between the poet and the young man into a sentimental and sexual rivalry about their shared mistress. Hugo added footnotes to explain his logic. Because he included several sonnets to the fair youth in sections ostensibly about a woman, Hugo ended up tacitly reassigning the addressee's gender in several key sonnets without having to change the text.

There were no fewer than four more attempts at reordering the sequence in France after Hugo's, with a view to solving the moral and aesthetic scandal posed by the *Sonnets*. The critic Alfred Copin obviously took his cue from Hugo, although his translation was entirely in rhymed alexandrines, when he reorganized the *Sonnets* into six slightly different sections to illustrate his thesis: "the Sonnets could be entitled: Shakespeare's Confessions" (Shakespeare 1888, 6). In 1919, poet and translator Abel Doysié reorganized the sonnets again, allegedly to "clarify" the narrative line, which was always more or less a variant of the same, with its focus on the poet's love affair with a mistress who betrays him with his best friend (Shakespeare 1919). The eccentric civil servant Edmond L'Hommedé was more original in this respect when, in 1932, he divided up the sequence, translated in rhymed decasyllables, into twelve sections to prove his extravagant thesis: the poems, he claimed, were jumbled to hide the identity of Shakespeare's patron, the Earl of Essex, who had commissioned the poet to write invitations for him to marry in

---

[6] François Guizot was de facto the first to offer to the French public a complete translation of the sonnets in the Thorpe order, and he published them without any comments about their "immorality" (Shakespeare 1862).

order to distract the queen's attention away from his affair with a lady—most probably Penelope Devereux, Lady Rich—with whom the poet was also infatuated (Shakespeare 1932). As for the rival poet of Sonnet 86, he must be either Robert Greene or Christopher Marlowe. The translation comes furnished with intertitles and long glosses to clarify the development of the love affair, and offers titles for each sonnet. The last attempt to date at reorganizing the sequence is that of academic Fernard Baldensperger, who inexplicably argued, in 1943, that the manuscript of the sonnets must have accidentally been printed from back to front (Shakespeare 1943b).

While not all translators who felt ill at ease with the immorality of the *Sonnets* went to the extreme of reorganizing the sequence, most simply left out the most "embarrassing" poems (such as Sonnet 20), or silently altered personal pronouns to reassign some of their passion to the "right" gender. However, at least two translators (from French-speaking Belgium) chose explicitly to reclaim the homoeroticism of the sonnets: in 1942, Giraud d'Uccle (aka Léon Kochnitzky) published a translation of the first 126 sonnets, which he dedicated to his friend (Shakespeare 1942); and in 2010, William Cliff, who defines himself as a gay poet, admitted to choosing the sonnets precisely because of their queerness (Shakespeare 2010). D'Uccle and Cliff stand out among a host of translators who admitted to finding the homoeroticism of some of the sonnets uncomfortable,[7] although this was not always for moral reasons. Belgian poet Marcel Thiry candidly confesses that, because, as a straight man, he cannot share Shakespeare's "homoerotic Eros", he is unable to offer a literal translation (Thiry 1970, 19), and therefore treats the sonnets as a basis for new pieces about the passing of time and an older man's hankering after youth. Thiry thus produces original poems which only have a distant relationship with the *Sonnets*, but can nevertheless be described as creative imitations. In many cases, however, translators tend to underplay or erase, often silently, explicit references to homoeroticism, or they resort to glosses explaining it away by "conventions" of friendship and patronage. One of the most extreme cases of such "rationalizing" efforts is Baldensperger's version, which accumulates

---

[7] A recent translator can still feel entitled to pass homophobic comments on Shakespeare's "perverted morals" (Mourthé 2009, viii–ix).

references to precedents and contemporaries of Shakespeare to contextualize his use of the topoi, including the conventions of "Renaissance" friendship (Shakespeare 1943b).

Another major dividing line between translators concerns key issues of metre and rhyme, which reflect how they position themselves in relation to the literary tradition. From the first, Shakespeare's *Sonnets* were enrolled under the banner of modernity by opponents to the French formalist tradition: the early major translations of the *Sonnets* are thus all in prose (Hugo, Guizot, Montégut, Shakespeare 1857, 1862, 1873), rather than verse. Copin was the first to offer an integral version in rhymed alexandrines in 1888, just before Simone Arnaud, one of only four women who translated the *Sonnets* (Shakespeare 1919), and Fernand Henry (Shakespeare 1900)—but this came after the very partial forays in the same form by Philarète Chasles and de Wailly, both in 1833, Auguste Barbier in 1882, and of course Ernest Lafond's 1856 substantial selection. Translators thus found themselves taking sides in the *querelle* between the classicists—upholders of the French poetic tradition who believed in the canonicity of the rhymed alexandrine—and the Romantics—who opposed the "monotonous" music of what Mallarmé (after Victor Hugo) called "our national cadence" (Mallarmé 1945, 363). Pichot, whose prose translation of Byron was already widely acclaimed, opened the way when he chose prose, in conformity with a Romantic generation opposing what they saw as the tyranny of the rhymed alexandrine. François-René de Chateaubriand famously expressed the sentiment of this generation when, in his essay on translating Milton in1836, he called for a modern form of translation, more literal than the imitative, free translations that had held sway for two centuries. This, he argued, would have to be a new medium, a rhythmic, poetic prose or prose poetry, free from the shackles of verse (Chateaubriand 1837, iii). Chateaubriand translated three sonnets as an illustration of his method in his essay, but the result is curiously inconclusive, and misses out some lines, in spite of some audacious traits, perhaps because the sonnets were entirely devoid of the epic breadth of Milton's grand style which he captured so aptly in his celebrated version.

Meanwhile, the upholders of rhyme and the alexandrine never gave up. When François-Victor Hugo published his prose version of the *Sonnets* in 1857, even before his translation of the drama, it was perhaps in reaction to Lafond's verse translation the previous year (Shakespeare 1856). Lafond was clearly a traditionalist in formal, as well as moral, terms: he alternates between the rhyme schemes of the Italian and French sonnets,[8] with five or seven different rhymes, although he also experiments with the Shakespearean sonnet for the first time in French. In the context of the emerging Romantic conception of translation, his enterprise must be seen as a defence of rhyme against prose. Lafond argues that "the least we can do is give the author the physiognomy he favoured" (Lafond et al. 1848, viii), because only a sonnet can render a sonnet. His "translation", however, completely ignores Shakespeare's natural diction, his light humour and his irony; it is an adaptation which ennobles, and at times beautifies, the original text through an abundance of poetic topoi and archaic words. Lafond thus integrates Shakespeare into the nineteenth-century tradition of the "beau style" ("noble style") without making any concession to the experience of reading a Renaissance sonnet.

In fact, reading translations of the *Sonnets* can be tantamount to reading a counterhistory of French poetry. Twentieth-century translations thus understandably manifest a much less reverential attitude to both rhyme and the alexandrine, in the wake of the poetic revolutions accomplished by symbolist and modernist poets successively. After Mallarmé's and Verlaine's experimentations with verse, which extended the realm of formal possibilities, the translation of the sonnets could now take many more forms, from prose to a variety of metres from decasyllables to four-teeners, and free verse. The twentieth and twenty-first centuries are still periodically polarized by renewed oppositions between upholders of a strict sonnet form, mostly in rhymed alexandrines, and proponents of more freedom. While the alexandrine still holds sway, with over half of the fifty-six translations published since 1900 in that metre (twenty-one in rhymed, nine in blank, alexandrines), twelve are in free verse (21%), and four only in prose (7%).[9] As for the rest, four are in rhymed deca-syllables, one in (unrhymed) hendecasyllables and five are in a mixture of metres (including fourteeners). Abel Doysié was the first, in 1919, in the era of modernism, to offer a French translation of the *Sonnets* in unrhymed alexandrines, thus responding to Mallarmé's critical revision of that metre in the late nineteenth century (Shakespeare 1919). Mallarmé had famously called for the liberation of the alexandrine from

---

[8] The Italian sonnet generally follows the rhyme scheme ABBA ABBA CCD EED, while the French sonnet is usually ABBA ABBA CCD EDE.

[9] For a selective anthology and an exhaustive bibliography, see Cottegnies 2021, 972–76.

the strict rules that governed its usage in the Classical tradition, including the mandatory presence of a distinct pause, the caesura, between the first and second hemistichs, and a very codified use of the final "e" within the line—voiced before a consonant but silent before a vowel sound or a punctuation mark. Doysié was soon followed, in 1927, by Émile Le Brun, a friend of Verlaine's, whose version is distinctive for its very light punctuation (Shakespeare 1927), and later by Giraud D'Uccle (Shakespeare 1942), Henri Thomas (Shakespeare 1961), Pierre Leyris (Leyris 2002), Robert Ellrodt (Shakespeare 2002), and, more recently, Jean-Michel Déprats (Shakespeare 2021). It is only in the 1960s that the first translation in free verse appeared, with unrhymed lines of unequal lengths, that of Armel Guerne (Shakespeare 1964). This line of translators includes other distinguished poets, like René Char (with Tina Jolas, Char and Jolas 1981), or, more recently, Jacques Darras in his first (selective) version (Darras 1995) and Yves Bonnefoy (Shakespeare 2007). Other metres were also experimented with, like the rhymed decasyllable, a dense metre used by French Renaissance sonneteer Maurice Scève, among others, which some see as the closest equivalent to the rhymed pentameter (Daniel and Geneviève Bournet, Shakespeare 1995; Henri Meschonnic 1999; William Cliff, Shakespeare 2010), or the hendecasyllable, a line of eleven syllables, inspired by Verlaine's own experiments with uneven metre (Hennequin, Shakespeare 2016). Finally, a handful of translators, who are often published poets themselves, have chosen to go against the grain by returning to prose poetry, like Frédéric Roger-Cornaz (Shakespeare [1929]), Maurice Blanchard (Shakespeare 1944) or Pierre Jean Jouve (Shakespeare 1950).

While this review allows the reader to distinguish general trends, it is a peculiarity of this history of the integration of the *Sonnets* into French literary culture that the questions of the rhyme, and the alexandrine, pose themselves over and over again, in spite of the poetic revolutions of the twentieth century. As seen above, the proportion of contemporary translators who have chosen the rhymed alexandrine is overwhelming, in spite of other poetic experimentations, so strong is the weight of the literary tradition. Many still contend that a poem written as a sonnet must be translated as a classical sonnet, in order to transpose in French the experience of reading a Shakespearean sonnet, even if it is at the expense of excessive formalism, or, sometimes, archaism. A strong divide thus opposes the proponents of strict classical forms (rhymed alexandrines or decasyllables, and strict rhyme schemes), who believe in creative constraint, and the champions of metrical freedom, who prefer to think of the sonnet as a rhythmic and musical experience which can be transposed and recreated through different means. Jean Fuzier or Jean Malaplate's perfectly orthodox alexandrines (Shakespeare 1959, 1992) thus run the risk of sounding at times like pastiches of Renaissance sonnets, and the same can be said of Meschonnic's and Daniel and Geneviève Bournet's experiments with rhymed decasyllables (Shakespeare 1995). This is due to the numerous archaic words and phrases, the use of poetic inversions, and the elision of articles made necessary by formal constraints. French is a language that is notorious for possessing far fewer monosyllables and for being less concise and economical than English. This poses technical problems, and makes the decasyllable in particular a real challenge. An alternative trend has led to a much more relaxed attitude towards metre, however, and even sometimes, among the translators who have adopted "free" verse or a mixture of various metrical forms, to prosaic slackness—a possible corollary of the democratization of translation and publishing media. For it is a fact that translation today is no longer the affair of specialists, whether professional translators, academics, or published poets; and that the great variety of publishers and media has made it easier for enlightened amateurs to publish their own versions of the *Sonnets*. It is not even necessary to read English fluently to translate Shakespeare, when so many translations and scholarly editions are so easily available.

For all translators, however, retranslating Shakespeare's *Sonnets* is a personal challenge, a way of confronting an iconic text that is notoriously obscure and complex, and for many it opens up a space of formal experimentation. It is not surprising therefore that so many published poets should have confronted the *Sonnets*, including major figures of the French-speaking poetic scene, like René Char and Tina Jolas, Pierre Jean Jouve, Yves Bonnefoy or Jacques Darras. No fewer than twenty translators of the *Sonnets* since 1900 are acclaimed poets in their own rights—a stunning 40%. Other distinguished figures include Swiss poets Armel Guerne, Frédéric Roger-Cornaz and Pierre-Louis Matthey; Belgian poets Giraud d'Uccle, Mélot du Dy (Robert Mélot), Marcel Thiry and

William Cliff, and French poets André Prudhommeaux, Maurice Blanchard, Henri Thomas, Jean Rousselot and Patrick Reumaux.[10] For most of these, the experience of translating Shakespeare is both an intellectual and poetic challenge and a personal contest. Translations by poets are often "adaptations"; they stand out because the poets' original voices tend not to dissolve in the translating process: couched in their own poetic idioms, their versions retain much of their distinctive worlds, although this might be an obstacle to accuracy, and can occasionally play against the text. A poet's fidelity to Shakespeare is generally more to the spirit than the letter of the text, and is placed at the level of poetic experience. Darras perfectly synthesizes this form of "adaptation" by defining translation as interpretation in the musical sense of the term, a form of re-enactment and re-possession that is necessarily subjective (Shakespeare 2013, 9). This is confirmed by Jouve (Shakespeare 1959) and Bonnefoy (Shakespeare 1994, 2007), who have also produced intensely personal rewritings of the *Sonnets* that are unmistakably theirs. Jouve's translation, in prose, is characterized by the combination of prosaic simplicity and mannered archaism that is the hallmark of his own poetry, a balance which produces, according to critic Patrick Hersant, "obscurity that conceals no enigma" (Hersant 2004, online). Meanwhile, critics have described Bonnefoy's version in free verse as intensely lyrical and musical, much more so than the original. Bonnefoy significantly ignores Shakespeare's predilection for rhetorical effects such as repetitions and his reliance on topoi, to freely expand on the lyricism and the passion suggested in the poems.

For some poets-cum-translators the confrontation with Shakespeare's *Sonnets* is prolonged over decades, and occasionally over a lifetime: the number of poets who revise earlier versions, or decide to offer a new version based on different principles, is overwhelming. Matthey, for instance, first published a translation of forty-nine sonnets in 1944, but tirelessly revised his text over the successive editions, and he was still working on revisions at the time of his death—the posthumous edition of his works includes a version based on the very last authorial manuscripts (Matthey 1944, 2016). Yves Bonnefoy also thoroughly revised his 1994 translation of twenty-four sonnets (Shakespeare 1994)

---

[10] Char and Jolas 1981, Shakespeare 1950, 1994, 2007, Darras 1995 and Shakespeare 2013, 1919, [1929], Matthey 2016, Shakespeare 1942, Shakespeare 1943a, Thiry 1970, Shakespeare 1944, 1945, 1961, 1969, Reumaux 2018.

for his 2007 complete edition (Shakespeare 2007). While both versions, in free verse, share similar principles, Bonnefoy objects, in 2007, to his earlier attempt for letting sonnets spill over into poems of sixteen or seventeen lines, with lines of varying lengths. He now feels that, rather than slackness, the rhythm of the sonnets demands concentration (Shakespeare 2007, 37). His 2007 version is thus more compact and focuses more on issues of rhythm. Meanwhile, Jacques Darras's conversation with the *Sonnets* has been going on for over twenty years, and is perhaps not over: he first included a selection of thirty-five sonnets in free verse in a 1995 miscellany, before publishing a very different, integral version in 2013, in rhymed alexandrines (Shakespeare 1995, 2013). Still poring over the sonnets in 2018, he published the two versions of twenty-two of the sonnets (revised) as parallel texts in a new collection (Darras 2018).

Critic Christian Mouze has recently argued that "a translation is not the rival of another translation, but a flower added to the bouquet" (cited in Déprats 2021, lix). Yet for French translators Shakespeare's *Sonnets* have consistently served as an experimental battleground over which were fought *querelles* that traverse the field of French poetry: between the Romantics who defended prose versus the Classicists who fought for the poetic tradition; between the guardians of fixed metre versus the proponents of blank or free verse, and between the supporters of "beau style" ("noble style") and those of a more "natural" style. *Pace* Mouze, new French translations are always, in some sense, the rivals of previous translations, if only because each translator is convinced that he can improve on his predecessors' attempts, in spite of all claims to modesty. A translator does not just grapple with a challenging text, therefore, when he or she tries to render the experience of reading the *Sonnets* in French, but with a whole poetic line that determines his or her position in the history of the translations of the *Sonnets*, and, beyond it, in the very field of French literature. If the Shakespeare of the *Sonnets* was treated as a rival poet in the nineteenth century, it is first because he came to represent an alternative to a stifling national literary tradition and allowed poets and translators to express their aspiration to literary freedom; and, conversely, for the upholders of French classicism, because the *Sonnets* appeared then as a slightly barbarous Other, the product of an incomprehensible culture. For contemporary translators, working in a less constrained environment, in a time when the weight of the literary tradition is less prevalent and literary *querelles* perhaps less heated, the *Sonnets* have often been treated as the ultimate touchstone, the holy grail of poetry, each sonnet an almost magically perfect form whose delicate, organic machinery cannot be expressed by the sum of its parts, and must be felt and experienced, as well as understood. Sparring with them means confronting a form of genius that was recognized early in the nineteenth century when critic Delécluze saw in them "the imprint of a genius of the first order" (1848, 517). But as Darras has recently argued: "knowing that there will never be a definitive version […], to translate Shakespeare's *Sonnets* is to embrace the principle of unsatisfaction" (Shakespeare 2013, 7–8).

REFERENCES

Acker, Faith. 2020. *First Readers of Shakespeare's Sonnets, 1590–1790*. New York and London: Routledge.

Arnaud, Simone. 1891. "Les Sonnets de Shakespeare". *Nouvelle revue* 71: 537–555.

Barbier, Auguste. 1882. *Chez les poètes. Études. Traductions et imitations en vers.* Paris: E. Dentu.

Berman, Antoine. 1995. *Pour une critique des traductions: John Donne*, Paris: Gallimard, Collection Bibliothèques des idées.

Besterman, Thomas, ed. 2008. *Voltaire on Shakespeare*. Berne: Peter Lang.

Char René, and Tina Jolas. 1981. *La Planche de vivre, poésie. Raimbaut de Vaqueiras, Pétrarque, Lope des Vega, Shakespeare, et. al.* Paris: Gallimard.

Chasles, Philarète. 1833. *Caractères et paysages*. Paris: Mame-Delaunay.

Chateaubriand, François-René de. 1836. *Essai sur la littérature anglaise et considérations sur le génie des hommes, des temps et des révolutions*. Paris: Furne et Charles Gosselin, 2 vol. T. 1.

Chateaubriand, François-René de. 1837. *Œuvres complètes. Le Paradis perdu de Milton*. T. XXXV. Paris: Purrat Frères.

Cottegnies, Line. 2021. "Les traductions françaises des Sonnets". In Shakespeare 2021. 961–1020.

Cottegnies, Line. 2018. "Les traductions de Shakespeare en Europe: du 'sauvage ivre' à 'notre Shakespeare'". In *Les Routes de la traduction. Babel à Genève*, ed. Barbara Cassin and Nicolas Ducimetière. 259–267. Paris: Gallimard - Fondation Bodmer.

Darras, Jacques. 1995. *L'Embouchure de la Maye dans les vagues de la Manche.* Bruxelles: Le Cri.

Darras Jacques. 2018. *L'Embouchure de la Maye. Poème.* Bègles: Le Castor astral – In'hui.

Delécluze, Étienne Jean. 1848. *Dante Alighieri ou la poésie amoureuse*. Paris, Amyot.

Déprats, Jean-Michel. 2021. "Traduire les Sonnets". In Shakespeare 2021. lix–lxvi.

Dobson, Michael. 1992. *The Making of the National Poet: Shakespeare, Adaptation and Authorship 1660–1709*. Oxford: Clarendon Press.

Dugas, Don-John. 2006. *Marketing the Bard: Shakespeare in Performance and Print, 16601740*. Columbia, University of Missouri Press.

Hazlitt, William. 1848. *Characters of Shakespeare's Plays* [1817]. 4th ed. London: C. Templeman.

Hersant, Patrick. 2004. "Shakespeare en miroir: Pierre Jean Jouve". *Études Épistémè*, 6. https://journals.openedition.org/episteme/3814 (accessed 03/08/2021).

Kingsley-Smith, Jane. 2019. *The Afterlife of Shakespeare's Sonnets*. Cambridge: Cambridge University Press.

Kingsley-Smith, Jane. 2022. "'Distinguished by the Letter C': Edmond Malone and Edward Capell as Rival Editors of *Shake-speare's Sonnets*". *Shakespeare Quarterly*, 2022; quac023. https://doi.org/10.1093/sq/quac023 (advance publication: 12/08/2022).

Kirwan, Peter. 2021. "The Shakespeare Canon from the Sixteenth to the Twenty-First Century". In *The Arden Research Handbook of Shakespeare and Textual Studies*, ed. Lukas Erne, 150–167. London and New York: Bloomsbury.

Lafond, Ernest, and Edmond Lafond, trans. 1848. *Dante, Pétrarque, Michel-Ange. Sonnets choisis*. Paris: Comptoir des Imprimeurs.

Leyris, Pierre. 2002. *Rencontres de poètes anglais*. Paris: Corti.

Lintott, Bernard (ed.) 1711. *A Collection of Poems in Two Volumes*. London: Bernard Lintottt, s.d.

Mallarmé, Stéphane. 1945. *Crise de vers*. In *Œuvres complètes*, ed. H. Mondor. Paris: Gallimard, Bibliothèque de la Pléiade.

Matthey, Pierre-Louis. 2016. *Poésies complètes*. Chavannes-près-Renens: Editions Empreintes. 5 vol. T. V.

Matthey, Pierre-Louis. 1944. *Un Cahier d'Angleterre: poésie célèbres transcrites*. Lausanne: H. L. Mermod.

Meschonnic, Henri. 1999. *Poétique du traduire*. Lagrasse: Verdier.

Mourthé, Claude. 2009. "Avant-propos". In *Shakespeare. Sonnets*. Trans. C. Mourthé. Saintes: Editions de l'Atlantique.

Reumaux, Patrick. 2018. *Quarante Sonnets noirs*. Nancy: Isolato.

Roberts, Sasha. 2007. "Reception and Influence". In *The Cambridge Companion to Shakespeare's Poetry*, ed. Patrick Cheney, 260–280. Cambridge: Cambridge University Press.

Shakespeare, William. 1609. *Sonnets*. London.

Shakespeare, William. 1640. *Poems*. London.

Shakespeare, William. 1709. *The Works of Mr. William Shakespear; in Six Volumes*. Ed. Nicholas Rowe, London, J. Tonson.

Shakespeare, William. 1710. *The Works of Mr. William Shakespear. Volume the Seventh.* Ed. Charles Gildon. London, E. Curll. Vol. 7.

Shakespeare, William. 1745–1746. *Le Théâtre anglois.* Trans. Pierre Antoine de La Place. Londres [Paris]. 4 vol.

Shakespeare, William. 1776–1783. *Shakespeare.* Trans. Pierre Le Tourneur. Paris: Veuve Duchesne. 20 vol.

Shakespeare, William. 1780. *Supplement to the Edition of Shakespeare's Plays Published in 1778 by Samuel Johnson and George Stevens.* Ed. Edmond Malone. London: C. Bathurst.

Shakespeare, William. 1821. *Sonnets.* Trans. Amédée Pichot. In *Œuvres complètes, traduites de l'anglais par Letourneur. Nouvelle édition, revue et corrigée par F. Guizot et A. P. Traducteur de Lord Byron.* Paris: Ladvocat. 13 vol. T. 1.

Shakespeare, William. 1856. *Poëmes et sonnets de William Shakespere, traduits en vers.* Trans. Ernest Lafond. Paris: Typographie de Charles Lahure.

Shakespeare, William. 1857. *Les Sonnets de Shakespeare traduits pour la première fois en entier.* Trans. François-Victor Hugo. Paris, Michel Lévy Frères.

Shakespeare, William. 1862. *Sonnets.* In *Œuvres complètes de Shakspeare, traduction de M. Guizot, Nouvelle édition entièrement revue.* Trans. François Guizot. Paris: Didier et Cie, 1860–1862. 8 vol. T. 8.

Shakespeare, William. 1873. *Œuvres complètes.* Trans. Émile Montégut. Paris: Librairie Hachette, 1867–1873. 10 vol. T. X.

Shakespeare, William. 1888. *Les Sonnets de Shakespeare en vers français.* Trans. Alfred Copin. Paris: A. Dupret.

Shakespeare, William. 1900. *Les Sonnets de Shakspeare. Traduits en sonnets français.* Trans. Fernand Henry. Paris: Librairie Paul Ollendorff.

Shakespeare, William. 1919. *Les Poëmes intimes et le pélerin passionné.* Trans. Abel Doysié. Paris: La Renaissance du livre.

Shakespeare, William. 1927. *Sonnets.* Trans. Émile Le Brun. Paris: J. Schiffrin, Collection Classique des éditions de la Pléiade.

Shakespeare, William. [1929]. *Shakespeare. Sonnets.* Trans. Frédéric Roger-Cornaz. Paris: Payot, Bibliothèque Miniature, n. d.

Shakespeare, William. 1932. *Le Secret de Shakespeare. Les Sonnets.* Trans. Edmond L'Hommedé. Paris: Henri Didier.

Shakespeare, William. 1942. *Sonnets.* Trans. Giraud d'Uccle. Alger: Edmond Charlot, Collection Poésie & Théâtre.

Shakespeare, William. 1943a. *XXV Sonnets de Shakespeare.* Trans. Mélot du Dy. Bruxelles: Éditions du Cercles d'Art.

Shakespeare, William. 1943b. *Les Sonnets de Shakespeare, traduits en vers français et accompagnés d'un commentaire continu.* Trans. Fernand Baldensperger. Berkeley and Los Angeles: University of California Press.

Shakespeare, William. 1944. *Douze Sonnets.* Trans. Maurice Blanchard. Paris: Editions des Quatre Vents.

Shakespeare, William. 1945. *Les Sonnets de Shakespeare. Essai d'interprétation poétique française*. Trans. André Prudhommeaux. Porrentruy: Editions des Portes de France, Collection de l'Oiselier.

Shakespeare, William. 1950. *Shakespeare. Sonnets*. Trans. Pierre Jean Jouve. Paris: Editions du Sagittaire.

Shakespeare, William. 1959. *Sonnets*. Trans. Jean Fuzier. In *Shakespeare.Œuvres complètes*. Ed. Henri Fluchère. Paris: Gallimard, Bibliothèque de la Pléiade. 2 vol. T. I.

Shakespeare, William. 1961. *Sonnets*. Trad. Henri Thomas. In *Œuvres complètes de Shakespeare*. Ed. Pierre Leyris et Henri Evans. Paris: Club français du livre, 1964–1961. 12 vol. T. VII.

Shakespeare, William. 1964. *Sonnets*. Trans. Armel Guerne. In *Œuvres complètes*. Ed. José Axelrad. Bruges: Desclée de Brouwer, 1961–1964. 4 vol. T. 4.

Shakespeare, William. 1969. *Sonnets, Texte Anglais*. Trans. Jean Rousselot. Paris: Editions Chambelland.

Shakespeare, William. 1992. *Les Sonnets*. Trans. Jean Malaplate. Lausanne: L'Âge d'homme.

Shakespeare, William. 1994. *XXIV Sonnets de Shakespeare, précédé de « Traduire les sonnets de Shakespeare »*. Trans. Yves Bonnefoy. Paris: Les Bibliophiles de France.

Shakespeare, William. 1995. *Shakespeare. Sonnets*. Trans. Daniel and Geneviève Bournet. Paris: Librairie A-G. Nizet.

Shakespeare, William. 2002. *Sonnets*. Trans. Robert Ellrodt. In *Œuvres complètes, Tragicomédies II, Poésies*, ed. Michel Grivelet et Gilles Montsarrat. Paris: Laffont, Collection Bouquins.

Shakespeare, William. 2007. *Les Sonnets, précédés de Vénus et Adonis, Le Viol de Lucrèce, Phénix et Colombe*. Trans. Yves Bonnefoy. Paris: Gallimard, Collection Poésie.

Shakespeare, William. 2010. *Shakespeare. Sonnets*. Trans. William Cliff. Bruxelles: Editions du Hazard.

Shakespeare, William. 2013. *Sonnets*. Trans. Jacques Darras. Paris: Bernard Grasset.

Shakespeare, William. 2016. *Sonnets de Shakespeare, version revue et corrigée*. Trans. Pierre Hennequin. Online https://phennequin.wordpress.com/2016/11/ (accessed 3 August 2021).

Shakespeare, William. 2021. *Sonnets*. Trans. Jean-Michel Déprats. In *Œuvres complètes*. Ed. Jean-Michel Déprats et Gisèle Venet. Paris: Gallimard, Bibliothèque de la Pléiade, 2002–2021. 8 vol. T. VIII.

Thiry, Marcel. 1970. *Attouchements des sonnets de Shakespeare*. Bruxelles: André de Rache.

Tournu, Christophe. 2017. "The French Connection' among French Translations of Milton and Within Du Bocage's Paradis Terrestre". In *Milton in

Translation, ed. Angelica Duran, Islam Issa and Jonathan R. Olson, 140–164. Oxford: Oxford University Press.

Wailly, Léon de. 1834. "Sonnets de Shakspeare". *Revue des deux mondes*. 3rd series. IV: 679–697.

Willems, Michèle. 2007. "L'excès face au bon goût: la réception de Gilles-Shakespeare de Voltaire à Hugo". *Société française Shakespeare* 25: 224–237.

CHAPTER 4

A Stylistic Analysis of Montale's Version of Sonnet 33: Translation, Petrarchism and Innovation in Modern Italian Poetry

Allison L. Steenson and Luca Trissino

The Cultural Context

This essay consists of an in-depth analytical and stylistic comparison of Shakespeare's Sonnet 33 and the translation of the same poem in Italian on the part of Eugenio Montale (1896–1981), an emblematic figure in the Italian poetry of the Novecento. After an analysis of the formal features that inform the structure and meaning of the original English poem, this essay offers a close reading of Montale's translation, with particular regard to its formal aspects (structure, metre, syntax, sound and speech figures), in order to illustrate his specific strategies in the reception

A. L. Steenson (✉)
University of Sussex, Falmer, UK
e-mail: A.Steenson@sussex.ac.uk

L. Trissino
Università della Svizzera italiana, Lugano, Switzerland
e-mail: luca.trissino@usi.ch

© The Author(s), under exclusive license to Springer Nature Switzerland AG 2023
J. Kingsley-Smith and W. R. Rampone Jr. (eds.), *Shakespeare's Global Sonnets*, Global Shakespeares, https://doi.org/10.1007/978-3-031-09472-9_4

and translation of foreign poetry. The text of Sonnet 33 as translated by Montale provides a clear illustration of one of the main aspects of literary translation, i.e. its function as a site for cultural mediation and to provide a space for the negotiation of cultural (linguistic, ideological) constructs. In so doing, literary translation activates both centripetal and centrifugal forces that shape reception and inform individual poetic choices at the metrical, stylistic and semantic level. More significantly for the aims of this volume, Montale's version of Sonnet 33 is also a clear example of the role of Shakespearean poetry in informing modern literary traditions in languages other than English. Montale's sonnet confirms the persistence of Shakespeare's influence over time: his poetry has been periodically revitalized and has provided foreign literary languages with innovative means of expression.[1]

In Italy, the practice of poetic translation became firmly established in the 1930s, when Italian poets adopted it, both as an individual exercise and a collective pursuit, as the outward expression of their conscious effort in renovating Italian culture and "balancing European tendencies with national identity" (Mengaldo 1978, XXXII). This historical period saw Italian poets engaged in the reception of the stylistic innovations developed by European symbolism, while, on the other hand, striving to reclaim the language of their national poetic tradition, which was at this point close to being abandoned, if it had not been altogether dismissed. In the 1930s, the relationship between the Italian and foreign literary traditions was being fundamentally redefined, and the period is marked by irreversible fractures in the traditional metrical system and by the demise of closed poetic forms. Therefore, it became necessary to adopt a form that could accommodate foreign text without misinterpreting it or distorting it, but that could at the same time imbue it with unique stylistic value. In this context, it is clear how and why establishing a poetic form that was functionally identical to the original was a core objective for contemporary Italian poets. As a result of this situation, the translation of poetry by poets saw an exceptional growth between the 1930s and the first half of the 1940s; immediately after World War

---

[1] Paragraph 2, "Shakespeare's Sonnet 33", has been written by Allison Steenson, who is also responsible for translating the text into English (including direct quotes from authors and critics, unless otherwise specified). Paragraph 3, "Montale's Italian Version of Sonnet 33", has been written by Luca Trissino. The introductory paragraph "The Cultural Context" has been written collaboratively.

Two, poetic translation in Italy could comfortably live on "the extensive application of the methods and the results" (Fortini 1987, 359) of the previous decade. Thanks to poetic translation, the Italian lyrical tradition could rediscover its legacy *ab extra*, incidentally reclaiming the sonnet, one of the most iconic among Italian poetic forms, through a mediation process that involved both English sonnets and Italian attempts at re-elaborating the Shakespearean sonnet pattern. It is not a coincidence that this operation took place in the same span of time that saw historical events threatening Italy's culture and the country's fundamental values. Through the practice of literary translation in the interwar period, the Italian lyrical language was both consolidated and mitigated in its lexicon, syntax and available structures; translation of foreign texts enacted both a formal and ideological transfer, with the ultimate aim of recovering a (foreign) tradition in order to rebuild a national one.

Through the 1930s and the beginning of the 1940s, in a crucial moment in the country's history, foreign literary experiences, past and present, provided Italian national poetry with a unique reforming potential, and Italian poets consequently found themselves at the core of the osmotic relationship between different poetic traditions and individual poetic expression. Overall, Montale's Sonnet 33 represents a perfect example of this type of literary encounter, amalgamating the poetics of the translated text with the personal poetics of the translator. It is in this specific context that Montale's version of Sonnet 33 must be interpreted: in Montale's text, translation moves from a process of absorbing and recovering, towards "an individual reclaiming of specific models from the past" (Mengaldo 1996, 142).

SHAKESPEARE'S SONNET 33

Sonnet 33 belongs to the first part of Shakespeare's *Sonnets* (1–126); here, most poems are addressed to an unnamed "fair youth", a character that has been generally identified with William Herbert, Earl of Pembroke and one of Shakespeare's patrons. Although the transmission and publication history of the *Sonnets* remains unclear, the 1609 edition is generally accepted as presenting the poems in the order decided upon by their author, a fact which allows for several considerations regarding Sonnet 33 (Burrow 2002, 95). In the economy of the collection, Sonnet 33 and the ones that follow it have long been considered as a self-contained cluster, nestled inside the first partition of the sequence. The sonnets in this section, which appears to consist of chronologically linked poems, were probably composed in the mid- to late 1590s, when the craze for writing and reading sonnet sequences was at its height in England, although single poems might have been revised at a later time and closer to their publication date (Burrow 2002, 103–108). The cluster to which Sonnet 33 belongs also includes Sonnets 34 and 35; within this group, Sonnet 33 is more closely linked with the poem that directly follows it, which continues to employ the same protracted metaphor linking the fair youth to the image of the sun (Paterson 2012, 98).

This group of poems, sometimes known as "estrangement sonnets" and termed a "notorious problem spot" (Hedley 1994, 1) in the collection, marks an unexpected change in the mood of the sequence, which becomes noticeably darker (Hammon 1981, 42; Paterson 2012, 98–99). The group suggests a period of estrangement and introduces into the sequence the first inklings of deception, disloyalty and disaffection (Duncan-Jones 1997, 176). This change in mood running through Sonnets 33–35 has been associated with a separation of the lovers, the reason for which can be identified in a romantic betrayal on the part of the fair youth. This reading is supported by textual evidence: the unspecified "stain" in Sonnet 33 is further explained as a "strong offence" in Sonnet 34, and then finally identified as a "sensual fault" in Sonnet 35. The group concludes with the dejected poet acknowledging that he cannot stop loving the fair youth and "grovelling in a pit of self-humiliation" (Slater 2016, 167). Finally, Mark Schwartzberg has suggested that the change to a darker psychological mood, mirroring a similar shift in Shakespeare's later dramatic works, could be due to the loss of Shakespeare's young son Hamnet, who died in 1596, close to the composition of this part of the sequence. According to Schwartzberg, the evidence for this can be found in l. 11 ("he was but one hour mine") and in the closing pun between the words "sun" and "son" (Schwartzberg 2002, 14, mentioned below). Shakespeare's text reads as follows:

> 1   Full many a glorious morning have I seen
>   Flatter the mountain tops with sovereign eye,
>   Kissing with golden face the meadows green,
>   Gilding pale streams with heavenly alchemy,
> 5   Anon permit the basest clouds to ride
>   With ugly rack on his celestial face,
>   And from the forlorn world his visage hide,
>   Stealing unseen to west with this disgrace:
> 9   Even so my sun one early morn did shine
>   With all triumphant splendour on my brow;

> But out, alack, he was but one hour mine,
> The region cloud hath masked him from me now.
> 13   Yet him for this my love no whit disdaineth;
> Suns of the world may stain when heaven's sun staineth. (Burrow
> 2002, 447)

As far as the content is concerned, the poem is built around an extended metaphor linking the poet's beloved to the image of the morning sun, which is sustained and reworked throughout the poem, giving Sonnet 33 a tight thematic coherence (Fineman 1986, 68; Hammond 1981, 42). Sun-imagery is not uncommon in sonnets, and had been used before by Shakespeare, for instance in Sonnet 7 (beginning "Lo! in the Orient when the gracious light"), which, however, lacks the deeply personal sorrow and the barely concealed bitterness of 33. In Sonnet 33, the sun metaphor is not only a clever conceit, but functions as a powerful structuring element in conjunction with the more technical aspects of the poem. The poem has long been recognized as playing with the proverb "the morning sun never lasts the day", an idea that is here materialized, and linked to the fickleness of the fair youth (Booth 1977, 186). More to the point, the sun metaphor in Sonnet 33 functions across several juxtaposed layers of meaning, intertwined through the semantic connotations of the words involved. The most literal is the visual and meteorological layer: in this sense, the poem describes a promising bright morning transformed into foul weather by the arrival of dark clouds obscuring the sun. A further layer of the metaphor is psychological, linking natural phenomena to the poet's passions and using nature as a mirror for the lover's emotions. The connection between nature and human feelings had a long history in sonnet writing, dating back to Petrarch's *Canzoniere* and to Sonnet 35 (beginning "*Solo e pensoso*"). An additional layer alludes to the sun in the context of astrology and alchemy (with words such as "heavenly alchemy"), two connected exoteric practices that had a significant weight in contemporary knowledge. Alchemy in popular culture was linked to the creation of gold (alluded to in ll. 3–4), and a reference to the sun "playing the alchemist" and turning matter into gold is contained in *King John* (Act III, scene 1; Burrow 2002, 446). One last semantic layer links the metaphor of the sun to courtly and political discourse, a *milieu* that is often referenced in sonnets from the Elizabethan period. To this level allude such terms as "glorious", "sovereign" and "flatter"; these word choices bring readers inside the world of the Tudor court, where poems (especially sonnets) could be used to curry favour with the powerful and were often understood as vehicles for covert political messages. Finally, several critics have also highlighted the presence of "vague and unharnessed" religious suggestions in words such as "heavenly" and "heaven's sun", connected both to "incarnation and crucifixion" (Booth 1977, 188) and to "the sanctified political and cosmological order" (Fineman 1986, 69); this last interpretation hinges on the pun between the words "sun" and "son" that seals the sonnet.

The logical development of the poem, and with it the development of the metaphor which constitutes its thematic core, is heavily dependent on the sonnet's main metrical partitions, which function as a structuring device, enclosing three self-contained metrical modules, which correspond to three separate units of meaning. The three main parts of the poem can be identified with, respectively, the first two quatrains, the third quatrain and the final couplet (Booth 1969, 39–41). The first two quatrains consist of a single sentence, which is built by stacking together two different periods corresponding to the two rhyming quatrains (ll. 1–4 and 5–8). The first period sets the stage for the extended metaphor that is the main *motif* of the poem, which is presented in its first layer of meaning, describing the rising sun (l.1, "glorious morning") and its effects on, respectively, "mountain tops" (l. 2), "meadows" (l. 3) and "streams" (l. 4.). This first quatrain achieves a remarkable visual and mimetic effect (Vendler 1997, 176), with each line expanding on the previous one, and creating a surprisingly dynamic depiction of a landscape at dawn, where the sun can be seen descending from the mountain tops, down to the surrounding meadows and finally shining on the water of a nearby brook.

The second quatrain operates a reversal of this blissful image, describing how the sun is suddenly ("anon", l. 5) obscured by menacing clouds, which hide the sun's face and leave the world "forlorn". This abrupt change in weather mirrors the change in the poetic tone of the whole sequence, with Sonnet 33 introducing explicitly negative emotions into the narrative (Booth 1977, 186). The prosody of this quatrain similarly serves the content: if the first quatrain sees four units of meaning juxtaposed using asyndetic coordination to create a cumulative effect, this second quatrain features longer sentences connected by a conjunction ("and", l. 7) and several adjective+ noun pairs, especially in the first two lines ("basest clouds", "ugly rack", "celestial face", "forlorn world", ll. 57). Here, the longer periods and the series of word-pairs allow the rhythm of the poem to reach a slower pace, and mimetically express the sense of creeping menace symbolized by the clouds. These first two quatrains have been seen as resembling the organization of poetic material in Italian sonnets, where a structural and thematic differentiation is found between an initial octave and the following sestet. In 33, this feeling is reinforced by the third quatrain, separated from the first two by a sort of *volta* signalled by the thematic and syntactic break between ll. 8 and 9, and by the contrastive beginning of l. 9 (Booth 1969, 39; Boyd 2014, 46). The third quatrain (ll. 9–12) perfectly mirrors the content of the octave, with ll. 9–10 and 11–12 recalling, respectively, ll. 1–4 and ll. 5–8. Here, the second layer of the metaphor is laid bare, linking natural phenomena to human psychology. The final couplet is an independent unit, syntactically and prosodically self-sufficient and separated from the rest of the poem by the change in metre (from alternate to couplet) and rhyming syllable. The last line contains the key to the extended metaphor that lies at the heart of this sonnet, in the comparison between "heaven's sun" and "suns of the world". The two concepts in the metaphor, the sun and the person, symmetrically occupy each half-line of l. 14 (Vendler 1997, 176). Finally, according to many critics l. 14 contains a hidden pun in the phrase "suns of the world", which could be read as "sons of the world", making the founding metaphor even more explicit (Hammond 1981, 43–44; Paterson 2012, 100).

The vocabulary contributes to reinforcing the strong structural parallelisms and symmetries between stanzas that are established at the prosodic and metrical level. Lines 1–4 contain overtly positive words connected to the lexical fields of kingship. The sun is "glorious" and "sovereign" like a monarch sitting high on his throne, whose gaze "flatters" its lower-standing subjects; the scene is visually dominated by the idea of gold ("golden face" l. 3, "gilded streams" l. 4). Line 4 contains an allusion to the spiritual and mystical world ("heavenly alchemy"), evoking ideas of nobility and virtue. The vocabulary of the second quatrain operates a complete reversal on the scene just described, with several negative and pejorative terms ("basest clouds", "ugly rack", "forlorn world", "stealing", "disgrace"; Boyd 2014, 46). The use of the adjective "base", with the contemporary political and social meaning of "vile", "low-born" (*OED s.v.*) in particular, is in sharp and painful contrast with the images evoked by the language of the previous stanza (Booth 1977, 187; Burrow 2002, 446). The lexicon of the third quatrain similarly contributes to the structural design of the poem, with symmetrically placed reminders (in l.

10 "triumphant splendour", and l. 12 "region cloud", both positioned in the first half-line of an even-numbered line) pointing to the opposed landscapes depicted, respectively, in the first and second quatrains.

Several aural repetitions also contribute to enhance both the appeal of the piece and its overall thematic and stylistic coherence. The alliteration involving only the opening fricative sounds in line 12 links the two lines and widens the pace of the opening sequence. From there, the extended metaphor that lies behind the poem is sustained throughout by several instances of alliteration that also respond to structural reasons. In the first quatrain, the alliteration on the letter "m" links together content-heavy words such as "morning", "mountain" and "meadows", while alliteration on the letter "g" links together "glorious", "golden" and "gilding" with "green" for a powerful visual effect (Boyd 2014, 46). Sustained alliteration on the letter "s", runs through ll. 9–14, linking the "sun" (ll. 9, 12) to several words situated in close ("splendour", l. 10) or conflicting lexical fields (l. 14 "stain", "stained"). This has the effect of partially erasing the marked separation between the third quatrain and the couplet, contributing to the coherence of the piece; at the same time, the semantic relationships between the alliterating words complicate the initial metaphor with suggestions of negative attributes, and cast doubt on the resolution expressed in the couplet.

The metre also exhibits the same regularity and structural parallelisms displayed by other aspects of the sonnet, contributing to a piece that is remarkably coherent in its relation between form and content. The fourteen lines of the poem are all iambic pentameter, with very small recourse to variation; when this is present (as happens in the final couplet), it shows the poem's considerable restraint, especially when compared to Shakespeare's usual metrical virtuosity. Variation is present in the form of an extrametrical unstressed syllable at the end of ll. 13 and 14 (commonly called a feminine ending), as well as of a few trochaic inversions, where the first iamb in a line is substituted by a trochaic foot (ll. 2, 3, 4, 8 and 14). Divergent rhymes are few, and include the eye rhyme "eye": "alchemy", the desinential rhyme "disdaineth": "staineth" and possibly an internal rhyme "rack": "alack" (although involving lines in two separate stanzas; Duncan-Jones 1997, 177). This kind of minimal metrical variation is rather frequent in sonnet diction, and strategies like these were used extensively by many other sonneteers to vary the uniform pace of the pentameter line without causing disruption in the rhythm of the poem. Here, the limited recourse to metrical *variatio* within the tight patterning of the sonnet serves to avoid excessive monotony, but also to single out significant textual *loci*, as in l. 14, where the stress on the first syllable of the line brings the main point of the poem to the fore.

This stylistic restraint contributes to the expressive power of Sonnet 33. Within the framework of its seemingly rigid structure, several variations are possible on a small number of images, and the many structural symmetries are masterfully exploited to create parallelisms in the arrangement of the different units of meaning that bring home the poem's message. In the case of Sonnet 33, form and content are inextricably linked into a cohesive and powerfully expressive mixture; this poem is also quite unique in Shakespeare's collection, due to the single concept it expresses and to the exceptionally tight internal architecture that upholds its discourse. As the following comparison will show, it is possibly these features, heavily reminiscent of the careful construction and architectural balance of Petrarchan sonnets, that would attract the Italian poet Montale to this specific text, in a sort of "return journey" of Petrarchist poetics that was firmly grounded in the translation and re-elaboration of poetic form.

MONTALE'S ITALIAN VERSION OF SONNET 33

1 Spesso, a lusingar vette, vidi splendere
   sovranamente l'occhio del mattino,
   e baciar d'oro verdi prati, accendere
   pallidi rivi d'alchimìe divine.
5 Poi vili fumi alzarsi, intorbidata
   d'un tratto quella celestiale fronte,
   e fuggendo a occidente il desolato
   mondo, l'astro celare il viso e l'onta.
9 Anch'io sul far del giorno ebbi il mio sole
   e il suo trionfo mi brillò sul ciglio:
   ma, ahimè, poté restarvi un'ora sola,
   rapito dalle nubi in cui s'impiglia.
13 Pur non ne ho sdegno: bene può un terrestre
   sole abbuiarsi, se è così il celeste.[2]

---

[2] Eugenio Montale, *L'opera in versi*, ed. by Rosanna Bettarini and Gianfranco Contini (Torino: Einaudi, 1980), 712. This represents the reference edition for Montale's works as quoted in this article: *Ossi di seppia*, 1925; *Le occasioni*, 1939; *Finisterre*, 1943; *La bufera e altro*, 1956; *Quaderno di traduzioni*, 1948.

To escape censorship by the Italian fascist regime,[3] Montale published his *Finisterre*, described as a "Petrarchist experience", in Lugano in 1943 (Montale 1976, 568). Four Elizabethan-style sonnets can be found in the collection, consisting of three quatrains in alternate rhyme and a closing couplet. In the same period, Montale was testing his technical and expressive resources by translating some of Shakespeare's sonnets: in the "Note" that prefaces the first edition of his *Quaderno di traduzioni*, published in 1948 and collecting the "crumbs" of the "banquet" of his major translations, Montale claims that "the re-elaborations of the three Shakespearean sonnets were also written before '38" (Montale 1980, 1154). Montale's versions of Shakespeare's Sonnets 32 and 33 were first published in the magazine *Città* on 7 December 1944. As such, Shakespearean influence formed an integral part of Montale's engagement with the English language, which in turn represented for him both a formal crossroads and an extended lyrical and poetic training. Montale only translated three sonnets from Shakespeare, choosing the ones that contain thematic clusters close to his own imagery and that allowed him to investigate his relationship with the character of Clizia.[4] From the point of view of metrical choices, Montale modelled his re-making of Shakespeare's original onto a pattern that he had already experimented with in his own poetry, compressing the iambic pentameter of the original into the lesser space of an hendecasyllable. He also reproduced the rhyme scheme of the original, and inserted clean breaks between stanzas, which are separated by a change in rhyme pairs and sealed by punctuation. Generally, Montale adopted a tight metrical partitioning, albeit with several variations, that is close to Shakespeare's clinched structure in 33.

---

[3] "The booklet, with its quotation from d'Aubigné, against blood-thirsty princes, was not publishable in Italy in 1943. Therefore, I printed it in Switzerland, and it came out shortly before the 25th of July" (Montale 1976, 568), which is the day the fascist regime in Italy was overthrown. All of the poems in the collection, except for *Serenata indiana*, which would be published in magazine form along with the Shakespearian translations, had been published previously in significant Italian literary magazines. However, the coupling of the texts and the initial quotation attached to *Bufera*, alluding to the ongoing war and dictatorship, would have resulted in a problematic piece of writing.

[4] Clizia is the *senhal* which Montale attributed to Irma Brandeis, an American Italianist who had Jewish origins, who, following the racial laws of 1938, had emigrated to the United States and could not return to Italy. Thus, a relationship begun in 1933 and characterized by recurrent abandonment was finally ended. Its centrality in Montale's poetry and biography is evident in the promotion of Clizia to a protagonist in *Occasioni* and in most of *Bufera*, where she personifies the idea of the woman bringing salvation.

Montale's strong enjambments at first sight seem to distance his version from the original, with its rhythmically and syntactically autonomous lines; however, the enjambments allow Montale to broaden the confines of single lines by overstepping the line-length. Differing from Montale's practice in his other Elizabethan sonnets, here the syntactic breaks correspond to the single stanzas. In so doing, enjambed lines display one of Montale's usual strategies in translation, used as they are here to dilate the pace of the language, so different from the original. At the same time, the enjambments are confined to within single stanzas, and they do not involve the third quatrain, a place where the poem gathers pace in anticipation of the *tour de force* of the final couplet, where the epigrammatic *coup de théâtre* hinges on the marked enjambment "*terrestre / sole*". The final couplet highlights the foundational thematic core of the poem, similarly to the symmetrical half-lines in l. 14 of the original. In ll. 1 and 3, the predicatives "*splendere*" and "*accendere*" (rhyme words that conjure Petrarchist, Dantean and personal echoes), generate enjambments with a cataphoric function (according to the definition in Soldani 2003, 247–248) that dilate the initial description and act as a foreboding.

Montale's version of Sonnet 33 embodies an intimate connection between Shakespearean and Montalian poetics, a reciprocity of poetic means that finds its realization both synchronically, in Montale's own contemporary poetic production, and diachronically, in his encounter with the English poets of the past. An example of this is provided by the word "*fumi*" (l. 5), which is closely connected to *Occasioni* on the syntactic, semantic and thematic level, and to the semantic field relating to smoke and fog. Several occurrences of words related to this field are found in Montale's poetry, where they stand as a metaphor for the poet's struggle in reaching the truth, obscured as it is by "*nubi*" and fog. These words are in polar opposition to the semantic field represented by words such as "*lampo-barbaglio-scintille-barlume*", here exemplified by the pair "*accendere / mi brillò sul ciglio*". The phrase "*vili fumi*", diverging from Shakespeare's "basest clouds", is part of a stylistic feature that is quite common in Montale's poetry, the pairing of a bisyllabic adjective with "*fumi*" in an hendecasyllable. These occurrences show the degree to which Montale's "Petrarchist" phase in *Finisterre* was nourished by his Shakespearean translations.

Moreover, Montale's version displays an overall solidarity between the metrical and syntactical level and the poem's logical development, as

this is articulated in its internal partitions: punctuation marks boundaries between sections; syntax regulates metrical partitions and highlights
the development of the poetic argument and any tension is resolved
within single stanzas. Within the formal structure of the poem, syntactic
transitions follow thematic mutations, and reproduce the comparison
between nature's landscape and the poet's soul that acts as the ideological foundation of the original. Montale's "lack of faithfulness to rhythm"
(Lonardi 1980, 153) as a translator is first of all an issue of syntax and
is deeply connected to his reworking of aural patterns. By adapting and
readapting the tensions of his original, Montale ends up being exceptionally faithful to Shakespeare's text. For instance, the transition from
"basest clouds" to "*vili fumi*" (l. 5) maintains the opposition between
sounding and soundless consonants in "permit" vs "basest" and moves
the high-low opposition of Shakespeare's sonnet to an even lower level;
similarly, the courtly metaphor in the original is temporarily removed,
only to be evoked in the translation of "disgrace" with "*onta*". With
the word "*onta*", part of the quasi-stilnovistic and chivalric lexicon of
Montale's version, the poet aims at retrospectively re-collocating his
translation within its Italian and contemporary ideological landscape. In
Montale's translation, this kind of "summoning" is not limited to the
Italian national tradition, but instead engages with the whole reception
of poetry in English: "the forlorn world" becomes "*desolato / mondo*",
which recalls Eliot's *The Waste Land* as translated by Mario Praz (1932),
but also Montale's own translations of Eliot and Dickinson. Other structural affinities tie Montale's translation of 33 more closely to his own
poetic production, such as his virtuosity in compensating for the lack of
perfect rhymes, in accordance with a process of legalization of imperfect
rhymes that characterizes the Italian Novecento. Montale's version reproduces the rhyme scheme of the original, only maintaining one perfect
rhyme but making it proparoxytone ("*splendere: accendere*"), and avoids
more exact sounding rhymes, possibly to suggest a certain distance from
the sounds of the original, in full agreement with contemporary poetic
innovations.

The aural and metrical levels emphasize the poem's semantic depth.
The rhyming pair "*ciglio: impiglia*", typical of Montale (and before of
Dante), moves from a concept that is not present in Shakespeare's poem.
If in Shakespeare's poem the clouds are only masking the sun, in Montale
the latter is snatched away ("*rapito*") by the clouds; Montale's version
offers a more dynamic and dramatic version that directly proceeds from

his "unfaithfulness to the content" (Lonardi 1980, 154), stressing the sun's innocence and offering additional justification for the beloved's behaviour by citing external circumstances and the sun's impotence (see l. 11 "*poté restarvi*"). The allusion to the theme of erotic abduction, of mythological and metaphysical derivation, in Montale's version represents his poetic signature superimposed onto Shakespeare's lines, as this idea features prominently in the poems to Clizia, his "visiting angel", as he himself termed her. Several other instances exemplify the solidarity between this piece and Montale's own poetry, such as the choice of the same rhyme words and the discontinued presence of the beloved, whose relationship with the poet is based on a series of encounters and partings. For Montale, Sonnet 33 becomes the place to recall a distant Clizia, through the use of several *senhals* associated with her: eyes, forehead (*"fronte"*), brow (*"ciglio"*), and the chromatic opposition between dark and light. It is perhaps Clizia's memory that causes the deviation from the original in the third quatrain, shifting the definition of Montale's translation towards that of an imitation, an hermeneutic and stylistic exercise in shaping an archetype according to the *leitmotifs* of individual poetry.

The sonnet's rhyme series is closed by the imperfect rhyme "*terrestre: celeste*", hinged on the polar opposition that acts as the semantic foundation of the entire poem. Here, the antithesis between low and high, which does not only involve the spatial level, is finally perfected and highlighted by the strong enjambment that separates the true *mot-clé* of the text, "*sole*", from the rest of the poem. According to a stylistic feature common in Montale's poetry, the enjambment separates the noun from its adjective, with the latter at the end of a line. The foundational dichotomy of the poem, a key to the conceptual and stylistic world of Petrarchism, is also given prominence through a discernible aural pattern that serves to underline visual accumulation: the alliteration between "*nubi – abbuiarsi*", the assonance between "*fumi: nubi*", the iconic aural density of the voiceless-voiced opposition in "*pur – può – abbuiarsi*" and finally the intensifying rhythm of the close, with its concatenation of monosyllabic and bisyllabic truncated words, beginning in l. 9 with the internal rhyme "*anch'io: mio*". The recursive presence of "i" in a stressed position runs through the entire text, starting from the first indicative that highlights the speaking subject ("*vidi, mattino, rivi, alchimie, divine, vili, viso, io, mio, mi, rapito, impiglia, così*"), possibly acting on suggestions from the original, with its insistence on "I". At the same time, syllabic iteration lends the poem a halting rhythm that reproduces the binary pattern of the original, in a syncopated motion that contributes to the accurate mimetic conversion of Shakespeare's poem. Elision and especially syntactic breaks greatly enhance this rhythmic arrangement, highlighting half-line breaks and suggesting rapid aphoristic movement. This is another of the strategies employed by Montale as a translator, one that the poet had developed during his "fight to dig another dimension into our poly-syllabic language" and perfected in his "forced and unwelcome activity as a translator" (Montale 1976, 567).

The dense euphonic pattern, made of repetitions, alliterations, asso-nances and consonances, redeems the many imperfect rhymes, creating a secondary rhythm juxtaposed to the prosody that builds a further struc-tural framework; at the same time, this alternative pattern offers a chance to recover those semantic ties that have been cancelled out in the trans-lation process. An example of this procedure, characterized by an effort towards both variation and synthesis, is offered by the blend of "glorious" and "sovereign" in the adverb "*sovranamente*" (l. 2), a polysyllabic word occupying the beginning of an *a minore* hendecasyllable: here, the regal quality expressed by the two English words is condensed into a single term, alliterating and in assonance with both "*vette*" and "*splendere*", which corresponds perfectly to the initial alliteration on the fricative in the original (ll. 1, 2). If the alliterating pair "golden"—"gilding" (ll. 2, 3) is elided semantically, its presence is recovered through the repetition of "d"; similarly, the repetition of the word "face" (ll. 3, 6) in the orig-inal is partially but meaningfully maintained ("*fronte*" l. 6, where the word is similarly placed in a rhyming position). Finally, the internal rhyme "kissing: gilding" (ll. 2, 3) is substituted by the internal rhyme "*lusingar: baciar*", symmetrically placed and identically desinential in nature. Here, the infinitive is lightened via the use of an apocope, which creates a break in sound, in keeping with the swift motion of the rhyming proparoxytone words and underlining the rise in poetic register signalled by the phrase "*a lusingar vette*". The recovery of the images present in the original, and of the metaphorical framework they uphold, is another of Montale's stylistic features as a translator who preferred omitting a word and recovering its meaning through syncretism and substitution, re-elaborating the original and enhancing its visual impact. In 33, "gilding", closely connected to "golden", is deleted, but its meaning is maintained in the image evoked by the verb "*accendere*", which belongs both to the Italian tradition and to Montale's own poetic vocabulary. A similar procedure is behind the translation of "did shine with all-triumphant splendour" with "*e il suo trionfo mi brillò*": here, too, Montale compresses the meaning of the phrase into a single noun while other meanings are absorbed by the predicative, with the syntactic clinch of the coordination establishing rhythmic and lexical connections. Montale's variation is finalized in the promotion of "*ciglio*", the *senhal* of Clizia and the result of a selection by synecdoche starting from the original "brow".

Another feature signalling Montale's presence within the Shakespearean textual material is the synthesis operated by the phrase "*occhio del mattino*", where the direct object is changed into a specification within the metaphorical construction, in a virtuoso shortcut encapsulating several different elements. The phrase is the literal translation of another line by Shakespeare, "the morning's eye", found in *Romeo and Juliet* (Act III, scene 5, a text that was undoubtedly known to Montale), where it also occupies the beginning of a line; the words "mountain tops", "pale", "brow" and "heaven" are also found in the same passage in a similar thematic configuration. In Montale's version of 33, the contamination of poetic *loci* between *Romeo and Juliet* and the *Sonnets* cannot be considered coincidental. This procedure is in accordance with Montale's translation technique, based on eliding and amalgamating, and characterized by *concinnitas*, incisive imagery, and by formal variation displaying a marked faithfulness to the original text.

Concerning the positioning of adjectives, Montale reproduces the inversion in "meadows green", operated for reasons of rhyme, mirroring the English text and transposing the collocation of the adjective in "*verdi prati*", where the positioning of the colour adjective before the noun intensifies its value and emulates the marked phrasing of Shakespeare's sonnet. Similarly, with the phrases "suns of the world" and "heaven's sun", arranged in a chiastic structure in the final line, Montale operates another reshuffling based on compressing and restructuring his original. The revelation of meaning is centred on the metrical and syntactic profile of the last two lines, and specifically in their deviations from the original, i.e. the strong enjambment "*terrestre / sole*" and the quasi-rhyme "*terrestre: celeste*", which has here more foundational and structural value than any perfect rhyme could ever have. Montale the translator noticed how the two opposed dimensions were cohabiting in the same line and mirroring each other, and chose to disassemble and re-assemble, and to use his own metrical and syntactic choices to underline the antinomies evident in the original. The final couplet, the characterizing structural variant associated with the Elizabethan sonnet, is also the place to finally bring home stylistic tensions and rhythmical suggestions. The syntactic isolation contributes to the final couplet's epigrammatic and definitive tone, according to a stylistic move that is also markedly Montalian; in Montale's poetry, final lines aim at sanctioning the results of the poetic reflection via the lyrical synthesis of a *fulmen in clausula*, that in 33 clarifies both the whole reasoning and its final *correctio*.

If the symmetries in Shakespeare's sonnet are finalized by iterations, Montale chose instead to employ variation, a technique with a "Petrarchan vocation" (Lonardi 1980, 154). The only exceptions to this are the etymological figure of speech in "*celestial—celeste*" and the keyword *sole* redoubling the ending of l. 9, both excluded due to their specific semantic significance, highlighted by the enjambment. In Montale's version, the final couplet allows for a separation of the poem in two moments— *descriptio* e *meditatio*—that is typical of Montale's short poetry in *Ossi di seppia* and *Mottetti*, where the density of the close is a symptom of inevitability and necessity, two key concepts in Montale's poetry. The rivalry between metre and syntax displayed by Montale's final lines, with their strong enjambment and mid-line caesuras, can also be found in the final couplets of the other two sonnets by Shakespeare translated by Montale, and in the Elizabethan-style sonnets contained in *Finisterre*. Overall, in his translation Montale made use of a framework based on the high style of the Italian sonnet tradition, while at the same time treasuring Shakespeare's formal exhortations and adapting the idea of faithfulness to the form to his own poetic score. His stance as a translator is opposite to the one that produces the a-linear translation of the same sonnet by Giuseppe Ungaretti, developed in the same years and published in 1946, where the Elizabethan sonnet form is treated as if it were merely a formal icon, a hollow container to be filled with meaning and an instrument of metrical coercion.[5] Montale chose instead to empower the function of signifiers and meanings in the original text by putting them in a dialogue with his own production. Sonnet 33 shows the typically Montalian restructuring of poetic form, that upsets tradition and revitalizes it with modern suggestions: the intensified rhythm generating homogeneity, reiterated sounds, the effort to condense semantics, the refined lexical additions and the clarification of key images. As

---

[5] These considerations are the result of a cursory glance, and of preliminary research results which will shortly be published.

Leopardi wrote in his *Zibaldone,* "exactness has nothing to do with faithfulness"; the content is found in the form, especially when the latter is conceived as a fact to be challenged and disobeyed, with the ultimate aim of reaching true faithfulness to the foreign text.

References

Booth, Stephen. 1969. *An Essay on Shakespeare's Sonnets.* New Haven: Yale University Press.

Booth, Stephen. 1977. *Shakespeare's Sonnets.* New Haven: Yale University Press.

Boyd, Brian. 2014. "Verse Versus Story. Open Versus Convergent Pattern". *Sewanee Review* 122: 34–54.

Burrow, Colin. 2002. *Shakespeare: The Complete Sonnets and Poems.* Oxford: Oxford University Press.

Duncan-Jones, Katherine. 1997. *Shakespeare's Sonnets.* Nashville: Thomas Nelson & Sons.

Fineman, Joel. 1986. *Shakespeare's Perjured Eye: The Invention of Poetic Subjectivity in the Sonnets.* Berkeley: University of California Press.

Fortini, Franco. 1987. *Traduzione e rifacimento.* In *Saggi italiani.* Milano: Garzanti.

Hammond, Gerald. 1981. *The Reader and Shakespeare's Young Man Sonnets.* London and Basingstoke: MacMillan.

Hedley, Jane. 1994. "Since First Your Eye I Eyed: Shakespeare's Sonnets and the Poetics of Narcissism". *Style* 28: 1–30.

Lonardi, Gilberto. 1980. *Fuori e dentro il tradurre montaliano.* In *Il Vecchio e il Giovane e altri studi su Montale.* Bologna: Zanichelli.

Mengaldo, Pier Vincenzo. 1978. *Poeti italiani del Novecento.* Milano: Mondadori.

Mengaldo, Pier Vincenzo. 1996. *Aspetti e tendenze della lingua poetica italiana del Novecento.* In *La tradizione del Novecento. Prima serie.* Torino: Bollati-Boringhieri.

Montale, Eugenio. 1976. *Intenzioni (Intervista immaginaria).* In *Sulla poesia,* ed. by Giorgio Zampa. Milano: Mondadori.

Montale, Eugenio. 1980. *L'opera in versi,* ed. by Rosanna Bettarini and Gianfranco Contini. Torino: Einaudi.

Paterson, Don. 2012. *Reading Shakespeare's Sonnets: A New Commentary.* London: Faber.

Schwartzberg, Mark. 2002. "Shakespeare's Sonnet 33". *The Explicator* 61: 13–14.

Slater, Eliot. 2016. "A Psychiatrist's View of Shakespeare's Sonnets". *The Oxfordian* 18: 155–174.

Soldani, Arnaldo. 2003. "Procedimenti inarcanti nei sonetti di Petrarca. Un repertorio ragionato". *Atti della Accademia roveretana degli Agiati*. CCLIII: 243–342.

Vendler, Helen. 1997. *The Art of Shakespeare's Sonnets*. Harvard: Harvard University Press.

CHAPTER 5

Addressing Complexity: Variants and the Challenge of Rendering Shakespeare's Sonnet 138 into Italian

Valerio de Scarpis

And simple truth miscalled simplicity
(Shakespeare's *Sonnets* 66.11)

Clarity is a prerequisite of simple, effective communication; poetry, however, often exploits complexity, polysemy, ambiguity and oblique reference. Sonnet 138 ("When my love swears that she is made of truth") presents considerable problems of interpretation for its complexity, relating to the emotive stance of the speaker (the lyric "I"), the referential situation alluded to, the interaction with the woman implied, and the reader's expected response to the poem. Such a hermeneutic quandary raises a question about the aim of the author in devising so cryptic and sophisticated a text. A possible explanation is offered by Shakespeare's

V. de Scarpis (✉)
Ca' Foscari University of Venice, Venice, Italy
e-mail: dscarpis@unive.it

J. Kingsley-Smith and W. R. Rampone Jr. (eds.), *Shakespeare's Global Sonnets*, Global Shakespeares, https://doi.org/10.1007/978-3-031-09472-9_5

method of revision and correction, as evident in an early version of the same sonnet (printed in 1599), which resulted in the final version included in the 1609 Quarto. The existence of such an early version allows us to make significant inferences about the intention or effect of revisions. That is, the variants adroitly deployed throughout the corrected version strongly suggest the author's deliberate pursuit of greater complexity by intensified ambiguity and indeterminacy.[1] Translators of this sonnet confirm that complexity as they face the difficult detective task of having to make explicit the poem's web of elusive meanings and its contradictory clues.

The first part of this essay aims at highlighting the multi-layered complexity accrued by the English text in its authorial revision: the result of a deliberate strategy implemented by Shakespeare.[2] The second part concerns the practice of translating the sonnets into Italian by focusing on the endeavours of three accomplished Italian translators in dealing with the significance of this sonnet and comparing their diverse solutions. As the present investigation will make clear, the practice of translating into another language may prove a valuable means available to hermeneutics, by rendering explicit what otherwise tends to elude interpretation.

Shaping Complexity in Sonnet 138

The following section is based on a comparison between the two versions of this sonnet and the analysis of its variant readings. The sonnet appears first in *The Passionate Pilgrim*, a miscellany of poems attributed to Shakespeare by William Jaggard in 1599, where it appears as poem number 1, and subsequently in the 1609 *Shake-speares Sonnets*, where it appears as

---

[1] Complexity entails an interpreting agent and a frame of reference; engagements with complexity require systemic approaches (Ladyman and Wiesner 2020).

[2] One of the many strategies exploited by Shakespeare in the *Sonnets*, as conclusively argued by Vendler (1997, 31).

number 138.[3] It is worth noting that in the latter version the time dimension has generally been undervalued by readers.[4] It functions both as topic (age *vs* youth) and, structurally, as constitutive process: a chronological disarray affects the comprehension of the entire poem. The sequential unfolding of its clusters of meaning is hampered by the repeated intersecting of its two leading isotopies: truth-deceit and sex-unfaithfulness, highlighted by a striking succession of rhetorical devices, causing serious problems of interpretation. The intricacy of this poem is signalled at the outset by the paradox that faces the reader in line two: belief and un-belief combined. Immediately following the paradox of contradictory beliefs, one encounters a spurious (disclaimed) hypothetical clause, then a jaded euphemism; next, the polyptoton quibbling on simplicity, a syntactic parallelism between lines, two proverbial saws, a chiasmus formed by the pronouns standing for the protagonists and the concluding witty paradox (pleasure in being deceived). The role played by rhetoric appears crucial in this sonnet and demands to be further examined when coming to consider the reception of the text.

The first perusal of this love-sonnet engenders increasing misgivings about sincerity, specifically the earnestness of the lovers' contorted relationship. In the process of reading the poem, one is made aware that the understanding of the referential situation, as reported, gets progressively destabilized by frequent ambivalent words and expressions (see Q text, below). The full extent of the referential implications raised by this polysemy is recognized as the process of reading concludes, reaching its climax with the manifest duplicity of the keyword *lie*. The word is encapsulated in an explosively polysemic syntactic structure: one in which a plethora of interpretations hinges on the humble preposition *by*. The syntactic

---

[3] *The Passionate Pilgrim* is henceforward referred to as PP, and the quarto edition of the *Sonnets*, published by Thomas Thorpe in 1609, as Q. The textual situation of Q 138 has been extensively studied by Rollins (1944). Three editions of the *Passionate Pilgrim* have survived: the first, fragmentary, dated approximately 1598/99 (though lacking its frontispiece, in the only surviving copy now preserved at the Folger Library in Washington D.C.); the second and the third, respectively 1599 and 1612, both derived from the first and dependent on it (with only very slight spelling changes and a single variant reading at line 11: *habit's in a s.* PP 1598/1599] *habit is a s.* PP 1599 and PP 1612). Following Rollins, I shall take for my comparison the text of sonnet number one from the first edition of PP (1598/1599) and that of sonnet 138 in the 1609 edition. The texts are displayed below, side by side.

[4] The exception is Helen Vendler (1997, 586–587), who has remarked on the effect of a progression in the reader's perception of mood throughout the sonnet.

And in our faults | by lies | we flatter ed be:

1) "We flattered be / in our faults by lies"

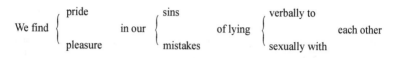

2) "In our faults / we flattered be by lies"

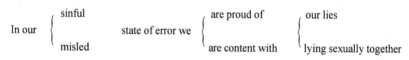

Fig. 5.1 The sibylline ibis

amphibology that emerges, also known as an *Ibis*, generates two main utterances, according to whether the reader relates the middle segment to the beginning or to the end of the line (Fig. 5.1).

Here, the leading dichotomy that runs through the poem, of (in)sincerity *vs* sexual (mis) behaviour, comes powerfully to the surface, while the number of combinations among the shades of meaning is striking, and consequently the interpretations multiply. Readers are, therefore, compelled to reconsider the whole sonnet and embark on a process of semantic reclaiming of the entire text, or "re-semanticising of the duplicate". In other words, the ending forces a reconsideration of the whole poem from the beginning and imposes the need for closer scrutiny. This leads to a fresh experience of the poem's unfolding, or "time of the utterance", the *énoncé* (Benveniste 1974), which becomes redoubled.

At this second reading, the matter of deception appears more serious: it involves not just the age of the protagonist, one suspects, but also infidelity in the relationship. Thus, the speaker of the sonnet feels ensnared and suffers from a gnawing desire to learn the truth about his relationship: is the young mistress only a well-meaning fibber,[5] or is she cynically dissembling her disloyalty? It may be better, he reflects, still to bear,

[5] Cf. footnote 13.

with a sardonic smile, the apprehensions of uncertainty, rather than to renounce the pleasure of her alluring company. Yet their physical closeness also elicits in the speaker some feeling of revulsion: he cannot eschew disturbing visions of promiscuous unfaithfulness on her part. For their mutual peace of mind, truth must be "*suppressed*". He realizes that in the complexity of his cognitive plight (the truth being far from "*simple*"), reluctantly, he must abide in his subjection to the enticements of the flesh and keep on hypocritically defying truth. However, this inferred second reading does not entirely supplant the reader's first unsuspecting surmise, giving rise to persistent interpretative doubts, since the reader is in a position rather like that of the lover.

The many ambiguities and the several paradoxes of the Q 138 text have been noted by most critics, who have produced diverging explanations of its introspective content and of the stance of the speaker. Helen Vendler (1997, 586) noticed two conflicting stances emphasized by different commentators: "the depravity readers favouring the octave, the comedy readers favouring the sestet". In search of evidence, one critic (Snow 1980) has invoked a conjectural method of explication of collated variants in the two extant versions (Q 138 and PP 1).[6] The underlying

---

[6] The range of responses to this sonnet has been impressive: as early as 1978 Allen (1979, 130–131) noticed the lack of agreement among critics over the tone of Sonnet 138 and reported their comments ranging from "an enjoyable jeu d'ésprit" to "a tragically embittered poem". In the wake of Booth's (1977, 478) exemplary investigation of polysemy in the *Sonnets*, most subsequent editions have continued to emphasize the paradoxical ambiguity of Q 138. Booth's glosses to this sonnet considered also some variants in respect to the PP text, about which he seemed hesitant: "If one were foolish enough to pursue the topic, one might posit an early version of the Q poem and guess that the PP text is a garbled version of that". Snow (1980, 462–483) is the only critic to have attempted an extensive comparison of the two versions of this sonnet. The main shortcoming of his line-by-line analysis consists in the lack of a global, systemic, approach to the complex of authorial revisions; and also in the focusing on the psychology of the love-relationship from the angle of the protagonists rather than that of the reader's response. About the difference between versions in Q and PP, the Italian scholar, Melchiori (1979, 278) observed that "the 1609 version introduces some significant variations, endowing it with an inflection of self-cruelty and of conscious moral dejection". The poem's taxing linguistic and logical peculiarities have repeatedly invited close examination: e.g. Bade et al. (2015), a team of linguists and critics, have systematically investigated the truth-conditions of the poem's discourse, foregrounding its ambiguity. It is a pity they did not consider the work of revision on the early version which would have shown the importance of rhetorical "*aequivocatio*" in the conceiving, shaping and destination of the poem. Also the semiotic critique of Beccone (2008, 57–76) in its perceptive investigation of Shakespeare's applied poetics deals only with the Q138 version.

persuasion (also governing the present enquiry) is that PP1 constitutes an early authorial version, later revised before inclusion in the 1609 collection.[7] It is necessary to begin by examining this version, before tackling the revisions in Q 138.

THE *PASSIONATE PILGRIM* VERSION

I provide below the text of the sonnet in the PP reading, numbering in subscript the lines for easy reference, and, next to it, I place the text of Sonnet 138 from the 1609 Quarto for subsequent consideration (both reproduced from Rollins, *Variorum*, I, 353–354).[8]

PP 1	*Q 138*
$_1$When my Love sweares that she is made of truth,	$_1$When my love sweares that she is made of truth
$_2$I do beleeve her (though I know she lies)	$_2$I do beleeve her though I know she lyes,
$_3$That she might thinke me some untutor'd youth	$_3$That she might thinke me some untuterd youth,
$_4$Unskilful in the worlds false **forgeries**	$_4$Unlearned in the worlds false subtilties
$_5$Thus vainly thinking that she thinkes me young,	$_5$Thus vainely thinking that she thinkes me young,
$_6$Although I know my yeares be past the best:	$_6$Although she knowes my dayes are past the best,
$_7$I smiling, credite her false speaking toung,	$_7$Simply I credit her false speaking tongue,
$_8$Outfacing faults in love, with love's **ill rest**	$_8$On both sides thus is simple truth supprest:
$_9$But wherefore sayes my love that she is **young**?	$_9$But wherefore sayes she not she is unjust?
$_{10}$And wherefore say not I, that I am old:	$_{10}$And wherefore say not I that I am old?
$_{11}$O, Love's best habit's in a **soothing toung**,	$_{11}$O loves best habit is in seeming trust,

(continued)

---

[7] On examining the variants most critics now agree that PP1 constitutes an early version of Q138 (cf. Duncan-Jones 2005; Roberts 2002). Edmondson and Wells (2020, 24–25) consider the first draft of this poem within Shakespeare's early output and posit revisions of the *Sonnets* taking place "over an almost thirty-year period".

[8] I have corrected *u* and *v*, *s* and *f*, leaving however *i* and *y* (occasionally interchangeable, as in *lie/lye*) unregularized. The numbering of lines in subscript will be used in quoting words throughout this paper.

(continued)

PP 1	Q 138
12And Age in love, loves not to have yeares told	12And <u>age</u> in love, <u>loves not t'have yëares told,</u>
13Therefore I'le lye with Love, and love with me,	13Therefore I <u>lye</u> with her, and she with me,
14Since that our faultes in love thus **smother'd** be	14And in our <u>faults</u> by lyes we flattered be
[bold face = altered endings/rhymes]	[underlining = polysemy]

The PP version is generally of the Shakespearean sonnet type. The main peculiarities of its rhyme scheme lie in the interlinking of the lines, from quatrain two to three, by repeating rhyme C (abab*Cd*C*d*C*e*C*e*ff); and in the pairs of identical rhymes: *young* (ll 5, 9) and *tongue* (ll 7, 11), which emphasize continuity across the formal and logical boundary separating octave from sestet. The content follows the love-sonnet convention with its copious repetition of the term *love,* as noun and as verb (occurring as many as ten times throughout). The concept of love is explored across the multiple facets offered by its antithetical realizations: abstract and general love vs love incarnate in one woman; mature love vs youthful love; sincere love vs feigned love; physical love vs Platonic love. Conceptually, the occurrences of *love* give rise to widespread equivocation: there is the expression 8*faults in love with love's ill rest*, where the two instances of *love* can be taken as either the epithet, "my beloved", or reflections on the condition of being in love. And again, 11*Love's best habit's in a soothing tongue* is bisemic, the woman's or Cupid's. Similarly, the final occurrence of 14*love*, found in the repeated syntagm 8*faults in love*, allows for both interpretations. Copious chiming resonates in lines 7–8, where several formal devices abound: homoioteleuton linking *Smil***ING**, 7*Speak***ING** and 8*outfac***ING**; alliteration in /s/ comprising also 7*fal***S***e*, 8*fault***S***, 8*love***S***, 8*re***S***t*; and the sound-compressing device that links both ends of these lines by echo 7*Smiling c***RE***di***T***e* ... 8***REST***. Also thickened /l/ phonemes appear towards the end: *fau***L***ts, **L***ove, **L***ove, i***LL*** (present in other keywords throughout: *fa***L***se, **L***ies, be***L***ieve, smi***L***ing, o***L***d*).

These devices, in lines 7–8, mark the importance of the conclusion of the octave, where a major step in the conceptual development of the sonnet occurs: the pun between 7*false* and 8*faults* (homophones), emphasized by all that chiming, uncovers the attitude of the speaker.

His ironical detachment is revealed by the qualifier 7*smiling*, that legit-
imizes the ambivalence of 8*outfacing faults in love*: the resolve to overlook
defects or the recognition of guilt in the mistress. The preceding statement 7*false speaking toung* clarifies the kind of faults: both insincerity and
dissimulation. Line 8, therefore, presents a first climax, before the divide,
in the sonnet's development (a halt in the perceived reading time); and so
the thematic unity of the sonnet, centred on the concept of love, appears
fragmented into a variety of conflicting attributes, ironically exposed in
the self-indulgent epigrammatic ending.

EFFECTING THE REVISIONS

We may now consider the alterations made to *The Passionate Pilgrim* text,
leading to the variants present in the 1609 Quarto. A first-sight comparison of the two versions reveals major lexical substitutions of certain
keywords in rhyming position, as shown above. The variant readings fall
into two types:

i. VARIANTS AIMED AT ELIMINATING IDENTICAL RHYMES. And
causing the removal of ties between the inner quatrains. This alone
proves the chronological precedence of PP over Q, when set against
the developments of European poetics from late sixteenth to early
seventeenth centuries with more exacting norms for rhyming. If this
seems merely a technical intervention, limited to two rhyming positions (9*young* and 11*toung*, turned into 9*unjust* and 11*trust*), it looks
different if considered according to Q's new system. The change
affects the entire formal and logical structure. The new lexical items,
in fact, do not supply synonyms for the rhymes that are expunged,
but alter the general balance of the poem (Fig. 5.2).

ii. VARIANTS AIMED AT ENHANCING THE LOGICAL STRUCTURE AND
ALLUSIVENESS OF THE SONNET. In Q, there is a clearer presentation of the governing antinomies: to *false* (with *lyes* strengthened)
vs *truth* (reinforced by repeating the word in l. 8) are now added
"trust" vs "unjustness", and "simplicity" vs "subtleties" (near-
antonyms). Accompanying changes occur: the principle of reciprocity is introduced in Q by 8*both* and by the increased symmetry of
the syntactic parallelism 9*wherefore sayes she not she is* and 10*wherefore
say not I that I am* and also by the improved climax and the more
effective polysemy of Q's conclusion with that sharing of faults

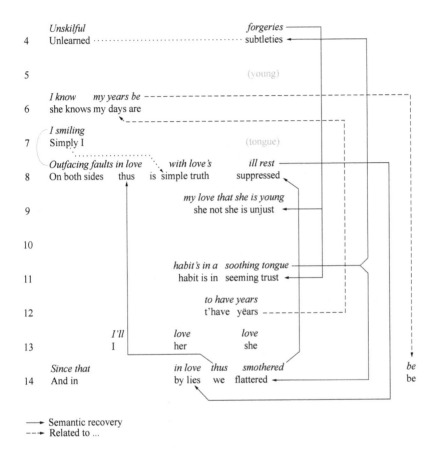

Fig. 5.2 Sonnet 138: semantic shifts (Valerio de Scarpis)

($_{14}our$) emphasized by $_{14}we$.[9] Some redundant expressions are left out: i.e. $_9young$ disappears (formerly opposed to $_6yeares...past$ *the best*), likewise the now superfluous $_{11}soothing$ *tongue* (opposed to $_7false$ *speaking...*—see below). The repetition of $_8faults$ (key term) is also eliminated by retaining only one instance in the concluding line. Furthermore, the repetition of *yeares* in lines 6 and 12 is cancelled

[9] See also the change of the subject in line 6 from "*I*" to "*she*" which balances the responsibility for hiding his age.

by dropping the former (see below). Also phonemic patterning remains strong in Q: lines 7 and 8 (the largest revision) become even more incisive thanks to added alliteration in /s/: $_7$*SimPly i cREdiT...$_8$SuPPREST*.

The *Ibis* figure is preserved across versions: in line 14 the multiple ambiguity of: *faults||in love||smothered* gives way to the corresponding scheme of: *faults||by lyes||flattered*, as observed. Thus, more irony is bestowed on the sonnet, which turns from an opposition *love/lies*[1]/*lies*[2] to a much subtler opposition *truth/lies*[1]/*lies*[2], by shifting its thematic dominant.

ANALYSIS OF THE VARIANCE ACROSS SYSTEMS. By comparing the PP and Q systems, it appears that there is a web of trans-positions and semantic recoveries that develop in the process of correction (Figs. 5.2 and 5.3): Starting from the second occur-rence of $_{11}$*toung*, one of the identical rhymes dropped in revision, the concept of suave falsity/flattery present in that $_{11}$*soothing toung* of PP, once expunged, gets to be partly recovered by one of the interpretations given to the Q reading of $_4$*false subtilities*—i.e. false refinements—and furthermore is recovered in Q by the more balmy $_{14}$*flattered*, that has replaced the allusively physical $_{14}$*smothered*.[10] The concept itself of stifling the culpable truth, in the expunged word $_{14}$*smothered* (literal meaning "suffocate" or metaphorically "steep in") is retrieved by the connotations attached to the aggres-sively crude $_8$*supprest*. The rhyming position occupied in Q by this verb corresponds in PP to that of the strongly polysemic segment $_8$*with loves ill rest*.[11] As noted, this segment makes explicit in advance the bawdy innuendo, thereby prefiguring Q's mischievous bisemic segment $_{14}$*faults by lyes*, allusive of sexual misconduct. In Q's line 4, the more pregnant $_4$*false subtleties* ("alluring subterfuges") reaffirms the alleged naïveté of the counterfeit young speaker and conse-quently provokes the other revision in the same line from $_4$*unskilful*

---

[10] This is metaphorical in *Venus & Adonis*, 17–18, "Here come and sit ... and being set, I'll *smother* thee with kisses".

[11] See *Richard III*'s use of this phrase, to mean lack of repose/sinful lying in bed: "Anne: And thou unfit for any place but hell [...] Gloucester: Your bed-chamber; Anne: *ill rest* betide the chamber where thou liest; Glo. So will it, madam, till I lie with you" (110–3).

("lack of dexterity" in PP) to $_4$*unlearned* (in Q, "cognitive ineptitude", more pervasive). However, the twice negative meaning of the expression $_4$*false forgeries* ("deceptive frauds")—so important in the economy of the early version—is recovered in two other revisions of Q: the allusively disparaging $_9$*unjust* ("unfaithful", "disloyal") and $_{11}$*seeming trust* ("apparent honesty", *or*, "to pretend trustworthiness").

A different tone in Q is suggested by the altered phono-prosodic and syntactic lay-out as seen in its rhythmic pacing, which is more varied and supple, with greater counterpoint between language and metre, and in the frequent foot-reversals: e.g. in place of $_9$*that shé is young* (PP) in Q we have $_9$*she ìs unjust*; in place of $_{11}$*habit's ìn a soothing* (PP) we have $_{11}$*ìs in seeming*. The word [*t'have*]$_{12}$*yëares* in Q becomes onomatopoeic, being stretched in metrical time (bisyllabic with hiatus), suggesting a longer timespan. Thanks to these adjustments, the tone of Q appears colloquial and discursive, reflecting the aloof, ironical attitude of the speaker, as foretold by the expunged PP expressions $_8$*Outfacing faults in love...* and $_7$*I smiling*.

GRAMMAR-BASED ALTERATIONS. Two modifying connectives are altered in the process of revision. The $_{14}$*thus* attached to $_{14}$*smothered* follows the semantic recovery of the latter and therefore shifts from line 14 of PP to line 8 of Q to join $_8$*supprest*, becoming a hinge for the logical turn of a culpable reciprocity. The other revision ushers in the conclusion, no longer as a follow-up to the rhetorical questions

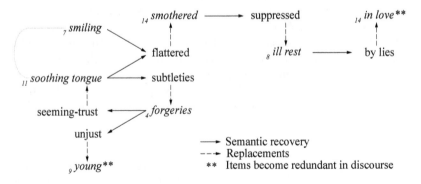

Fig. 5.3 Sonnet 138: recoveries (Valerio de Scarpis)

and answers of PP, but less determinate, through a mere conjunction, $_{14}and$. Furthermore, the indefinite, semi-finite mood in $_6I$ *know my yeares be* (PP) is captured by the descriptive vagueness of Q's metaphoric $_6dayes$, which replaces $_6yeares$ (literal), leaving the other occurrence of $_{14}be$ unique in Q, and thus emphasizing the indeterminacy of the final, clinching polysemy. Another revised tense is the intentional future in PP, $_{13}I'le\ lye\ with\ love$, revised as $_{13}I\ lye$ *with her* (in Q), which reveals either a resolution or a prediction. The use of the present tense here enhances the obliqueness of the verb $_{13}lye$: to the former "since we are stifled", Q adds a *carpe diem* exhortation. Such corrective tendencies all point towards indeterminacy, and this endows the text with greater referential complexity. There is also felt greater introspection on the part of the speaker, who seems divided between an attitude of nonchalant aloofness and one of sardonic bitterness.

The Translator's Challenge in Addressing Sonnet 138

On the basis of the above analysis of the sonnet, examined across its two versions, we are in a position to appreciate the complex hermeneutical task facing both the reader and the translator. Translators into another language, setting out to tackle this problematic text, would necessarily need to conjecture for themselves an explication and consequently develop their individual interpretive strategies. We ought therefore to consider some notable translations of Sonnet 138 into Italian, for some diverging responses to this challenge.[12] The most clear-cut interpretations follow two opposite directions: that of a straight-forward, more candid reading, and that of a probing, malicious reading, both substantially legitimized by the ambivalence of the text.

To the first type I would assign the following free verse translation of the sonnet by Massimo Rizzante (2013), poet, essayist and translator.

---

[12] Concerning the *Sonnets*, an overview of Italian translators' poetics can be found in the preceding essay in this collection by Steenson and Trissino. It is significant that Q138 did not meet the taste of the two leading Italian poet-translators (Ungaretti and Montale), who, more receptive to the appeal of "romantic lyricism", excluded it from their selections.

Quando il mio amore giura che è sincera
io le credo, anche se so che mente,
perché pensi a me come un giovane insipiente,
ignaro delle sottili falsità del mondo.
Così pensando invano che giovane mi pensi,
benché sappia che i miei giorni migliori son persi,
do credito soltanto alla sua lingua mendace:
tanto che per entrambi la semplice verità si tace.
Ma perché non mi dice che è bugiarda?
E perché io non le dico che son vecchio?
Oh, è meglio mostrar fiducia in amore,
e in età non amare il computo degli anni!
Perciò io le mento e lei a me,
e, mentendo, ci lusinghiamo colpevolmente.

This is a valuable rendering of the source text, coherent in respect to the opposition *Truth vs Insincerity*, which brings to light the complicity of the protagonists in the relished, nonchalant skirmishes of love they play with each other. They emerge from this interpretation as a sophisticated, sceptical pair of ill-assorted lovers, who defy the censure of the world. The truth of their relationship is merely (*soltanto*) not spoken (*si tace*). According to him she is a fibber (*bugiarda*)[13] and, therefore, it suits him best to show trust (*mostrar fiducia*). So they exchange lies (*le mento e lei a me*) and they are both pleased (*ci lusinghiamo*) while telling lies (*mentendo*) and feeling guilty (*colpevolmente*). This rendering of the source conjures up a playful atmosphere that recalls the ethos of the Tuscan novella, where, typically, the male protagonist sets out to hoodwink his friend/partner and ends up cheerfully hoodwinked himself[14]; and it also reminds us of certain self-ironical sonnets by Sir Philip Sidney, where pretending is just part of the social game.[15]

To the second type I would assign the translation by Alessandro Serpieri (1991, 343), who has felt the need to probe deeper into the convoluted psychology of the speaker:

[13] The distinction in Italian between "bugiarda" and "menzognera" is here rendered by that between puny "fibber" and serious "liar".

[14] He knows that she knows that he wants to hide his age even if he is conscious that she understands that he does not believe she believes him: a hypocritical game entertained by both subjects.

[15] *Astrophil and Stella*, Sonnet 87, "When I was forced from Stella ever dear".

Quando il mio amore giura di essere tutta fedeltà,
io le credo, anche se so che mente,
affinché possa pensarmi un giovane inesperto,
ignaro delle false sottigliezze del mondo.
Così, con vanità pensando che giovane mi pensi,
sebbene lei sappia che son passati i miei giorni migliori,
ingenuamente presto fede alla sua lingua bugiarda;
e così da tutte e due le parti la semplice verità è cancellata.
Ma perché non dice lei d'essere infedele?
E perché non dico io d'essere vecchio?
Oh, il miglior costume dell'amore è l'apparente fiducia,
e la vecchiaia innamorata non ama che le siano contati gli anni.
Perciò io mento giacendo con lei, e lei con me,
e, nelle nostre colpe, siamo lusingati da menzogne.

This is a masterly translation by one of the most distinguished Italian philologists and Shakespeare scholars. It preserves that progression towards the final climax, with the dénouement of the clinching pun on the bisemic expression "to lie", here rendered through a periphrasis which makes explicit both meanings of the double entendre (*mento giacendo con lei*: we lie down together and we deceive each other).

Other keywords align themselves across the sonnet to sustain an anguished, self-searching process of introspection on the part of the speaker, divided between trust and diffidence, and between guilt and self-indulgence. This emphasizes the traditional ethos of the sonnet type, which developed as a personal meditation in which the speaker is the only real protagonist, and the context is represented by his emotional reaction to the conflicting thoughts and memories that occupy his mind (cf. Petrarch). The suppleness of the language employed by the translator does justice to Shakespeare's lexical variety. The woman, here, assures the speaker that she is absolutely faithful (*tutta fedeltà*) and he, out of pride (*con vanità*), pretends to believe her, with the result that they both destroy all mutual sincerity (*verità cancellata*). Presumably she is unfaithful (*infedele*) and will not admit it: is this because he too pretends that he is not getting old (*d'esser vecchio*)? Love's disguise (*costume*) is fake trust (*apparente fiducia*); and so they have sex together and deceive each other (*mentiamo giacendo*) and they wallow in those sinful lies (*nelle colpe lusingati da menzogne*). This interpretation recalls the sombre atmosphere of suspicion in *The Winter's Tale* or the workings of jealousy in Othello's mind. It uncovers the disturbing, obscure side of human nature.

A different type altogether is represented by the translation of Lucia Folena (2021, 277), unusual among translations of the sonnets in being in metre, specifically the Italian hendecasyllable line.

Quando proclama la sua buona fede,
alla mia donna, anche se so che mente,
credo, affinché mi reputi un pivello
ignaro di mondani sotterfugi.
Nell'illusione che mi pensi giovane,
mentre sa che ho passato il fior degli anni,
do credito alla sua lingua fallace:
così la nuda verità aboliamo
entrambi. Ma perché lei non confessa
i suoi misfatti, ed io la mia vecchiezza?
Fanno bene all'amor la fiducia
simulata ed il non contare gli anni;
perciò giacciamo insieme e ci inganniamo,
colpevoli blanditi da bugie.[16]

The regular metre gives greater polish to the language, which acquires a declamatory stateliness. At the same time, the rhythm tends to the colloquial with its spontaneous intonation patterns that dictate a pace unfettered by line divisions; one notes four enjambments between lines and several caesuras scattered across them. Folena, herself, admits to having had to condense the utterances of the source texts in her translation of the *Sonnets* because of the greater length of the Italian and the strictures imposed by metre. The tone, therefore, appears terse and emphatic; the lexicon is incisive (e.g. *sotterfugi* "guiles", *fallace* "devious", *aboliamo* "abolish", *misfatti* "misdeeds"). Like Shakespeare's original, the poem has an excellent recitability. Here, the protagonist comes across as flippant, and aloof from the subject matter of his account (*fa*

---

[16] Since the latter metrical translation is less close to the source-text than the former ones, I here provide an English back-translation with significant choices underlined: "When she proclaims her <u>honesty</u>,/my lady, though I know she tells lies,/I believe, so that she may think me a simpleton,/ignorant of <u>worldly guiles</u>./In my delusion of being thought young,/notwithstanding she knows that my <u>prime of life</u> is over,/I give credence to her <u>devious</u> tongue:/thus we <u>abolish</u> naked truth/both of us. But why does she not <u>confess</u>/her <u>misdeeds</u>, and so do not I my old age?/Love <u>benefits</u> from trust that is/<u>feigned</u> and from reluctance to add up years;/Therefore <u>we lie down together</u> and we <u>deceive</u> each other,/<u>culpable</u>, being <u>coaxed</u> by the lies that are told".

bene all'amore...fiducia simulata: feigned trust benefits love; *colpevoli ci inganniamo:* culpable we deceive ourselves). And the final attribute given to the couple (*blanditi*: coaxed) reveals the same self-ironical flippancy conveyed by the tone of the source.

It is interesting to reflect retrospectively on two clues about the original intention of the author seen in the PP version: "outfacing faults in love", that is to say, overlooking some flaws in the relationship, and the "smiling" that reveals a hidden facet of the speaker's outlook and, particularly, the veiled attitude of the author regarding his artefact: one of amused complacency. Folena's translation seems to have taken into account this former indication. Her interpretation, though attentive to the sombre build-up of sexual innuendoes in the body of the poem, strikes a note of cheerful zest in the sceptical conclusion (*fanno bene all'amore...fiducia simulata...giaciamo e ci inganniamo...blanditi da bugie*: feigned trust is beneficial to love...and we trick each other, in lying down, coaxed by our lies). This brings to mind the titillating eroticism of *Venus and Adonis*. As done by Serpieri, the crucial pun on "lie" is similarly split into two overlapping meanings, impossible to collapse into a single Italian word.

A further precious aid to the interpreter, that confirms the correctness of the above sensuous reading of Q 138, comes from that verb tense found in the final couplet of PP: the future of "I'll lie with Love and Love with me" (indicating a blithe intention rather than a crude statement of fact). It gives away the original inspiration of the poet while working out his psychological context. No wonder that so many shrewd readers of this sonnet have compared its scenario with that of *Antony and Cleopatra*. Both protagonists of that play, in fact, are ambivalent in the eyes of the audience: Cleopatra, earnestly in love but given to deceiving, and Antony, gullible though conscious of being manipulated.

Each of these translations is true to the inferred tone of the source text, since they respond to three distinct interpretative designs. These renderings bridge the gap between the reading and the performance of the text in the act of reception. In terms of Jakobson's (1975, 366–367) useful scheme about verse production, the third step, that of "delivery design", is where the strategies of both author and interpreter (translator) come together and are compelled to negotiate an accord. In the case of Q 138, to the text instance there corresponds a twofold delivery design (the result of the "semantic re-claiming of the duplicate"). Overlapping designs generate a complexity that needs to be made intelligible when transferred into another language by eliminating competitive accounts.

In conclusion, these three translations, suggesting diverging responses to the source text, have made apparent the intention of the author to leave the interpretation of the scenario indeterminate and open to the critical disposition of readers. The fact that critics still continue to address this text from different angles can only prove its inherent vitality. But why did Shakespeare choose to spend so many technical resources on such a cognitively demanding sonnet? Presumably the answer lies in the Elizabethan frame of mind: the result of Humanist learning and education. Peter Mack (2002, 73–75) in his *Elizabethan Rhetoric* has shown how prominently dialectic figured in those days in the syllabi of grammar school and university. "Dialectical reading" was the principal heuristic tool of the day, until it was displaced by the scientific method.[17] Nevertheless the "tutored youths" of Shakespeare's generation needed to be extremely learned in the skills of language, conceived in terms of their competence in handling rhetoric and dialectic.

This sonnet (through the author's progressive honing of the text) must have appeared to his first privileged circle of recipients, those "private friends" referred to by Meres, as a brilliant compositional stunt, a veritable rhetorical showcase.[18] This is what can still be observed here through the eyes of the translators, who are obliged to make explicit what cannot be left indeterminate in the target language. What is interesting is the way Shakespeare applies dialectical reading in forecasting the reception of his work, all the way up: from the single word to the entire text. Words like the verb "lie" or the noun "habit" get dissected into their semantic components; sentences appear ambivalent, thanks to their grammar and syntax; even whole texts may acquire more than one significance, as our translators' work has so aptly illustrated.

REFERENCES

Allen, Michael J.B. 1979. "Shakespeare's Man Descending a Staircase: Sonnets 126 to 154." *Shakespeare Survey* 31: 127–138.
Bade, Nadine, Matthias Bauer, Sigrid Beck, Carmen Dörge, and Angelika Zirker. 2015. "Ambiguity in Shakespeare's Sonnet 138." In *Ambiguity: Language and Communication*, ed. Susanne Winkler, 89–110. Berlin: De Gruyter.

[17] See Nauert (1995, 207–209).

[18] See the literary links between Shakespeare and the learned circle surrounding the Earl of Pembroke: Kingsley-Smith (2019, 44–45).

Beccone, Simona. 2008. *"I Do Believe Her Though I Know She Lies". Il sonetto 138 o l'apologia shakespeariana della poesia*. Roma: Aracne.

Benveniste, Émile. 1974. *Problèmes de linguistique générale 2*. Paris: Gallimard.

Booth, Stephen. 1977. *Shakespeare's Sonnets: Edited With Analytic Commentary By Stephen Booth*. New Haven and London: Yale University Press.

Duncan-Jones, Katherine. 2005. *Shakespeare's Sonnets*. London: The Arden Shakespeare, Thomson Learning.

Edmondson, Paul, and Stanley Wells. 2020. *All the Sonnets of Shakespeare*. Cambridge: Cambridge University Press.

Folena, Lucia (ed.). 2021. *William Shakespeare: Sonetti*. Torino: Einaudi.

Jakobson, Roman. 1975. "Closing Statement: Linguistics and Poetics." In *Style in Language*, ed. Thomas Sebeok, 350–377. 6th ed. Cambridge, MA: M.I.T. Press.

Kingsley-Smith, Jane. 2019. *The Afterlife of Shakespeare's Sonnets*. Cambridge: Cambridge University Press.

Ladyman, James, and Karoline Wiesner. 2020. *What Is a Complex System?* New Haven: Yale University Press.

Mack, Peter. 2002. *Elizabethan Rhetoric: Theory and Practice*. Cambridge and New York: Cambridge University Press.

Melchiori, Giorgio. 1979. *William Shakespeare: Sonetti*. 5th ed. Torino: Einaudi.

Nauert, Charles. 1995. *Humanism and the Culture of Renaissance Europe*. Cambridge: Cambridge University Press.

Rizzante, Massimo. 2013. "William Shakespeare, Sonetti 13, 27, 138." *Archivio di Traduzione* 1. Accessed June 15, 2021. http://www.massimorizzante.com/pdf/sonetti.pdf.

Roberts, Sasha. 2002. *Reading Shakespeare's Poems in Early Modern England*. Basingstoke: Palgrave Macmillan.

Rollins, Hyder E. (ed.). 1944. *A New Variorum Edition of Shakespeare: The Sonnets*. 2 vols. Philadelphia: Lippincott.

Serpieri, Alessandro. 1991. *William Shakespeare: Sonetti*. Milano: Rizzoli.

Snow, Edward. A. 1980. "Loves of Comfort and Despair: A Reading of Shakespeare's Sonnet 138." *English Literary History* 47: 462–483.

Vendler, Helen. 1997. *The Art of Shakespeare's Sonnets*. Cambridge, MA: Harvard University Press.

CHAPTER 6

"Far from Variation or Quick Change": Classical and New Translations of Shakespeare's Sonnets in Hungary

Bálint Szele

The most important year in the history of the Hungarian *Sonnets* is probably 1921, when a young poet of 21, Lőrinc Szabó (1900–1957), published his new translation of the full cycle. This translation was the ambitious work of a young man, who used all philological data available to him to understand as much about the poems as possible, and who also wrote an introduction to the book and detailed notes to the individual sonnets. This achievement was unprecedented in Hungary at that time and met with critical acclaim. Before this, two translations of the *Sonnets* had been published, in 1878 and 1916, both inadequate in language and content. To understand the significance of the young poet's work, it is

B. Szele (✉)
Kodolányi János University, Székesfehérvár, Hungary
e-mail: bszele@kodolanyi.hu

© The Author(s), under exclusive license to Springer Nature Switzerland AG 2023
J. Kingsley-Smith and W. R. Rampone Jr. (eds.), *Shakespeare's Global Sonnets*, Global Shakespeares, https://doi.org/10.1007/978-3-031-09472-9_6

necessary to go back in time until the beginning of the nineteenth century to have a brief look at the development of the Hungarian language, and the unfolding cult of Shakespeare in Hungary.

THE EARLY HISTORY OF THE *SONNETS* IN HUNGARY

Since the early sixteenth century, the kingdom of Hungary was at least partly under Hapsburg rule, and from the beginning of the eighteenth century, the Hapsburg dynasty ruled the whole country until 1918. Consequently, Latin and German were the languages used for administrative purposes (Latin being the official language until 1844), and Hungarian was only used by country populations and the lower middle classes, preserving an archaic, outdated language, lacking in many lexical items for contemporary life. People committed to reviving the Hungarian language formed a loose alliance to carry out the enormous work of a "language renewal", mostly between 1790 and 1820, forming new words and reforming orthography and grammar rules. This activity was also seen as a crusade to overcome the rival German language. Hungarian literati wanted to create a literary Hungarian language that had the same capabilities as German.

The work of spreading the reformed Hungarian language to people in an age when nationalism was the most progressive idea of the day was partly done by theatres and theatrical troupes, travelling actors and actresses, who, lacking plays written in Hungarian, began to use translations and adaptations of Latin, Greek, and, most significantly, German plays. There was a constant need to clarify the theoretical rules and practical issues of translating, and more and more translations were made, as translating was seen as a patriotic activity. The first English plays to be translated were *Richard II* (1785), *Romeo and Juliet* (1786), and *King Lear* (1795), although it would be more accurate to call them adaptations rather than translations, as these texts lacked any kind of equivalence to the original in structure or content. The initial requirements were rather different from what we call literary translation today: in 1792, a theoretician demanded that translators "have a duel with the author" to "get a translation that is just as good, or even better than the original"[1] (Péczeli

---

[1] All translations from Hungarian in this paper are by the author.

1996, 45). He also declared that "improper parts" should not be translated word by word. "Improving" and selecting from the original was encouraged so that only "the best and nicest pieces enrich our culture" (Péczeli 1981, 308).

During their search for texts, theatre companies discovered the "German Shakespeare", which had already been naturalised and considered by many Germans as "Unser Shakespeare". Not much was known about Shakespeare's plays in Hungary at that time, and there were hardly any people in Hungary who read English. The first proper translation of *Macbeth* was published in 1830 by Gábor Döbrentei (1785–1851), who was the first translator to use the English original text as his source. One year later, the Hungarian Academy of Sciences—established in 1827 "to strengthen, spread and refine the Hungarian language"—set up a theatrical committee, which put twenty-two Shakespeare plays on its list containing seventy-one foreign plays worthy of translation. At that time, Hungarian literati were optimistic about their language being capable of rendering the English plays just as well as German. When, in 1836, Mihály Vörösmarty (1800–1855), the famous Romantic poet, started to translate *Julius Caesar* into Hungarian, the feat was considered heroic enough to get into the news sections of contemporary papers.

After the Revolution of 1848 and the failed War of Independence, the country was depressed, subdued under Hapsburg rule again. Translation became one of the ways of upholding Hungarian culture and it gave solace to many writers and poets. From the 1860s, Shakespeare translators, now drawing on accumulating experience, began to identify the most relevant problems of translation (cf. Szele 2006, 2013), such as the number of syllables in a line and how to reproduce the rhymed parts, as well as the contrast of elevated feelings and low comedy within one play. Shakespeare's plays became part of Hungarian literature and education; a Shakespeare cult developed. Sándor Petőfi (1823–1849), the fiery revolutionary and romantic poet, had said in 1847: "Shakespeare in Himself is half of Creation" (Petőfi 1984, 160). The work was done when the first complete Hungarian Shakespeare was published between 1864 and 1878 by the famous and authoritative Kisfaludy Society in nineteen volumes, with usually two plays to a volume.

The nineteenth volume contained all of Shakespeare's poems, including the *Sonnets*, translated by Károly Szász (1829–1905) and Vilmos Győry (1838–1885). Their work perfectly follows the form and structure of the original, but the imagery is weak, the language contorted, many metaphors and puns are omitted, and moods and feelings are not conveyed adequately.

Following the tradition of contemporary Hungarian poetry, translators had been looking for fixed meanings, clear ideas, to give "to airy nothing/ A local habitation and a name", and they were afraid of multiple interpretations, possible misunderstandings, obscene meanings or connotations. Károly Szász claimed that the English Renaissance sonnet was an artificial, unnatural, unhealthy creation springing from Italian influence, and declared that the English sonnet "did not imitate life in its entire reality, did not even make an attempt to idealise it, but created something entirely different using sheer imagination; in action, it looks for the novelistic, even frivolous; in feelings, it looks for the exalted and extreme, in presentation, the overburdened, the picture-laden [...] Dismissing the natural, its caprice carries it away to extremes" (Szász 1869, 75–76). Károly Szász was puzzled, even disturbed by the level of ambiguity in the sonnets: "how many approximations and how little certainty! How many lines, ideas, and poems misunderstood and too hard to understand! [...] As a red line, there is an effort running through all the poems: do not let readers understand, let them just suspect a lot. This seems to go contrary to the purpose of poetry, of any kind of writing" (Szász 1869, 104).

In this period, literary people in Hungary did not know how to approach the *Sonnets*, thinking they were bad, incomprehensible, obscure poems. The theoretician of Shakespeare translation in Hungary, the renowned poet and translator János Arany (1817–1882), who translated three of the plays and did a lot of reviewing and editing too, summarised the main requirements of Shakespeare translation for fellow translators, but this did not include the *Sonnets* as they were seen as marginal pieces. (Trying to find anybody mentioning them during the nineteenth century is quite impossible; if anyone ever wrote about Shakespeare, it is about the plays they wrote). Arany shared Szász's ideas that poetry must be able to convey the intended meaning of the author without any misunderstandings. Whereas Shakespeare's Early Modern English was still flexible and ready to accommodate new, foreign influences, Hungarian after the "language renewal" was past its malleable period, and, having fixed the meanings, poets were determined to defend them. Under such circumstances, obscurity and ambiguity were seen as dangerous. This idea led to a rigid dismissal of obvious and hidden obscenities or ambiguities. In Sonnet 87, the translator either voluntarily or by accident dismissed the sexual allusions in the lines "For how do I hold thee but by thy granting?" or "Thyself thou gavest, thy own worth then not knowing", simply using neutral phrases, but still keeping the legal vocabulary characteristic of the sonnet: "Hisz birtalak csak ingyen kegyelembül" [I just possessed you as a gratis grace], and "Becsed nem tudva, adtad át magad te" [you handed yourself over not knowing your value]. The feeling that the Hungarian *Sonnets* still did not come up to standard—they were hard to read and their story was not fully revealed—and the realisation that translating them was an extreme task even for the best of poets, led to a new attempt by the famous classicist poet, Mihály Babits (1883–1941), who translated two sonnets in 1916 after claiming that "of all our translations of Shakespeare, the *Sonnets* are the least comprehensible", while also admitting that "translation is of the utmost hardship because of the closed form and the multitude of unclarified questions" (Babits 1978, 432). It was his disciple, Lőrinc Szabó, who, in 1921, transformed all the sonnets into a contemporary, modern, clear Hungarian version, expressing both his thankfulness to and his disagreement with his mentor. In the following section, I will sketch in the theoretical background against which Lőrinc Szabó's and later translations need to be assessed.

THEORY AND PRACTICE IN THE EARLY TWENTIETH CENTURY

The unwritten rules of literary translation in Hungary have been observed ever since János Arany laid down the basic principles in 1860: "translators should aim at faithfulness both in form, and substance or content" (Arany 1984a, 213). However impossible it may sound, translators need to abide by this rule, broken down into a strict list of requirements that bind the translator in terms of form and content, depending on mode and genre. The translator must rely on his/her taste, experience, and previous readings, and may be helped by a reviewer or proof-reader who spots mistakes and helps the translator with advice.

The formal requirements adapted for the case of the *Sonnets* are the following: the number of syllables in a line must be kept; the rhyme scheme must be kept and rhymes must be rendered with rhymes; and the rhythm must be iambic, as far as possible. The requirements concerning the content are the following: special vocabulary (legal, medical, etc.) must be kept; images and metaphors must be kept, possibly throughout the whole cycle; conceits must be kept; ambiguities and paradoxes must be rendered, as much as possible; the sonnet must have a strong couplet; and the translation in general must be clear and comprehensible.

The difficulties of translating Shakespeare's Sonnets into Hungarian have been summarised in a previous paper (Szele 2016), which discusses the abovementioned problems in more detail. The first problem is the number of syllables and the length of words in English and Hungarian. The average number of letters in English words is about 4.7–4.8, whereas Hungarian is an agglutinating language which uses various affixes that can be added to a word to increase its length (and change its meaning). It is almost impossible to compare the two languages systematically in this respect, but it can be stated that Hungarian words tend to be longer. To fit the ten or sometimes eleven syllables of a line in a sonnet into the same number of syllables in Hungarian is almost impossible. As an example, we can quote Lőrinc Szabó's two lines, six words, from Sonnet 35: "túlzott mentéssel túlzom bűneid; | értelmezem érzékiségedet" [I exaggerate your sins with exaggerated excuses, I interpret your sensuality]. In the original two lines we find 17 words: "Excusing thy sins more than thy sins are: | For to thy sensual fault I bring in sense". The translator had to make an extreme effort to condense the text so that it fits into the sonnet form.

Choosing the right words in translation is also problematic because of the rhymes. The rhyme scheme of the sonnet is rigidly fixed, and while Shakespeare had a chance to use short, one-syllable words and masculine rhymes, Hungarian translators have a hard time finding the right words for the rhyme. For example, Sonnet 84 has 7 rhymes, six one-syllable masculine rhymes, and one feminine rhyme. The masculine rhymes are "more – store", "you – grew", "dwell – tell", "writ – wit", "clear – where", "curse – worse". The only feminine rhyme is "glory – story". Lőrinc Szabó's translation of this sonnet uses feminine rhymes and good or bad assonances (usually alternately, so that the bad ones fall on odd, and the good ones on even lines), and the clearest rhyme is found in the couplet. The numbers show the number of syllables in the line.

Mondjon legtöbbet, ki mond többet annál	11
a gazdag bóknál, hogy te csak te vagy?	10
Annyi kincsre hol és kiben akadnál,	11
hogy versenyre hívd benne másodat?	10
Kór ínség lakja a pennát, amely	10
semmi dicsfénnyel nem emeli tárgyát,	11
de aki rólad csak azt mondja el,	10
hogy te te vagy, már örök glóriát ád	11

(continued)

(continued)

Másolja csak, mi beléd íratott,	10
s ne rontsa meg természetes derűd:	10
szellemét oly képmás hirdeti, hogy	10
ámulat lesz stílusa mindenütt	10
Te szép áldásod átokkal tetézed:	11
dicsvágy, dicsfényed rontja a dicséret!	11

The number of syllables per line is not as even as in the original. Szabó, who is famous for his negligence concerning music in poetry, in the sonnet above takes good care of the couplet, which is a challenge in itself for the translator: it must be clear, epigrammatic, and effective. The music of the sonnets does not only come from the rhymes, but internal repetitions of sounds and rhythms, too. Even if the Hungarian language has an inherent iambic tendency (see line 10 here: "s ne **ron**tsa **meg** ter**mésze**tes **derűd**"), it is hard to keep most of the sonnet iambic. Hungarian is a syllable-timed language, so it is not the alternation of stressed and unstressed syllables that gives the rhythm, but the alternation of long and short syllables.

So far, only formal requirements have been discussed. The *Sonnets*, however, have other, more substantial components, too. It is enough to mention vocabulary, conceits, allusions, as well as ambiguities and paradoxes that need to be taken care of in translations. As an example, we might consider the famous couplet of Sonnet 138, where Shakespeare plays with "lie to" vs. "lie with", which Lőrinc Szabó translated as "Ezért hazudik nekem, s én neki, | vétkünk a hazugságot élvezi" [therefore she lies to me and I to her,/ our sin enjoys the lies]. It is obvious that such a pun cannot be rendered in any other language.

Another practical problem is that before the age of digital text processing and modern research tools a lot of meanings and philological facts we are aware of today were simply unknown to translators. We know from their accounts that early translators used all the sources available to them, for example, Vörösmarty used a copy of the Schlegel–Tieck edition (Maller 1984, 17), but later translators also used contemporary English essays and German translations and commentaries, especially the German Delius edition, which was equipped with explanations and footnotes (Arany 1984b, 210). Although they read the original texts, none of the translators *spoke* English at the time, so the sound of the poems, their many puns, internal rhymes, and other subtleties, remained undiscovered.

Translators who interpret the sonnets for readers have to take their own standpoint concerning questions which might be described as the background of the *Sonnets*, namely whether the sonnets are based on real events, even Shakespeare's own life, and who the characters in the *Sonnets* are and what the relationships are between them. As has been shown, Szász, Győry, and then Babits and Lőrinc Szabó, mainly saw the sonnets either as descriptions of autobiographical events, or as *études*, poetic exercises. Neither approach helped them to find the "real meaning" of the poems. The interwoven layers of meaning, the continuous play with language that we today see as the greatest feature of the *Sonnets*, seemed rather a burden to all early translators. Babits saw the sonneteer Shakespeare as a secretive poet who, instead of writing about his own life, condensed his feelings into tight forms, as if he were attracted to some kind of excessive formalism. "Shakespeare did not write songs, and he did not express his own feelings in his resounding words. In his youth, as everyone, he did write love poems, but these would only show his personality in a one-sided and semi-developed form, even if the poems had all come from his own soul, and if they were not just polite witticisms made for specific occasions" (Babits 1978, 58). However, both Babits and Lőrinc Szabó believed that at least some of Shakespeare's life must have found its way into the *Sonnets*. Szabó, in his introduction, wrote that "Shakespeare in his youth did use the strange conventions of his age, the complicated trains of thoughts and oddities of Euphuism", but he also added that "the conventions are in full contradiction with the uncommonly passionate voice and the tense, dramatic power of the *Sonnets*" (Szabó 1921, XXXIII, XXXIV). When publishing his second translation, in 1948, Szabó went further and declared that "a serious reader finds it impossible that a poet, a poet of such capacity as Shakespeare, wrote his poems as virtuosic rhythmic or style exercises, as riddles, in the names of others. Life itself bleeds in them, the key actually unlocks the door to a heart, the pounding secrets of a giant heart" (Szabó 1948, 14). The writings of English critics such as A. C. Bradley, whose influential book might have been available in Hungary, and O. Smeaton, whose books Lőrinc Szabó used, support the Hungarian translators' beliefs that the *Sonnets* are substantially dramatic poems about real-life events: "The *Sonnets* are lyrical poems of friendship and love. In them the poet ostensibly speaks in his own person and expresses his own feeling" (Bradley 1965, 312).

One example of the change between Lőrinc Szabó's old and new translations is Sonnet 12, which, in the first lines, evokes the sounds of a clock, then plays on the contrast between day and night, and, finally, emphasises contrasting colours. Here, the first four lines are shown together with an English gloss:

1921

Harangot hallva, mely órákra ver,	hearing a bell that tolls every hour
s látva: a boldog napra éj borúl,	and seeing happy day covered by night
hogy tavasz multán még ibolya kel	that the violet still comes up after spring
s fekete fürtre évek hava hull,	and black hair is covered with the snow of years

1948

Számolva az óramondó időt,	counting the hour-telling time
s látva, hős nap rút éjbe hogy merül,	and seeing how heroic day is immersed in foul darkness
hogy kókkad az ibolya nyár előtt,	how violets wither before summer
s ezüst zúzt hogy kap a fekete fürt;	and how black hair gets a silver frost

The first translation is much more musical and poetic: the reader can hear the bell. The images are simple and only slightly extended (cf. "snow of years") compared to the original. In the second version, there is little music. The rhymes are dull, the words are more exalted, and the imagery is more complicated. The translator tried to cram as much meaning into the poem as possible, which makes reading harder and overburdens the text; what is more, he used the same words he used in his translation of *Macbeth* (1939), another piece that has time as one of its main characters, making the poem as dramatic as possible. In both translations, however, the translation of the third line is incorrect.

There is also a clear shift in how the translator saw the poems. Sonnet 16 was an impressionistic and emotional song in the 1921 translation, whereas the 1948 version is denser and more metaphorical. Where the earlier version starts with a theatrical outcry "Hervadsz! —mért nem erősíted magad/ jobb fegyverekkel, mint meddő dalom?" [you are withering!—why do not you have better weapons than my barren song?], the final version says "romlásodtól mért nem óv üdvösebb/ eszköz, mint a száraz dalok?" [why is there no better tool to protect you from your decay that these dry songs?]. The earlier version of Sonnet 90 includes an exalted question: "El akarsz hagyni? — Hagyj el most" [Do you want to leave me? — leave me now], whereas the final version shows the speaker's true distress behind a calm facade: "Ha el akarsz, hagyj" [If you want to leave me, leave me]. What had been seen as a Renaissance poetic exercise in 1921 turned into heartfelt agony in 1948.

Szabó's translation remained the only "authorised version" for a long time for a number of reasons. Translators in Hungary have always had to cope with some kind of censorship, as sexual topics and immoral ideas were simply unacceptable in print until 1989 and the fall of socialism. This in itself is a big problem, as the *Sonnets* are very non-traditional love poems. Nineteenth-century taste condemned open references to immorality, sexuality, and homosexuality, and later, the period between the two World Wars (1920–1944)—characterised by strong clerical influence and revisionism—and the age of socialism in Hungary (1948–1989)—characterised by strong-handed state control over cultural matters—were both unfavourable for unfolding the real meanings of the *Sonnets* (cf. Szele 2017). Once a good, acceptable translation was at hand, leaders of the cultural life of Hungary did not support new translations. In theatrical translations, there were attempts at loosening the control and smuggling some "improper" low comedy back into the plays—if not in print editions, then in the theatres—but this did not happen in the case of the *Sonnets*.

Lőrinc Szabó's translations have served the public well since 1921. The poet allowed only one reprint of his first translation as he was dissatisfied with his first version, and continuously worked on new versions until 1948, when his second translation was published. This second version, which put much less emphasis on sound and music, but highlighted the intellectual content and again softened the improper parts of the sonnets, was well-accepted by communist and socialist administrations. A third version, a small volume, came out in 1956, with a few major and a lot of minor modifications, so today this is regarded as the final version of Lőrinc Szabó's *Sonnets*. As Szabó's translations were regarded as final, there was no need to publish a new translation or ask any other translator to do the work. It was only after the end of socialism that new generations of translators began to rediscover the *Sonnets* in Hungary and use new approaches and methods in their translations.

CONTEMPORARY APPROACHES

Since the middle of the twentieth century, several exhaustive studies have been written on the *Sonnets* (e.g. Booth 1969, 2000; Duncan-Jones 1997; Kerrigan 1986; Mahood 1968; Muir 1979; Vendler 1997), all extensively analysing Shakespeare's language play. Some essays in Hungarian have also made attempts at analysing how the *Sonnets* can be and have been translated (Kiss 1975; Fabiny 1997; Kardos 1965; Kéry 1961; Lutter 1956; Szentkuthy 1985). These essays focus primarily on the formal characteristics (rhyme, metre, sound effects) and the subject matter of the *Sonnets*—the characters and the story Shakespeare presented— putting less emphasis on the language play and ambiguity in the poems (Szele 2018). There is currently a process of rediscovering the *Sonnets* in Hungary using the latest philological information, also including the reconstructed pronunciation of Shakespeare's time. Four contemporary translators and their versions of some sonnets are introduced in the final section. Two are Tibor Csillag (1928–2007) and Anna Szabó T. (1972–), both poets, and Sándor Fazekas (1975–), a literary historian. A fourth translator, Zsolt Farkas (1964–), has recently published some prose translations.

Csillag produced his translation around the time of great political changes, between 1987 and 1994. The volume was first published in 2004. In the essay closing his book, Csillag admits trying to "compete with" Lőrinc Szabó by "following the original even more closely than he did" (Csillag 2015, 101). However, his translations cannot be considered as modern and faithful, first, because of the obsolete, archaic language forms he used, and, second, because of the overarching compulsion to fit the rhyme scheme. This is what Italian calls *tirannia della rima*, tyranny of rhymes, its equivalent in Hungarian being "rímkényszer" [force of rhyme], which can effectively hinder finding the word the poem actually needs and force the translator into including a word which fits the rhyme scheme but not the poem. Csillag, however, tried to translate some double-entendres and obscenities more clearly than his predecessors, for example, in Sonnet 135, he dared to speak about "member", "swollen", or "eruptive". In many sonnets, he highlighted the (long forgotten) corporeal aspect of the text.

Anna Szabó T. is one of the most distinguished poets in Hungary and she is also an expert on the *Sonnets*. Her ambition is to keep the music of the original poems and to preserve their original ambiguities, to synthesise these two aspects of language play. In her translations, she adopts George Steiner's ideas: "we learn to listen. [...] We discard the static or ready explanation, of scattered association, of personal commentary, in order *to listen totally*. [...] It is only when we apprehend the 'meaning of meaning', *the expressive totality* integral to a given set of verbal, syntactic, language-specific units, that we understand fully" (Steiner 1975, 376). She knows the English language inside out, and accommodates music, language play, puns, and sexual language gracefully and elegantly. It is also worth noting that she introduces a rare female perspective into translating the sonnets. In her translation, Sonnet 60 preserves its music, the assonances are strong, the language is easy to understand and modern, and the poem shines in its own simplicity. The following translations are coupled with their English glosses.

Mint hullámzás a kavicsos fövenyre,	as waves to the pebbled shore
a vég felé úgy futnak perceink,	our minutes run towards the end
egymás nyomában küzdve és sietve	they struggle and hurry one after the other
előre ringnak mért ütem szerint	swinging forward in a measured beat
Az újszülöttet fénytenger füröszti,	the new-born is bathed in a sea of light
élete delén koronát visel,	wears a crown in the middle of his life
de dicsfényét a torz sötét kikezdi,	but his glory is challenged by misshapen darkness
s az idő mindent visszakövetel	and time claims everything back
Az idő minden virágzáson átüt,	time grows through every blooming
árkokat ás a szépség homlokára,	digs ditches on the forehead of beauty
felemészti a természet csodáit,	wears away the wonders of nature
és rendre mindent levág a kaszája	and its scythe cuts everything down
De versem időtállón hirdeti	but my poem durably propagates
dicséreted, és ellenáll neki	your praise, and resists time

It is also worth reading the first four lines of Sonnet 12 in Anna Szabó T.'s translation to see how music, sound, light, darkness, and colours are represented in the translation. Not only is the language clear and simple, and the rhymes perfect, but the meaning is also as close to the original as possible.

Ha számolom, ahogy az óra üt,	when I count as the clock chimes
és látom, hogy lesz fényességből éj,	and I see how light becomes darkness,
s az ibolya hogy hervad mindenütt,	how the violets wither everywhere,
s a hollóhajból hogy lesz hófehér,	and how raven hair becomes snow white

Sándor Fazekas (1975–) defines his task as leaving the Lőrinc Szabó-era behind and making a completely new translation of the *Sonnets* based on the latest information available.

As he says in his introductory essay, "I want to make the sonnets more easily comprehensible for the new generations […] make the *Sonnets* available for secondary school pupils, university students, educated chief accountants, bored wives of millionaires, open-minded brigadiers, priests preparing for their preaching, and innovative car part dealers too" (Fazekas 2019). In contrast, he stipulates the strictest translator's rules: he intends to keep feminine and masculine rhymes, iambic and spondaic lines, and to use archaisms only if Shakespeare used archaic language himself. He even declares that "the translating practice in Hungary is much more loose than it should be" (Fazekas 2020). "I treat the poems as a literary historian: I am trying to create a translation faithful in form and content, as such a translation is still not available" (Fazekas 2019). Fazekas sees the key to good translation in a rigid formal equivalence, but since he has not published the most challenging sonnets so far, it is impossible to see whether his method really works. He admits that we "cannot speak about one and only correct translation or interpretation" and declares that "the real power of the *Sonnets* lies in plain speech concerning emotional intimacy, but this plain speech usually means hidden, sometimes obscene double-entendre", but he also opens up escape routes: "footnotes might take us closer to the text by explaining the delicate points" (Fazekas 2019).

In the few instances he has already published, Fazekas shows his readers both the positive and negative outcomes of his extreme form-centred translation approach. In Sonnet 42, the approach works, and one of the famous conceits is rendered in a clear, modern language (shown here with an English gloss).

Ha elveszítlek, hát övé leszel,	if I lose you, you will be hers
s barátomé lesz, ha elveszteném;	and she will be my friend's if I lose her;
duplán vesztek: a pár egymásra lel,	I lose twice: the couple find each other,
s tőlük kapom nehéz keresztem én	and I get my heavy cross from them
Egy vagy velem, ez itt az élvezet:	you are one with me, this is the pleasure
Szép öncsalás! Csupán engem szeret!	nice self-cheating! she only loves me!

In Sonnet 130, however, many of the aforementioned translators' woes appear: the evil force of rhyme and the small number of syllables per line, which result in contorted sentences and obsolete words, and a lame couplet, which also includes a run-on line. This list recalls the problems and mistakes of nineteenth-century translators. It is not worth quoting Fazekas' Hungarian translation here; there is still hope the translator will amend it. But the limitations are made clear: the sonnet form, with its fixed and tight structure, does not easily accommodate its Hungarian version.

Careful contemporary translators usually adopt an approach Stephen Booth suggests: "the substance of the sonnets is paradox, so the style is paradoxical" (Booth 1969, 104). Booth notes about Sonnets 135 and 136 that they are "festivals of verbal ingenuity in which much of the fun derives from the grotesque lengths the speaker goes to for a maximum number and concentration of puns on *will*" (Booth 2000, 466–467). If the translations of Lőrinc Szabó and Anna Szabó T. are compared, we can see a huge distance between the two poems; Lőrinc Szabó, in Sonnet 135 had written "Villik rajzanak körül, száz lidérc,/ villik, szeszélyek, vágy, kéj, ezer álom". [villis swarm around you, a hundred incubi,/ villis, caprices, lust, pleasure, a thousand dreams]. The translator used the word "villi" to render the wordplay on "will", but this word is far from well-known: it is not used in everyday Hungarian language, at least not in ordinary texts. Some occurrences can be found in nineteenth- and twentieth-century poetry with the meaning "lustful fairy". The sound itself implies a diminutive of "villám" (Hungarian for "lightning"), and it has a connotation of the fairy-like/supernatural. Thus, the whole meaning of the poem is shifted from sexual pleasure to a *Midsummer Night's Dream*-like supernatural world.

Anna Szabó T., however, gives the reader a new and playful sonnet, with accentuated rhythm, good rhymes, lots of wordplay and alliterations, and some bawdy language, while she also distances the text from the target audience by retaining the word "Will", emphasising the game with the poet's name. Here is the sonnet with its back-translation into English:

Mi kell a nőnek? Kell a vallomás,	What does a woman want? She wants confessions,
és kell a vágy, s ha Willt vállal, sokat,	and wants lust, and if she takes on a lot of Wills,
vállának nem sok a váltott nyomás,	to her shoulders the changing pressure is not too much
válogatatlan vállal másokat	she takes on others without any selection
Tágas vágyadba venni vágyamat	It would be fit to take my lust into your
illő volna – miért nem vállalod?	spacious lust – why do not you take it on?
Más Willek vágya áldja ágyadat,	Other Wills' lust blesses your bed,
de vágyam, valló Willed vágya, sok?	but my lust, the lust of your confessing Will, is much?
Ládd, beveszi a tenger az esőt,	See, the sea takes in the rain,
bővében van, mégis befogadó –	there is plenty, still it is keen to accept –
ha mást elvállalsz, vállald hát el Őt:	if you take on others, do take Him on as well:

(continued)

(continued)

illik hozzád, mert Will beléd való	he befits you, Will perfectly fits your lust (body)
E vallomásra nem mondhatsz nemet:	You cannot say "no" to this confession:
sok Will helyett válassz egy Williamet	instead of many Wills, choose one William

This kind of playfulness is liberating for the poem, especially if the translator sticks to the strict sonnet form.

From the examples above, it is clear that some sonnets allow a good Hungarian translation within their formal limits and some do not. In this latter case, when the limitations of the sonnet kill the Hungarian poem, it might be worth shifting the paradigm altogether, and translating the sonnets into simple prose. This idea has been adopted by poet and essayist Zsolt Farkas. As he says, "I share the opinion, as many others also do, that prose translations are much better reflections of the original poems than verse translations, which rewrite and restructure the original text in the name of an ideal that is impossible to follow" (Farkas 2021). It is indeed a liberating feeling to have a lot of syllables at hand and not have to make sacrifices to the god of rhymes. Here is Sonnet 12, faithfully rendered in Hungarian prose:

> Mikor az órát figyelem, amint az időt ketyegi,
> és nézek, hogy a bátor nap rémisztő éjbe merült;
> mikor észreveszem, a bíbor hogy elszürkült, és
> a fekete tincsek még ezüstösebbek lettek; mikor
> a magas fákon nézem, hogy nincs lomb, ami
> egykor a forróságtól óvta a csordát, és a nyár
> zöldjét kévékbe kötve viszik, halotti szekéren,
> boglyas, őszes szakállal; akkor a szépséged
> kérdése is felmerül, hogy Te is mész, a tékozló
> idő hulladéka közt, hisz a kedves és a szép is
> elhagyatnak és meghalnak oly gyorsan, ahogy
> az ifjak nőnek, és semmi sem véd az Idő
> kaszájától, csak sarjadó magjaid: legyőzted,
> vihet.

Conclusion

Examples in this chapter have shown that formal equivalence is of extreme importance in Hungarian literary translation. It seems to overwrite other aspects of Shakespeare's *Sonnets*, and puts translators under extreme pressure when working. As has been shown, the greatness of the original poems lies in poetic perfection, the enigmatic social game Shakespeare played through the cycle, the eternal truths and catchphrases that have become popular with readers, and the meticulous composition of the whole cycle. These together make the *Sonnets* great; foregrounding or neglecting any will result in a significant loss.

All literary translations are but approximations of the original pieces. Hungarian translators have to find a new starting point and realise that perfection of form is not a merit in itself, the sonnet form is just the external shell; and as the social game is now almost incomprehensible for us, it is the feelings and thoughts in the *Sonnets* that are more interesting and comprehensible even after centuries, together with the complicated linguistic and semantic forms they take: idiosyncrasies, imagery, and ambiguities to be interpreted and understood. Lőrinc Szabó put aside formal perfection for the sake of saving as much meaning as possible. Sándor Fazekas fixes his eyes on the perfection of form, but his translation is still to be published and evaluated. Anna Szabó T. focuses on language play and ambiguities and, as a practising poet, has a natural talent for balancing form and content. Zsolt Farkas votes for prose translation. Hungarian literary translators continue to look for ways of contributing to the long tradition of translation in Hungary, keeping it an organic, living tradition within European literature.

REFERENCES

Arany, János. 1984a. "A Magyar Shakespeare megindítása". In *Magyar Shakespeare-tükör*, ed. Maller Sándor, Ruttkay Kálmán, 212–216. Budapest: Gondolat.

———. 1984b. "Levél Tomori Anasztáznak". In *Magyar Shakespeare-tükör*, ed. Maller Sándor, Ruttkay Kálmán, 209–210. Budapest: Gondolat.

Babits, Mihály. 1978. *Esszék, tanulmányok*. Budapest: Szépirodalmi Könyvkiadó.

Booth, Stephen. 1969. *An Essay on Shakespeare's Sonnets*. New Haven and London: Yale University Press.

———. 2000. *Shakespeare's Sonnets*. New Haven and London: Yale University Press.

Bradley, A.C. 1965. "Shakespeare the Man". In *Oxford Lectures on Poetry*, A.C. Bradley, 311–357. New York: St Martin's Press.

Csillag, Tibor. 2015. *William Shakespeare: Szonettek*. Budapest: Petit Real Kiadó.

Duncan-Jones, Katherine. 1997. *Shakespeare's Sonnets*. London: Thomson Learning.

Fabiny, Tibor. 1997. "Előszó". In *Shakespeare: Szonettek*, 5–10. Budapest: Akkord.

Farkas, Zsolt. 2021. "Shakespeare Vilmos: Prozettek". *Jelenkor*, 21/04: 356–358.

Fazekas, Sándor. 2019. "Triptichon. Részlet Shakespeare szonettjeinek új, teljes fordításából". *Anyanyelvi Kultúraközvetítés*, 2(1): 24–31.

Fazekas, Sándor. 2020. "The Sonnets in Hungarian". Shakespeare.org.uk. https://www.shakespeare.org.uk/explore-shakespeare/blogs/sonnets-hungarian. Accessed 20 September 2021.

Kardos, László. 1965. "A 73. szonett magyar útja". In *Shakespeare-tanulmányok*, ed. Kéry László et al., 56–79. Budapest: Akadémiai Kiadó.

Kerrigan, John. 1986. *William Shakespeare: The Sonnets and a Lover's Complaint*. Harmondsworth: Penguin Books.

Kéry, László. 1961. "Shakespeare költeményei". In *Shakespeare összes művei. VII. kötet. Versek*, 299–312. Budapest: Európa Könyvkiadó.

Kiss, É. Katalin. 1975. *Shakespeare szonettjei Magyarországon*. Budapest: Akadémiai Kiadó.

Lutter, Tibor. 1956. "Bevezető". In *Shakespeare szonettjei*, 5–16. Budapest: Corvina.

Mahood, Molly. 1968. *Shakespeare's Wordplay*. London: Routledge.

Maller, Sándor. 1984. "Shakespeare-örökségünk". In *Magyar Shakespeare-tükör*, ed. Maller Sándor, Ruttkay Kálmán, 11–54. Budapest: Gondolat.

Muir, Kenneth. 1979. *Shakespeare's Sonnets*. London: George Allen & Unwin.

Péczeli, József. 1981. "A fordításokról". In *A magyar kritika évszázadai. Rendszerek. A kezdetektől a romantikáig*, ed. Tarnai Andor, Csetri Lajos, 307–308. Budapest: Szépirodalmi Könyvkiadó.

———. 1996. *Henriás* (1792). Budapest: Balassi Kiadó.

Petőfi, Sándor. 1984. "III. Richárd király". In *Magyar Shakespeare-tükör*, ed. Maller Sándor, Ruttkay Kálmán, 159–163. Budapest: Gondolat.

Steiner, George. 1975. *After Babel*. Oxford: Oxford University Press.

Szabó, Lőrinc. 1921. *Shakespeare szonettjei. Fordította Szabó Lőrinc*. Budapest: Genius.

———. 1948. *William Shakespeare szonettjei. Fordította és bevezette Szabó Lőrinc*. Budapest: Franklin-társulat.

Szász, Károly. 1869. "Shakspere kisebb költeményei". *Székfoglaló. A Kisfaludy Társaság Évlapjai*, 1869: 73–107.

Szele, Bálint. 2006. "A magyar Shakespeare-fordítás története. Műfordításelméleti áttekintés 1785-től 2005-ig". *Fordítástudomány*, 2006/2: 78–94.

————. 2013. "Translating Shakespeare for the Hungarian Stage: Contemporary Perspectives". *AHEA: E-journal of the American Hungarian Educators Association*, Volume 6. http://ahea.net/e-journal/volume-6-2013/19. Accessed 20 September 2021.

————. 2016. "Fordítási nehézségek Shakespeare szonettjeiben". In *Ikon, nyelvi jel, szimbólum: nem természetes jelek a kommunikációban*, ed. Gecső Tamás, 182–188. Budapest: Kodolányi János Főiskola, Tinta Könyvkiadó.

————. 2017. "Translators and the Literary Politics of Socialism in Hungary". *Freeside Europe Online*. Issue 7. http://www.kodolanyi.hu/freeside/issues/issue70. Accessed 10 September 2021.

————. 2018. "Ambiguity and Language Play in Shakespeare's Sonnets – Approximations in Hungarian Translations". In *Egy- és többértelműség a nyelvben*, ed. Gecső Tamás et al., 226–231. Budapest: Kodolányi János Egyetem, Tinta Könyvkiadó.

Szentkuthy, Miklós. 1985. "Shakespeare szonettjei". In *Múzsák testamentuma*, Szentkuthy Miklós, 183–192. Budapest: Magvető Kiadó.

Vendler, Helen. 1997. *The Art of Shakespeare's Sonnets*. Cambridge: Harvard University Press.

CHAPTER 7

Sonnets in Turkish: Shakespeare's Syllables, Halman's Syllabics

Melih Levi

Shakespeare's *Sonnets* have been translated into Turkish multiple times. The first translations, in the late nineteenth century, were made into Ottoman by Mehmet Nadir (forty-two sonnets) and Muallim Naci (eight sonnets). Both used François Victor-Hugo's French translations of Shakespeare and aimed for different poetic effects. For example, while Naci's translation mostly renders Shakespeare's images into those familiar from the Ottoman poetic tradition, Nadir's translations are more "faithful" in their rendering of Shakespearean imagery (Enginün 227). Ultimately, as İnci Enginün's comprehensive study demonstrates, these late Ottoman translations were very much a part of the "prose poetry fashion" [mensur şiir cereyanı] of the late nineteenth century, which Ottoman writers had cultivated through influences from French Symbolist and Parnassian poetry.

M. Levi (✉)
Boğaziçi University, Istanbul, Turkey
e-mail: melih.levi@boun.edu.tr

© The Author(s), under exclusive license to Springer Nature   107
Switzerland AG 2023
J. Kingsley-Smith and W. R. Rampone Jr. (eds.), *Shakespeare's Global Sonnets*,
Global Shakespeares, https://doi.org/10.1007/978-3-031-09472-9_7

Apart from a few stand-alone translations (e.g., Can Yücel's translation of Sonnet 66), the *Sonnets* were not systematically translated into modern Turkish until 1961, when Talât Sait Halman began a project that would take him almost thirty years to complete. In 1979, the scholar translators Saadet and Bülent Bozkurt produced a prose translation of the *Sonnets* and revised this translation fifteen years later within a more formal and poetic structure. In recent years, additional translators have stepped up to the task. However, Talât Sait Halman's translations have remained the most formally rigorous and accomplished versions. Aesthetic claims aside, it certainly was the earliest most systematic attempt to make the whole sequence available to a Turkish readership.

This chapter studies Talât Sait Halman's translations of Shakespeare's *Sonnets* into Turkish through a comparative prosody angle. Halman (1931–2014) was a prolific poet, scholar, translator, and bureaucrat, who served as Turkey's first Minister of Culture and dedicated his life to making Turkish literature available to wider audiences across the world. He is recognized for the formal and epigrammatic ingenuity of his original poetry, prolific practice as translator into and from Turkish, international academic career, comparative grasp of poetic traditions on a wide historical and cultural spectrum, and meditative stance as a cultural theorist. He worked on his Shakespeare translations between 1961 and 1989, opting for syllabic verse, one of the two dominant metrical structures in Turkish poetry, the other being *aruz,* a quantitative scheme based on syllable length.

When we study the journey of these two metrical forms through the twentieth century, syllabic verse emerges as a curious choice from both a historical and a biographical standpoint. By the 1960s, both metrical forms had gone out of fashion. While *aruz* almost entirely disappeared, syllabics entered a period of dormancy. Halman himself, like many in the Turkish poetic tradition, initially regarded syllabics as the aesthetically inferior prosodic pattern, incapable of reproducing Shakespeare's rhythmic and musical effects. On top of this, syllabics was historically associated with the plainer folk poetry, therefore not immediately attractive for the translation of a highly stylized Renaissance poet.

Shakespeare, too, was writing in the final stretch of a complex prosodic landscape. Prosodists of the sixteenth century typically struggled to distinguish between the structures of celebrated historical models (Latin and Greek) and the emergent rhythmic characteristics of the English language. Many poets were suspicious of a prosodic pattern based solely on the number of syllables (Attridge 1974). Having learned and imitated Latin and Greek in schools and universities, many poets felt that a quantitative prosodic structure (based on syllable length) was more complex and therefore superior, and tried to establish it in the English language. Poets writing in native meters after the mid-Tudor period certainly followed a consistent syllable count. However, regarding accentual arrangements, most demonstrate an intuitive grasp. While it is true that mid-Tudor plain style poets such as George Gascoigne regularized the pentameter line with discernible regularity in accentual alternation (Dolven 2010), no poet or prosodist of the period seems to have been able to outline a coherent poetic system based uniquely on accentual distinctions until Samuel Daniel in 1603 with *Defense of Rhyme* (Dolven 2010).

A comparative glance at the two prosodic histories is especially interesting since both Shakespeare and Halman opted for meters which were associated with native origins, nationalism, and plainness. Syllabics in Turkish had already been heralded, somewhat ideologically, as a more national style, unencumbered with Persian and Arabic vocabulary, and praised for its ability to sustain the rhythms of the more native and folk poetic traditions. Likewise, in the English context, iambic pentameter was often distinguished as native, unencumbered with the semantic memory of Latin and Greek. In addition, as already indicated, it was the mid-Tudor poets, typically associated with the plain style, who had given the pentameter its most systematic articulation. In particular, they had proven this verse suitable for an epigrammatic style, which would become strategically central to the final couplets in Shakespeare's sonnets. The association of these meters with plainness in either national context will prove integral to my analysis.

In the first part of this chapter, I situate Halman's translation as part of the prosodic debates in modern Turkish poetry. I show that Halman chose syllabics for the translation of one of the most accomplished poets in history at a time when it had largely gone out of fashion and in the face of his own initial skepticism about its aesthetic capabilities. Nonetheless, he managed to breathe life into a prosodic structure which had been eclipsed by the rise of free-verse poetry soon after reaching aesthetic maturity between the 1920s and 1950s. Halman thus redefined the possibilities that syllabic verse continues to represent for Turkish poetry. This argument becomes more pressing when we notice the relatively recent reemergence of a syllabic movement in Turkish, in the early 1990s, with Süleyman Çobanoğlu's volume *Şiirler Çağla*.

In the final part, I step away briefly from the Turkish context to rethink Shakespeare's verse within the metrical debates of the sixteenth century. Reading a syllabic rendition of Shakespeare without the accentual paradigm allows us to raise an experimental question: What if Shakespeare had, in fact, written in syllabics? History gives this provocative question some unexpected justification. As much prosody scholarship shows, it was more likely for poets and readers of the period to arrange their lines by numbers rather than by accents. Surely, poets must have had a sharp and intuitive ear for accentual patterning. After all, the accentual pattern, in the making ever since Chaucer's time, had acquired a systematic articulation through the plain style poets of the mid-Tudor period.

Nevertheless, as Shakespeare's own scheming and monosyllable-heavy language demonstrates, he is also likely to have undermined this newly emergent prosodic norm on purpose. The *Sonnets*, with their mono-syllabic opulence, unsettle the metrical scheme both to accentuate the inevitably subjective nature of poetic meter and, more importantly, to arrest those rhythms which tend to sustain the fallacies and truisms by which humans and poems tend to live. In other words, returning to Shakespeare's historical context with Halman's translations in mind gives us an opportunity to revisit the prosody debates of the sixteenth century and to reevaluate the ingenuity of Shakespeare's poetic form.

Debates Concerning Syllabics and *Aruz* in Turkish Poetry

To demonstrate the complexity behind Halman's prosody, I first need to summarize the journey of these two metrical forms in the late Ottoman and early Republican eras. The history begins in the second half of the nineteenth century, during the reformation period called the Tanzimat Era, when contact with Western literary traditions gains momentum. Modern Turkish poets such as Ziya Paşa, Nâmık Kemal, and Abdülhak Hâmid Tarhan begin modest experiments with syllabics, at times trying it out in their plays and translations and, occasionally, in individual poems (Kolcu 37). Though the poets of this generation (1860–1895) only show tentative interest in syllabics and mostly end up declaring *aruz* as their ultimate preference, their probings, nevertheless, plant the seeds of the prosody debates to come.

It is with the Servet-i Fünun Era writers (1896–1901/1912), heavily influenced by aestheticist principles and French literary movements like Symbolism and Parnassianism, that large-scale transformations in prosody begin to take place. Tevfik Fikret, for example, famously advocates for varying *aruz* units within the space of a single poem and for using the verse in a mimetic manner, whereby the movement of the verse more directly imitates the psychological states described in the poem (Erbay 2003). These attempts to psychologize verse structures give poets license to modify established metrical templates and to question where verse ought to originate: from tradition or from the psychological rhythms and emotional cadences of the poet?

In the literary journals of the Servet-i Fünun era, debates begin over which of the two metrical schemes—syllabics and *aruz*—Turkish poets ought to choose. Among those defending syllabics is H. Nâzım [Ahmet Reşit], who argues in 1896 that *aruz* is "foreign," forcing Turkish poets to adjust words beyond their ordinary inflections. H. Nâzım also argues that promoting a uniform metrical pattern in a poem limits rhythmic variations necessitated by the content, often causing the formal structure to overwhelm the meaning (Kolcu 2007). Similarly, Menemenlizâde Mehmed Tâhir offers the use of syllabics in French poetry as an example to show that syllabics can indeed generate a strong poetic tradition and makes the case for eliminating strict caesural divisions to cultivate more variety within a single poem.

Debates reach a peak during the final decades of the Ottoman Empire and the period leading up to the establishment of the modern Turkish Republic. This is also when syllabics becomes entangled in the ideological rhetoric of movements such as Pan-Turkism, which advocates for the promotion of a Turkish ethnic identity. In 1899, Mehmet Emin Yurdakul publishes *Türkçe Şiirler* (*Poems in Turkish*) which, as the title indicates, features poems in plain Turkish and syllabics. Pan-Turkism has an overwhelming influence on many poets in this period, especially as the War of Independence begins and nationalist sentiments gain strength. Writers associated with the Genç Kalemler (Young Pens) group, such as Ömer Seyfettin and Ziya Gökalp, systematize the correlation between syllabics and national belonging. Many writers (e.g., Halit Fahri Ozansoy, Şükûfe Nihal Başar, and İbrahim Alaettin Gövsa) waver between the two meters before finally settling on syllabics (Aker 2018).

Despite the growing popularity of syllabics, some continue writing in *aruz*. For example, Cenap Şehabettin remains an adamant advocate for *aruz*, both in his own practice and in his impassioned contributions to literary journals. More importantly, three prominent poets—Mehmet Akif Ersoy, Ahmet Haşim, and Yahya Kemal Beyatlı—also continue writing in *aruz*, often successfully renovating the meter and adapting it to modern Turkish. Despite his commitment to *aruz*, Beyatlı has a more metaphysical understanding of verse. He cautions poets and critics not to make essentializing arguments about any prosodic form, calling them mere tools. Instead, Beyatlı foregrounds the concept of "deruni ahenk" [interior rhythm], emphasizing the music which stems from subjective experience and coalesces into a harmonious unity. Beyatlı (2005) therefore holds that syllabics has just as much claim to aesthetic autonomy and success as *aruz*, even writing one of his poems ("Ok") in syllabics.

Meter in Modern Turkey

Soon after the establishment of the modern Turkish Republic, a series of language reforms consolidates the campaign for syllabic verse. A 1929 law officially replaces the Ottoman script with the Latin alphabet along with attempts to simplify the language by dropping Arabic and Persian vocabulary. The plain-sounding syllabic meter, which had already come to be associated with nationalist sentiments, thrives even more in this political context. Some critical accounts, such as Erhan Altan's *Ölçü Kaçarken* (2011), tend to subordinate the journey of syllabics to these ideological paradigms. Though partly true, such linear accounts of prosodic history risk losing sight of poets who forged compelling bridges with the long history of syllabics in folk poetry, as well as of the aesthetic potential of syllabics which later generations of poets were able to unleash.

In fact, a systematic account of how syllabic verse came to be aestheticized by the poets of the modern Turkish Republic remains to be written. There are prosody manuals which explain the technical arrangement and varieties of syllabic verse, as well as independent studies of poets who wrote in syllabics. However, there is no scholarly work offering a systematic articulation of its newly discovered aesthetic possibilities in the modern period, e.g., what themes came to be associated with which syllabic forms; how artistic or literary trends (symbolism, modernism, imagism) disrupted or transformed the meter; the kinds of rhetorical modes and attitudes supported or dramatized by syllabic verse. Most recently, Abdülhâlik Aker, who happens to be one of the skilled poets writing in syllabics today, wrote a Master's Thesis (2018) which begins with a historical overview of syllabics in Turkish literature starting from the late nineteenth century. The recent revival of syllabics in Turkish poetry suggests more studies of this kind in the future.

Members of two prominent poetic movements (Beş Hececiler and Yedi Meşaleciler), along with independent poets, mostly born at the turn of the century (e.g., Ahmet Hamdi Tanpınar, Ali Mümtaz Arolat, Halide Nusret Zorlutuna, Kemalettin Kamu, Necip Fazıl Kısakürek, Cahit Sıtkı Tarancı, Ahmet Kutsi Tecer, and Ahmet Muhip Dıranas) begin the work of exploring the aesthetic possibilities that syllabics might offer for a modern poetic voice. While some use the relative freedom of this form as a stepping-stone for later explorations with free verse, most make meaningful uses of the possibilities ingrained into it by hundreds of years of native and folk poetic traditions. Even when these poets adjust the form to animate complex, philosophical ideas (e.g., Tanpınar's interest in Bergsonian duration) or various aestheticist or avant-garde impulses (e.g., Tarancı's psychologizing Symbolism), they all continue to observe the plainspoken attitude which had become entrenched in the language of syllabic verse.

Nonetheless, it is also right at this time, in the 1920s, that Nureddin Ferrûh's premature invitation to "liberate poetry from verse" in 1896 comes to life (Kolcu 2007). Nâzım Hikmet, who had already ventured into poetry with syllabics, travels to the Soviet Union and comes into contact with the more experimental forms of Futurist poets. He departs from syllabics in search of more experimental formal structures. Thus, the winds of free verse begin to blow. Later in 1941, a new poetic initiative, *Birinci Yeni* or *Garip* (The First New or Strange) emerges, with a manifesto explaining why "the belief that poetic harmony is dependent on meter and rhyme is needless and harmful" (Wade and Murad 2015). Garip becomes a breakthrough, bringing about wholesale transformations in poetic taste. However, theirs is a style based on attitude and voice. Their rejection of traditional structures does not impede the ongoing advances in syllabics, since both remain committed to the possibilities of plain poetic registers.

The subsequent venture emerging in the 1950s, the *İkinci Yeni* (The Second New), is a different story altogether. This movement, often misleadingly branded as the "modernist" moment in Turkish poetry, emphasizes linguistic self-consciousness and imagistic attitudes to such an extent that it is often accused of hermeticism. This style is diametrically opposed to the plainspoken registers of syllabic poetry. As the popularity of *İkinci Yini* grows, syllabic verse quickly turns old-fashioned. Yalçın Armağan (2021) demonstrates how the acceptance of this movement's poetic style pushes many now-old-fashioned poets into changing their techniques or, in some cases, even abandoning poetry. Hence, it would not be wrong to claim that syllabics runs out of steam toward the end of the 1950s. Put another way, the journey of syllabics gets cut short right when it is in the process of proving itself compatible with the concerns of modern poetry.

TALÂT SAIT HALMAN'S PROSODY

This is where Halman comes in. He begins to take an interest in prosody at the beginning of the 1940s. While only nine years old, he teaches himself *aruz* by reading Divan poetry, and one of the most important modern renovators of *aruz*, Mehmet Akif Ersoy (Halman 2003). Halman first encounters Shakespeare as a student at Robert College, the prestigious American high school in Istanbul, and soon after his graduation, before traveling to Columbia University, he translates *Macbeth* into Turkish with *aruz* in 1951 (Warner 2017). Two years later, in *Tercüme* (1953), a journal focusing on literary translation, he explains his rationale for preferring *aruz*. He begins by raising questions about the existing syllabic translations of Shakespeare's dramatic works:

> Forget that our syllabic verse, in all its simplicity, cannot accommodate qualitative differences. It does not even have a quantitative basis. It is simply the repetition of a set number of syllables per line. That's why syllabic verse cannot work for translating Shakespeare.... [Syllabics], especially when used without rhymes, would yield such a weak and rudimentary rhythm that one could hardly call this finger-count a type of verse (64). [Finger-count, or parmak hesabı, is a synonym for syllabic verse in Turkish.]

At the end of the article, Halman reiterates his defense of *aruz*: "Syllabic verse is too weak to be able to compete with Shakespeare's rhythm. *Aruz*, on the other hand, even without rhyme… is the one and only way to translate Shakespeare into Turkish; I believe that is the truth" (65). Accordingly, in his translation of *Macbeth*, Halman uses *aruz* in a flexible manner. Rather than following a set scheme throughout the translation, he varies the metrical pattern from line to line in an effort to replicate Shakespeare's dynamic dramatic meter.

Halman's devotion to *aruz* would continue for the rest of his life. He would often lament the fact that *aruz* had virtually disappeared from poetic culture and that its teaching in schools had become too mechanistic (2003). In his original poetry, too, Halman almost always used *aruz*, even developing new metrical patterns which could prove more compatible with the rhythms of modern Turkish. For example, in a 2003 interview, he explains possible ways of "reforming" *aruz*, such as by populating the verse units with more short syllables. His strong defense of *aruz* and skepticism about the rhythmic capabilities of syllabics are especially striking if we remember that he would end up choosing syllabics for his translations of the *Sonnets*.

Halman's original poetic output is also quite remarkable, often exclusively devoted to short epigrammatic one-liners and couplets. He was inspired to work with these short forms from the long history of aphoristic and epigrammatic statement in Turkish literature. In these poems, Halman masters the art of condensation, squeezing an intellectually complex sentiment, a deep emotion, or state of mind into the space of a short one-liner or couplet. In the introduction to "Bin Bir," for example, Halman describes these poems through their "internal unity" (1974). Here too, Halman remains rather skeptical about syllabics: "My intention... was to apply *aruz* to our alive and dynamic modern Turkish as well as to realize a harmonious and rich reverberation that could not have been possible with free verse or finger-count [syllabics]" (10). Apart from his curious dismissal of syllabic verse, Halman's practice with these short epigrammatic forms proves generative for his translations of Shakespeare. After all, the epigrammatic impulse is at the core of Shakespeare's style and his management of the final couplets in the *Sonnets*.

Halman begins translating the *Sonnets* for literary magazines such as *Varlık*, *Yeditepe*, *Türk Dili* and *Dost* in 1961. By 1964, he finishes 40 sonnets and puts them together in a slim publication to commemorate Shakespeare's four-hundredth birthday (Halman 2009). This slim volume marks the beginning of a much longer journey that would take him twenty-five more years to complete. The work would be interrupted by many significant events: an academic career in the US, busy diplomatic work for Turkey, a crucial post as Turkey's first Minister of Culture, and the tragic loss of Sait, his son (Warner 2017). In 1989, Halman finishes his translation of the sequence, making it available to Turkish readers for the first time.

Halman's Shakespeare Translations

Despite his earlier reservations about syllabics, Halman, nevertheless, ends up settling on a particular arrangement of syllabic verse for the *Sonnets*: fourteen-syllable lines divided with a caesura in the middle (7+7). In his introduction (2009), Halman explains his preference for this 7+7 variety by emphasizing its maneuvering capacity and "kıvraklık" [agility, quickness]. The word "kıvraklık" also appears in significant ways throughout the translation itself. For example, he renders the self-conscious first lines of Sonnet 76 as follows:

> Why is my verse so barren of new pride?
> So far from variation or quick change? (Shakespeare 2000)

> Şiirim niçin yeni ses ve süslerden yoksun,
> Ne çeşnisi yeterli, ne de kıvraklığı var? (Halman 2009)

> [Why is my poetry lacking in new sounds and ornaments,
> Having neither the necessary seasoning nor dynamism/agility?]

There is a delightful contradiction between what the speaker of the poem claims about his style and rhetoric—it lacks "quick change" or kıvraklık—and what Halman emphasizes about Shakespeare's handling of the poetic form: "ritmik ve kıvrak vezni" [its rhythmic and quick/dynamic meter]. This semantic coincidence illuminates one of the *Sonnets'* central conceits: the speaker's tendency to brag and moralize about his constancy, even as the language jolts between different moods, images, and metaphors.

Halman does not only convey this tension between constancy and mutability in the *Sonnets* through his diligent rendering of Shakespeare's sensuous imagery, he also uses the syllabic meter to great effect. For example, in the opening lines of Sonnet 76 above, Halman omits the medial caesura in the first line, making readers get through the line in one breath and returning to the 7+7 arrangement that readers would have long become accustomed to over the course of the sequence. Shakespeare is similarly inventive and self-conscious with language. The two lines have a completely different texture. While the first line employs "barren" sounds and a mostly monosyllabic diction—a mainstay of Shakespeare's verse—the second line hits the reader with the word "variation" right where the diction itself experiences discernible variation. At the end of the line, the speaker offers a near-synonym of variation but this time the monosyllabic pace picks up again, describing a kind of "change" that is perhaps sharper and swifter.

George T. Wright (2000) relates this effect to the ongoing and delightful "play *between* the metrical line and the rhythmical phrase": "The phrasing is extremely various; that is, we hardly ever find the same phrasing-patterns in successive lines (except for deliberate echoes), and the movement from line to line and quatrain to quatrain permits us to savor a great many line-forms" (78). The pentameter allows the arrangement of these phrasal possibilities in the space of a single line and, in so doing, once again raises the possibility that numbers and syllabic distinctions mattered more to Shakespeare than any desire to sustain accentual currents through the line.

In using syllabics with such delightful caesural variations, Halman follows in the footsteps of syllabic poets like Ahmet Muhip Dıranas, Cahit Sıtkı Tarancı, and Faruk Nafiz Çamlıbel who had begun the work of giving the form a more elastic texture. It is no surprise that the 7+7 line had been one of the most popular verse structures with these earlier poets as well (Onay 1996). Just as the pentameter line engenders a kind of intuitive standard (the perfect length for a full sentence) and then stages departures from this normative syntactic intuition, 7+7 proves perfect for juggling two clauses or even sentences in the space of a single line and keeps the reader wondering what the exact nature of the relationship between them will be. Will it be one of dependence or independence, or will the poet dodge the caesura altogether?

Thus, the even division of the line under the 7+7 structure promises a recurring pause where the grammatical screws of the line can tighten. Variations from this norm confuse the reader's sense of syntax and grammar, at times threatening the autonomy of the poetic voice. The occasional eruption of this vulnerability, the momentary staging of a loss of control, was exactly the psychological effect that poets like Tarancı had pursued when employing caesural variations within syllabics. Syllabics proves perfect for capturing this tension between experiential stability and variability, between sustained conviction and self-deception. By adapting syllabics to a work which really dramatizes this dynamic, Halman discloses the metaphysical and experiential potential of this verse form.

THE *SONNETS* AND SHAKESPEARE'S SYLLABLES

The formal arrangement of the *Sonnets* offers a similar portrait of a mind struggling to extract from experience truths by which it can live and truisms to which it can return. The final rhyming couplets of the poems often convey a sense of finality, control, and authority. Aurally and syntactically, these epigrammatic couplets create the impression of a maxim extracted from experience with great conviction. However, these couplets often contain puns, syntactic ambiguities, contradictory sentiments, and, most importantly, remarkable rhythmic versatility which disturb this sense of an unshakeable conclusion. As Heather Dubrow (1981) explains, "Shakespeare's couplets explore and often exemplify an issue with which the whole sequence is very concerned: our predilection for deceiving ourselves and others... In sonnets like these, the couplet form itself becomes a symbol of our cursed rage for order, our tendency to simplify and sanitize our experience, even at the expense of truth" (65).

Shakespeare achieves this versatility by intensifying a linguistic tendency that is omnipresent throughout the sequence: the use of monosyllables. The monosyllabic richness of these final couplets opens the whole question of an "iambic" pattern up to debate. At times, monosyllables confuse our sense of meter to such an extent that any perceived iambic pattern falls apart. The experiential rhythms and patterns suddenly fail or disappear in these seemingly conclusive couplets. A good example of this is the final couplet of Sonnet 130 (Shakespeare 2000):

> And yet by heav'n I think my love as rare
> As any she belied with false compare.

As Joel Fineman (1984) explains, the "she" in this couplet "is logically, as well as grammatically, both subject and object of 'belied with false compare,' comparable, therefore, only to the way comparison has failed" (68). The speaker clearly demonstrates control and authority through the sharp turn ("and yet"), the metrical precision of the first line, the alluring management of a complex, comparative logic, and the sense of closure engendered by the rhyme. Nevertheless, as is often the case in the final couplets, the metrical regularity gets undermined by monosyllables which proliferate the tonal and syntactic possibilities of the line: the difference between "*any* she" and "any *she*" is significant. Is the speaker comparing the Dark Lady here to other figures who have received formulaic praises in the busy history of epideixis? Or is the Dark Lady dismantling the entire comparative operation and undermining the performed authority of the speaker?

Halman was acutely aware of the monosyllabic core of Shakespeare's poetry. For instance, in a 2008 interview, he offers the following assessment while contrasting English to the agglutinative structure of Turkish: "The diction of the sonnets—with a rough estimate—is eighty percent monosyllabic. Look at the last line of the 73rd sonnet: 'To love that well which thou must leave ere long.' Ten individual words in a ten-syllable line. In Turkish you would get six words in a fourteen-syllable line. It is so difficult to strike a similar rhythm" (236). Here is Halman's translation of the above couplet from Sonnet 130 (Halman 2009):

> Şu var ki ozanların boş lafına karnı tok,
> [literally: However, had enough of the poet's empty talk [as in satiated and cannot take any more]
> Mecazı fos çıkararan, sevgilinin eşi yok.
> [literally: There is no match for the beloved, the one who made all metaphor a sham.]

Unlike in the previous example, Halman here observes the medial caesura in both lines, but he still maintains the ambiguity over the "she." He achieves this by planting caesural uncertainties in both lines which can only be realized when the poem is read out loud. In the first line, there is no dominant caesura, but depending on where we entertain brief pauses, the line could mean either of the following: the poets had enough of her empty talk; or, she has no room left for poets' empty talk. The former is surely more likely; however, this slight ambiguity already begins the work of loosening the syntax of what seems to be building toward a sturdy epigrammatic statement.

The second line consolidates the ambiguity by containing the following two possibilities: there is no match to the beloved who has revealed the falsity of all metaphors (where she is the subject doing the falsifying). Or read with the feeling of an apostrophic self-address (as in, o poet!): here is no match for this beloved who reveals this whole business of metaphors to be a sham (where she is the object, and the rhetorical mastery now belongs to the poet). Halman achieves this beautiful ambiguity by reclaiming the standard caesural pattern in the final line. It is evenly and perfectly divided, with a medial caesura after the seventh syllable.

In accomplishing this effect, Halman imitates Shakespeare's manipulative ingenuity over poetic form and style. Both Shakespeare and Halman show that genuine originality emerges from within the tradition, when individual management of form suddenly supersedes the internalized rhythms and wisdoms of received forms.

Furthermore, Shakespeare's use of monosyllables to engender these rhythmic uncertainties and contradictory possibilities is significant. He seems at once to be continuing a tendency that was observed by mid-Tudor poets with certain nationalistic undertones. As most monosyllabic words are of Anglo-Saxon origin, their employment in verse was also deemed by many versifiers to signal national identity and belonging. Most famously, for example, George Gascoigne (1575) had claimed: "The more monasyllables [sic] that you use the truer Englishman you shall seeme, and the lesse you shall smell of the Inkehorne" (468). Jeff Dolven (2010) explains how this monosyllabic tendency "conspires with a general preference for nativist English diction" (373). Shakespeare, however, differs from these mid-century poets because he often intentionally uses monosyllabic diction to destabilize a metrical pattern that was cultivated so meticulously by these poets.

Shakespeare could very well have intended to expose the fallacy of this newly emerging pattern. Practitioners of this emergent pentameter often celebrated it as the preferred native alternative to quantitative meters of foreign import. However, somewhat ironically, the oft-celebrated native protagonists of this verse—monosyllables—made it difficult to sustain such accentual regularity across a line. As Glenn Spiegel (1980) shows, polysyllables were "among the most important tools a poet has for controlling the sound of his line, since they are relatively unsusceptible to having a rhythm imposed on them" (209). Hence, just as Shakespeare exposes the deceptive fallacies of experiential truisms, he also exposes the deceptive ideological layers that his contemporaries associated with certain poetic and formal conventions. After all, the speaker of the *Sonnets* repeatedly emphasizes his poetry as a performative departure from tradition by explicitly targeting Petrarchan tropes.

Finally, monosyllables also expose the fallacy of a plain style, which too was cultivated by the poets of the mid-Tudor era. Anglo-Saxon monosyllables were typically celebrated for their directness and simplicity, as opposed to the fancier-sounding polysyllabic words derived from Latinate languages. Yet, by using monosyllables to ambiguate the seeming directness of the final couplets, Shakespeare discloses what makes a plain style so poetically and experientially enchanting. What gives an epigrammatic statement its force is not necessarily the truth of its claims but rather its ability to dramatize the manner of finding and articulating that truth—in other words, the *experience* of truth as it appears to a mind adorned with certain experiential grammars.

In short, Shakespeare's monosyllables psychologize the speaker's epigrammatic formulations and subvert the sense of plainness associated with this native prosodic form to turn both into dramatic opportunities for poetry. George T. Wright (1991) describes this achievement by calling attention to how in Shakespeare "a varied verse line and a heightened (or suddenly plain) poetic language can combine to present complex psychological states of mind and elevate the opposite sides of personal and public quarrels into profound philosophical issues" (288).

Monosyllables, as we have seen, also undermine the historical claims attached to an emergent prosodic form by brief obfuscations of accentual patterning.

Conclusion

Halman's syllabic rendering of the sonnet (which does not have an accentual basis in Turkish) apprehends an imaginary version of the original that Shakespeare might actually have wanted readers to experience. What if we read Shakespeare's *Sonnets* as undoing or challenging the work of mid-Tudor poets, distorting the emergent links between a native tradition, a plain style, and an accentual patterning? Ultimately, most of these links do not hold up under scrutiny. A plain, epigrammatic style often fails to engage readers unless its truisms are supported or complicated by dramatic complexity. As Yvor Winters (1967) once said, "The wisdom of poetry of this kind lies not in the acceptance of a truism, for anyone can accept a truism, at least formally, but in the realization of the truth of the truism: the realization resides in the feeling, the style. Only a master can deal successfully in a plain manner with obvious matter" (263).

Accentual regularity is also almost a utopian conception, for, at the end of the day, there remains something relative and subjective about accentual distinctions. When scholars analyze prosody debates in the sixteenth century with the hindsight of a formal literary history, they tend to call attention to widespread confusion regarding poetic terms, especially concerning distinctions between accent and syllable length. Yet, as Sharon Schuman (1977) reminds us, "they may not have been confused at all, only accommodated to one another in different ways at different points in an ad hoc kind of application" (344). Likewise, according to Eleanor Berry (1981), "most of the Elizabethan prosodists did not make a distinction between quantity and accent, and most regarded the line of the native mode as being based simply on the number of syllables" (117). These scholarly interventions demonstrate that our eagerness to observe accentual distinctions in most sixteenth-century, syllabic verse might actually prevent us from appreciating the flexibility of an emergent and plastic form. Shakespeare's heavy reliance on monosyllables also provocatively and intentionally destabilizes the metronomic regularity that any contemporary or future reader might hope to find in poetry.

The syllabic version of Shakespeare in Turkish thus provides exciting insights into the original text and its literary context. Conversely, by applying an eclipsed prosodic form to one of the most skilled poets in history, one can also disclose the overlooked opportunities syllabic meter still holds for Turkish poetry. It is my hope that this study will insert Halman's achievement into histories of meter and syllabics in literary scholarship, because, by featuring the capabilities of this form through the translation of an English poet, Halman's project conveniently relaxes the staunch, nationalist sentiments associated with the form. In addition, Halman worked on these translations exactly between those years when syllabic meter was eclipsed by the rise of free-verse forms (1950s) and when syllabics returned to the Turkish poetry scene in the early 1990s. Accordingly, the translations provide a somewhat coincidental but nevertheless noteworthy testament to the endurance of this verse form.

Most importantly, a comparative approach to debates concerning verse and poetic form in these divergent contexts reveals conceptual entanglements that are strikingly similar in nature: the association of syllabic verse with plainness, a native style, nationalism, and a desire for epigrammatic rhetoric. Even though these are the attributes often associated with these meters, the poets who manage to equip them with the most imaginative and exciting possibilities happen to be the ones who intelligently subvert these associations. Shakespeare employs plainness and an epigrammatic style as a kind of rhetorical strategy to reveal their capacity for self-illusion and manipulation. Similarly, in the history of Turkish syllabics, the meter often comes to life most vividly when poets bend its now-historical capacity for plainness and epigrammatic delivery to dramatize the rhetorical reflexes of an individual speaker or community. Halman's masterful rendering of Shakespeare with syllabics captures this possibility exceptionally well. Finally, the speaker of the *Sonnets* repeatedly performs departures from the linguistic or poetic conventions of the larger community. He keeps situating himself within and against the sonneteering and Petrarchan traditions of the period. At every opportunity, he tries distancing himself from other poets and the oft-used Petrarchan tropes. Still, by adamantly reiterating this rejection, he perversely proliferates them and ends up calling attention to his own rhetorical insecurity.

The poetic form itself performs a similar function. Shakespeare combines two linguistic and formal features both of which had come to be heralded for their national significance: syllabic verse and monosyllables. However, provocatively, in Shakespeare's hands, these two features brush against one another, allowing him to foreground that delightful tension, as Wright emphasizes (1991), between the metrical and the phrasal like no other poet before. This tension becomes mimetic of the tension between the individual and a larger (poetic) community.

It is by first affirming an emergent traditional form that Shakespeare trains our ears to overhear both the fallacies of the form and the promise it holds for future departures. Halman's landmark translation, produced at a time when syllabics had been losing steam in the Turkish context, suddenly reminds us that those aspects of poetic form which had been labeled as restrictive or ideological, in fact, provide productive grounds for poetic innovation. It would therefore be interesting, in a future project, to look at the syllabic revival in Turkish poetry from this perspective: how might Halman's translations of Shakespeare have, consciously or unconsciously, informed the Turkish poets of the new syllabic revival in the nineties?

References

Aker, Abdulhâlik. 2018. *Modern Hece ve Süleyman Çobanoğlu* [Thesis]. Selçuk University Social Sciences Institute. Department of Turkish Language and Literature.

Altan, Erhan. 2011. *Ölçü Kaçarken*. İstanbul: 160. Kilometre.

Armağan, Yalçın. 2021. "Melih Cevdet Anday'da Etkilenme Arzusu ve Kanon". *Birikim* 389: 6–13.

Attridge, Derek. 1974. *Well-Weighed Syllables: Elizabethan Verse in Classical Metres*. New York: Cambridge University Press.

Berry, Eleanor. 1981. "The Reading and Uses of Elizabethan Prosodies". *Language and Style* 14, 2: 116–152.

Beyatlı, Yahya Kemal. 2005. "Vezinler I [1922]". In *Edebiyata Dair*, 109–120. İstanbul: İstanbul Fetih Cemiyeti.

Dolven, Jeff. 2010. "Tudor Versification and the Rise of Iambic Pentameter". In *A Companion to Tudor Literature*, ed. Kent Cartwright, 364–380. Oxford: Blackwell.

Dubrow, Heather. 1981. "Shakespeare's Undramatic Monologues: Toward a Reading of the Sonnets". *Shakespeare Quarterly* 32, 1: 55–68.

Erbay, Erdoğan. 2003. *Yenileşme Dönemi Türk Edebiyatında Aruz Arayışları*. Erzurum: Aktif Yayınları.

Fineman, Joel. 1984. "Shakespeare's 'Perjur'd Eye'". *Representations* 7: 59–86.

Gascoigne, George. [1575] 1907. "Certayne Notes of Instruction Concerning the Making of Verse or Ryme in English". In *The Complete Works of George Gascoigne Volume 1*, ed. John W. Cunliffe, 465–473. New York: Cambridge University Press.

Halman, Talât Sait. 1953. "Shakespeare'in Manzum Tercümesi Meselesi ve Aruz". *Tercüme* 10, 55: 63–73.

Halman, Talât Sait. 1974. *Bin Bir (Özdeyiş Şiirleri)*. İstanbul: Milliyet Yayınları.

Halman, Talât Sait. 2003. "Interview with Cahide Birgül (Sesveren)". In *Aklın Yolu Bindir*. İstanbul: Türkiye İş Bankası Kültür Yayınları.

Halman, Talât Sait. 2008. "Çeviri Sanatı Üzerine Söyleşi [Interview with Gülenay Börekçi]". In *Çiçek Dürbünü: Edebiyat ve Kültür Yazıları*, 233–237.

Halman, Talât Sait. 2009. *William Shakespeare: Soneler*. İstanbul: Türkiye İş Bankası Kültür Yayınları.

Kolcu, Hasan. 2007. *Türk Edebiyatında Hece-Aruz Tartışmaları*. Ankara: Akçağ.

Onay, Ahmet Talat. 1996. *Türk Şiirlerinin Vezni* [1933], ed. Cemal Kurnaz. İstanbul: Akçağ.

Schuman, Sharon. 1977. "Sixteenth-Century English Quantitative Verse: Its Ends, Means, and Products". *Modern Philology* 74, 4: 335–349.

Shakespeare, William. 2000. *William Shakespeare's Sonnets*, ed. Stephen Booth. New Haven: Yale University Press.

Spiegel, Glenn S. 1980. "Perfecting English Meter: Sixteenth-Century Criticism and Practice". *The Journal of English and Germanic Philology* 79, 2: 192–209.

Veli, Orhan, Melih Cevdet, Oktay Rifat. 2015. "*Garip*: A Turkish Poetry Manifesto" (1941). Trans. Sidney Wade and Efe Murad. *The Critical Flame: Journal of Literature & Culture* 39.

Warner, Jayne L. 2017. *Turkish Nomad: The Intellectual Journey of Talat S. Haman*. New York: I.B. Tauris.

Winters, Yvor. 1967. "The 16th Century Lyric in England: A Critical and Historical Reinterpretation". In *Elizabethan Poetry: Modern Essays in Criticism*, ed. Paul J. Alpers, 93–125. New York: Oxford University Press.

Wright, George T. 1991. *Shakespeare's Metrical Art*. Berkeley: University of California Press.

Wright, George T. 2000. "The Silent Speech of Shakespeare's Sonnets". In *Shakespeare's Sonnets: Critical Essays,* ed. James Schiffer, 135–158. New York: Garland Publishing.

CHAPTER 8

New Words: Language and *Shakespeare's Sonnets* in the Global South

Anne Sophie Refskou and Tabish Khair

In a 1997 interview by Philip Nanton, Jamaican poet John Figueroa makes an evocative reference to his first encounter with Shakespeare's *Sonnets* as a schoolboy at a Jesuit High School in his native Kingston.[1] The interview opens with a conversation about Figueroa's early writing before he began the career that would lead to his important contribution to Anglophone Caribbean literature, both as a poet and as the editor of the seminal two-volume anthology *Caribbean Voices* in the 1960s. When asked by Nanton what he first wrote that he was proud of, Figueroa responds:

> When I was about 13, I visited *The Nelson* in Kingston Harbour and wrote about that. The piece was used in the High School Journal and was called

[1] The interview took place two years before Figueroa's death and was included in a special edition of *Caribbean Quarterly* dedicated to his memory.

A. S. Refskou (✉) · T. Khair
Aarhus University, Aarhus, Denmark
e-mail: litasr@cc.au.dk

© The Author(s), under exclusive license to Springer Nature Switzerland AG 2023
J. Kingsley-Smith and W. R. Rampone Jr. (eds.), *Shakespeare's Global Sonnets*,
Global Shakespeares, https://doi.org/10.1007/978-3-031-09472-9_8

127

"Some Confusion". When I went up to Holy Cross, the very first year that I was there as a freshman, quite unusually, I got a poem published in the College magazine which was respected in New England. That was a sonnet. I was proud of that, but unnecessarily proud because it was not as good as it should have been. The end was fixed up by the editor for me. The piece that I wrote that I realise was outstanding was a poem called "Winter Night". It's published in my collection, *The Chase*. I realised that it was good because it has been translated into German. Now the way that I came to write sonnets was that when I was a boy at George's College, a Jesuit High School in Jamaica, I was walking about and I saw a little smouldering fire. In the fire was some books that had been attacked by silver worms. I pulled one out and it was a book of Shakespeare's sonnets printed on lovely paper. I took it home and read it. The sonnets enchanted me and so I always wanted to write sonnets. That was in 1937 or 38. I don't think that I wrote anything really good till 1941. (Nanton and Figueroa 2003, 61)

It is hardly possible to read Figueroa's description of finding a copy of Shakespeare's *Sonnets* somewhere in the grounds of his Jamaican high school without also feeling the historical implications of Shakespeare's presence in that memory. The volume of Shakespeare's verse, "printed on lovely paper", is also unavoidably imprinted with the legacy of colonialism's cultural and educational intrusion. Something of that legacy—with its ongoing hierarchical topography of European "centres" and postcolonial "peripheries"—perhaps finds its way, consciously or not, into Figueroa's wry comment on realising that his poem "Winter Night" was "good because it has been translated into German". On the other hand, Figueroa's remarkable rescue of the worm-eaten *Sonnets* from the smouldering fire—worm-eaten, presumably, because the colonial subjects for whom they had been intended had stopped reading them—subtly inverts some of the hierarchies and power structures lingering from the colonial past. Having rescued a dilapidated Shakespeare text from the colonial ashes, the young Figueroa brings home the *Sonnets* and is enchanted by them. Part of what seems to delight him—although he does not say so explicitly—is the formal language of the *Sonnets*, because the encounter makes him want to write sonnets of his own. This appreciation of the sonnet form through Shakespeare is something he shares with several fellow Caribbean writers, some of whom we will return to in this chapter.

Figueroa's description of an encounter with Shakespeare's *Sonnets* that is marked by a colonial past—and that is also somehow both appreciative and subversive—is emblematic of the kinds of reception of the *Sonnets* we would like to explore in this chapter. We look at the ways in which certain twentieth- and twenty-first-century writers and translators from a broad geographical and cultural range—India, Bangladesh, the Caribbean, Brazil and Canada—have engaged directly and indirectly with the *Sonnets*. All our examples negotiate to some extent what engaging with the *Sonnets* might mean for a postcolonial identity, but we have grouped them under the geographical/critical term "the global South" rather than "the postcolonial", even if postcolonial criticism nevertheless necessarily underpins our readings. Recently introduced into Shakespeare studies—particularly within the field known as Global Shakespeare—the idea of "the global South" encompasses a multiplicity of locales and identities across the southern hemisphere, many of which share histories of colonial dispossession and ongoing disempowerment. However, as Sandra Young writes, "[w]here specific histories have yielded particular stories of power, resistance and transformation, postcolonialism's familiar dichotomies may prove limiting" (2019, 2). For instance, the postcolonial resistance implied in the familiar notion, coined by Salman Rushdie, of "writing back" to the colonial centre does not always apply to the examples we discuss here, especially not in the cases of diasporic identity or dual heritage.

The global South instead offers a broader, lateral view of what Young calls "connections and affinities between diverse contexts across the South" (2019, 6), and extends to diasporic "southern" identities in the global North, in this case Canada. Moreover, we want to suggest that studying the reception of Shakespeare's *Sonnets*—rather than that of Shakespeare's plays—within the framework of the global South contributes an important critical perspective on Global Shakespeare both as a phenomenon and as a scholarly field. This is not only because Global Shakespeare tends almost exclusively to address afterlives of the plays, not the poems, but also because deploying the *Sonnets* as a case study in global reception requires first and foremost an unavoidable literary focus on the poetics of texts and their languages.

Since Dennis Kennedy's rejection, in his pioneering 1993 collection *Foreign Shakespeare: Contemporary Performance*, of Shakespeare's (English) text as the fundamental basis for critical analysis of Shakespeare's ongoing presence around the world, scholarship in this field has not been primarily concerned with text-focused studies.[2] This includes translation studies, which have occupied at best a marginal position. In a more recent and oft-cited contribution to the field, Douglas Lanier conceptualises Shakespearean adaptations across the globe through a helpful rhizomatic model which, true to its name, dispenses with the idea of Shakespeare's text as the root of subsequent iterations: "within the Shakespearean rhizome, the Shakespearean text is an important element, but not a determining one" (2014, 29). The turn away from the Shakespearean text to an engagement with how global theatre, cinema and popular culture more broadly reinvent and reinvigorate Shakespeare in ways that need not directly include his text has been important to the establishing of Global Shakespeare as a scholarly field and underwrites many of its methodologies. In this sense, decentring the Shakespearean text is a natural and in many ways liberating critical move.

Similarly, the interdisciplinary focus of Global Shakespeare—which has drawn extensively on performance and film studies, for instance— has created room for the analysis of signifiers other than the linguistic in global Shakespearean afterlives, such as the visual, aural or material components of performance as well as cinematic techniques or, more recently, digital remediation. This has arguably created a rich and diverse understanding of "Shakespeare's Language", taking scholarship far beyond more philological modes of critical thinking.

But downplaying, or downright dispensing with the Shakespearean text and what Kennedy calls "the deep study of the linguistic clues in the text" (1993, 2) may also have left Global Shakespeare with a critical paradox. That is, in leaving textual and linguistic poetics behind to focus on other media, scholarship might unintentionally overlook the rich literary and linguistic traditions of the global cultures that have engaged with the Shakespearean canon and continue to recreate it. Moreover, while Kennedy's championing of "Shakespeare Without His Language" (the title of his introduction to *Foreign Shakespeare*) opened the door for non-Anglophone Shakespeares and challenged the idea that Shakespeare can be contained within a single (linguistic) culture, Global Shakespeare has

---

[2] Sonia Massai, however, has recently demonstrated a shift in the more general trend to forego language-focused studies in *Shakespeare's Accents: Voicing Identity in Performance* (2020), which both outlines histories of British resistance to hearing Shakespeare in other languages and demonstrates the influence of non-Anglophone productions on diversifying accents on the British Shakespearean stage.

arguably not yet managed fully to shift the fundamental understanding of "Shakespeare's Language" as essentially Anglophone. In fact, paradoxically, the increased study of plural multilingual Shakespeares might unintentionally risk facilitating the continued vision of a singular Anglophone "Shakespeare". As Sandra Young points out, there has sometimes been a regionalising tendency in Global Shakespeare that "positions Shakespeare as the dominant figure in the creative partnership of, say, 'Indian Shakespeare' or 'Shakespeare in Africa'. Shakespeare remains the dominant figure—the noun—and the region under focus is positioned as a colourful variant, qualifying the primary" (2019, 3).

Examining the global reception of the *Sonnets* offers an important opportunity to continue the critical negotiation of "Shakespeare's Language" in a global context and arguably in a more direct and distilled way than focusing on the remediation of the plays. The hierarchical relation described by Young is difficult, perhaps impossible, to level out, but one way to do so is a counterintuitive "return" to text-centred analyses that pay attention to "linguistic clues", as Kennedy puts it. In the case of Shakespearean afterlives in the global South, paying attention to unintentional recycling of hierarchies—ones that might contain echoes of colonial history—is not surprisingly even more important. But, at the same time, it may also be in longstanding postcolonial traditions of literary and linguistic resistance in writing from or connected with the global South that Global Shakespeare may look for critical cues, as seen in John Figueroa's account of his meeting with the *Sonnets*.

The Barbadian writer George Lamming's pioneering reading of *The Tempest*, for instance, which predates the institutionalisation of postcolonialism as a field of study, embodies a strong and complex response to the role of language in colonial history. Caliban, Lamming writes, "can never be regarded as an heir of [Prospero's] Language, since his use of Language is no more than his way of serving Prospero; and Prospero's instruction in this Language is only his way of measuring the distance that separates him from Caliban" (1960, 110). And more recently, Ngũgĩ wa Thiong'o has reintroduced the Caliban-Prospero trope in works such as *Something Torn and New: An African Renaissance* in order to signify the ongoing linguistic displacing, or "othering", of the colonised self (2009, 16). Indeed, given the engagement with *The Tempest* in the critical tradition of linguistic decolonisation as well as the impact of postcolonial critical engagement with Shakespeare, as exemplified in work by critics such as Ania Loomba and Jyotsna Singh, it seems even more important for Global Shakespeare to include a heightened focus on language.[3] Equally, given Kim Hall's work on racial epistemologies in the *Sonnets*, it seems crucial for studies of the reception of the *Sonnets* in certain regions and locales—such as those we address in this chapter—both to build on these scholarly traditions and to express them in new ways.[4]

The creative writers and translators whose work we refer to in the following sections engage implicitly or explicitly with the complicated, sometimes difficult, historicity of their language. Even when their first language is not English—as is the case for the Brazilian translator, Geraldo Carneiro—their language is still inextricably connected with colonial history. The main point is that writers in and from the global South have engaged directly with "Shakespeare's Language" and continue to do so, as any case study centred on the *Sonnets* must make very clear. Our examples also clearly indicate that as "Shakespeare's Language" travels, it does not remain unchanged by those who choose to use it. Instead Shakespeare's words represented by the *Sonnets* are incorporated into new formal and semantic settings. The result may be that Shakespeare's Language" is not so much "his" any longer—or, rather, that any invisible hierarchical demarcations between "Shakespeare's Language" and its global reception become productively unstable.

SHAKESPEARE'S *SONNETS* AND THE GLOBAL SOUTH

As Young explains, the global South is limited as a critical tool if it is used only to signify a set of geographical regions. Its main value lies in offering a critical perspective that emerges *from* those regions. "The global South", she observes, "draws attention to what is barely visible within colonial modernity. By identifying the existence of an alternative set of interests and material conditions, the global South challenges the normativity of the view from the North" (2019, 7). In their 2012 article, "Theory from the South: Or, how Euro-America is Evolving

---

[3] See for example Loomba, *Shakespeare, Race and Colonialism* or Singh, *Shakespeare and Postcolonial Theory*, particularly her third chapter on "The Legacies of Decolonization: Aimé Césaire, George Lamming, Roberto Fernández Retamar, Kamau Brathwaite and Ngũgĩ wa Thiong'o".

[4] See, for example, Hall, "'These bastard signs of fair': Literary Whiteness in Shakespeare's Sonnets".

Toward Africa", and their monograph of the same title, Jean and John Comaroff offer an influential framing of this alternative critical perspective. Comaroff and Comaroff propose a hierarchical inversion of "North" and "South" epistemologies, suggesting that it is to the South that we must look for the theories needed to understand global modernity. Importantly, they diagnose the previous (and ongoing) hierarchy as one in which theory from the North is applied to "raw" data from the South, much in the same way as former European colonisation derived raw materials from the colonies to be refined at home (2012, 1). For the field of Global Shakespeare to avoid repeating this pattern, it may be helpful to think of "Shakespeare" as a raw material which is being refined by global iterations—and, in many instances, this is implicit in the critical attention afforded to adaptations of Shakespeare's plays by scholars in the field. Yet, for as long as "Shakespeare's Language" remains distinct and separate from the "Shakespeares" produced around the world, that critical task feels incomplete.

Although translations of the *Sonnets* from English into other languages feature in the following sections, our overall focus is on the cultural politics of reception—which includes, importantly, translation. We realise that in assembling examples drawn from across wide distances, both temporal and geographical, we risk producing a disjointed framework in which nuances will inevitably be lost, but this is one of the inevitable flipsides of the deployment of the global South as a critical framework. What we hope to show is an emerging network of connections and affinities of the kind described by Young. By introducing that network, we in turn aim to provide a creative and critical view from the global South on the question of "Shakespeare's Language" in a global context. At the same time, by taking this cross-over approach, we seek to avoid the kind of regionalism that seems to have been necessary, as an initial tactic, in the establishment of Global Shakespeare—a mapping out of the geographical spread of the field—but which risks upholding "Shakespeare" as the dominant signifier in respect of the regional case study.[5] In the necessarily brief sections that follow, we seek to identify and focus on certain affinitive themes: an approach to the *Sonnets* as "raw material" available for creative transformation, sometimes in ways that are irreverent and explicitly or

---

[5] The rhizomatic model proposed by scholars such as Lanier (2014) has helped to displace this hierarchy. See also Young (2019, 3) for a critique of the region-based framework.

implicitly subversive; the literary form of the Shakespearean sonnet as providing (perhaps counterintuitively) creative freedom and opportunity for nonconformity (with emphasis on the "form" in "nonconformity"); and, thirdly, the complicated relation of "self and other" in the *Sonnets*, which finds new cultural and political expression in the work we look at here.

REINCARNATIONS IN INDIA

Recent criticism addressing the reception of Shakespeare's plays in India—including in cinematic adaptation both within and beyond Bollywood—has uncovered a wealth of new creative and critical lexica for studying Indian Shakespeares.[6] But, as is the case elsewhere, the reception of the *Sonnets* has attracted less attention. There is, however, a long and rich tradition of translating the *Sonnets* and incorporating them into Indian literary history while also negotiating the colonial history that brought them there. Rabindranath Tagore (1861–1941), the only Nobel laureate in Literature from India, wrote intermittently about Shakespeare, whose work he greatly admired, though he never published any extensive study. Tagore's great poem "Where the Mind is Without Fear"—arguably the most widely recited poem in any language in India—is considered to have been inspired by the sonnet form that he encountered in Shakespeare. Tagore dedicated another sonnet directly to Shakespeare in *Balaka* (*Flight of Cranes*), published in 1916. His obvious appreciation of Shakespeare, as well as the thematic similarities between some of his plays and those of Shakespeare, continue to be a topic of study and performance in Bengali culture, as in the event "William Tagore Meet", organised at the "Sonnet in Kolkata" in 2016. During that event, Biplab Dasgupta and Anasua Mazumdar recited excerpts from the works of Tagore and Shakespeare, and had the former pose a question—one that seems to combine appreciation and irreverence—to Shakespeare in an enactment of a hypothetical conversation: "How could you write so little in one lifetime?"[7] It is not

---

[6] As exemplified in the recent edited collection by Poonam Trivedi and Paromita Chakravarti: *Shakespeare and Indian Cinemas: Local Habitations* (2018).

[7] https://www.telegraphindia.com/west-bengal/if-tagore-met-shakespeare/cid/147 1074. Accessed 27 June 2021. The other (and earlier) foundational figure of Bengali literature, Michael Madhusudan Datta (1824–1873), also shows the influence of Shakespeare's *Sonnets*, as outlined by Sisir Kumar Das.

surprising that the spheres of Bengali culture—including its Anglophone offshoots—are penetrated by Shakespearean remembering. Kolkata, after all, was the heart of British India and its capital until 1931 when the British shifted to Delhi, a mere sixteen years before the Raj came to an end in 1947. Shakespeare's *Sonnets* have been variously translated and trans-created in Bangla. This has happened both in India, with various Bangla translations of the *Sonnets* by Sudhin Datta and Swapan Baran Acharya, and in Bangladesh, where at least two significant translations exist.[8]

But perhaps just as extensive a response to Shakespeare's *Sonnets* exists in the South Indian cultural and linguistic sphere of Malayalam. The leading Malayalam critic and writer, K. Satchidanandan—one of the major writers of contemporary India—who has just published a significant verse and prose translation of the *Sonnets*, notes that the sonnet "has existed in Malayalam poetry for more than a century, as the form (*Geetakam* in Malayalam) came to be known widely when the English language was introduced in Kerala, particularly through the missionary schools. Generally, it is the 4+4+4+2 form that has been in use".[9] He adds that it is not a popular form, and only a few poets have used it in Malayalam. However, it is interesting that the sonnet has been given an indigenous name "*geetakam*" in Malayalam, while in many other languages, such as Bangla and Urdu, it is simply transliterated, for instance as "*sanit*" in Urdu.[10] At least some of the *Sonnets* have been translated into Urdu, and various translations of Shakespeare's *Sonnets* also exist in Hindi, the two being mutually intelligible languages, though usually written in very different scripts.

There are, it is true, relatively few instances of creative reuse or rewriting in the Indian reception of the *Sonnets*—especially in comparison with other postcolonial lines of reception, such as those we look at in the following sections. While translations and pedagogic uses and even stage/performative adaptations abound, the *Sonnets* seem not often

---

[8] See *William Shakespearer sonnet samagra* translated by Selim Sarwar (2007), and the earlier *Shakespearer sonnet* translated by Zillur Rahman Siddiqui (1977), both of which were brought to our attention by Professor Kaiser Haq, Dhaka, Bangladesh.

[9] Email correspondence, d. 26th June 2021. The sonnets translated by K. Satchidanandan were published in 2000.

[10] *Urdu Shairi Mein Sanit* by Haneef Kaifi is a study of the sonnet (transliterated as "sanit") and its uses in Urdu poetry, and it inevitably refers to Shakespeare's *Sonnets*.

to have been put to specifically creative uses by Indian poets. Even in English, one can only trace faint resonances in two of the most formalist of the poets of the older and the current generations—Dom Moraes and Vikram Seth—and no real study exists to ascertain if these are direct borrowings or only due to the formalist structure of the poems. Yet, as this brief overview makes clear, the extensive and continuous tradition of translating the *Sonnets* into Indian languages offers rich opportunity for scholars to ask new questions about the meaning of "Shakespeare's Language" in Indian contexts.

CARIBBEAN REWRITINGS: UNA MARSON'S *TROPIC REVERIES*

The longstanding and widespread Caribbean engagement with Shakespeare—exemplified by figures as culturally and linguistically diverse as Lamming, Aimé Césaire or Roberto Fernández Retamar—has also included an engagement with the *Sonnets*, even if a less obvious one than that of *The Tempest*. Late twentieth-century Caribbean poets, such as Figueroa, Derek Walcott and Lorna Goodison, have in different ways responded to Shakespeare's *Sonnets* as part of a larger response to the English literary canon introduced by the colonial education system in the Caribbean. As seen in our opening reference to Figueroa's encounter with the *Sonnets*, absorption of the sonnet as a literary form has been important for these poets, but they have displayed a tendency to use the form freely, increasingly subverting it in ways that are visible, for instance, in the "sonnets" by Derek Walcott that make up his long poem, "Tales of the Islands" (Walcott, 22–27). Walcott's sonnets are of 14 lines, but the iambic line often exceeds five feet, and both the rhymes and slanted rhymes are loosely structured. It can also be difficult to trace direct Shakespearean references in Caribbean creative reuses of the *Sonnets*, especially in the latter half of the twentieth century. This ought also to be seen in the context of Caribbean poetry's moving towards a greater realisation of the distinctiveness of the Caribbean "language", as in Edward Kamau Brathwaite's formulation of "nation language" in the 1970s.[11]

---

[11] Kamau Brathwaite sets out the concept of "nation language" in his 1984 book *History of the Voice*.

Looking back to Una Marson's first collection of poetry, *Tropic Reveries*, published in 1930, however, we find arguably one of the most complex and interesting Caribbean engagements with Shakespeare's *Sonnets*. The collection contains a series of sonnets that clearly evoke a Shakespearean presence, both in Marson's choice of the sonnet, formal as well as thematic, to draw—albeit in deeply ambivalent ways—on the Elizabethan imagery of courtly love. The collection also contains a sonnet-like rewriting of Hamlet's soliloquy, "To be, or not to be", in which Marson directly appropriates Shakespeare to comment on a choice between spinsterhood and marriage, re-titling the soliloquy, "To wed, or not to wed". Despite (or accentuated by) the parenthetical "with apologies to Shakespeare" at the end of the poem, the appropriation signals both feminist and cultural resistance to the Shakespearean text, including, perhaps, a reminder to the reader that Hamlet's famous soliloquy is immediately followed by his misogynistic outburst at Ophelia. Marson overwrites Hamlet's soliloquy by substituting and rearranging the words, but without changing the iambic metre. The result is a humorous, irreverent and effective defamiliarisation of the Shakespearean content that is, in fact, underpinned by the deployment of the familiar form.

As Alison Donnell has argued in her work on Marson, much of the early critical reception of *Tropic Reveries* failed to appreciate the full extent of its resistance to colonial, cultural and linguistic domination.[12] While several forms of resistance feel quite explicit in the irreverent "To wed, or not to wed", it becomes a more elusive task to trace these in the sonnet sequence, which, as Donnell also acknowledges, is "somewhat disturbing" (1995, 51). A sonnet such as "In vain" describes female love as enslavement, opening with the lines

> In vain I build me stately mansions fair,
> And set thee as my king upon the throne,
> And place a lowly stool beside thee there,
> Thus, as thy slave to come into my own. (Marson, 27)

The combination of Elizabethan form and love tropes with the imagery of female submission and enslavement is difficult to read, because Marson, at first glance, makes no effort to inject any form of resistance into the speaker's voice. However, if, as with Marson's subversive rewriting of Hamlet's

---

[12] See Donnell (1995, 1997).

soliloquy, we read "In Vain" alongside Shakespeare's Sonnet 57, "Being your slave, what should I do but tend/ Upon the hours and times of your desire", it becomes easier to read her sonnet against the grain and perhaps detect notes of irony among those of submission. While we do not suggest that Marson's sonnet functions as a direct rewriting of Shakespeare's Sonnet 57, it seems safe to assume her familiarity with it and, therefore, look at how the two poetic perspectives collide on the subject of love as enslavement. It is revealing, for instance, that while the speaker in both Marson's sonnet and Sonnet 57 wait in vain for the Master-Lover, Marson's speaker is extremely busy, as an actual slave would be, building the Master's "mansion", setting up his "throne", etc., while Shakespeare's speaker has "[n]o precious time at all to spend,/ [n]or services to do" (4–5). Behind a very similar wait, in Marson's version there lies a history of endless labour by the slave for the "king" or master.

Tropic Reveries should be seen in the context of Marson's subsequent explicitly anti-racist, anti-colonial and feminist work, as well as of her enormous importance for Caribbean literature and culture as the founder of the BBC's *Caribbean Voices*, which had an immense impact on the careers of Figueroa and Walcott, among many others. Marson's early response to Shakespeare—and especially to Shakespeare's language and form—holds a different kind of value, one that arguably serves as an important precedent for later receptions of the *Sonnets* in the postcolonial world.

Translating the *Sonnets* in Brazil

The Brazilian poet and translator, Geraldo Carneiro, has translated Shakespeare intermittently since the 1980s and 1990s and is one of the country's most sought-after Shakespearean translators for contemporary theatre productions. He has translated a good number of the *Sonnets*, published in the collection *O Discurso do Amor Rasgado* (*Speeches of Torn Love*, 2013).

As Gisele Dionísio da Silva has noted, Shakespeare's reception in Brazil since the first half of the twentieth century shows a sustained tendency to associate the work with elitist culture, even to the extent of establishing "Shakespeare" as the representative of a "superior cultural paradigm in relation to Brazil" (2009, 834). As Dionísio da Silva explains, this tendency also influenced early Brazilian translators of Shakespeare's

Sonnets, resulting in some overly scholarly and complex translations.[13] However, another strand in Brazilian Shakespeare reception shows a distinctly more democratic mindset and incorporates Shakespeare into popular Brazilian culture in ways that overtly or implicitly subvert the notion of Shakespeare as the representative of superior (European) culture.

Carneiro's translations of the *Sonnets* (as well as his translations of the plays) arguably belong to this other strand. To begin with, his translations of the *Sonnets* into Portuguese are characterised by a clarity that makes them quite accessible to a wide, contemporary readership. This is partly attributable to Carneiro's ability to maintain a ten-syllable line and his prioritisation of monosyllabic word choices wherever possible, which, as Alfredo Michel Modenessi (himself a prolific translator of both the plays and the *Sonnets* into Mexican Spanish) has pointed out, is not easily achieved with Latinate languages.[14] Interestingly, it is precisely Carneiro's choice to conform as closely as possible to Shakespearean metre that enables him to create this highly readable style. At the same time, the rhythmic fluidity of his lines often recreates a musical pattern that is deeply embedded in Brazilian Portuguese and Brazilian musical culture.[15] Carneiro's translation of Sonnet 15 is a good example of this:

> Quando penso que tudo quanto cresce
> Só guarda a perfeição por um momento,
> Que o palco deste mundo só oferece
> Aquilo que dos astros ganha o alento;
> Quando vejo que os homens como as plantas
> Crescem e declinam sob o mesmo céu,
> Se jactam e depois, a alturas tantas,
> Decaem sem memória do que é seu,
> Então a percepção da impermanência
> Te faz mais moço aos olhos meus agora,
> Em que combatem o Tempo e a Decadência
> Para mudar em noite a tua aurora.
> E, combatendo o Tempo por teu amor,
> Se ele te toma, eu te faço maior.

---

[13] Exemplified by the 1953 translation by Péricles Eugênio da Silva Ramos. See Dionísio da Silva's analysis of Ramos' translation (2009, 835–838).

[14] Modenessi, 'Immersed in translation'.

[15] See also Carneiro and de Carvalho (2019) on this aspect of Carneiro's translations.

In his translation of the final couplet of Sonnet 15 ("And all in war with time for love of you / As he takes from you, I engraft you new"), Carneiro uses the verb *"tomar"* ("to take") which is used colloquially and informally in Brazilian Portuguese with a range of meanings, from "taking" to "consuming". The first part of the line, *"se ele te toma"*, moreover, has an uninterrupted, soft rhythmic quality, thanks to Brazilian phonetics: the Brazilian Portuguese pronunciation of *"te"* is closer to the English "chi", which means that the line avoids the harder-sounding repetition of "t" plus vowel. The second part of the line, which translates "I engraft you new" into *"eu te faço maior"* maintains this combination of the colloquial and the musical, which is characteristic of Carneiro's work.

However, a remarkable aspect of this translation is also what appears to be a subtle intertextual reference in that final line. Carneiro's *"eu te faço maior"* (literally, "I make you bigger") invokes, almost verbatim, the line of a much-loved Brazilian samba from the 1970s: "Escurinha" by the equally loved "sambista", Angenor de Oliveira, known as "Cartola":

> Escurinha tu tem de ser minha de qualquer Maneira
> Te dou meu boteco te dou meu barraco
> Que eu tenho no morro de Mangueira
> Comigo não ha embaraço
> Vem que eu te faço meu amor
> A rainha da escola de samba
> Que o teu preto e diretor
> Quatro paredes de barro, telhado de zinco,
> Assoalho de chão, só tu escurinha
> É quem esta faltando no meu barracao
> Sai disso bobinha só nessa vidinha, levando a pior
> Lá no morro eu te ponho no samba
> Te ensino a ser bamba te faço a maior

Whereas Shakespeare's Sonnet 15 is addressed to the "fair youth", Cartola's samba is addressed to a young black woman. Essentially a love-poem, "Escurinha" features a young man inviting his sweetheart to join him in his tin-roofed shack in the *Mangueira favela* of Rio de Janeiro (famous for its samba school), promising to make her the queen of the samba school. Through an intertextual reference that works so naturally within the translation that it is hardly noticeable, Carneiro accomplishes multiple cultural inversions. First, he thoroughly democratises the elitist status Shakespeare's *Sonnets* might still have for some Brazilian readers by inserting an iconic element of Brazilian popular culture. At the same time, he destabilises the dichotomous fair youth/dark lady trope in the *Sonnets* by effectively writing a young black woman into the procreation sequence.

An insertion of such subtlety—one that is hardly noticeable at first—appears rather more direct when read alongside a 2017 column by Carneiro in the Brazilian newspaper *O Globo* in which he lamented certain historical tendencies to exclude Afro-Brazilian female authors from the Brazilian literary scene.[16] Carneiro concluded the column by citing his own translation of Shakespeare's Sonnet 65 and implied that his translation of the final couplet "O none, unless this miracle have might:/ That in black ink my love may still shine bright" ("Ninguém: só se um milagre faz-se impor/ E em tinta negra esplende o meu amor") unambiguously celebrate the "Tinta negra" (which in Portuguese can include the colour black as well as "black ink"). The language here may still be "Shakespeare's" yet the meaning of the words is productively destabilised as they are incorporated into a new linguistic and cultural setting. Translations may be expected to transport, rather than transform, the semantic contents of a text but we should perhaps not underestimate the role they play in creating new versions of "Shakespeare's Language", even if they may do so on a less perceptible level than, say, theatre performance. Again, looking to the global South and to a specific "southern" cultural politics of translating Shakespeare helps to make this clearer.

LOOKING TO THE GLOBAL NORTH: CONCLUDING REMARKS

The network of examples in this chapter—to which many others could be added—on one level resembles the rhizomatic model frequently deployed by Global Shakespeare studies, but with the key difference, *pace* Kennedy, that Shakespearean language, the Shakespearean text—exemplified by the Shakespearean Sonnet—*is* the determining element. What emerges during the process of establishing this text-centred network, we would argue, is a diverse global understanding of "Shakespeare's Language". What constitutes the Shakespearean text and its language, in other words, becomes an open question, reformulated and answered by other and new

---

[16] https://oglobo.globo.com/ela/gastronomia/tinta-negra-21588640. Accessed 20 September 2021.

texts. The translators and writers we have looked at here—coming, as they do, from diverse linguistic and cultural traditions—all demonstrate an engagement with "Shakespeare's Language" that resists linguistic hierarchies. That is, they demonstrate quite clearly that "Shakespeare's Language" can be thoroughly democratised when it is divorced from past hierarchies and continuously recreated, even if this is no easy process.

In this sense, the view from the global South may also provide an illuminating perspective on affinitive engagements with "Shakespeare's Language" in the global North. In a very recent engagement with Shakespeare's *Sonnets*, the Canadian poet and critic, Sonnet L'Abbé—in her aptly entitled collection of prose poems *Sonnet's Shakespeare*—deploys a process of rewriting that speaks directly to other examples in this chapter. While L'Abbé's rewritings of the *Sonnets* represent a personal twenty-first-century poetics, situated in the global North, they also demonstrate the author's connection to past and present postcolonial identities in the global South. The striking inversion of authorial authority in the title of the collection—made possible by L'Abbé's first name—both establishes the personal voice and gestures at the literary legacy of those identities. The inversion in the title also effectively "others" Shakespeare, allowing for a different poetic self (L'Abbé's) to emerge. Writing as a mixed-race Canadian woman, L'Abbé demonstrates a sometimes painful process of negotiating her relationship with the Shakespearean text while she rewrites it. In her poem CXXVII (a rewriting of Shakespeare's Sonnet 127), lines such as "Informed since I could read by the monarchy's hand on the throat of English, I've put on an enunciative face, trusting the figure of speech's power to fair the ink of English thinking" show that dismantling linguistic hierarchies—ones that also underwrite racial hierarchies—is far from simple.

L'Abbé draws on the poetics of erasure to rewrite the *Sonnets*, but she does so by rearranging each letter of the original Shakespearean Sonnet into a new, and lengthier, prose version which subsumes and over-writes both the content and form of the original. The palimpsestic result becomes a reverse metaphor for historical processes of colonisation, as L'Abbé methodically breaks up and rearranges Shakespeare's language, eventually regenerating it in a different idiom. She may be writing in the Global North—geographically speaking—but her creative tactics suggest a clear alignment with the Global South: her collection thus participates in a network of engagements with the *Sonnets* which continues to deconstruct and reconstruct "Shakespeare's Language" in a global context. As Ngũgĩ wa Thiong'o puts it in a recent interview: "When you crush hierarchy, and replace it with network, then the cultures held in the different languages generate oxygen. They cross-fertilize" (2018). Counterintuitive as it may at first sound, re-inserting and re-assessing "Shakespeare's Language" into studies of his global reception—above all in the Global South—turns out to perform an equivalent cultural cross-fertilisation.

REFERENCES

Brathwaite, Edward Kamau. 1984. *History of the Voice: The Development of Nation Language in Anglophone Caribbean Poetry*. London: New Beacon Books.

Burnett, Mark Thornton. 2019. *'Hamlet' and World Cinema*. Cambridge: Cambridge University Press.

Carneiro, Geraldo. 2013. *O Discurso do Amor Rasgado*. Rio de Janeiro: Nova Fronteira.

Carneiro, Geraldo and Vinicius Mariano de Carvalho. 2019. "We Are All Cannibals: Reflections on Translating Shakespeare". In *Eating Shakespeare: Cultural Anthropophagy as Global Methodology*, ed. Anne Sophie Refskou, Marcel Alvaro de Amorim and Vinicius Mariano de Carvalho, 27–41. London: Bloomsbury Arden Shakespeare.

Comaroff, Jean and John L. Comaroff. 2012. *Theory from the South: Or, How Euro-America Is Evolving Toward Africa*. Boulder, CO: Paradigm Publishers.

Dionísio da Silva, Giselle. 2009. "Shakespeare's Sonnets in Brazil: Striking a Balance Between Losses and Gains in the Translation Process". *Meta: Journal des traducteurs/Translators Journal* 54, 4: 833–841.

Donnell, Alison. 1997. "Sentimental Subversion: The Poetry and Politics of Devotion in the Work of Una Marson". In *Kicking Daffodils: Twentieth-Century Women Poets*, ed. Vicki Bertram, 113–124. Edinburgh: Edinburgh University Press.

Donnell, Alison. 1995. "Contradictory (W)omens?—Gender Consciousness in the Poetry of Una Marson". *Kunapipi*, 17, 3: 43-58.

Hall, Kim F. 1998. "'These Bastard Signs of Fair': Literary Whiteness in Shakespeare's Sonnets". In *Post-Colonial Shakespeares*, ed. Ania Loomba and Martin Orkin, 64–83. London and New York: Routledge.

Kennedy, D. 1993, rev. edn. 2008. *Foreign Shakespeare: Contemporary Performance*. Cambridge: Cambridge University Press.

L'Abbé, Sonnet. 2019. *Sonnet's Shakespeare*. Toronto: Penguin Random House Canada.

Lamming, George. 1960. *The Pleasures of Exile*. London: Pluto Press.

Lanier, Douglas. 2014. "Shakespearean Rhizomatics: Adaptation, Ethics, Value". In *Shakespeare and the Ethics of Appropriation*, ed. Alexa Alice Joubin and Elizabeth Rivlin, 21–40. New York: Palgrave Macmillan.

Loomba, Ania. 2002. *Shakespeare, Race and Colonialism*. Oxford: Oxford University Press.

Marson, Una. 1930. *Tropic Reveries*. New York: Gleaner Co.

Massai, Sonia. 2020. *Shakespeare's Accents: Voicing Identity in Performance*. Cambridge: Cambridge University Press.

Modenessi, Alfredo. "Immersed in Translation: Challenging Misconstructions of Translating, Via Shakespeare". Conference Paper.

Nanton, Philip and John Figueroa. 2003. "Interview". *Caribbean Quarterly* 49, 1/2: 61–65.

Raut, Tanuj. 2017 (updated in 2018). "Interview with professor Ngũgĩ wa Thiong'o". *Project Myopia*. https://projectmyopia.com/interview-with-professor-ngugi-wa-thiongo/. Accessed 1 September 2021.

Singh, Jyotsna G. 2019. *Shakespeare and Postcolonial Theory*. Arden Shakespeare and Theory. London: Bloomsbury Arden Shakespeare.

Sisir Kumar Das. 1966. "Michael Madhusudan Datta and the Sonnet in Bengal". *Mahfil*, 3, 4: 102–105.

Thiong'o, Ngũgĩ wa. 2009. *Something Torn and New: An African Renaissance*. New York: BasicCivitas Books.

Trivedi, Poonam and Paromita Chakravarti. 2018. *Shakespeare and Indian Cinemas: Local Habitations*. London: Routledge.

Walcott, Derek. 1992. *Collected Poems 1948-1984*. New York: Farrar, Straus & Giroux.

Young, Sandra. 2019. *Shakespeare in the Global South: Stories of Oceans Crossed in Contemporary Adaptation*. London: Bloomsbury Arden Shakespeare.

CHAPTER 9

The Pauper Prince Translates Shakespeare's *Sonnets*: Ken'ichi Yoshida and the Poetics/Politics of Post-war Japan

Reiko Oya

君を夏の一日に喩えようか。
Shall I compare thee to a summer's day?

In 1978, Akiko Yoshida began a memoir of her late father Ken'ichi by quoting from his Japanese rendition of Shakespeare's Sonnet 18. Ken'ichi was a prolific writer—his posthumous "Collected Works" consists of 32 thick volumes—but it was this poem that "kept haunting" the daughter.[1] Her mother, who loved Ken'ichi's *Sonnets*, had originally recommended the translation to Akiko. Sonnet 18 reminded the daughter of her childhood home and of the pale pink roses over the fence as they glowed in the

---

[1] Unless otherwise specified, all English translations from Japanese are mine.

R. Oya (✉)
Keio University, Tokyo, Japan
e-mail: reikooya@hotmail.com

© The Author(s), under exclusive license to Springer Nature
Switzerland AG 2023
J. Kingsley-Smith and W. R. Rampone Jr. (eds.), *Shakespeare's Global Sonnets*,
Global Shakespeares, https://doi.org/10.1007/978-3-031-09472-9_9

slanting evening light of early summer (Yoshida A 2013, 93). The association of Sonnet 18 specifically with twilight scenery is unusual—there is no direct reference to a time of day in the poem itself—but it was part of a family tradition dating back to Ken'ichi's first encounter with the *Sonnets* about half a century earlier.

Author and literary critic Ken'ichi Yoshida (1912–1977) was born into an illustrious family of aristocrats and statesmen and had a privileged, international upbringing. He had one of the founders of modern Japan, Toshimichi Okubo, as a great-grandfather and counted a couple of prime ministers, a count, and a princess among his immediate family members. His father, the future Prime Minister Shigeru Yoshida, was a diplomat at the time of the birth of his eldest son. Ken'ichi would spend his childhood in Qingdao, Paris, London, and Tianjin, as well as in Tokyo, becoming as proficient in English as in Japanese (Morita 2007). One day, the talented young man came across "an advertisement for a perfume or some such item" on a magazine page, where an image of the English countryside was accompanied by a single line: "And summer's lease hath all too short a date" ("Sheikusupia-no juyongyoshi-ni tsuite" ["On Shakespeare's *Sonnets*"], 1954, 6:342–43).[2] In a later retelling of the memory (1966), the landscape and the verse were "printed on a nice-looking chocolate box" (Yoshida K 2007, 68–69). Either way, he was smitten by the brilliant piece of poetry even though he had yet to know who the sonneteer was. The beautiful landscape and line 4 of Sonnet 18 would influence Yoshida's perception of England and its literature for the rest of his life.

The following essay will explore Yoshida's engagement with English literature, with special reference to his *Sonnets* translation, against the backdrop of the rapidly democratizing Japanese society of the late 1940s through to the 1960s. Yoshida's idiosyncratic Japanese, which entailed long complex and compound sentences and difficult words, was much maligned by fellow writers as "recondite" and "incomprehensible," but his *Sonnets* translation would crucially influence Japanese contemporary poetry. Most importantly, Yoshida's engagement with Shakespeare's *Sonnets* afforded him insight into, and visions for, Japanese literature and society in the years following World War Two.

---

[2] Unless otherwise specified, quotations from Ken'ichi Yoshida are from Yoshida K (1978–1981), and are given parenthetically by the volume and page numbers. The *Sonnets* are quoted from Shakespeare (2002).

THE FATHER AND THE SON

In 1930, Yoshida enrolled at King's College, Cambridge to read English literature, and instantly became a favourite student of F. L. Lucas and Goldsworthy Lowes Dickinson. However, in less than half a year, he withdrew from the university. He offered several explanations about this decision. His sudden dislike for England was one of them: "When I left for England in the early Showa period, I frankly could not stand the country called Japan, but after I left Japan, I developed an antipathy to the country called England" ("Ryugaku-no koro" ["My Study Abroad Experience"], 28:204). Moreover, he had an ambition to become a "*bunshi*" [man of letters] and to devote his life to literature. Studying English at Cambridge did not seem to him to help achieve that objective:

> ... I had made up my mind to become a *bunshi* when I returned to Japan. I came to question if spending my teens and twenties studying English literature in England would lead to that goal. (*Koyuroku* [*Memories of Old Friends*], 22:37)

Dickinson understood the young student's anxiety and advised that one should be on one's native soil to fulfil one's literary ambitions. Against his father's wishes, he left Cambridge in February 1931 and spent the next few years studying French at the Athénée Français in Tokyo. He then launched his literary career, primarily as translator of such French writers as Jules Laforgue and Paul Valéry. It was not until after WW2 that the self-styled "Pauper Prince" would turn to English literature once again to address the ideological and literary crises in the shattered, defeated nation.

Although a hard-liner concerning Chinese matters, Shigeru Yoshida was firmly against war with the United States and the United Kingdom. His sympathy with the Allied nations cost him his diplomatic career: he resigned as ambassador to Britain in 1939. Back in Japan, he held no official positions during WW2, but still tried to get the government to negotiate peace with the Allies. He was arrested and kept in custody by military police in April 1945. Following Japan's surrender and the Allied occupation in August the same year, he was appointed the Prime Minister in 1946 and served five terms until 1954. Known for his pro-American, pro-British ideals, he was instrumental in creating a constitutional democracy in Japan in the crucial decade after the traumatic war.

Ken'ichi, meanwhile, was drafted into the Imperial Japanese Navy in May 1945 but was not actually sent to the frontline. When the war ended, he restarted his literary career, producing a prolific output that included critical writings, translations, essays in culinary culture, short stories and novels. He had long turned his back on his family's wealth and power: the first collection of his essays was aptly entitled *The Prime Minister's Son—in Reduced Circumstances* (Yoshida 1954). Notorious for his sardonic sense of humour, he went on publishing books with titles such as *Kojiki oji* [*The Pauper Prince*] (1956) and *Sanmon sinshi* [*The Hack-Writer Gentleman*] (1956). In the latter, he claimed (truthfully or not) that he once sat outside a publishing house to collect alms from the editors and fellow writers (2:251). His literary and real-life antics notwith-standing, the Pauper Prince was also in search of new ideals for post-war Japan through the study of Shakespeare and other English writers.

Some fifteen years after he quit Cambridge, Yoshida rekindled his passion for English literature in the midst of the Americanization of Japanese culture. During the U.S. occupation (1945–1952), the Japanese were heavily exposed to the culture and ethos of the former "enemy state." To the destitute citizens of the defeated nation, the material prosperity of the victorious country and the "American Dream" were alluring in themselves. A Japanese-*American* (not "English") conversa-tion manual (*Nichi-bei kaiwa techo*) was published just a month after the end of the war in 1945, and went on to sell 3.5 million copies. In 1946, the NHK (Japan Broadcasting Corporation) started the popular radio programme *Amerika dayori* [*Letters from America*] introducing the American way of life, while Hollywood movies and jazz music were welcomed enthusiastically (Tsutsumi 1996). In 1949, defying the rapid assimilation of American culture, a group of anglophile politicians, busi-nessmen, academics, and writers formed a small society called the Albion Club. To the members, British culture and society offered a possible alter-native to the American model for post-war Japan. Yoshida was a founding member of the Albion Club and edited the first several issues of its maga-zine, *The Albion* (1949–1960). His critical engagements with Shakespeare in the post-war era were part of this elite cultural movement.

Among Yoshida's prodigious post-war publications was a trilogy of studies in English literature: *Eikoku-no bungaku* (*England's Literature*, 1949), *Sheikusupia* (*Shakespeare*, 1956), and *Eikoku-no kindai bungaku*

(*England's Modern Literature*, 1959).[3] Yoshida habitually discussed "England's literature," tenaciously avoiding the term *Ei-bungaku*, the customary Japanese translation for "English literature." This was partly due to his antipathy to the institutionalized English studies at the author-itarian Tokyo University and other higher education institutions in Japan. Even more importantly, Yoshida was gesturing that his books explored not only the literature but also the people, culture, and society of the country. English studies were for him not simply a literary pursuit but a broader, cultural project, and his ultimate goal was to create a new ethos and literature suitable for post-war Japan.

THE *SONNETS* AND THE "SUMMER'S DAY"

Shakespeare's *Sonnets* held a special place in Yoshida's literary and critical writings. *England's Literature*, which was his first monograph, offered a sweeping survey of Chaucer and Malory down to E. M. Forster and A. E. Housman. In the first chapter, he quoted his favourite line 4 of Sonnet 18, to explain how the uniqueness of England's natural environ-ment gave special poignancy to the verse (Yoshida K 1949, 9–10). To him, the sonnet was equally about the poet's fair friend and about the fleeting "summer's day" to which the young man was compared. The critic would quote the same line 4 yet again in "Eikoku-no shiki" ["On the Four Seasons in England"], to argue: "Summer is incessantly fleeting in Sonnet 18, and the people in the age of Elizabeth I were acutely aware of the brevity of human life as contrasted with the immortality of literature" (9:271).

In *England's Literature*, Yoshida went on to discuss the whole of Sonnet 18, describing the evening scenery that the poem never failed to evoke in him:

> The poem inevitably reminds one of the summer evening of England with the gorgeous slanting sunrays in the western sky scattering gold dust in the atmosphere. People of the Orient are unacquainted with a resplendent natural phenomenon such as this except through Western poetry, music,

---

[3] The word "Eikoku," which appears in the two titles in the trilogy, normally means "Britain," but in his books, Yoshida focused on the works written in English by English authors. In the following discussion, Yoshida's "Eikoku" will be translated as "England."

or painting. They are equally ignorant of the gloominess of the English winter. (Yoshida K 1949, 12–13)

The landscape called forth by Sonnet 18 would also help define the English national character. The critic continued:

> The ugliness of English winter is inversely proportional to the beauty of its spring, summer and autumn ... English people do not survive the winter on the strength of the spring and summer. Rather, they can endure the overwhelming beauty of the spring and the summer precisely because they are robust enough to survive that bleak winter. They are equally resilient to the extremes of beauty and ugliness. (Yoshida K 1949, 13)

Interestingly, the manifesto of the Albion Club, also published in 1949, similarly pointed to the resilience of the English during and after WW2, emphasizing the need for the Japanese to learn from their good example:

> British citizens remained calm and strong, understood the essential evil and misery of war, and survived the unprecedented national crisis... now is the time for us Japanese to study the history and culture of Britain and British people in a concerted effort to rebuild our country. (The Albion Club 1949, 104)

Yoshida's reading of Sonnet 18 resonated with the cultural project outlined in the Albion Club manifesto: interpreting Shakespeare's love poems, the critic was in search of ideals for the newly democratized Japanese society.

LANDSCAPE AND LOVE: YOSHIDA READS THE SONNETS

Yoshida constantly identified the narrator of the *Sonnets* with Shakespeare. In both *England's Literature* and *Shakespeare*, published three years later, the critic followed the conventional division of the sonnet sequence and traced the playwright's changing relations with the young man (Sonnets 1–126) and with the dark woman (Sonnets 127–54). To him, Sonnet 18, like the rest of the poems in the first sub-sequence, was addressed to a young man, even though the gender of the addressee is not specified in the 14 lines. He commented:

Shakespeare expressed his ardent love for this young man in many of the 150-odd sonnets, while the second sub-sequence portrayed his affair with a married woman. When the young man and the woman cheated on him, the sonnets took a dark, tortured tone unimaginable from the early poems. The sonnets in the first group proved Shakespeare's credentials as an exceptional lyrical poet while the later poems expressed what the French call *l'amertume* to an extent unparalleled even by the French literature itself. (Yoshida K 1949, 48)

Yoshida's reading might sound naively biographical but in fact he was not interested in the factual details of Shakespeare's life or in the identity of the young man and the dark woman. Rather, he was highlighting the fullness and vitality of human experience underlying early modern literature, contrasting it with the diminishing human interest and preoccupation with the specifics of language and technique in modern European literature. Being an avid reader and translator of Valéry, Yoshida had in mind the detachment of poetry from the poet's life experience as epitomized by Poe's "The Raven," Baudelaire, and ultimately the French symbolist tenet of "la poésie pure."[4] Indeed, French symbolists were always at the back of Yoshida's mind as he discussed the *Sonnets*. He observed:

Sonnet 18... reminds us of Baudelaire ("Bientôt nous plongerons dans les froides ténèbres...," and "Je te donne ces vers afin que si mon nom..."), but compared with this sonnet, the poems of *Les Fleurs du mal* lose their sheen. This probably shows the difference between true poetic genius and mere talent. (Yoshida K 1949, 49)

To Yoshida, Shakespeare's *Sonnets* epitomized the prelapsarian innocence in English literature where (to misquote Jean Moréas's "The Symbolist Manifesto," 1886) "the pictures of nature, the actions of human beings, all concrete phenomena *would* themselves know how to manifest themselves."[5] He believed that Shakespeare's life experience permeated and invigorated the *Sonnets*, and that the poet's artistry was not an end but a means to immortalize the beautiful friend. He continued:

---

[4] See Takamatsu (1994) for the influence of symbolism on Yoshida's literary criticism.

[5] Moréas explained that in symbolist poetry, "the pictures of nature, the actions of human beings, all concrete phenomena would not themselves know how to manifest themselves" (Moréas [1886] n.d.).

This is the basic tenet of traditional English poetry. Both Wordsworth's emotion recollected in tranquillity and Shelley's idea of the poet as prophet assume that the poet has real emotions and experiences and when he gives them expression, he would cultivate his poetic talent and techniques. Words are just one of many objects of the poet's passion and are not his overriding objective in themselves. Poetry is a passion, but it is not a passion for language. (Yoshida K 1949, 50)

Yoshida even believed that Shakespeare's love affair with the young man and the dark woman brought about the transition from the comedies of the middle period, such as *Twelfth Night*, to the tragedies from *Julius Caesar* onwards.

While postulating Shakespeare's life underlying the sonnet sequence, Yoshida was actually against biographical studies. Poems are not confessions, and Shakespeare's total mastery of poetic expression gave the *Sonnets* an independent life as an aesthetic object. He believed that "the poetic voice in the *Sonnets* is as detached from Shakespeare as the speeches assigned to the characters of his plays" (Yoshida K 1949, 51). Shakespeare's lived experience was important only in so far as it deepened his understanding of human psychology. It is worth recalling that, in the English literature trilogy, Yoshida was interpreting the *Sonnets* for the readers of the war-torn native country. While studying the relations between human experience and poetry, he was also exploring the relevance of English literature to Japanese readers. This was made clearer in a later essay, "Eikoku-no gendaishi-ni tsuite" ["On England's Contemporary Poetry"] (1967), where French symbolists were contrasted with "the practical-minded English people":

French symbolists substituted verbal expression for real-life issues, whereas English poets lived their poems.... Shakespeare's *Sonnets* portrays the same sort of anxiety as modern poetry, and Baudelaire's poems sometimes sound like French translations of Shakespeare... English poets did have "modern" anxieties. However, Shakespeare used the *Sonnets* to escape from the abyss. His later works, such as *The Tempest* and *The Phoenix and the Turtle*, show that he succeeded in doing so. (Yoshida K 2014, 223–24)

Yoshida's Shakespeare lived through the "modern anxiety," and matured as a person as a result. Here, the English playwright set a great example for the Japanese to follow.

THE TRANSLATOR AS ARTIST

Yoshida was a prodigious translator: a chronology of his life and work lists around 50 full-length books translated by him (32:351–450). While translation was partly a way for him to make a day-to-day living, two more factors influenced his signature translation, *Juyongyo-shi* [*The Sonnets*] (Yoshida K 1955): his comparative approach to literature and his theory of translation. Having spent his childhood in many different cultures, Yoshida was not only fluent in Japanese and English, but well versed in Chinese and French literature. As a consequence, he understood individual literary works in wider European and east-Asian contexts. In "Higashi-to nishi" ["The East and the West"] (1966) and "Seiyou" ["The Occident"] (1966), he emphasized that Japanese readers should grasp the basic tenet of Western love poetry to understand Shakespeare's *Sonnets*. Love can be a consuming passion for a Western poet, whereas a Japanese poet would always write about love in conjunction with something else: Japanese love poetry is not simply about two people in love but about the world surrounding them. Yoshida also argued that, when Japanese poets happened to write about love pure and simple, they were indeed "translating" Western literature (14:243–61, 279–94). This is an interesting observation as Yoshida himself literally "translated" many of Shakespeare's sonnets into Japanese.

For Yoshida, translation was a creative act. The first sentence of his essay, "Hon'yaku ron" ["On Translation"] (1960) reads: "Translation is a form of criticism" (12:343). A critic would analyse a literary work and reconstitute the impressions and emotions it evoked into a new, critical entity. According to Yoshida, a translator would be engaged in the same process of analysis and reconstitution. The analogy between the translator and the critic is significant as Yoshida was an admirer of Oscar Wilde: he read the *Intentions* during the war and felt "as if things I had always wanted to say were all verbalized in the book" ("Osuka Wairudo-no koto" ["On Oscar Wilde"], 32:35). After the war, he not only translated "The Critic as Artist" (1951), but famously opened *England's Modern Literature* by declaring: "The modern age in England arrived with Wilde." By linking translation with criticism, Yoshida was in effect postulating "the translator as artist."

The 1955 anthology contained 43 out of the 154 sonnets.[6] Yoshida apparently worked on more poems—a manuscript for Sonnet 62, which was omitted from the selection, is reproduced in a posthumous publication (Kobikisha 1995, 35)—but some of the sonnets proved untranslatable in the end. In *Shi-ni tsuite* [*On Poetry*] (1975), he compared Spenser and Shakespeare and concluded that the former's "Sweet Thames, run softly till I end my song" in the *Epithalamion* cannot be put in any other language, as the beauty of the verse consists in the precise order of these specific English words. Shakespeare's poems, meanwhile, are beautiful not only because of the words used, but because of the feelings and thoughts captured in them. Even so, he could not translate some of the poems. He cited Sonnet 98 as an example.

> From you have I been absent in the spring,
> When proud-pied April (dressed in all his trim)
> Hath put a spirit of youth in every thing,
> That heavy Saturn laughed and leapt with him.
> Yet nor the lays of birds, nor the sweet smell
> Of different flowers in odour and in hue,
> Could make me any summer's story tell,
> Or from their proud lap pluck them where they grew.
> Nor did I wonder at the lily's white,
> Nor praise the deep vermilion in the rose;
> They were but sweet, but figures of delight
> Drawn after you, you pattern of all those.
>   Yet seemed it winter still, and, you away,
>   As with your shadow I with these did play.

This was "among the most beautiful sonnets in the sequence," but was ultimately not translatable, for "all the words are mundane in themselves and lacking in character, and white lilies and red roses are so hackneyed by overuse in Japan and would give a wrong impression of the original poetry" (12:357–359).[7] As a result, Yoshida omitted from his

---

[6] The sonnets in Yoshida's anthology are: 18, 20, 21, 22, 23, 24, 25, 27, 28, 29, 30, 32, 33, 34, 35, 42, 43, 44, 48, 55, 64, 71, 81, 87, 90, 91, 93, 96, 107, 110, 127, 129, 130, 132, 133, 134,137, 138, 144, 147, 149, 150, 152.

[7] See also "Eigo-to eibungaku" ["English and English Literature"] (1957), 9:166–67, where Yoshida observed that the beauty of Sonnet 98 consisted in the specific arrangements of the specific English words in the 14 lines.

selection such obvious "anthology pieces" as Sonnets 60 ("Like as the waves make towards the pebbled shore..."), 94 ("They that have power to hurt and will do none..."), and 116 ("Let me not to the marriage of true minds...").

While using the most generic 私 (*watashi*) to translate the "I" of the *Sonnets*, Yoshida used two different second personal pronouns to reflect his views on the young man and the dark woman. Japanese has many second personal pronouns conveying the gender and social status of the addressee, levels of formality, and psychological distance. Yoshida used 君 (*kimi*) to translate both "thou" and "you" in the first sub-sequence.[8] *Kimi* is used mainly by men to address a male peer or someone of lower status. It can sound rude and presumptuous when used with elders, superiors, or strangers. Yoshida's predecessor, Shoyo Tsubouchi, who translated all the sonnets in 1928, mixed *kimi* with the more reverential 御身(*onmi*) and polite 我君(*wagimi*) to match poetical contexts. For Yoshida, the addressee of the first sub-sequence was primarily the poet's younger friend and lover, rather than a social superior. It was probably no accident that his anthology omitted poems that depict the two characters as a feudalistic master and his vassal, as in Sonnets 26 ("Lord of my love..."), 57 ("Being your slave..."), and 58 ("That god forbid, that made me first your slave..."). Yoshida's "democratic" rendering of the relations between the two male characters would be passed down to later translators, including poet Junzaburo Nishiwaki (1967), Nobutaro Nakanishi (1976), Yuichi Takamatsu (1986), and Yushi Odashima (1994), who likewise used 君or きみ(which is *kimi* in hiragana characters) or more neutral あなた(*anata*).

Meanwhile, Yoshida's understanding of the dark woman was openly misogynistic. While idealizing Shakespeare's deep love (as opposed to mere friendship) for the young man, Yoshida saw a damning disgrace in the poet's relationship with the dark woman and described it by using such words as "inferno," "darkness," and "filth" (1:293, 6:343, 14:253). Reflecting his view of the woman, he consistently used お前 (*omae*) to translate the second person pronoun in Sonnets 127–54. *Omae* is used

---

[8] As for Shakespeare's use of the second person pronouns, Andrew Gurr (1982) distinguishes between a "literary" singular (thou) and "a more human and social" plural (you) in the first sub-sequence. The "thou" form is used consistently in the second sub-sequence, the only exception being the so-called "Ann Hathaway" sonnet (Sonnet 145).

almost exclusively by men to address someone of equal or lower social standing. It carries an endearing connotation when used inside a close circle of family and friends but insulting and discourteous outside it. Compared with other translators, most of whom used a more neutral *anata* or *kimi*, Yoshida's *omae* in the dark woman sonnets carried a slight derogatory undertone. Takamatsu partly followed Yoshida but used the hiragana form おまえ (*omae*), which has a softer, more affectionate note. By using *kimi* and *omae*, the translator underscored his interpretation of the relations among the poet, the young man, and the dark woman of the *Sonnets*.

THE *SONNETS* AS CONTEMPORARY JAPANESE POETRY

In "Chachiru-to bungaku" ["Churchill and Literature"] (1954), Yoshida reflected on how the Japanese language was disrupted by the Meiji Enlightenment. The rapid Westernization exposed the Japanese to ideas and technologies imported from the US and Europe. To make sense out of them, people learned to use their native tongue in a new way, inventing "a whole new structure" of language use. Traditional everyday speech was distorted and lost as a result. Even after WW2, the Japanese had yet to create a colloquial style suitable for their society (4:59–60). Since the Meiji period, the Ministry of Education had implemented a series of reforms "to craft a modern language appropriate for mass education, literary writing, and social discourse" (Shockey 2016, 303), and in 1946, to align with the policies of the Occupation authorities, the Shigeru Yoshida administration also tried to simplify the writing system by limiting the number of *kanji* taught at schools and introducing a new *kana* usage to align with modern pronunciation.[9] The Prime Minister's son spurned these government-led language reforms.[10] He would resolutely stick to the old-style orthography throughout his life and, in his singleminded pursuits as a Japanese *bunshi*, would develop a highly idiosyncratic style of modern writing. He would even rewrite the whole of *England's Literature* in the new colloquial style in 1963. As novelist Shohei Ooka once

---

[9] See Nanette Gottlieb (1994) for the language reforms after WW2.

[10] Yoshida repeatedly attacked the post-war government's language reforms as inconsistent and irrelevant. See, among others, "Nihongo-ni tsuite" ["On Japanese"] (1958), 7: 379–81; "Kotoba Sonota" ["Words, etc."] (1969), 28:298–301; "Kotoba" ["Words"] (1977), 32:127–28.

observed, translation of English and French literature greatly facilitated Yoshida's experiment with Japanese (Kakuchi 2014, 70). His two renderings of Sonnet 18 aptly illustrate the ambitious language project. The first version in *England's Literature* read (with underlines showing the difference between the two versions):

君を夏の一日にも喩へようか。
君は更に美しく、更に優しい。
心ない風は五月の蕾を散らし、
又夏の期限が余りにも短いのをどうしたらいいか。
烈日の熱気は堪へ難く、
又時にはその黄金の面は雲に遮られる。
如何なる美も美ではなくなる時があり、
辛い目に会うのでなければ自然の変遷に害はれる。
併し君の夏は尽きることがなく、
君の美が褪せることもない。
これら永遠の詩句に君が生きる時、
死は君を己れの影の裡に包んだと言ふことは出来ない。
人間が地上にあって盲にならない間、
君はこれ等の詩句とともに忘れられることはないだらう。

(Yoshida 1949, 11–12)

In this first version, Yoshida's translation was already in modern Japanese (even though his *kanji* and *hiragana* scripts were in the old style). Unlike Sofu Taketomo, who translated the same sonnet by using the 5–7 syllabic metre (Taketomo [1951] 1982), Yoshida's lines did not conform to the metrical patterns of traditional Japanese poetry. In 1955, he opened his *Sonnets* anthology with a new translation of his favourite poem[11]:

---

[11] The orthography in the 1955 anthology was modernized very probably by the editor of the book. Yoshida himself followed the old usage throughout his life.

君を夏の一日に喩えようか。
君は更に美しくて、更に優しい。
心ない風は五月の蕾を散らし、
又、夏の期限が余りにも短いのを何とすればいいのか。
太陽の熱気は時には堪え難くて、
その黄金の面を遮る雲もある。
そしてどんなに美しいものもいつも美しくはなくて、
偶然の出来事や自然の変化に傷つけられる。
しかし君の夏が過ぎることはなくて、
君の美しさが褪せることもない。
この数行によって君は永遠に生きて、
死はその暗い世界を君がさ迷っていると得意げに言うことは出来ない。
人間が地上にあって盲にならない間、
この数行は読まれて、君に生命を与える。

(Yoshida 1955, 173)

Yoshida modified postpositional particles so that the new quatrains make up a rhyme scheme of ABBA CDCD CECE.[12] He also replaced such literary idioms as " 烈日" (scintillating sunray; "the eye of heaven" in line 5), " 変遷" (alteration; "changing course" in line 8), and " これ等の詩句" (these verses; "this" in line 14), with more common " 太陽" (the sun), " 変化" (change), and " 数行" (lines). Lines 7 and 8 were revised wholesale. While replacing antiquated idioms with more contemporary ones, Yoshida changed the abstract term " 美" (beauty), with " 美しいもの" (beautiful things). By reinterpreting the "fair" in the original ("And every fair from fair sometime declines") as a fair person or thing rather than as intangible fairness, the translator provided the Japanese version with concrete reality and immediacy.

Yoshida's *Sonnets* anthology influenced two important contemporary poets. In 1980, Hiroshi Yoshino (1926–2014) published a guide to contemporary poetry, analysing how some of his favourite poems were composed and explaining the thematic, lexical, and phonetic components that touched his heart. He devoted two chapters to Yoshida's *Sonnets* and studied the poetic subjectivity and human relations inscribed in the love poems. Particularly noteworthy is the title of Yoshino's book: *Gendaishi*

---

[12] I owe this observation to Nahoko Miyamoto Alvey. Other pieces in the 1955 collection were unrhymed.

nyumon [*An Introduction to Contemporary Poetry*]. Thanks to Yoshida's translation, the Elizabethan sonnets were assimilated into Japanese contemporary poetry.

Shuntaro Tanikawa (1931–), the star poet in Japan since the early 1950s, also acknowledges his indebtedness to Yoshida's *Sonnets*. Tanikawa does not usually like poems in translation, but the *Sonnets* anthology, alongside Toyoki Ogasawara's rendition of Jacques Prévert, was an exception: "I was naturally impressed by the earnestness and ingenuity of Shakespeare's poetic expression but more importantly, I was attracted to the rhythm of Yoshida's colloquial Japanese." After quoting Sonnet 81, Tanikawa observed that the "sinuous and interminable" flow of the verse was attributable to the translator, rather than to the poet, and that the translation had "a unique tonality: the Japanese version is not in rhyme, but it is musical nonetheless." Tanikawa even penned several poems, including "*Sheikusupia-no ato-ni*" ["After Shakespeare"] (1975), by "consciously imitating Yoshida's style" (Tanikawa 1981). The testimonies of these two distinguished poets show that, through translation, the Pauper Prince created a new language for contemporary Japanese poetry. Yoshida may have bidden farewell to English studies at age 18, but Shakespeare's *Sonnets* formed an integral part of the *bunshi*'s contribution to Japanese literature.

Acknowledgements I should like to thank Ann Thompson, Matthew Hanley, and Nahoko Miyamoto Alvey for kindly reading and commenting on an earlier version of this essay. I am grateful to Tetsuo Kishi, Hisaaki Yamanouchi, and Yuji Kaneko for their helpful suggestions concerning the final version. All the remaining errors are mine.

References

Gottlieb, Nanette. 1994. "Language and Politics: The Reversal of Postwar Script Reform Policy in Japan." *The Journal of Asian Studies* 53, no. 4: 1175–98. https://doi.org/10.2307/2059238.

Gurr, Andrew. 1982. "You and Thou in Shakespeare's *Sonnets.*" *Essays in Criticism* 32 (1): 9–25.

Kakuchi, Yukio. 2014. *Kenburijji gaeri-no bunshi* [*A Bunshi from Cambridge*]. Tokyo: Shinchosha.

Kobikisha, ed. 1995. *Yoshida Ken'ichi*. Tokyo: Shinchosha.

Moréas, Jean [1886] n.d. "Symbolist Manifesto." Translated by C. Liszt. Accessed 11 November 2021. https://enjoymutable.com/home/thesymbol istmanifesto.

Morita, Norimasa. 2007. "Yoshida Ken'ichi (1912–77)." Vol. 6. *Britain and Japan: Biographical Portraits*. 9 vols. 224–35. Folkestone: Global Oriental.

Shakespeare, William. 2002. *The Complete Sonnets and Poems*. Edited by Colin Burrow. Oxford: Oxford University Press.

Shockey, Nathan. 2016. "Toward a New Word Order: Early Twentieth Century Orthographic Reform and Its Discontents." *Japanese Language and Literature* 50, no. 2: 303–45. http://www.jstor.org/stable/24892015.

Takamatsu, Yuichi. 1994. "Commentary." In Yoshida 1994, 249–56.

Taketomo, Sofu. [1951] 1982. *Houonrin* [Houon Collection]. Vol. 1. *Taketomo Sofu Senshu* [Selected Works of Sofu Taketomo]. 2 vols. Edited by Fujii Haruhiko. Tokyo: Nan'undo.

Tanikawa, Shuntaro. 1981. "Tegami-no kotonado" ["On a Letter from Mr. Yoshida"]. In a newsletter attached to vol. 31 of Yoshida 1978–81.

The Albion Club. 1949. "Arubiyon kurabu souritsu-no shushi" ["The Albion Club Manifesto"]. *The Albion* 1, no. 1: n.p.

Tsutsumi, Shiro. 1996. "Sengo 50-nen: gendai Nihon-no shakai shinri" ["Fifty Years After WW2: Social Psychology of Contemporary Japan"]. *Meisei University Research Bulletin of Sociology* 16 (March): 53–66.

Yoshida, Akiko. 2013. *Chichi Yoshida Kenichi* [My Father, Ken'ichi Yoshida]. Tokyo: Kawadeshobo shinsha.

Yoshida, Ken'ichi. 1949. *Eikoku-no Bungaku* [England's Literature]. Tokyo: Ondori-sha.

———. 1954. *Saisho onzoshi hinkyusu* [The Prime Minister's Son—In Reduced Circumstances]. Tokyo: Bungeishunju shinsha.

———. 1955. *Juyongyo-shi* [The Sonnets]. Vol. 1. *Sekai Shijin Zenshu* [Poems of the World]. 24 vols. 173–85. Tokyo: Kawadeshobo.

———. 1978–81. *Yoshida Ken'ichi chosaku-shu* [The Collected Works of Ken'ichi Yoshida]. 32 vols. Tokyo: Shueisha.

———. 1994. *Eikoku-no bungaku* [England's Literature]. Tokyo: Iwanami shoten.

———. 2007. *Rondon-no aji* [London Flavours]. Edited by Yuko Shimauchi. Tokyo: Kodansha.

———. 2014. *Eikoku-no seinen* [Youths of England]. Edited by Yuko Shimauchi. Tokyo: Kodansha.

Yoshino, Hiroshi. 1980. *Gendaishi nyumon* [An Introduction to Contemporary Poetry]. Tokyo: Seidosha.

CHAPTER 10

Translational Agency in Liang Shiqiu's Vernacular Sonnets

Alexa Alice Joubin

Literary translations appeal to readers by virtue of echoes they evoke between cultures, because translations work with, rather than work out of, the space between languages. Translation exposes the fundamental instability of languages as systems of communication by drawing attention to shifting meanings of words or cognates, as Michael Saenger has theorized (3–5). Translations can, on the one hand, erase difference, and, on the other hand, *recognize* difference, with an eye toward equality. An example of this type of contemporary translational agency is Paul Edmondson and Stanley Wells' paraphrase of the sonnets in their recent collection *All the Sonnets of Shakespeare*. Their prose "translation," found in a section entitled "literal paraphrases" in the appendices, highlights the many ambiguities, from the gender of the addressee to semantic meanings, in the sonnets (233–290). The translator's agency, rather than superficial compatibilities between languages, has led to the phenomenon

A. A. Joubin (✉)
George Washington University, Washington, DC, USA
e-mail: ajoubin@gwu.edu

© The Author(s), under exclusive license to Springer Nature Switzerland AG 2023
J. Kingsley-Smith and W. R. Rampone Jr. (eds.), *Shakespeare's Global Sonnets*, Global Shakespeares, https://doi.org/10.1007/978-3-031-09472-9_10

of modernization of literary meanings. As André Lefevere's study shows, literary translation primarily serves nonprofessional readers who cannot, or choose not to, access the source text (14). In this context, the translational agency is one of artistic creation rather than reproduction of semantics or musicality. The translational agency emerges from an artist's negotiation with the powers that be—political, cultural, poetic. Translators confront various forms of linguistic and cultural otherness and produce just enough familiarity to engage their readers while preserving part of that otherness.

Like Virginia Woolf's 1928 novel *Orlando: A Biography*, the autobiographical and ambiguous nature of *Shake-speares Sonnets: Never before Imprinted* (1609) challenges the binaries between genders and between the vernacular and the literary across history. Many themes in the sonnets, including their addressees, remain open for interpretation. Over the centuries and around the world, translators have taken up this challenge. Some have turned the poems into expressions of humanism, as is the case of Taiwanese essayist and lexicographer Liang Shiqiu's (1903–1987) translation.[1]

Taking a cue from what Susan Bassnett calls the cultural turn in translation studies and the translation turn in cultural studies (123–140), I consider the linguistic and cultural aspects of translational agency by examining both textual and extratextual materials. In the process, I attend not only to word choice but also to literary patronage as well as the translator's own rationale for the project, for, as Lawrence Venuti notes, "every step in the translation process—from the selection of foreign texts to the editing ... and reading of translations—is mediated by the diverse cultural values that circulate in the target language ... in some hierarchical order" (308). This chapter close-reads Liang's annotated translations of the *Sonnets* within the contexts of his stated rationale and of early and mid-twentieth-century historical contexts. To highlight Liang's translational agency, I also offer comparative analyses of his translations and those of his contemporaries.

---

[1] Liang is his last name. East Asian names appear in the order of family name followed by given name, in respect of East Asian customs, except when they are more familiar inverted (for instance, scholars who publish in English). I adopt the pinyin romanization system for Chinese.

THE POLITICS OF VERNACULAR TRANSLATION

Widely known in the Sinophone world as the first and, so far, the only person to have single-handedly translated and annotated all of Shakespeare's plays, poems, and sonnets into modern vernacular Mandarin Chinese, Liang Shiqiu uses translations of the Western canon to promote the written vernacular (*baihua wen*, or "written colloquial language") during a time when classical Chinese was regarded as the preferred vehicle for literature, especially the translation of canonical, pre-modern foreign literature.

It is valuable for global Shakespeare studies to attend to ideological and sonic differences in translations into languages far removed from European languages, such as the Mandarin vernacular being created and championed by Liang. The challenges he faced are distinct from those confronted by his European peers, because European languages share "patterns of sound-symbolism" with English. Linguist Stephen Ullmann identifies these patterns in the following examples:

> Verbs for snoring in many languages contain an /r/ sound (English *snore*, German *schnarchen*, Dutch *snorken*, Latin *stertere*, French *ronfler*, Spanish *roncar*, Russian *chrapét'*, Hungarian *horkolni*, etc.), and those for whispering an /s/, /ʃ/ or /tʃ/ (English *whisper*, German *wispern* and *flüstern*, Norwegian *hviske*, Latin *susurrare*, French *chuchoter*, Spanish *cuchichear*, Russian *sheptát*, Hungarian *súgni, susogni, suttogni*, etc.). (69)

The sonic and semantic differences between Chinese and Anglo-European languages, for Liang, create linguistic and cultural opportunities in enriching the vernacular and articulating anew poetic sensibilities for both Liang's and Shakespeare's works.

Liang's translational agency emerges from the island republic's history of art patronage and immigration. Historically, Taiwan has been open to elements from different cultures, partly through colonization and partly through international trade.[2] An island off the southeast coast of China, Taiwan has had complex relationships with the dominant Mandarin-Chinese culture across the strait and with Japan to the north. It was first colonized by the Dutch (1624–1661), before being partially governed by

---

[2] For a compelling history of Taiwan in relation to Chinese modernity, see Spence, 46–49 and 51–57.

Zheng Chenggong (known as Koxinga in Europe) from 1661 to 1683 who is best known as the pirate-turned-general who defeated the Dutch colonizers and reclaimed, on behalf of the Chinese Ming dynasty, Taiwan as a territory. The Chinese Qing imperial court took over Taiwan from 1683 to 1895. After China's defeat in the Sino-Japanese War in 1895, Taiwan was ceded to Japan for fifty years. As a result, Japanese forces colonized Taiwan and mandated education in the Japanese language for residents of the island. At the end of World War II in 1945, the Japanese forces in Taiwan surrendered to the government of the Republic of China, known as the Kuomintang Nationalist government.

Currently, some of the main languages spoken on the island are Mandarin, Taiwanese, Hakka, Japanese, and the indigenous Formosan languages. The version of Mandarin used in Taiwan differs from that in China in writing system, pronunciation, and vocabulary. Mandarin in Taiwan (Guoyu), for example, is characterized by its traditional, complex-character writing system (rather than simplified Chinese script). The Standard Mandarin (Putonghua), in use in China, features the frequent addition of a final -r sound to a syllable (known as *erhua* accent). Both versions of Mandarin have four pitched tones. Meanwhile, Taiwanese, an octatonic dialect that exists primarily in oral form, shares linguistic features with Southern Min, the tonal dialect spoken in China's Fujian province as well as parts of Southeast Asia, such as Singapore. Mandarin speakers in Taiwan and China—despite their distinctive vocabularies—are mutually intelligible, but not speakers of Taiwanese and Mandarin. The multilingual, immigrant society of Taiwan influenced Liang's decision to further promote Taiwan's Mandarin vernacular, written in traditional characters, rather than translating Western works into classical Chinese or publishing in the simplified Chinese script that was promoted by the Communist Party in China.

Liang's agenda is twofold. On one hand, he believes in the role of translation in extending the life of the canon. From Liang's perspective, his translational agency is shaped by the moral responsibility of giving his readers access to what he deems world-class literature. On the other hand, he is invested in enriching the modern Mandarin vernacular, a new form he promotes through the translation of pre-modern English litera-ture. In an essay on the sonnet, he championed his perceived connections between Shakespeare's sonnets and his moralist intentions by quoting from William Wordsworth's poem ("an advocate of vernacular literature") in praise of the sonnets (1964: 197):

Scorn not the Sonnet; Critic, you have frown'd,
Mindless of its just honours; with this key
Shakespeare unlock'd his heart; the melody
Of this small lute gave ease to Petrarch's wound.

Literary translation, for Liang, is both an artistic endeavor and a form of cross-cultural labor to give new life to the vernacular and to extend the afterlife of Shakespeare. A translator's role is to select the best poetry and reproduce its beauty, for literature is the product of "a few geniuses" rather than the masses (1987, 2: 204–205).

Guided by these principles, Liang produced a copiously annotated translation of the sonnets. His translation is enhanced by reproduced illustrations from Charles and Mary Cowden Clarke's nineteenth-century edition. Some notes provide criticism and interpretation, while others unpack words or expressions to supply meanings the translation is unable to contain.

LITERARY PATRONAGE

Born in Beijing in 1903, Liang relocated to Taipei in 1949 when Chiang Kai-shek's central government of the "Republic of China" moved to Taiwan and when Mao Zedong's army took over China and established the People's Republic of China. Liang's relocation to Taiwan was also spurred by fierce attacks on his work by leftist Chinese writer, Lu Xun (the penname of Zhou Shuren, 1881–1936), who called Liang "a homeless dog [*sang jia gou*] serving capitalists" (qtd. Bai 166).[3] In the China of the 1940s, Liang was derided as a bourgeois and elitist writer due to his preference for literary genres and subject matters far removed from the "revolution" and his rejection of the politicization of literature.[4] It is the subject matter, rather than his preference for the vernacular, that made Liang a "bourgeois" writer who keeps his distance from the causes of the revolution.

His relocation to Taiwan was a pivotal turning point for his ambitious translation project. Having escaped the tumultuous Cultural Revolution

---

[3] Unless otherwise noted, all translations from Chinese and German back into English are my own. On the severity of the pejorative phrase "homeless dog," see Li (2010).

[4] For a succinct account of Lu Xun's criticism of the bourgeois and elitist tendency of Liang Shiqiu and the Crescent Moon Society, see Wong (2008).

(1966–1976), where foreign works, including those by Shakespeare, were banned, and having been ostracized from the Chinese literary circle, Liang worked steadily and persistently on his translation of Shakespeare in the relatively stable political environment of Taiwan. Part of Liang's unarticulated agenda was to revitalize the Mandarin vernacular in the traditional script and distance it from the language, in simplified characters, used in the People's Republic of China which increasingly incorporates Soviet-inspired neologism (Chen 2015; Hsia 1956) and "proletarian" vocabulary such as *gàn* (to do, to make, to kill; also refers to sexual intercourse) and *tóngzhì* (comrades, referring to one's lovers as well as coworkers, supervisors, friends, family). Liang translates the sonnets into a distinctively non-Communist vernacular.

Translating all of Shakespeare's writing was a monumental task that occupied Liang from 1930 to 1967. A large majority of his project was completed after he took up residency in Taiwan, having fled the wars from China under the patronage of influential philosopher Hu Shi (1891–1962). Hu Shi initiated the vernacular movement known as *baihua wen yundong* in 1917. The campaign called for the government, educational establishments, writers, and public media to adopt the modern vernacular. Among the eight principles proposed by Hu are the elimination of "old clichés," an aversion to using couplets, and the intentional use of popular expressions (357–360), all of which are reflected by Liang's translation of the sonnets. Hu also played a key role in the completion of Liang's translation. Liang wrote that "even though Mr. Hu did not possess in-depth knowledge about Shakespeare, he knew the importance of translating Shakespeare and made all the arrangements. Without his enthusiastic support, I would not have taken the path less traveled" (1970: 98). Hu was himself a major supporter of the vernacular movement of the time, and, under Hu's patronage, it comes as no surprise that Liang opted to render the sonnets in vernacular prose. In a time when the Chinese Communist Party was taking over China with Soviet-Marxist ideologies, Liang promoted what he saw as humanist values associated with Shakespeare as a countermeasure.

In 1930, while chairing the translation committee of the China Foundation for the Promotion of Education and Culture, Hu Shi invited five scholars—Liang Shiqiu, Wen Yiduo, Xu Zhimo, Ye Gongchao, and Chen Tongbo—to translate and produce a definitive edition (*dingben*) of all of Shakespeare's works. Having earned a PhD from Columbia University and served as China's ambassador to the United States (1938–1942) and President of the Academia Sinica, Hu was one of the most influential public men of letters in modern China (Chiang 2004). His pursuit of definitive editions of the Western canon was informed by his role in China's modernization movement and his position as a purveyor of Western knowledge within East Asia. Detailed plans were made by Hu, including style ("we shall experiment with verse and prose before deciding on the best approach to translate the texts") and compensation ("the highest possible stipend will be offered, because this collection will sell" (Liang 1970: 94). As part of the "discovery by experiment" scheme, Hu commissioned Wen and Xu to translate Shakespeare into verse, and Liang and Chen to translate the same texts into vernacular prose.

By 1931, it had been decided that only the written vernacular would be used in the translation, that annotations should be added where necessary, and that all proper names should be transliterated into the Chinese script following standard Mandarin pronunciations (e.g., Shakespeare as Shashibiya) rather than translated semantically (e.g., Mistress Overdone as Gan Guotou [Trying Too Hard]). One drawback is that Anglo-European personal names can become long and unwieldy in Chinese, because Chinese names are commonly only two to three syllables in length. Since Chinese is a monosyllabic language, a name of six syllables (first and last names) will require at least six characters. As it turned out, due to the ongoing wars, Liang was the sole person in the group to complete the work. The large-scale team project fell apart, and eventually Liang single-handedly completed the translation of all of Shakespeare's works.

Liang became a major figure in cross-cultural exchange in Taiwan. Shakespeare's sonnets have not been as popular as his tragedies and comedies there. As Liang himself readily acknowledged, there were few satisfactory translations of the sonnets. "Among the genres of poetry, essay, novel, and drama," wrote Liang, "poetry is the most difficult to translate, especially from English into a language as distant as Chinese." Mandarin prosody is based on changes in pitch as well as in accent of the written character. He reasoned that because "the language of poetry is refined, allusive, subtle, and elusive, it is very hard to reproduce all of the aspects that constitute the experience of poetry" (1987, 2: 200–201). He does not wish to translate suggestive language into explicit declarations of intent, and believes that, to the extent possible, one has to attend to rhyme, rhythm, and form. Liang has played an important role in expanding local readership of the sonnets and helped add the sonnets to the curriculum. His translation of *The Complete Works* has been a staple in the classroom since the mid-twentieth century.

In terms of poetic forms, Liang's choice in his translation stands out among his peers. The early modern sonnet is commonly known in Chinese as "fourteen-lined poetry," which emphasizes the genre's formalistic feature above all else. Liang opted for rhymed prose to reproduce the metric form of ABAB/CDCD/EFEF/and GG, as in, for instance, lines ending with the words shengyù (to give birth)/bùxiǔ (immortal) and siqù (to die)/fengliú (merry) in Liang's translation of the first 4 lines of sonnet 1. The lines in Liang's translation, however, have varying numbers of Chinese characters and syllables. The final words in each line, when possible, may share the same vowel and/or tonality, but Liang does not adhere to strictly defined rules of meter.

In contrast, other translators, such as Yu Erchang (1903–1984), another scholar who moved to Taiwan in 1949 and exerted a great deal of influence on Taiwan's Shakespeare studies, translated the sonnets using the heptasyllabic verse (*qiyan shi*), a poetic form that emphasizes even tonality, parallelism, and antithesis. Insisting on fidelity to the original form, Yu used the seven-syllabic format which was perceived to hold the same cachet and prestige in the Chinese literary tradition since the eighth century as the sonnet did in the Renaissance. Each line has the same number (7) of Chinese characters and syllables. Based on the Arden edition, Yu's translation appeared in an English-Chinese facing-page bilingual edition in 1961. Yu recreates a historical distance for his readers, while Liang attempts to modernize the sonnets for the mid-twentieth century. Yu contended that most Chinese translations of the sonnets no longer feel poetic, as "they are at most prose interpretations of the sonnets and read like essays, which has done great injustice to Shakespeare" (1996: 1–5). Yu's translation features fourteen lines with the same number of written Chinese characters (seven in each line) and the same rhyming scheme as Shakespeare's sonnets.

Yu gave priority to diction and classical allusions, while Liang believed it more efficient and accurate to translate the sonnets in rhymed prose with jagged lines. The pleasure afforded by translation lies in the alternating revelation and concealment of the shifting meanings of the sonnets.

Unique Feature: Annotations

Few East Asian translations of Western works come with such copious notes. Liang's translation features lengthy annotations that elaborate upon the meanings that could not be adequately rendered. Liang reiterated his principles in an essay entitled "A Translator's Tenet":

> A good translator should avoid awkward expressions or patterns in the target language. Avoid literal translation at all cost. Annotate all allusions and difficult phrases. Provide sources of citations from authoritative studies in the notes. (qtd. Wu 1998: 51)

There are several instances where Liang admits to not being able to find better words in Mandarin or not being able to fully convey the meanings of the sonnets without interrupting the rhythmic flow of the lines. In a note on the word "conquest" in the last line of sonnet 6 ("Be not self-willed, for thou art much too fair/To be death's conquest and make worms thine heir"), Liang explains that "'conquest' does not refer to possessions acquired by brute force" (which is what the reader would assume from his translation, *qiangzhan,* acquisition by force) but instead, as the *Oxford English Dictionary* states, to "the personal acquisition of real estate with any means other than by inheritance" (1985, 12: 29).

Liang's patron played a role in his decision to add the annotations. While annotations are a staple feature of Liang's translation, his initial plan was to render the *Sonnets* enjoyable by Mandarin-speaking readers without having to refer to notes. As he wrote in his memoir: "I wanted my translation to be readable and enjoyable without any notes. Therefore, I started out without annotation. As I progressed, Hu Shi urged me to annotate key features or passages. Eventually I developed a great interest in annotating everything" (1970: 110).

Liang Shiqiu's Humanist Agenda and Translational Agency

Liang's humanist agenda drives his translational agency. Liang was influenced by Irving Babbitt's New Humanism, as he studied under Babbitt at Harvard University. In an article in the June 1928 issue of *Crescent Moon*, Liang went against the class-based view of literature of his time to contend that "human nature" should be "the sole standard for measuring literature" (1996: 310). As a humanist, Liang was interested in the universal literary experience and its artistic rather than political function. For example, in his note to the first sonnet, Liang draws on the allegory of poetry as a vehicle for immortality. He writes:

> Sonnets 1-17 form a self-contained unit dedicated to a young man. The sonnets revolve around the narrator's plea to the young man to get married and have offspring to carry on his beauty. This thought is not unusual, for any middle-aged person, having seen the contingency of life, will realize that only procreation will extend one's blood line. (1985, 12: 182)

His note glosses over the question of the speaker's affective feelings toward the young man. Without mentioning self-censorship, he does acknowledge that Shakespeare's texts are full of "profanity" and indecency, and states that he will convey Shakespearean impropriety to the best of his ability.

Liang derives his moralistic view from the first sonnet cycle in Shakespeare's collection, regarded as "ethically complex and narratively diffuse" (Schoenfeldt 2007: 129). The first sonnet declares: "From fairest creatures we desire increase / That thereby beauty's rose might never die." The convention of extolling idealized chaste women established by Sir Philip Sidney and Edmund Spenser in the previous decade is appropriated here to urge a young aristocratic man to "pity the world" and procreate so that his "tender heir" will "bear his memory" and carry on his beauty beyond the cruelty of time. Perceiving these lines to be evidence of the moral burden of literature, Liang takes to translating Shakespeare's sonnets, "the best poetry in the world that has withstood the test of time," arguing that if one drinks anything at all, one should "drink only first-rate tea and wine," and if one wishes to read anything, one would do well to read only the classics (1987, 2: 204).

Liang is influenced by Babbit as well as the Victorian poet Matthew Arnold, who pronounced unequivocally in 1869 that great works of art embody "the best which has been thought and said in the world" (viii). The moralist idea of literature's socially reparative value, which Liang subscribes to, has a long history, though reparative interpretations of the canon have taken many different forms. In the twenty-first century, Martha Nussbaum has written extensively about how literature makes readers better people by enabling the good life of self-reflection (32–34). Some artists are invested in offering a corrective to the canon to promote social justice. They reclaim the classics from ideologies associated with colonial and patriarchal practices. Other artists such as Liang, in contrast, draw on the canon's authority to "repair" and renovate performance genres, poetic expressions, and the vernacular. Liang uses the sonnets to claim cultural merit for the vernacular.

The Vernacular *Sonnets*

To elevate the status of the vernacular, both Liang and his patron emphasize its utilitarian value. They demonstrate its value by translating Shakespeare into the Mandarin vernacular with modern punctuation—which is absent in classical Chinese. Liang's project bears nationalist significance, since the Mandarin vernacular also operates as a lingua franca across the Sinophone world and within the Chinese diaspora. Educated speakers of different versions of modern Mandarin (in China and Taiwan) and dialects (such as Taiwanese, Southern Min, Hakka) can all read written Mandarin in some form. Since Liang opposed the Communist rule of China and the Beijing government's adoption of simplified Chinese characters as the People's Republic of China's official writing system (Tsu 214), he published his translations in the traditional script known as the complex-character writing system which has been in use since the second century CE. It should be noted that the simplified writing system is also in use in Malaysia and Singapore, while the traditional script is widely adopted in Taiwan, Hong Kong, Macau, and the Sinophone diaspora. Throughout his illustrious career, Liang never explicitly stated his political stance regarding an independent Taiwan, but his decision to publish in the traditional script suggests his intention to enhance the vitality of the Mandarin vernacular in Taiwan as a form of cultural expression. Literary translation, therefore, is not merely a vehicle of communication but also a tool to renovate Chinese literary forms. Examples below reveal how Liang achieves this, and how his versions contrast with those produced by his peers.

Based on the 1943 reprint of W. J. Craig's Oxford edition, Liang's annotated translations of the *Sonnets* gloss over what he considers unpalatable sexual references. The translation also brushes aside the (then sensitive) question of a male speaker asking a young man to reproduce in sonnets 1–17. Since gendered pronouns are sometimes interchangeable in the Chinese language, with the contexts determining the exact meanings of the pronouns (Iljic), Liang glossed over a male speaker's praises of the beauty of a young man. In other instances, Liang avoided assigning male or female identities to a speaker in the poems. In his translation of the first sonnet, for instance, he uses the neutral term *zuimei de ren* (the most beauteous person) for "fairest creatures." It is notable that Liang translates "fair" elsewhere with different vernacular phrases beyond "beautiful." Likewise, the word "blood" in the final line of sonnet 2 is translated by Liang simply as blood, with a subtle hint at the significance of "blood line" (sonnet 2: "... see thy blood warm when thou feel'st it cold").

Liang's gender-neutral choice stands in stark contrast to the translation by Gu Zhengkun, director of the Institute of World Literature at Beijing Foreign Studies University, as semen and sexual desire ("when your semen is devitalized and blood vessels have turned cold, you can reignite their warmth through the body of your offspring"). Gu's footnote explains his masculinist reading by emphasizing male desire as the primary force of procreation: "This line refers to familial blood line as well as semen" (161 and 258n.11). In other instances, Liang seems to bend backward to ensure heterosexual themes. He translates "if thou thyself deceivest / By wilful taste of what thyself refusest" in sonnet 40 into something oddly specific in terms of gender and interpersonal relationships: "if you lower yourself to mingle with a woman whom you do not love." The "gentle thief" in the next line takes on a moralistic tone: "promiscuous robber." While Liang pursued a vernacular translation with a conservative agenda, his version turns out to be ahead of his time, as the revisionist approaches of Paul Edmondson and Stanley Wells demonstrate that the addressees in many sonnets cannot always be gendered because the context is fluid and ambiguous (27).

Liang has indeed enriched the vernacular by drawing on intuitive and subtle distinctions between various expressions in Chinese. For example, he translated the word "fair" in sonnet 127 ("In the old age black was not counted fair, / Or if it were it bore not beauty's name") as *biaozhi* (comely or good-looking) and the word "beauty" as *mei* (aesthetically beautiful). In classical texts, the word *biaozhi* often refers to the attractiveness of female facial features. As such, it is more clearly gendered than *mei* (beauty in the metaphysical sense). The word *mei* circulates more widely in the vernacular—both written and spoken—but the somewhat more literary *biaozhi* was introduced into the vernacular by Liang and eventually became part of the modern vernacular. Liang's work reflects the phenomenon noted by Umberto Eco, that literary translation tends to "modernize the source to some extent" by building in new relevance of the work to contemporary readers (22). Plays such as *Hamlet*, as I have examined elsewhere, have the potential to become a more politically charged work or to be used as a platform to discuss sensitive topics (2021). Liang's sonnets, while they still thematize love, are a vehicle for the promotion of the vernacular.

While his contemporaries opted for the metaphorical in their translations, Liang favored a more colloquial vocabulary. For example, the "eye of heaven" in sonnet 18 is rendered as a giant eye in the sky (*tiankong zhi juyan*) by Cao Minglun (1995) and heavenly eye (*tianyan*) by Ruan Kun (2001). Liang simply translated it as the sun (*taiyang*) without any flourishes, for more immediate impact on his readers.

Liang's translational agency is evident in his word choices and transformation of the sonnets into vernacular prose, a bold move in his time. It is ironic that Liang was accused of being an elitist in China when he approaches the sonnets with such plain, vernacular language. For instance, he evokes the idea of a court session where a defendant recalls his memories in sonnet 30: "When to the sessions of sweet silent thought/ I summon up remembrance of things past." Sonnets 30 and 31 are a pair of melancholic sonnets that recall loved ones who are no longer there. The somber tone of sonnet 30 is accentuated by words with voiceless sibilants, such as "sessions," "sweet," "silent," "summon," and "past." Together with words with voiced sibilants such as "things," the sonnet offers sonic echoes of its sorrowful themes (Zhou 76–77). Edmondson and Wells interpret the idea of "session" as "happy and peaceful contemplation" in their paraphrasing, though they do gloss the word as "(court) sittings" (156, 266). In contrast, Liang renders this couplet as a scene in a court: "As I summon memories of past events, I arrive in the court (*gongtang*) of sweet, silenced thoughts." *Gongtang* often comes with negative connotations, as in the expression "legal confrontation" (*dui bu gongtang*, to accuse someone in a public courtroom or to take someone to court).

Liang's interpretations and translations of the sonnets have been influential on subsequent translators; for example, his successors ended up adopting the idea of *gongtang* (court of law) in their translations. Cao Minglun renders the lines with an element of legal judgment as "Whenever I summon dusty memories to the public court that judges meditative thoughts" (1995), while Liang Zongdai (not related to Liang Shiqiu) makes it explicit that the speaker has been summoned to court, using even more specific legal language: "When I appear in the court of musky (*shex-iang*), pensive thoughts, I summon memories of past events" (1992). Built around the idea of a court sitting, Liang Zongdai's version uses Chinese words with similarly voiceless sibilants to create a similar sonic impression: *shexiang* (musky) and *moxiang* (pensive thoughts). These are but many examples of how one word choice by Liang has influenced subsequent generations of translators who expand upon the seed Liang has sown.

Many translators acknowledge the challenges of translating such loaded words as "fair" in contrast to beauty. Renowned Egyptian playwright Mohamed Enani ponders: "How do you translate both words into Arabic so as to distinguish the sense of beauty denied a dark complexion?" He interprets beauty here as something purely physical ("white skin and blond hair"). This stands in contrast to "fairness" which refers to "the abstract qualities [of] goodness and righteous[ness]; the subjective element [that has] enabled the swarthy face to look ... attractive" (121). Enani, after some soul searching, chose حسناء (*hasnā'*) for "fair" and جمال (*jamāl*, a word derived from camel) for beauty. Likewise, in rendering variegated concepts of "beauty" fluidly relational (from superficially comely to transcendentally beautiful), Liang has expanded the vernacular and enriched the translation's fluctuating relationship to Shakespeare.

Exceptionally in his translations, which are usually full of annotations, Liang does not provide any annotation for *biaozhi* (fair) and *mei* (beauty). This choice most likely reflects Liang's satisfaction with his achievement of vernacular "clarity at a glance" (*yimu liaoran*) in translating this tricky couplet.

Liang's translation of sonnet 90 is another example of his occasional deference to the more immediate impact of vernacular expressions, thereby eschewing verbose annotations. Along with sonnet 89, sonnet 90 addresses the emotions of parting with a friend of unspecified gender. The keywords in the first quatrain are "wilt" and "spite of fortune":

> Then hate me when thou wilt, if ever, now,
> Now while the world is bent my deeds to cross,
> Join with the spite of fortune, make me bow,
> And do not drop in for an after-loss.

The opening line is glossed by Edmondson and Wells as "hate me whenever you will," with a more open timeframe ("whenever" 253). Liang, in
contrast, emphasizes the imperative form in the present ("now") in the
first line: "If you want to hate me, go ahead. If you wish, hate me now."
He continues with a liberal sprinkling of more loaded vocabulary than
sonnet 90:

> Now, right now, when people in the world are bent on beating me and,
> Working hand in hand with the god of fortune, to entrap me and force
> me to bow.
> Do not wait to catch me off guard and torture me in the future. (1985,
> 12:129)

Among the notable new elements Liang has introduced are the god of
fortune (replacing the "spite of fortune"), entrapment, and human foes
and gods working hand in hand against the narrator. He also repeats the
urgent, temporal designator "now" three times. Instead of footnoting the
quatrain, Liang augments the narrator's rhetorical plea ("If you want to
hate me") with the more dramatic situation of being entrapped by gods.

Liang's dramatization inspired Fang Ping (1921–2008), President of
the Chinese Shakespeare Society and honorary member of the Hong
Kong Translation Society. In his translation, Fang introduces the theme
of "career" (*shiye*) while maintaining the imperative in a rhetorical form:

> If you want to hate me, hate me now;
> Take advantage of this moment when people are sabotaging my career,
> To collude with ill fortune to conquer [*zhansheng*] me in battle.
> Do not catch me off guard later when you take sudden action. (257)

Setting Liang's and Fang's versions side by side, it is notable that some key
elements Liang introduced were carried over in Fang's rendition, such as a
tug of war between the narrator and their absent friend and the narrator's
rhetorical plea for the friend to take action now rather than catching them
off guard in the future. The simple imperative in sonnet 90 becomes, in
both Liang's and Fang's translations, a more full-fledged speech.

CONCLUSION

Translations create new communities. The new vernacular community Liang creates echoes the kind of community described by French philosopher Jean-Luc Nancy, a shared community of "being-together" that is defined by its "being-in-common" but not by universal sameness (xxxix). The concept of community can be applied to translation studies to reveal what translations share in common with the translated, namely "the being-in-common, the standing-in-relations between two texts." In expanding the meanings of the Sonnets and the vernacular without subjugating one to the other, Liang renders the otherness in familiar and uncanny forms.

Liang's revolutionary vernacular prose translations have been well received. Zhang Chong, Shakespeare scholar at Fudan University in Shanghai, for instance, praised the contribution of Liang's prose translation: "Prose as a form enables the translator to adjust the length of each line of the sonnet to more fully express cultural, historical, and linguistic subtexts. The sonnets in prose would appeal not only to general readers but also actors and audiences" (70). Reflecting on his decision to transform the sonnets into prose poetry, Liang remains open minded: "While I prioritize prose as a form, I very much support any translator who opts for the poetic form" (qtd. Ke 48). In conclusion, in Liang's sonnets, the form is part of his message.

REFERENCES

Arnold, Matthew, 1869. *Culture and Anarchy: An Essay in Political and Social Criticism*. London: Smith Elder.

Bai, Li-ping, 2001. "Patronage and Translation: Hu Shi's Influence Upon Liang Shiqiu's Translation of Shakespeare's Works [Zanzhu yu fanyi: Hu Shi dui Liang Shiqiu fanyi Shashibiya de yingxiang]," *Chungwai Literary Monthly* 30.7: 159–177.

Bassnett, Susan, 1998. "The Translation Turn in Cultural Studies," *Constructing Cultures: Essays on Literary Translation* , ed. Susan Bassnett and André Lifevere. Bristol PA: Cromwell Press, 123–140.

Cao, Minglun, trans., 1995. *Shakespeare's Sonnets* [Shashibiya shisi hang shi quanji]. Guilin: Lijiang chubanshe.

Chen, Ping, 2015. "Language Reform in Modern China," *The Oxford Handbook of Chinese Linguistics*, ed. William S-Y Wang and Chaofen Sun. Oxford: Oxford University Press, 531–540.

Chiang, Yung-chen, 2004. "Performing Masculinity and the Self: Love, Body, and Privacy in Hu Shi," *The Journal of Asian Studies* 63.2 (May): 305–332.

Eco, Umberto, 2001. *Experiences in Translation*, trans. Alastair McEwen. Toronto: University of Toronto Press.

Edmondson, Paul and Stanley Wells, eds. 2020. *All the Sonnets of Shakespeare*. Cambridge: Cambridge University Press.

Enani, Mohamed, 2016. "On Translating Shakespeare's Sonnets into Arabic," *Critical Survey* 28.3: 119–132.

Fang, Ping, trans., 2014. *The Complete Works of Shakespeare* [Shashibiya quanji], 10 vols. Vol. 10: Poetry. Shanghai: Yiwen chubanshe.

Gu, Zhengkun, trans., 2016. *Shashibiya shi ji* [William Shakespeare's Poems and Sonnet]. Beijing: Foreign Language Teaching and Research Press.

Hsia, Tao-Tai, 1956. "The Language Revolution in Communist China," *Far Eastern Survey* 25.10 (October): 145–154.

Hu, Shi, 1917. "Wenxue gailiang chuyi [A Preliminary Discussion of Literary Reform]," *Xin Qingnian* [*The New Youth*] 2.5 (January 1); English translation in *Sources of Chinese Tradition: From 1600 Through the Twentieth Century*, 2 vols., Vol. 2, ed. Wm. Theodore de Bary and Richard Lufrano. New York: Columbia University Press, 2000, 357–360.

Iljic, Robert, 2005. "Personal Collective in Chinese," *Bulletin of the School of Oriental and African Studies* 68.1: 77–102.

Joubin, Alexa Alice, 2021. "How Translating Shakespeare's Plays Reveals New Ideas—From China to Afghanistan," Interview by CBC-Radio Canada, November 3; https://www.cbc.ca/radio/ideas/how-translating-shakespeare-s-plays-reveals-new-ideas-from-china-to-afghanistan-1.6234629, accessed January 15, 2022.

Ke, Fei, 1998. "Liang Shiqiu on Translating Shakespeare [Liang Shiqiu tan fanyi Shashibiya]," *Foreign Language Education and Research* [Waiyu jiaoxue yu yanjiu] 1: 48.

Lefevere, André, 1992. *Translating Literature: Practice and Theory in a Comparative Literature Context*. New York: The Modern Language Association of America.

Li, Ling, 2010. "The Explanation of 'Sang jia gou' [The Homeless Dog]," *Contemporary Chinese Thought* 41.2: 54–53.

Liang, Shiqiu, 1964. "On the Sonnet [Tan shisi hang shi]," in Liang Shiqiu, *Prejudices* [Pianjian ji]. Taipei: Wenxing shudian. 197.

———, 1970. "On Translating Shakespeare [Guanyu Shashibiya de fanyi]," in Liang, Yu Guangzhong et al., *The Art of Translation* [Fanyi de yishu]. Taipei: Chenzhong chubanshe.

———, 1985. *The Complete Works of Shakespeare* [Shashibiya quanji], 12 vols. Vol. 12. Taipei: Yuandong tushu, 129.

——, 1987. *A Cottager's Sketchbook* [Yashe sanwen], 2 vols. Vol. 2. Taipei: Jiuge chubanshe.

——, 1996. "Literature and Revolution [Wenxue yu geming]," *Crescent Moon* [Xinyue] (June 1928); English translation in Kirk Denton, ed. *Modern Chinese Literary Thought: Writings on Literature, 1893–1945*. Stanford: Stanford University Press.

Liang, Zongdai, trans., 1992. *Shakespeare's Sonnets* [Shashibiya shisi hang shi]. Chengdu: Sichuan renmin chubanshe, 1983; Taipei: Chun wenxue chubanshe, 1992.

Nancy, Jean-Luc, 1991. *The Inoperative Community*, trans. Peter Connor, Lisa Garbus, Michael Holland, and Simona Sawhney. Minneapolis: University of Minnesota Press.

Nussbaum, Martha, 2011. *Creating Capabilities: The Human Development Approach*. Cambridge, MA: The Belknap Press of Harvard University Press.

Ruan, Kun, trans., 2001. *The Sonnets* [Shisi hang shi ji]. Wuhan: Hubei jiaoyu chubanshe.

Saenger, Michael, 2014. Introduction. *Interlinguicity, Internationality, and Shakespeare*, ed. Michael Saenger. Montreal: McGill-Queen's University Press, 3–22.

Schoenfeldt, Michael, 2007. "The Sonnets," in *The Cambridge Companion to Shakespeare's Poetry*, ed. Patrick Cheney. Cambridge: Cambridge University Press, 125–143.

Spence, Jonathan D, 1999. *The Search for Modern China, Second Edition*. New York: W.W. Norton and Company.

Tsu, Jing, 2022. *Kingdom of Characters: The Language Revolution That Made China Modern*. New York: Riverhead.

Ullmann, Stephen, 1964. *Language and Style*. Oxford: Blackwell.

Venuti, Lawrence, 1995. *The Translator's Invisibility*. London: Routledge.

Wong, Lawrence Wang-chi, 2008. "Lions and Tigers in Groups: The Crescent Moon School in Modern Chinese Literary History," in *Literary Societies of Republican China*, ed. Kirk A. Denton and Michel Hockx. Lanham, MD: Lexington, 299–305.

Wu, Xizhen, 1998. "In Memory of Liang Shiqiu [Daonian Liang Shiqiu xiansheng]," *Cultural Celebrities on Liang Shiqiu/Liang Shiqiu on Cultural Celebrities* [Yashe xian weng: Mingren bixia de Liang Shiqiu/Liang Shiqiu bixia de mingren], ed. Liu Yansheng. Shanghai: Dongfang, 51.

Yu, Erchang, 1996. *Shakespeare's Sonnets* [Shisi hang shi]. Taipei: Shijie shuju., 1–5.

Zhang, Chong, 1996. "Verse and Prose Translations of Shakespeare [Shiti he sanwen de Shashibiya]," *Foreign Language* [Weiguo yu] 6: 70.

Zhou, Min, 2013. "Echoing the Musicality of Shakespeare's Sonnets [Yiyi zhi huixiang: Shashibiya shisihang shi yinyue xiaoguo ji qi Han yi]," *Wide Translation* [Guangyi] 9: 67–91.

PART II

Sonnets in Performance: Theatre, Film and Music

CHAPTER 11

Playing the Poems: Five Faces of Shakespeare's Sonnets on Czech Stages

Filip Krajník and David Drozd

It could be seen as a kind of paradox that, although the direct cultural influence between England and the Bohemian Lands (today's Czech Republic) was historically limited, in the course of the nineteenth century William Shakespeare managed to become a firm part of Czech theatrical, literary and political cultures as an adopted national poet. The first crude translations of Shakespeare's plays into Czech appeared in print as early the 1780s and, by the end of the eighteenth century, adaptations of plays such as *Macbeth*, *Hamlet* and *King Lear* were staged in the first provisional Czech playhouse in Prague (the other theatres in the city played exclusively in German), showing off the ability of the Czech language to convey the words and ideas of the great European classics (still filtered through German translations rather than being directly based

F. Krajník (✉) · D. Drozd
Masaryk University, Brno, Czech Republic
e-mail: filip.krajnik@phil.muni.cz

D. Drozd
e-mail: drozd@phil.muni.cz

© The Author(s), under exclusive license to Springer Nature
Switzerland AG 2023
J. Kingsley-Smith and W. R. Rampone Jr. (eds.), *Shakespeare's Global Sonnets*,
Global Shakespeares, https://doi.org/10.1007/978-3-031-09472-9_11

on the English originals) (Drábek 2012, 75–102). By the mid-nineteenth century, Shakespeare had become a symbol of the Czechs' striving first for cultural and, later, political emancipation, with lavish Shakespearean festivities with clear political undertones organised in 1864 and 1916 to commemorate the tercentenary of Shakespeare's birth and death.[1] In this climate, a new collective translation of the entire Shakespeare dramatic canon was also commissioned (published between 1855 and 1872), the first such endeavour in any Slavonic language (Drábek 2012, 121–145).

When the first selection from Shakespeare's sonnets in Czech was printed in 1860, Shakespeare was already a Czech cultural phenomenon through his dramatic works and, as mentioned above, a proxy for expressing Czechs' political positions—a function that he retained for most of the turbulent twentieth century in Eastern Europe. The first effort to present Shakespeare's sonnet sequence in Czech as a whole started in the 1890s, with the preeminent Czech poet, author, playwright and translator Jaroslav Vrchlický (1853–1912) (Vočadlo, 603). Although his attempt remained unfinished (only a handful of sonnets were printed in Vrchlický's lifetime, with a collection of 122 pieces being published posthumously in 1954), it helped both to set the standards for the subsequent translators and to establish the prestigious position of Shakespeare's sonnets in the Czech literary tradition. The translation scholar and translator Stanislav Rubáš maintains that "Czech renditions of both individual sonnets and the entire sequence are an equally essential part of our [Czech] translated literature as Ovid's *Metamorphoses* or Dante's *The Divine Comedy*".[2] To date, nine complete Czech translations have been printed, with several more likely existing in manuscript (including that of František Nevrla, the first Czech to translate single-handedly the entire Shakespeare canon in the late 1950s and early 1960s (see Drábek 2005), but whose translations of Shakespeare's poetic works remain unpublished to this day). Rubáš counts more than 1,300 Czech versions of Shakespeare's sonnets published in journals and books between 1860 and 1997, including complete translations, several larger fragments of the cycle, as well as dozens of partial translations of no more than a few pieces by a single translator (Rubáš, 9). While selections from other

---

[1] On the political importance of the 1616 Shakespeare cycle, see Mišterová, "Inter Arma Non Silent Musae."

[2] Rubáš, *Devatero klíčů k jednomu srdci*, 9 (Working translation F. K. and D. D.)

early modern English poets and sonneteers have been published in Czech in recent decades—for instance, an edition of Philip Sidney's *Astrophil and Stella* (as *Astrofel a Stella*), published once in 1987 on the occasion of the quadricentenary of the author's death, or a slim volume entitled *Fénixovo hnízdo: Sonety Shakespearových předchůdců a současníků* (*The Phoenix's Nest: Sonnets of Shakespeare's Predecessors and Contemporaries*, 1991, reprinted 2001)—these were always largely understood in the context of Shakespeare, whose popularity among the general Czech readership, quite understandably, could not be matched.

The biggest wave of translations of Shakespeare's sonnets into Czech appeared roughly in the last decade of the twentieth century and the first of the twenty first. Indeed, between 1986 and 2008, seven new complete translations were printed, including those by two prominent members of the last generation of translators of Shakespeare's plays into Czech so far: Martin Hilský (whose rendition of the sonnet sequence was first published in 1998) and Jiří Josek (2008) (Drábek 2012, 263–302). Due to his continuous efforts to popularise Shakespeare among the general reading and theatregoing audiences, Hilský has become a household name in the Czech Republic over the years, and just as his translations of Shakespeare's dramatic works have been dominating Czech theatres since the 1990s,[3] his versions of the sonnets have enjoyed the most reprints and re-editions of all the aforementioned translations: according to the Czech National Library catalogue, at least twelve book editions of Hilský's sonnets have been published to date, as opposed to one or two of most of the other translators' versions. This testifies to two phenomena connected with the reception of Shakespeare's sonnets in the Czech Republic: the association of Shakespeare with a particular translator, whose name has become almost synonymous with the Renaissance author in the audience's mind; and, more importantly for the present chapter, the fact that Shakespeare's sonnets are closely linked with the Czech theatre tradition and, as we will see, are largely understood as a kind of dramatic text.

---

[3] David Drozd counts that, by 2011, when Hilský published his one-volume collected works of Shakespeare in Czech, the number of theatre productions of his translations had more than doubled those employing Jiří Josek's renditions (Drozd, 178–179).

Producing Shakespeare's Sonnets
in Czech Theatres After the Year 2000

In the context of world theatre, the best-known scenic version of Shake-speare's sonnets is Robert Wilson's *Shakespeares Sonette* (*Shakespeare's Sonnets*), which premiered in 2009 on the occasion of the quadricen-tenary of the publication of the first Quarto in 1609. Thanks to the popularity of the Berliner Ensemble, Wilson's production was met with considerable response and inspired similar endeavours in other countries, including the neighbouring Czech Republic. The performance consisted of a series of disparate lyrical images (or theatre clips, so to speak), which, through repeated situations and iconic figures (a fool, Queen Elizabeth, Shakespeare, Cupid, etc.), presented a chain of free associations based on the textual tropes of the sonnets.

In the Czech theatre tradition, a number of scenic adaptations of the sonnets (as opposed to recitations) have appeared in the past twenty years as well. The frequency of these productions could, on the one hand, testify to the ever-rising popularity of Shakespeare among Czech theatregoing audiences, but could also be a response to the numerous editions of Shakespeare's sonnets in various translations. Considering that Shakespeare is regarded in the Czech Lands not just as "our contem-porary", but also as "our national poet", approaches to his works are very diverse, sometimes pious and traditional, at other times irreverent and radical—but always stemming from the fact that Shakespeare and his works (including the sonnets) are deeply embedded in Czech cultural memory. Each of the productions envisions the iconic Shakespeare in its own way. As we will see, for Czech theatre producers it is possible to discover in Shakespeare's sonnets a medieval morality; a drastic vaudeville travesty; a polemic about the patriarchy; as well as a dramatic testimony about the enduring clash of the genders.

The first production to be discussed here, which was entitled *Sonety, pánové, sonety!* (*Sonnets, Gentlemen, Sonnets!*) and premiered in 2001, was part of a larger project: in 1998, the artistic director of the regional theatre in Hradec Králové (East Bohemia) announced his intention to stage the entire *oeuvre* of William Shakespeare. The project was given the (half ironic) title "God Save William Shakespeare!" and up to three pieces were produced a year, in both traditional and more radical adapta-tions. Although not all Shakespeare plays were ultimately staged, in 2001 a special performance based on Shakespeare's sonnets saw the light of day.

The dramaturge Zora Vondráčková clearly defined the datum of the production in the printed programme:

> In 126 sonnets, a woman is only mentioned as: 1) a potential mother, who should be happy that the man celebrated by the poem picked her ("For where is she so fair whose uneared womb / Disdains the tillage of thy husbandry") as the mother of his child—a son, of course; and 2) a woman who, for a time being, disrupts a friendship between men by having an affair with both of them. In 28 pieces, addressed to the Dark Lady, is a woman mainly subjected to reproach for the suffering that she causes to the poet and his friend; the poet gives rich insight into his and his friend's minds, being concerned chiefly with his own soul and not with the feelings of the woman to whom these 28 sonnets are dedicated. A certain number of sonnets written for a friend, where the addressee is not clearly described, can be read ambiguously in terms of gender. These sonnets are concerned with the fear of death, the changes of time that affect both the human soul and body, and other more general issues, and one can find consolation in the hope that, when writing this rich poetry, Shakespeare had women in mind as well.[4]

From this polemical position, the production's scenic concept emerged: it took place in a women's prison, where, as part of their daily routine, a group of female inmates, supervised by two (male) guards, reminisced and dreamed. The script confronted Shakespeare's love sonnets (usually pronounced either by men or by women, who through them expressed the unrealistic, idealised picture of "eternal" love)—in the then new and latest translation by Martin Hilský—with a very open confession of women tortured and traumatised by both partner and marital relationships, which was textually based on *The Love Story of the Century*, a feminist story in verse by the Finnish writer Märta Tikkanen (b. 1935). The world of the sonnets was thus exposed as a world of men that dominates and objectifies women. This contrast was present not only on the level of the production's main theme but on a formal level as well: the accurate, formally strict structure of the sonnet was juxtaposed with the authentic sounding poetry by Tikkanen, written in free verse. The production thus deconstructed the traditional image of Shakespeare as a "poet/singer of love", lending voice to the other side: the woman (or,

---

[4] All the following passages from the production scripts or associated printed materials are working translations by F. K. and D. D.

rather, women), present in the sonnets while being completely silent. The appearance of women on the stage, by contrast, made them so visible that it made it impossible not to let them speak (Fig. 11.1).

Although the production had a topical and polemical theme at its core, it still retained a certain poetic quality and timelessness. The director Jakub Krofta and dramaturge Zora Vondráčková had previously worked for the Drak (Dragon) Theatre, also in Hradec Králové, which focuses mainly on puppet and children's productions. With this experience, they imbued their *Sonety, pánové, sonety!* with playfulness and lightness. The space of the prison was marked by clean white bars, while the guards' costumes were brightly coloured (being "theatrical" rather than specifically historical or contemporary). The production thus wanted mainly to create a space for the actors' art and the audiences' imagination. The female prisoners delved into their dreams, playing a wedding or evoking their (dark and painful) memories. Despite the fact that most of the sonnets in the production were ascribed to the male guards, it is very

Fig. 11.1 *Sonety, pánové, sonety!* [*Sonnets, Gentlemen, Sonnets!*]: Women prisoners start their daily routine (*Photo* Luděk Taneček)

much symptomatic of the message of the play that the "cult" sonnet 66, starting with "Tired with all these, for restful death I cry", was pronounced by one of the women (in Czech, which is able to express the gender of the speaker and thus demonstratively appropriate to this originally "male" text).

Linking the male (Shakespearean) and the female elements of the final play text was so natural and the final form so compact that some of the reviewers did not hesitate to call the production an original dramatic piece. The fact is that *Sonety, pánové, sonety!* presented its own story about women, and its motifs and situations derived from Shakespeare's sonnets only indirectly. The subject matter of the production was explicitly feminist, while also transcending gender categories:

> In the Hradec Králové production, the issue is not only the micro-world of the prison—it talks about the need of a human (and, even more, of a woman) to break various boundaries that restrict them. It is about the desire to be free. At the end, the inmates metaphorically overcome the bars, climb from the darkness of their cells into the daylight world and liberate themselves.[5]

An even more radical approach to Shakespeare's cult status was taken by the scriptwriter Lucie Trmíková and director Jan Nebeský in their 2013 production, entitled *Kabaret Shakespeare* (*The Shakespeare Cabaret*). The starting point for their production was the text of the sonnets and the basic triangle contained in them between the Poet, the Fair Youth (the addressee of the first group), and the mysterious Dark Lady (the addressee of the second group). The framework, however, was vaudeville, dominated by songs or, rather, jazz rags and hits based on Shakespeare's sonnets (again in Martin Hilský's translation), interspersed by short dialogues. The authors ironically elaborated on the Shakespearean myth— the character of the Poet was clearly designated as "WS"; upon his first entrance on the stage, the Poet's friend, designated as "WH", named all the theories concerning who was behind the initials from the dedication epistle of the 1609 Quarto; and, similarly, the Dark Lady presented herself through the various speculations about her identity. The way in which this short introduction was concluded is symptomatic of the ironic tone of the production:

---

[5] Skokanová, "Shakespeare v kriminále", 9 (Working translation by F. K. and D. D.)

I must confess that I was amused by the opinion that I was one of the first English ladies that indulged in smoking. But then again, why not? *(One of her fellow actors immediately cadges a cigarette off a theatregoer, which the actress lights hedonistically.)*

The production, however, began with a soliloquy by a fourth character, inspired by the contemporaneous historical context: designated as the "Preacher", he quoted early modern Puritan sermons against theatres. At the very beginning of the play, the tall figure approached the audiences, his face hidden under the black cape, storming, "I take upon myself the task to chase you off the theatres!" The fictitious scenes inspired by the relationship between WS and WH (in the production, Shakespeare was depicted as an ageing man who was linked with his young patron and addressee of his sonnets by an openly homosexual relationship) alternated with repeated railing at the sinfulness of the theatre. The scriptwriter (and actress impersonating the Dark Lady) Lucie Trmíková intentionally subverted Shakespearean idolatry. Shakespeare was presented as a self-conscious man, fawning over his noble patron, who manipulated and despised him. Although the production worked with contemporaneous documents or was at least inspired by them, its visual part was entirely modern. It was set in a virtually bare space, which was only filled with the racks for the costumes, the microphones and the live band. The costumes, however, attracted much attention: on the one hand, the shapes of male costumes alluded to Renaissance fashion (everyone wore a ruff collar at some point); on the other, the materials were markedly ahistorical. The youthful WH was especially noteworthy: his pseudo-Renaissance outfit with a black-and-white tiger pattern was completed with modern trainers and an extravagant wig. During the play, he changed clothes multiple times (at one point, his dress was dominated by a giant tie; at another, by a pair of trousers lasciviously exposing his backside), and rather than a Renaissance gentleman he resembled a modern pop star (Elton John or David Bowie). It is in this style, with fierce acting and brilliant singing, that the actor and singer Miloslav König interpreted some of the sonnets, engaging both the audience and his fan, Shakespeare (to whom he, indeed, behaved like a stereotypical rock star). The vaudeville framework of the production, understandably, did not aim at complex psychological character portraits; rather, it sought to capture individual types in a condensed form: an extravagant, charming, irresistible, but also arrogant and superficial youth; a melancholic, weary,

overly sensitive and ultimately forsaken poet; and next to these, a mysterious, but also manipulative woman. All these ended up alone in the end.
They were simultaneously showing off before and hiding from each other.
(Most of the time, they were symbolically wearing black sunglasses.) The
acting style drew on slapstick, aiming at gags and irony. Even the topic
of homosexuality, perhaps controversial for some members of the audience, was travestied: before the "sex" scene, both of the actors put on
white working suits and transparent capes, so the physical act, in spite of
the erotic text that accompanied it, looked like an awkward fight by two
clumsy men, who passionately tore plastic capes off each other and help-
lessly writhed on the slippery floor. Regardless of all the love poetry, the
production thus emphasised the grotesque physicality of sexual acts and,
in the end, the loneliness of the characters, who were animated solely by
their lust.

While the performance began as an extravagant, perhaps even disre-
spectful travesty, the titular character of Shakespeare gradually sank into
existential moods and the themes of ageing, death and the end moved
into the foreground. The Fair Youth and the Dark Lady were changing
lavish costumes, while the Poet grew old and withered away. Sonnets with
existential flavour, as well as other similar texts (the Preacher at one point
quoted the Book of Job), entered the script and, in one of the last scenes,
Shakespeare conversed with his dead son Hamnet. At the very end, the
aforementioned existential topics completely took over the production, as
well as the character of WS, who finished his role with the words:

> And now… just compassion.
> For oneself.
> For all the creation.
> For our frailty.
> For our limitedness.
> Praise for God, compassion for every creature, humility for oneself.

On the one hand, the audience witnessed a vaudeville production, a party
with catchy Shakespearean songs (Emil Viklický's music for the play was
awarded the Alfréd Radok Award for the best scenic music in 2013); on
the other, it was a meditation on the transience of human life. Particularly
the second half of the piece quoted authors whom director Jan Nebeský
likes to insert into his productions: even the non-experts could recognise
the fragments of Samuel Beckett, T. S. Eliot and various passages from

the Bible. The text of the production thus worked as a complex montage that, at times, went into an amusing loop: for instance, when a passage from *The Waste Land* was recited—a work in which T. S. Eliot quotes Shakespeare. If one wanted to follow these intertextual clues further, one could argue that the entire production, with its cabaret and jazz style, was inspired by the following lines by Eliot (that, of course, are heard during the play):

> O O O O that Shakespeherian Rag –
> It's so elegant
> So intelligent

The openness of the vaudeville structure that presented the plot as a loose series of images, songs and dialogues thus enabled the creators to capture Shakespeare in a number of different, little-related forms. On the one hand, the play was about Shakespeare the icon—and one could say about show business as such; on the other, the brutal physicality of sexual relationships was thematised, with the Beckettian existential emptiness opening at times to the sound of cheerful singing. But it was always about Shakespeare after all, as can be illustrated from a short dialogue that contains both the first and the last words exchanged between Shakespeare and his young friend:

> WH: Everyone still talks a lot of nonsense. Sometimes I ask myself whether it wasn't all just a dream.
> WS: It's all gone.
> WH: I see I should go now.
> WS: Yes.

Another very different approach to the sonnets was taken in 2017 by the producers of the Municipal Theatre of Mladá Boleslav (Central Bohemia), who turned Shakespeare's poems into a linear story of a man and a woman (who are designated in the printed programme as Everyman and Everywoman, although their names are never pronounced on the stage). The cast is completed with four allegorical figures—Death, Power, Fear and Passion—creating a variation of the morality genre, entitled simply *Sonety* (*The Sonnets*). The play was set in a greenhouse—a transparent structure with trees inside, in which the man and the woman appear, as if having grown up in a little Paradise. The Biblical nature of the story is obvious: the two characters resemble Adam and Eve, with the twist that, instead of fig leaves, they cover their nudity with musical instruments. The simple plot captured the twists and turns of their relationship, going through a number of crises, until finally reaching mutual understanding. The sonnets moved the individual situations onto a more general level while commenting on them. The greatest emphasis was thus on the poet's words both recited and sung to more or less static images on stage. The production was both lyrical and atmospheric, with music playing a significant role—as if the relationship between the Renaissance harmonies of music and the relationship materialised here. And it was harmony and reconciliation that the play ultimately aimed at (the role of music in the production was even strengthened by the fact that it is the actors who play it—therefore, it originated from the characters themselves) (Fig. 11.2).

Although the dramatic situations contained plenty of humour, Shakespeare was never ironised or problematised: the creators believed in him and let his words be heard in their original fullness, with their original poetry and magic. It should be noted here that, unlike the previously

Fig. 11.2 *Sonety* [*The Sonnets*]: Allegorical characters in action (from left to right: Death, Everyman, Power, Passion, Fear) (*Photo* Martina Veningerová)

discussed productions, *Sonety* was based on the then-new Czech rendition by the aforementioned Jiří Josek, another translator of Shakespeare's drama (before his untimely death in 2018, Josek managed to translate 34 of Shakespeare's plays), whose Czech version of Shakespeare's sonnets has a distinctively modern idiom, with a particular acoustic and "theatrical" quality. As Jakub Nvota, the production's director, revealed in the printed programme, this was the reason why Josek's translation was selected for this adaptation. This belief in poetry on the artists' part was in a charming way observable even at the very beginning of the production: instead of the conventional announcement asking the theatregoers to switch off their mobile phones, an actor recited a modern sonnet on this topic, finishing with the explicit line, "Give poetry a chance. Why? Because it'll change thee!"

How the identity of the translator of Shakespeare's sonnets (or any of his works, for that matter) can be important in the Czech context could be observed two years earlier, in the semi-improvised production of the sonnets in Viola Theatre in Prague, entitled *Sváteční Shakespearova pošta* (*Shakespeare's Festive Letters*), where the aforementioned Czech Anglicist and translator Martin Hilský took a place literally next to the Bard himself to enter into a dialogue with him about the meaning and intricacies of the latter's poetry.

In many respects, *Sváteční Shakespearova pošta* was the most conventional performance of all the productions described here. In the beginning, the poet and director Miloš Horanský, impersonating Shakespeare (he wore a ruff collar and a big sandglass hanging from his neck), appeared on the stage, announcing that he had risen from the dead because he heard that he would be given the opportunity to meet his translator, Martin Hilský. Although it might be expected that "Shakespeare" would be the star of the evening, in fact, it was the charismatic translator who attracted most of the audience (after the production, the theatregoers were invited to have their copies of Hilský's translation of the sonnets signed by him), perhaps even more than the acclaimed Czech actress Hana Maciuchová, who accompanied the dialogue between "Shakespeare" and Hilský about the sonnets by reciting some of them.[6]

---

[6] As Drábek maintains, unlike other translators of Shakespeare's works into Czech, Hilský has become an "authorial figure" for Czech audiences (see Drábek 2009, 73)—a notion that is literally embodied on the stage by *Sváteční Shakespearova pošta*.

This was not the first time Hilský had entered the theatre stage to join the Shakespearean actors. Most notably, during the Summer Shakespeare Festival in Prague (and the cities of Brno, Ostrava and Bratislava), the oldest and largest Shakespearean open-air festival in Europe, Hilský played the role of the guide through the world of Shakespeare for the audience in special thematic programmes, including *Pocta Shakespearovi* (*Homage to Shakespeare*), which was staged in 2016 to commemorate the quadricentenary of the Shakespeare's death and which, too, included a selection from Shakespeare's sonnets (Krajník and Kyselová, 68–70). *Sváteční Shakespearova pošta* was thus a continuation of Hilský's previous efforts to popularise Shakespeare among the general Czech audience, albeit here in a much more intimate setting (Viola Theatre only offers 76 seats in a bar-like arrangement).

What is most significant in the context of the present chapter is Hilský's view of the relationship between Shakespeare's plays and his sonnets which might explain why all of the productions discussed here are based on renditions of the sonnets by professional translators of drama rather than those of poetry. In an interview, printed just a few days after the production's premiere, Hilský stated:

> The specific feature of the Sonnets is that they are written in a very condensed language, they are a small-scale Shakespearean stage, a miniature world stage of a kind. Moreover, it is obvious that they were written by a great theatre poet. They are very dialogical, as if their speaker responded to a line that is pronounced immediately before the sonnet starts—sometimes you can even formulate it—so the text of the sonnet jumps *in medias res* of a specific situation or issue. Additionally, the language of the Sonnets is very much performative. Of course, they do not contain any plots, but speech events, so each of the poems represents to my mind a theatre, a drama.[7]

The latest attempt so far at a stage adaptation of this miniature *theatrum mundi* has been the 2019 production of the creative duo SKUTR in Dlouhá Theatre in Prague, entitled simply, again, *Sonety* (*The Sonnets*). Besides the previous Shakespearean efforts of the duo (comprising the

---

[7] Hrdinová, "Shakespearovy Sonety jsou jevišťátko svět," 11. (Working translation by F. K. and D. D.).

dramaturges and directors Martin Kukučka and Lukáš Trpišovský)—including the 2013 production of *A Midsummer Night's Dream* and the 2021 staging of *The Tempest* at the Summer Shakespeare Festival—another reason suggests itself as to why they decided to produce Shakespeare's sonnets on the stage. Kukučka and Trpišovský very often base their productions on non-dramatic or documentary material, frequently opting for poetry. While, being primarily poetical works, Shakespeare's sonnets do fulfil the criterion of being non-dramatic texts, their intrinsic dramatic quality, as we have seen, had proven to offer rich and versatile employment for the theatre. From the following discussion, it will become clear that Kukučka and Trpišovský not only recognised this quality but were able to take it even further than all the previous producers.

Our guide through the production is a reader of the sonnets, an apparently worldly lady smoking a cigarette and sitting at her dressing table, raised on a round halfpace, as if in a private room. The main stage looks like a hotel lobby, the space being delineated by a crescent wall with several identical doors. At the same time, however, it appears to be abandoned, and devastated—a piece of wall is in ruins and a sole bathtub sticks into the space. In defiance of any logic, a tree grows from the floor. The scene is both interior and exterior, a space in which, for the aforementioned reader, the micro-dramas of the sonnets come alive (Fig. 11.3).

In Kukučka and Trpišovský's performance, these stories are enacted by three love trios (consisting of two men and a woman each), the first in roughly Renaissance costumes, the second dressed according to the inter-war elegant fashion, the third being contemporary homeless people. The overall interpretation is clear: amorous fights repeat themselves only with slight variations across history, with their substance remaining always the same. In the beginning, three mature men enter the scene with their female partners but abandon them almost immediately when three young men appear. Both the heterosexual and homosexual readings of the sonnets are again thematised—this time, however, without any grotesque travesty, but in all seriousness and with the consequences in mind. All three love triangles develop equally: first, the women come to terms with their men's leaving and, subsequently, returning to them; then the passage of time is thematised, with the partners growing old and dying (the sequence is concluded by the deaths of all three young men). In the third part, we find ourselves in an underworld of a kind, where the trios still fight their inexorable fight like grotesque dead puppets, still

Fig. 11.3 *Sonety* [*The Sonnets*]: The Reader of the sonnets at her dressing table, with lovers from three historical periods peeping in (*Photo* Pavel Hejný)

shaken by their insatiable passion. The last segment is mostly based on the sonnets for the Dark Lady, who is metaphorically transformed into death, which cannot be overcome. In terms of genre, the production oscillates between poetic images and slapstick, almost in Tim Burton style (which is supported by the original music, obviously inspired by Tom Waits).

Kukučka and Trpišovský's production consistently works with the notion that Shakespeare's sonnets are, in fact, dramatic monologues. The poems are played out within the frame of the dramatic situation: they are not recited, but really acted out, often interrupted by pauses and action. Sometimes the sonnet even becomes a dialogue between two speakers. Although it may seem that the poetic language might come to harm in this manner, the opposite is true: the actors still make sure that the metric and rhyme schemes of the sonnet are preserved while stretching it to the very limit. Dramatic suspense is thus created simply by the audience's knowledge that one more line, one more rhyme, must be pronounced and that the dialogue must continue.

This breaking of the poetic text becomes most radical in the penultimate sonnet of the production, when all the three love trios (that is, nine actors and actresses) address the reader-guide, pronouncing Sonnet 152, divided into lines and words, taking turns one at a time. Thus they ultimately speak as if they were one person, in which the multitude of all the gender differences between the characters is contained in unity. A motto of a kind for the production is the last line from Sonnet 154, with which the character of the reader concludes the play, "Love's fire heats water, water cools not love".

CONCLUSION

When considering all four theatre productions addressed in this study (if we leave *Sváteční Shakespearova pošta* aside, as a public lecture/recitation rather than a piece of theatre, though touching most of the issues discussed here), it is worth noting the parallels and differences in the staging strategies of the individual artists. It is obvious that Shakespeare is a singer of love and, as such, his sonnets must be (at least sometimes) sung. The array of music styles, however—ranging from jazz (with an ironic pop and musical vibe) to the musical slapstick in the Tim Waits style, to well-measured classic singing—shows how different ideas can be as to how the Swan of Avon should actually sound.

All the productions inevitably touched on the main tropes of the original sonnets, such as relationships, sex and sexuality, and gender politics. In this respect, however, the differences between the productions could hardly be bigger: the Hradec Králové feminist play openly attacked Shakespeare as a patriarchal author; the one in Mladá Boleslav, in contrast, leaned towards the traditional image of Shakespeare as an author of timeless love poetry; the remaining two productions foreground the issue of homosexuality, a frequent trope of both Shakespeare criticism and some of the popular renditions of his life of recent years. Moreover, Kukučka and Trpišovský's *Sonety* bravely destroys all the conventional gender differences in the end.

The strategies that the individual artists adopted in their adaptations of the sonnets also vary significantly. The play text could be respectful to the source in terms of employing solely Shakespeare's poems; however, the Renaissance texts have more often been complemented and enriched (or even problematised) with additional materials, be it other poetry (Tikkanen, the Bible), or non-literary works and historical documents (such as early modern sermons). The relationships between this kind of material and the sonnets vary as well. In the case of *Sonety, pánové, sonety!*, a tension existed between the textual layers of the script with the intention to question the image of love presented by the sonnets; in *The Shakespeare Cabaret*, the sonnets are idolised when they are turned into jazz songs, while Shakespeare's life is being unceremoniously travestied. Jakub Nvota's *Sonety*, in contrast, respects Shakespeare's poems in their original form, making them part of his morality play (which, too, is a very conventional genre). SKUTR's *Sonety* is the only production that is textually based solely on the sonnets, ingeniously treating them as dramatic monologues or dialogues.

The analysis could go on and address even more aspects of how Shakespeare's poetry is treated by contemporary Czech theatre. The main point of the present chapter, however, has been to show the rich array of possibilities with which Czech dramaturgy approaches Shakespeare, treating the author predominantly as its own cultural phenomenon that could be celebrated, but also freely appropriated, updated or rejected according to current needs. During their two and a half centuries of living with Shakespeare, Czechs have created an intimate relationship with the Bard, and the fact that even his poetry has entered the cultural mainstream through popular theatre adaptations (while the producers can choose from several complete translations of Shakespeare's sonnet cycle) testifies to Shakespeare's cultural importance for the Czech nation both in the past and the present.

References

Drábek, Pavel. *České pokusy o Shakespeara* [*Czech Attempts at Shakespeare*]. Brno: Větrné mlýny, 2012.

Drábek, Pavel. "Český Shakespeare mezi normalizací a koncem milénia [Czech Shakespeare Between Normalisation and the End of Millennium]." *Theatralia* 12, no. 1–2 (2009): 64–78

Drábek, Pavel. "František Nevrla's Translation of *Hamlet*." *Brno Studies in English* 31 (2005): 119–127.

Drozd, David. "William Shakespeare. *Dílo*. Překlad Martin Hilský: Vklady, výklady (a úklady) shakespearovského překladu [*The Works* of William Shakespeare translated by Martin Hilský: Contributions, Interpretations (and Intrigues) of Shakespearean Translation]." *Theatralia* 15, no. 1 (2012): 178–189.

Fénixovo hnízdo: Sonety Shakespearových předchůdců a současníků [*The Phoenix's Nest: Sonnets of Shakespeare's Predecessors and Contemporaries*], selected and translated by Zdeněk Hron. Praha: Supraphon, 1991.

Hrdinová, Radmila. "Shakespearovy Sonety jsou jeviŠťátko svět [Shakespeare's Sonnets are a Miniature World Stage]." *Právo* 25, no. 91 (18–19 April 2015): 11.

Kabaret Shakespeare [*The Shakespeare Cabaret*], script by Lucie Trmíková, directed by Jan Nebeský. Studio DAMÚZA, Prague, Czech Republic, premiere 25 April 2013, closing night 27 April 2015 (renewed premiere 6 December 2015, closing night 6 May 2016).

Krajník, Filip and Eva Kyselová. "Shakespeare at Four Castles: Summer Shakespeare Festival in Prague, Brno, Ostrava (Czech Republic) and Bratislava (Slovakia)." In *Shakespeare on European Festival Stages*, ed. Nicoleta Cinpoeş, Florence March and Paul Prescott, 55–74. London: The Arden Shakespeare, 2022.

Mišterová, Ivona. "Inter Arma Non Silent Musae: Shakespeare as a Symbol of the Czech ProAllied Attitude During the Great War." *Brno Studies in English* 41, no. 2 (2015): 73–89.

Rubáš, Stanislav. *Devatero klíčů od jednoho srdce* [*Nine Keys to One Heart*]. Praha: Univerzita Karlova, Filozofická fakulta, 2000.

Sidney, Philip. *Astrofel a Stella* [*Astrophil and Stella*], translated by Alois Bejblík and Gustav Francl. Praha: Odeon, 1987.

Skokanová, Eliška. "Shakespeare v kriminále [Shakespeare in Prison]." *Hradecké noviny* 10, no. 241 (16 October 2001): 9.

Sonety [*The Sonnets*], script and directed by Jakub Nvota. Městské divadlo Mladá Boleslav, Czech Republic, premiere 28 April 2017, closing night 27 June 2018.

Sonety [*The Sonnets*], script and directed by Martin Kukučka and Lukáš Trpišovský. Divadlo v Dlouhé, Prague, Czech Republic, premiere 23 November 2019 (as of January 2022, still running).

Sonety, pánové, sonety! [*Sonnets, Gentlemen, Sonnets!*], script by Zora Vondráčková, Jakub Krofta and the collective of playing actors and actresses, directed by Jakub Krofta. Klicperovo divadlo, Hradec Králové, Czech Republic, premiere 22 September 2001, closing night 14 June 2002.

Sváteční Shakespearova pošta [*Shakespeare's Festive Letters*], directed by Miloš Horanský. Divadlo Viola, Prague, Czech Republic, premiere 14 April 2015, closing night 30 September 2020.

Vočadlo, Otakar. Notes on the *Sonnets*. In *Historie II, Básně* [*Histories II, Poems*], by William Shakespeare, 600–618. Praha: Státní nakladatelství krásné literatury a umění, 1964.

CHAPTER 12

"Not [...] for the Faint Hearted": Volcano Theatre's *L.O.V.E.* as a Physical Theatre Adaptation of Shakespeare's Sonnets

Márta Minier

This chapter will examine *L.O.V.E*, a stage performance devised in response to Shakespeare's Sonnets by a Welsh experimental theatre company established in 1987, the Swansea-based Volcano. This widely discussed and globally showcased, award-winning production was first made in 1992, revived in 2003 for a tour of the Caucasus and recreated

---

The quotation in the title is from Paul Davies, "Nigel Charnock, 1960-2012" (2012) [accessed via Volcano archive].

M. Minier (✉)
University of South Wales, Cardiff, UK
e-mail: marta.minier@southwales.ac.uk

© The Author(s), under exclusive license to Springer Nature
Switzerland AG 2023
J. Kingsley-Smith and W. R. Rampone Jr. (eds.), *Shakespeare's Global Sonnets*,
Global Shakespeares, https://doi.org/10.1007/978-3-031-09472-9_12

with a new ensemble of performers in 2012 (in celebration of the company's 25th anniversary), also leading to a 2013 offshoot entitled *Women in L.O.V.E.*[1]

As a significant British example of physical theatre—a mode of theatre-making that uses the movement of bodies as a key part of the aesthetics—the original production of *L.O.V.E.* was directed and choreographed by physical theatre and dance practitioner Nigel Charnock (a founding member of acclaimed physical theatre company DV8)[2] as the first of four shows he directed for the company (alongside *Macbeth: Director's Cut* (a 1999 two-hander); the Ibsen-inspired 1996 *How to Live or Ibsenities* and the 1994 *Manifesto*, which revisited the *Communist Manifesto*). The dynamic and passionate rejuvenation of the Sonnets was composed for three performers. At the centre of the love triangle in this narrative dramatisation of the Sonnets is a young lover—thought of by the ensemble members as The Lovely Boy (Davies 2021)—who makes both the Poet figure and the Dark Lady jealous. The original cast consisted of co-creators Paul Davies, Fern Smith and Liam Steel, with Andrew Jones as the designer. The "role" of the Lovely Boy (if we may use this traditional term), performed by Steel, was soon taken over by James Hewison because of Steel's limited availability. Hewison toured the show with Smith and Davies in 2003 to Georgia, Armenia and Azerbaijan, with Volcano being the first performing arts group representing the UK there with British Council support. The 2012/2013 version, remounted with direction by Davies and movement direction by Hewison, featured Tibu Forte, Andrew Keay/Joseph Reay-Reid and Mairi Phillips. In arts commentator Peter Aspden's words, the three performers "indulge[d] in many permutations of congress in a vicious love triangle which [brought] out all the darkness of Shakespeare's most rapturous work" (Aspden 2003). Accompanied by very mixed responses—including booing, walkouts and even local cancellation in 2003 in Georgia apparently because of

---

[1] I spoke at length to Paul Davies, co-creator of and performer in the original production, who also performed in the Caucasian tour and directed the 2012 remake. He is the current Artistic Director of Volcano. I am very thankful to him as well as to Claudine Conway, the company's Executive Producer, who helped me access the relevant archival material.

[2] DV8 Physical Theatre was to a great extent responsible for initiating the widespread adoption of the term "physical theatre" within the profession (Murray and Keefe 2016, 18) after co-founders Lloyd Newson and Nigel Charnock gave the company this name in 1986.

an onstage male kiss—the touring performance shocked some spectators and shook up and challenged what was considered acceptable action in a theatre performance. At some of the more socially conservative international touring venues, *L.O.V.E.* was seen as iconoclastic, and a somewhat controversial choice from the British Council to promote British culture abroad. The infamous "carnal" kiss, which "reach[ed] Hitchcockian levels of languorous eroticism", gave the audiences, according to Aspden, "an extraordinary moment, and a moving one" (2003).

The ultimate appeal of the complex and visceral performance was that it was a highly physicalised and visualised dramatisation of Shakespeare's Sonnets, one that "harnessed the wonderful words of Shakespeare to a breakneck physicality", using "physical and emotional extremism" in performance, against an "anarchic" and "irreverent" backdrop (Davies 2012). The original director-choreographer Charnock, who saw himself primarily as an entertainer (and trained as an actor originally at the Royal Welsh School for Speech and Drama) had a non-elitist approach to creating work for performance. This attitude was clear in *L.O.V.E.* as well, where the dialogue between literary words and physical movement resulted in a performance with an "over-the-top urgency" (Davies 2012) and a fresh, if disturbing or unsettling, engagement with the Shakespearean text. The present chapter will explore the production with the aid of Peter Brook's insights into working with classics, Antonin Artaud's vision of radical theatre, and Eugenio Barba's conceptualisation of dramaturgy for physical theatre. The perspective will be broadly intertextual and contextual, with comparative points made where appropriate.

Physical Theatre as a Choice

Physical theatre is a style Volcano is widely known for, and the reviews that the production received—in its various iterations—demonstrate that this physical theatre take on the Sonnets was noted for its "frenetic action" (James 2012) and "explosive energy" (Burke 1993). As Murray and Keefe elucidate about physical theatre,

> To be *physical* is to be sexy and to resist the dead hand of an overly intellectual and cerebral approach. To be *physical* in performance connects you to territories not regularly associated with theatre—with, for example, sport [...], dance and club culture and (more theoretically) with contemporary

discourses that articulate and rehearse the nature of embodiment in a wide range of public, personal and intellectual spheres. (Murray and Keefe 2016, 17)

Very much characterised by the abovementioned fluidity of influences and stimuli (as will be discussed later)—as well as the "sexiness" of corporeality over the weight of erudition—the performance was an act of revolt against what the young makers of the show perceived as conventional theatre at the time. The commercial, artistically corrupt and often narrow-minded theatre they were critical of seems to have some kinship with the "deadly theatre"—an "outmoded and laboriously word based" mode of theatre (Murray and Keefe 2016, 17)—which disappointed Peter Brook early in his career. It is not easy to pin down the descriptor "deadly theatre" into a definable concept, but Brook's insight seems very apt when we look for ways to shed light on what Volcano rebelled against with their experimental dramatisation of the Sonnets: "the Deadly Theatre approaches the classics from the viewpoint that somewhere, someone has found and defined how the play should be done" (Brook 1996, 14). (Here that verbal text is the Sonnets rather than a play, but the same principle applies: artists may be up against ossified, overly canonical interpretations.) And, as Brook provocatively claims, "Of course nowhere does the Deadly Theatre install itself so securely, so comfortably and so slyly as in the works of William Shakespeare. The Deadly Theatre takes easily to Shakespeare" (Brook 1996, 10). Looking back at the original intentions and the creative process leading to L.O.V.E., Paul Davies emphasises that they wanted to mark their work as distinct from the tepid, bookish and predictable productions that they thought to have dominated the sector in their youth (2021). Fern Smith also highlights their intention to leave behind the talking-head style and "beautiful voices" (BBC Wales). It appears that Volcano and Charnock targeted, even if unconsciously, the "excruciatingly boring" and lifeless "deadly theatre" that Brook raised his voice against (1996, 10). Volcano and Charnock's answer to this issue permeating conventional theatre is a heightened reliance on physicality, movement and proximity (not only among the ensemble but also to the audience, and in both cases, to the extent of potential discomfort). Perhaps due to their varied disciplinary backgrounds, the original devisers of the performance had mistrust of overly verbal theatre and gravitated towards predominantly physical ways of working, even if the work was catalysed by a written text or textual corpus as in the case of L.O.V.E.

as well as other adaptations by Volcano, for example, the 1991 *Medea: SexWar* (choreographed by Charnock), juxtaposing Tony Harrison's take on Euripides' *Medea* with Valerie Salernas's *SCUM (Society for Cutting Up Men) Manifesto*.

In addition to emphasising the physical aspect of the work, we also need to highlight that the adaptation was devised: rather than somebody writing a script and the performers performing it (under the direction of Charnock), the performers and director composed the piece together: verbal text and physical action were not separated in the making but layered together collectively in rehearsals. In a blog review of the 2012 version, Bethan James addresses the balance between (verbal) script and physical score: "Shakespeare's re-invented texts are given equal footing to the dynamic choreography and are [complemented] by the frenetic action rather than smothered by it".[3]

The developmental rehearsals for the original production took place in an old-fashioned gym in Port Talbot, a steel town in southwest Wales. The ambiance of the gym and the tense dynamic between its regular customers—local working-class men working out—and the "studenty" theatre-makers found its way into the atmosphere of the performance, too. The suspicion of the local men training at the gym and the ongoing vigilance by both parties is mirrored in the recurrent instances of being on edge and on the lookout in the performance. The production experiments with exposure to risk and pain. There is a lot that can go wrong including a knife being held in the Dark Lady performer's mouth and also being pressed against the exposed skin of the Lovely Boy performer. As reviewer Jim Burke captures this scene, Fern Smith "produces a knife from a bunch of roses and performs some decidedly inimitable acts upon Davies's and Steel's semi-naked bodies" (1993). Hewison also mentions "the sceno-graphic perils of a treacherously wet, champagne-drenched floor" and other physical risk factors for the performers:

> Even the frantic action in, on and around, the large four-poster bed that formed the center-point of the set was potentially risky since beneath its

---

[3] I cite both magazine/newspaper reviews and blogs in the chapter if they appear suitable. The dividing line between these is to some extent blurred today and the critical quality of a blog is often not behind the standard of a newspaper, magazine or journal review. See for instance Radosavljević for a robust defense of theatre blogs.

lush red velvet drapes and black satin sheets, the bed was an industrially tough and unyielding iron structure. (Hewison 2019, 534)

With the risk of physical harm, the commitment and discipline required of the performers in this show are considerable. The production also makes us ponder about the importance of trust in a performance—among the performers but also between performer and audience. As we know from performer accounts (Hewison 2019; Davies 2021), things did at times go wrong even to the extent of the physical injury suffered by an actor.

On a related note, watching recordings of the show in the early 2020s—the Covid-19 era—the discomfort of seeing the quasi-forced proximity and invasion of the privacy of audience members is quite palpable. While it is a largely subjective viewing experience that I am documenting here, the show has, anecdotally, remained infamous for pushing a notional boundary between performers and audience too far for some audience members' comfort in a scene early in the show in which the three performers "[trawl] their way through the auditorium, seducing uneasy spectators" (Burke 1993). In this scene (which appears as "audience kissing" in the unpublished script) the performers mingle with the audience, at times sitting on people's laps, at times kissing them, caressing them, checking if they wear wedding rings, flirting with them. The way this interactive scene is devised is that the actor performing the Lovely Boy does this scene for longer than the other two performers who return to the stage earlier and recite Sonnet 96, with the Lovely Boy performer joining in from the auditorium with Sonnet 121. This sequence attempts to put the audience at unease from the start in a rather Artaudian way by ignoring—trespassing even—the proverbial "fourth wall". The unorthodox early twentieth-century theatre visionary Antonin Artaud spoke against "the idolatry of fixed masterpieces" in his essays on how to revitalise theatre (Qtd Bermel 2013, 6). As Artaud expert Albert Bermel reminds us, in Artaud's perception "[t]he theatre's veneration for 'what has already been created' […] 'petrifies us' and 'deadens our responses'" (Bermel 2013, 6). In Artaud's vision any classic is only to be revisited in the theatre "after subjecting them to a radical overhaul" (Bermel 2013, 6). The "overhaul" is not meant in a politically radical way but rather in the sense of freeing up audience members to connect more directly with the text, "surrendering[ing] themselves to a performance, liv[ing] through it and feel[ing] it, rather than merely thinking about it" (Bermel

2013, 7). On the whole, Volcano's production has some Artaudian characteristics, and this early scene from *L.O.V.E.* in particular raises significant questions about the symbolic contract between audience members and performance. What reviewer Ashley Smith notes when reminiscing about *How to Live* and commenting on *L.O.V.E.* is apt here: "The theatre space felt too enclosed for their ideas but also too big; I think they really wanted to perform sat on your lap" (Smith 2012). Audience reactions certainly varied, ranging from the most appreciative and responsive to firm rejections of unsolicited intimacy. It seems valid to question whether this scene gives enough freedom—and enough notice—for a spectator to opt out (of the entire show, of the scene, or even just of being touched or kissed by a complete stranger). Shakespeare's Sonnets are recruited here to challenge what the makers see as bourgeois theatre-going habits, where there tends to be a clear divide between audience and onstage business. The Sonnets, which carry the dialogic intimacy of poetry and pull the audience member/reader into an inner circle, are ideal for this purpose.

The first short (20-min or so) work-in-progress showcase of *L.O.V.E.* took place at a garden festival in the small provincial south Walian town of Ebbw Vale and, as the anecdote goes, not many audience members stayed to the end. The "shock" value continued to accompany the production in its full-fledged versions. Many reviews note the production's preoccupation with shocking audience members. This has to be taken with a pinch of salt as it is impossible to speak with full confidence about the overall audience response; it is also difficult to document audience dismay retrospectively (Volcano did not keep letters of complaint, but Davies does recall that there had been some). Davies maintains that the company did not set out to shock the audience (2021). Even if that was not the main intention, it seems that the show's advertising materials benefited from the negative responses (including outrage on the show's foreign tour) which were translated into badges of value and integrity. For example, the 2012 press release proudly reminisces over the 2003 Caucasian tour and "[running] into trouble in Georgia, where the show's exuberant sexuality (and specifically a lingering and tender embrace between two men) angered the Orthodox Church and led to sabotage and a near-riot. The same scene was met with boisterous cheering and wild applause in Azerbaijan" (Volcano 2012a, b). Marking the tour, the Welsh newspaper *Western Mail* also marks the story at the time, with an optimistic reading of the event in Georgia and expresses Paul Davies' pride over the show's, as well as implicitly perhaps the Sonnets', alleged civilising power: "the general perception is that much needed debate about issues such as church censorship, personal politics and female empowerment has been opened up in the country and local media in a very positive way" (*Western* Mail 2003). The element of shock, beyond its Artaudian resonances, also reminds us of the style of the much-debated in-yer-face theatre trend—a phenomenon within British theatre prevailing from the mid-1990s for a brief decade, which was characterised by the breaking of numerous taboos both in the language of the "new writing" at the time and the stage business in the plays' productions. Violence, obscenity and disturbing subject matters all contributed to the "shock" value which was part and parcel of this style. There is little wonder this heteroge-nous school of quasi-contemporary theatre writing is at times referred to as "the new Jacobeans" (Saunders 2002). Volcano's *L.O.V.E.* predates the emergence of this style—if anything, it may have been influential on these new writers via the Edinburgh fringe/tour circuit. This take on Shakespeare's Sonnets is to some degree in the vein of in-yer-face theatre, the thematic liberation of which it appears to be pioneering for the Welsh public and much beyond. As Paul Davies recalls, the collective was concerned with showing the private as "ugly, gauche and ridiculous", unveiling "our narrow demands on each other" (Davies 2021) while also conveying the drama of a *ménage à trois*. The company's interest in the French theatre tradition of Grand Guignol—alongside an interest in Bergson and Schopenhauer at the time (Davies 2021)—may be visible in the melodramatic, self-mocking obsession with love and hurt we see in the play.

WORKING WITH SHAKESPEARE: INSPIRATIONS AND HETEROGENOUS TEXTUALITY

The originators of the production were generally working class and tended to be first-generation university graduates in their respective fami-lies. They were new to the Sonnets at that time. Charnock was at a juncture in his career where he was distancing himself from dance and moving towards working with scripted texts. Volcano, however, were moving towards dance; it was a felicitous moment for them to collaborate.

They saw it in the news that Shared Experience, a theatre company specialising primarily in theatre adaptations, was doing a performance inspired by the Sonnets, entitled (freely after Sonnet 30) *Sweet Sessions*.

While the company did not see this production—a 1991 performance directed by Nancy Meckler and co-devised by Meckler and Paul Godfrey—they became aware of it and their impression from the promotional material was that it was a static, mainly literary event, engaging with the Sonnets as texts rather than an emphatically theatrical reinterpretation and physicalisation (Davies 2021). In a sense, Shared Experience's adaptation acted indirectly as a catalyst for *L.O.V.E.* Looking at the production and reception history of both of these plays, the case can be made that there is just as much that links these two productions together as what distinguishes or contrasts them with each other, and these shared features include a sense of postmodern playfulness in their dealings with the "towering" classic. Volcano attempts to bring the Sonnets closer to the contemporary public by pinning a batch of sonnets to the dramaturgical nodes of a highly physical drama, thus rendering to the audience a non-high art, heterogenous Shakespeare. While doing so, their approach does not shy away from making any audience member uncomfortable. Shared Experience's production, on the other hand, abounds in meta-critical features with a meticulous, almost positivist Shakespeare studies PhD student (performed by Emma Dewhurst) trying to catalogue the imagery of the Sonnets, "enumerat[ing] animate, natural, and human images" "in an effort to gain access to the writer's *imagination*" and, in reviewer P. J. S.'s words, elaborating on "taxonomic difficulties" along the way (1991, 84). If anything, the show seems to have lovingly mocked a quasi-positivist understanding of Shakespeare and the possibility of reducing the power of his language to tables and lists. *Sweet Sessions* also appears to be gently warning the viewer against the dangers of seeing Shakespeare purely as a book—something we may also glean from Volcano's adaptation. The PhD student turning to writing sonnets herself by the end of *Sweet Sessions* affirms the power of creativity the Sonnets channel across time.

The method of working with the Shakespearean texts involved all of *L.O.V.E.*'s co-creators choosing twenty sonnets each and explaining their choices in collaborative sessions (Davies 2021). If a sonnet was chosen by at least two people they would not veto the inclusion of that sonnet. They did, however, agree to exclude the first seventeen sonnets which were—in the performance collective's reading at the time—about procreation. In their view, these sonnets pinned the value of life on producing offspring—something the makers of *L.O.V.E.* were not willing to embrace. After the initial selection process, they went on to experiment with the text by working physically with the thematic content of the Sonnets (but with their own improvised words where the physical experimentation needed a verbal component). They only layered this formulating physical score with the actual verbal text at a later stage in the developmental process when they were comfortable enough with the progress made. It appears that the process of organic or dynamic dramaturgy (which Eugenio Barba identifies as "the composition of the rhythms and dynamisms affecting the spectators on a nervous, sensorial and sensual level") may have enjoyed priority in the making process, though at least after a certain point it overlapped with narrative dramaturgy, "which interweaves events and characters, informing the spectators on the meaning of what they are watching" (Barba 2000, 60). Importantly, in this production, there also seem to be glimpses of Barba's third and "most elusive" type of dramaturgy, the dramaturgy of changing states. This strand of dramaturgy, as Barba suggests, "distils or captures hidden significances, which are often involuntary on the part of the actors as well as the director and are different for every spectator. It gives the performance not only a coherence of its own but also a sense of mystery" (Barba 2000, 60). The way the production might viscerally and emotionally affect individual spectators and how it taps into both audience members' and performers' vulnerability night after night is not only Artaudian but also shows this "mysterious" form of dramaturgy at play.

Even the "finished" product of the 1992 performance (if we can speak of a "finished" product when it comes to such a transitory and always evolving form as live performance) retained some of the improvisatory techniques governing the research and development period. A remnant of this scaffolding process in the show is an early scene where the three performers get the audience "warmed up" by voicing seemingly random words we may associate with the early modern era (including "twas", "couldst", "didst", "wanton", "nay", "tis"). Some of the words and phrases—for instance, "wanton", "canker" and "wanton canker"—foreshadow the emotional complexity of the play to follow. This enumeration, alongside the aforementioned notorious "mingling" scene, establishes ground rules with the audience, both inviting them aboard a transtemporal journey and urging them to sit on the edge of their seats. The first words spoken, cleverly intended to attune the audience to the sound of the script, gives us a glimpse of the making process in a metatextual way not that far away from the playful conceit behind Shared Experience's production.

Some of the dialogue is couched in contemporary language entirely. There is, for instance, a short yet very modern bit of dialogue between the Lovely Boy and the Dark Lady, in which the Dark Lady flirts with the Lovely Boy and gives voice to her jealousy over what may be developing between the Poet and the youth. There is a little teasing going on about a mysterious piece of writing (a letter? a shopping list?) which turns out to be a rather awkward amateurish love poem. "That's not it!", exclaims the Dark Lady when she hears it, and the Lovely Boy does indeed give in and reads Sonnet 71 in his "Charlton Heston voice". The way the young man introduces his "recital" of Sonnet 71 is brimming with aggression and competition: "You see I am proper poet. Right I'll read you the real on [sic]; this is culture. It's a sonnet. I'm going to read it because you need culturing and I'm the person to do it." It is interesting that in this dramatisation the sonnet is attributed to his character and he refers to other parts of the Sonnets as well: "I'm not very good with titles, well 69 wasn't bad." And, after the two of them rip the sheet(s): "I'll have a big gap at CXXXI now". The chosen sonnet is used in this dialogue as cultural capital as the Lovely Boy "shows off", trying to demonstrate an intellectual advantage or superiority. He patronises the Dark Lady by translating "nay" to "no" and "woe" to "sad". He lets the Dark Lady read "For I love you so" and they discuss where the accent should be ("For I lurve you so"). One may perceive the contemporary addition to the dialogue as jarring with the early modern poems—the core textual matrix—but this jarring dramatises the work of interpretation quite explicitly in a postmodern fashion. Interestingly, Shared Experience's *Sweet Sessions* has also been found to have displeasing contemporary dialogue interspersed with the sonnets themselves: "the interpolated speeches which Paul Godfrey had written to fuse the sonnets into a coherent 'story' were poor" (P. J. S. 1991, 85). To me, this aspect of both performances is a very intriguing one as it problematises—and stages—the transtemporal encounter that we all experience when interpreting the Sonnets today. In this case of *Sweet Sessions*, the metatextual play is considerably more overt, with the Young Man, the Dark Lady and Shakespeare emerging from the crate of the aforementioned doctoral student.

There is no rephrasing of Shakespeare in the contemporary section of this dialogue (or anywhere else in the verbal script of the performance) other than an explanatory intralingual translation of specific words. These minimal added bits of dialogue constitute modern improvised text (as part of the wider Shakespearean fabric). The script—while it was eventually written down—was not intended to function as a "play" for reading either in a separate tie-in volume to go with the production or in an anthologised format. In a similar vein, Godfrey does not include the *Sweet Sessions* script in his Methuen collected plays either (Godfrey 1998). It appears that these scripts are more fluid, collaboratively authored and perhaps also more functional and stage-oriented—something that neither a single-volume nor an anthologised print publication may do full justice to.

Character formation in *L.O.V.E.* evolved during the rehearsal process, as did the action, and perhaps in the spirit of post-dramatic theatre as "theatre of the body" and "theatre of potentiality" (Lehmann 2006, 163), the creative process was fuelled rather than hindered by not knowing precisely where the ensemble was going with the material (Davies 2021). For instance, Davies' "character" ends up battering the Lovely Boy to death with a book—something they did not foresee when they started scaffolding the performance. They did, however, find it important to have a strong Dark Lady figure (Davies 2021): their Dark Lady is endowed with assertive and manipulative features à la Lady Macbeth. The fact that the unpublished script does not use character names but the first names of the performers also suggests that there is a touch of the post-dramatic here: the performing ensemble members do communicate loosely composed characters but they are primarily physical performers rather than actors delivering clear-cut dramatic roles. The information sheet produced for marketing purposes to accompany the 2012 production is visibly cautious in its avoidance of the term "character" (in the traditional sense of dramatic theatre): "Its [*L.O.V.E.*'s] story is based on the implied figures in the Sonnets—the poet, the 'lovely boy' and the 'dark lady'".[4]

While *L.O.V.E.* is an emphatically physical performance with a lot of bodily contact among the performers (and briefly with audience members), communicating a narrative is still important to some degree. As Julie Sanders notes, "we can see in this performance a conscious nod to the sub-biographical figures traditionally associated with the Shakespearian sequence" with "a deep sexual entanglement between this trio" (Saunders 2011, 126). The performance's relationship to narrative—as

---

[4] Volcano. (2012a). "Notes for Box Office and Marketing" [accessed via Volcano archive].

well as to character—places it in a liminal space between dramatic and postdramatic theatre, as conceptualised by Lehmann. To render a story (even if loosely) through movement and by voicing a selection of the Sonnets suggests an affinity with dramatic theatre. Yet, the dominance of physicality and the lack of (realist) character development shift the play towards the post-dramatic mode. So does the inclusion of violent action: the presence of actual violence, physical exhaustion and risk of injury carried by the performers also strengthen the case for this being a postmodern and in part post-dramatic adaptation of the Sonnets.

SHAKESPEARE AND ...

As is often the case with adaptations, regardless of the medium, the primary—declared and formal source text/textual corpus—is amply supplemented and gains further interpretive layers and nuances from the multiplicity of additional references the adaptation "product" is infused with. Volcano's work at the time was largely influenced by popular culture, mainly popular music (Shirley Bassey and beyond), and indie art films (Davies 2021). It is important to acknowledge and engage with this infiltration, as intertextuality in the performance is emphatically not only with Shakespeare's text but also with a range of other, perhaps no less important, texts drawn from a range of contemporary forms and media. Hewison points out the kitsch aesthetic of the performance in his discussion of the production (Hewison 2019). One may see this as a postmodern feature that relativises the adapted textual corpus but at the same time, perhaps somewhat paradoxically, also reiterates its significance by demonstrating its very adaptability, even if it is through the vocabulary of kitsch and pop. In Bickley and Stevens' words, "reinvention creates renewal" (2020, 2).

L.O.V.E. has an evocative soundtrack underscoring the dynamic physicality of the action. A range of Shirley Bassey songs ("Something", "Never Never Never", "The Look of Love", "It Must Be Him", "The Party's Over") and the work of industrial metal band Ministry ("N.W.O.") alternate with Bach (Concerto in F): a powerful juxtaposition and a postmodern touch in terms of forcing "high culture" and popular culture to encounter and offer a hybrid, heterogenous experience to the audience. Even if they did not intend to shock for shock's sake in a sensationalist way, I think it is safe to read the performance—the palimpsest of L.O.V.E.

performances enveloping over two decades—as one that has the potential to make audience members uncomfortable in an Artaudian sense. As mentioned above, the performance is situated on the borders between dramatic and post-dramatic theatre. While, for some audience members, story and dramatic structure may be very much present (and when talking about the performance retrospectively Davies summarises somewhat of a skeletal plot [Davies 2021]), for others the performance may offer an experience of being washed over by a lot of Shakespearean language in the form of the performed sonnets juxtaposed with some very contemporary dialogue, all closely intertwined with intense and highly physical stage action which looks stylised but is genuinely exhausting for the performers and carries actual risks of being hurt.

Davies recalls Roman Polanski's 1992 thriller, *Bitter Moon*, as a significant viewing experience at the time (Davies 2021). One may notice a touch of the ambiance and themes of *Bitter Moon* in the production's structure of feelings, where raw emotions as well as passionate, and even desperate, encounters are presented to us through physical action punctuated by the words of Shakespeare's Sonnets. Speaking of filmic intertextuality, Peter Greenaway's films were also an influence on *Volcano* at the time, and Davies himself suggests that the ending of *L.O.V.E.* owes something to *The Cook, The Thief, His Wife and Her Lover* (1989) (2021). As Ruth D. Johnston reminds us, Greenaway himself acknowledged that his film was a "critique of consumer society during the Thatcher years" (Johnston 1990, 19). The experience of living in the Thatcherite era was certainly a catalyst for *Volcano*'s work (BBC Wales) and Greenaway's creative response to this lived experience resonated with them.

Poet, playwright and seasoned adapter Tony Harrison (b. 1937) also had a considerable impact on *Volcano*'s work and thinking around that time. His way of addressing class divisions inspired their perspective on the potential of art. *Volcano* worked on Harrison's "V" (1985), the outspoken tone, atmosphere and themes of which very much resonated with them, and the fact that Harrison was from the north of England also paralleled their own somewhat marginal geographical location. In an indirect sense, the politics of the Britain of the late eighties and nineties very much underlies the production even though it is not a political performance per se. Motivated in part by Harrison's work, *Volcano* engaged with poetry as a literary genre that also had the capacity to work in live performance. Shakespeare's Sonnets are not an unusual choice in this context.

When discussing any theatrical influences on Volcano's work at the time, Paul Davies is quick to point out that they had no major theatrical stimuli—indeed, those above are from other art forms (Davies 2021). Yet, we must acknowledge that Volcano were not on their own at the time in the UK with their reliance on the collective creative practice of devising. In fact, their development was at least in part co-eval with the evolution of other major devised theatre companies such as DV8 itself and the Sheffield-based Forced Entertainment (founded in 1984). Nonetheless, Volcano only became aware of Forced Entertainment at a later stage. Speaking in 2021, Davies primarily sees Forced Entertainment as a company engaged with how to negotiate the contemporary form of capitalism.[5] Undoubtedly, Forced Entertainment came to adapt Shakespeare at a much later point in the company's history. Their *Complete Works: Table Top Shakespeare* (2015) and its *At Home* lockdown version (2020)—much viewed during the Covid-19 pandemic—is a theatrical delicacy with an everyday touch. While there is a lot that distinguishes the style of the two companies, the predominance of "physically-based devised theatre" (to use Bruce Barton's apt term (2005)), alongside a penchant for a punk aesthetic, is a common element and it helps us place Volcano firmly in the experimental theatre landscape in the last quarter of the twentieth century, even if there was no significant contemporary theatrical influence on Volcano's work that they would have been conscious of at the time.[6]

Even though it was primarily Northwest Arts that funded Volcano around then and they benefited from various invitations to perform in the Manchester area, alongside frequent participation in the Edinburgh fringe, they thought of themselves as a Welsh and European company. Welshness is another contextual—if not strictly intertextual—framework that helps us better position this production. In retrospect, Davies thinks

---

[5] Davies (2021) is conscious of Volcano potentially having influenced Tic Toc Theatre Company in Coventry as well as Boilerhouse but does not think that there were companies who would have worked in a similar way at the time for Volcano to look up to.

[6] It is perhaps ironic that Nancy Meckler is mentioned as an important practitioner of "US-inspired style 'physical theatre'" in *Physical Theatres: A Critical Introduction* (Murray and Keefe 2016, 42), which makes interesting reading in the light of Volcano's concern with the *Sweet Sessions* performance coming across as too bookish.

of *L.O.V.E.* as a quintessentially Welsh show (Davies 2021). While none of the original co-creators of the performance spoke Welsh, they were conscious of the challenges and necessity of creating work that is away from the London limelight and is instead made in pre-devolution Wales, a culturally very rich and often overlooked part of the UK.

L.O.V.E. AND …

As mentioned earlier, the production history of *L.O.V.E.* is not complete with the remounting of the piece for the company's 25th anniversary. Fern Smith, who was one of the original performers and co-creators, has also created a spin-off production, *Women in L.O.V.E.* in 2013, with Mairi Phillips, her "Dark Lady" counterpart from the 2012 version. This performance, with its unmissably Lawrentian title, used the production history of *L.O.V.E.* and its key props—physical metaphors—as raw material and has extended the performance's boldly iconoclastic approach to Shakespeare to the iconic (and iconoclastic), famous and infamous production itself. The photo gallery of this performance reveals some key props intrinsic to *L.O.V.E.*—the knife and roses—in addition to passport photo style pictures of all the performers over the years and press cuttings that aid the critical/creative "woman-handled" retrospection. The colour scheme of the acclaimed Volcano production is also reproduced in *Women in L.O.V.E.* The red roses scattered on the stage, the red party hat worn by Fern Smith and the black dresses worn by both performers recall the black/red colour scheme of *L.O.V.E.* itself, with its very many associations, including the Freudian opposing drives of Eros and Thanatos as well as the broader themes of blood and death. The photos of previous cast members (fed into a fire at some point), the newspaper cuttings and the CD player held by Fern Smith in one of the production photos all emphasise the preoccupation with looking back, talking back, rewinding, unwinding and creative debriefing that characterises this somewhat intratextual, largely metatheatrical and summative spin-off production of an intriguing Shakespearean item of the physical theatre canon.

CONCLUSION

Peter Brook points out the issue with the academic who goes to the theatre to have their theoretical conviction justified:

[...] there is always a deadly spectator, who for special reasons enjoys a lack of intensity and even a lack of entertainment, such as the scholar who emerges from routine performances of the classics smiling because nothing has distracted him from trying over and confirming his pet theories, whilst reciting his favourite lines under his breath. In his heart he sincerely wants a theatre that is nobler-than-life and he confuses a sort of intellectual satisfaction with the true experience for which he craves. Unfortunately, he lends the weight of his authority to dullness and so the Deadly Theatre goes on its way. (1998, 10)

This is the kind of theatre and audience that Volcano's *L.O.V.E.* wished to unsettle and challenge as they tapped into the Shakespearean texts' "extraordinary plurality and fluidity" (Bickley and Stevens 2020, 2) for their "collaboratively authored"—devised—piece (Murray and Keefe 2016). Working against calcified perceptions of "bookishness" and high literary value, the production brought the Shakespearean text into a thoroughly physical matrix. "[S]ensuality undermines sense", writes Lehmann of post-dramatic theatre generally, also helping us interpret this take on the Sonnets (2006, 162). *L.O.V.E.* very much borders on the area of post-dramatic theatre, fluctuating between a sense of character in a dramatic (Aristotelian sense) and mere performing figures in a post-dramatic sense. As Fern Smith also underlines in *The Slate* documentary about Volcano, the three artists on stage are not actors but performers who work in the theatre.[7] The Sonnets were a perfect arena for experimentation with the physical and the post-dramatic and there is small wonder that the 2003 tour of the show was rapidly followed by the company's take on another adaptation "staple" from the Shakespeare canon, *Romeo and Juliet* (2004–2005), which they "revitalised for the reality tv generation".[8]

As an experimental production, pressing various artistic and ideological boundaries, *L.O.V.E.* has also featured as a UK arts export item, of which the aforementioned British Council funded Caucasian tour is a prominent example. From a postcolonial perspective there may be some slight irony to this largely iconoclastic (but also, in its own way, paradoxically canon-upholding) production coming from Wales being pressed into the service of communicating British culture abroad, but

[7] BBC Wales, The Slate: *Volcano*.

[8] See website. https://volcanotheatre.wales/timeline/. Accessed on 11 February 2022.

the "Britishness" this artistic "package" delivered would not have been one smoothly adhering to stereotypes. So much so that public diplomacy expert Nicholas J. Cull (2011, 127) uses this production—and its South Caucasus tour—as an example of theatre diplomacy as dialogue, in light of the political debate the performance instigated in Georgia in particular. In my view, the performance also had something to do with some of the other functions of theatre diplomacy as outlined by Cull (prestige gift and cultural information), but Cull's emphasis on the show's contribution to (cultural) dialogue appropriately highlights the relentless and uncompromising creative critical probing of the Sonnets in this performance.

REFERENCES

Aspden, Peter. 2003. "Does this look like the best way to sell Britain?" *Financial Times Magazine*. 25 July 2003.

Barba, Eugenio. 2000. "The Deep Order Called Turbulence: The Three Faces of Dramaturgy" *The Drama Review*, 44.4: 56–66.

Barton, Bruce. 2005. "Navigating Turbulence: The Dramaturg in Physical Theatre", *Theatre Topics*, 15.1: 103–119.

BBC Wales. *The Slate: Volcano*. Producer/director Karen Whiteside. [accessed via Volcano archive]

Bermel, Albert. 2013. *Artaud's Theatre of Cruelty*. London: Bloomsbury. [2001].

Bickley, Pamela and Stevens, Jenny. 2020. *Studying Shakespeare Adaptation: From Restoration Theatre to YouTube*. London: Bloomsbury.

Brook, Peter. 1996. *The Empty Space: A Book About the Theatre: Deadly, Holy, Rough, Immediate*. New York: Scribner. [1968].

Burke, Jim. 1993. *"L.O.V.E."* [Review of *L.O.V.E.* at the Green Room, Manchester]. *Plays and Players*. [accessed via Volcano archive].

Cull, Nicholas J. 2011. "Staging the Catastrophe: The Tricycle Theatre's The Great Game: Afghanistan and Its Diplomatic Journey from London to the Pentagon, 2010-11", *Theatre Topics*, 21.2: 125-137.

Davies, Paul. 2012. "Nigel Charnock, 1960–2012." [accessed via Volcano archive].

Davies, Paul. 2021. Unpublished interview with author.

Davies, Sarah. 2013. "Volcano: *L.O.V.E.*" [Review]. *Total Theatre* August 2013. http://totaltheatre.org.uk/volcano-theatre-l-o-v-e/. Accessed on 23 October 2021.

Godfrey, Paul. 1998. *Plays 1*. London: Methuen.

Hewison, James. 2019. "Shakespeare and *L.O.V.E.*: Dance and Desire in the Sonnets". In *The Oxford Handbook of Shakespeare and Dance*, ed. by Lynsey McCulloch and Brandon Shaw. 525–544. Oxford: Oxford University Press.

James, Bethan Natalie. 2012. Review—*L.O.V.E.* by Volcano. National Theatre Wales Community. 30 October 2012. https://community.nationaltheatre wales.org/profiles/blogs/review-l-o-v-e-by-volcano. Accessed 23 October 2021.

Johnston, Ruth D. 2002. "The Staging of the Bourgeois Imaginary in *The Cook, the Thief, His Wife, and Her Lover* (1990)" *Cinema Journal* 41.2: 19–40.

Lehmann, Hans-Thies. 2006. *Postdramatic Theatre*. Tr. by Karen Jürs-Munby. London and New York: Routledge.

Murray, Simon and Keefe, John. 2016. *Physical Theatres: A Critical Introduction*. 2nd ed. Abingdon and New York: Routledge.

P. J. S. 1991. "*Sweet Dreams*" [A review]. *Cahiers Élisabéthains* 40.1: 84–86.

Radosavljević, Duška. 2016. "Theatre Criticism: Changing Landscapes" in *Theatre Criticism: Changing Landscapes*, ed. by Duška Radosavljević. 1–36. London: Bloomsbury Methuen.

Sanders, Julie. 2011. "The *Sonnets* as an Open-Source Initiative", in *Shakespeare as Cultural Catalyst: Shakespeare Survey* 64, ed. Peter Holland. 121–132.

Saunders, Graham. 2002. *'Love Me or Kill Me': Sarah Kane and the Theatre of Extremes*. Manchester: Manchester University Press.

Smith, Ashley. 2012. "Legendary Theatre comes to Derby", Derby Independent Theatre Network blog. 23 October 2012.

Volcano. 2012a. "Notes for Box Office and Marketing" [accessed via Volcano archive].

Volcano. 2012b. "Press Release: *L.O.V.E*," [accessed via Volcano archive].

Western Mail. 2003. "Volcano's 'corruption' sees steamy night in Georgia". 1 July 2003.

CHAPTER 13

Homoerotic Counter-Mythologies in Derek Jarman's *The Angelic Conversation*

Jim Ellis

Derek Jarman (1942–1994) was a queer artist, writer, gardener, and filmmaker, for whom the Renaissance in general, and Shakespeare in particular, was a life-long site of inspiration and contestation. His career spanned several generations of gay and queer activism, from his first feature *Sebastiane* (1975), which reflects the idealism of the gay liberationist movement, to his punk version of *The Tempest* (1979), through more overtly self-reflexive engagements with the past in films such as *Caravaggio* (1986), and, finally, his pointedly anachronistic adaptation of Christopher Marlowe's *Edward II* (1991), an anti-Thatcherite film that was heralded by B. Ruby Rich as one of the pioneering works

---

This chapter is a revised and expanded version of a section from Chapter three of Jim Ellis, Derek Jarman's Angelic Conversations, 99–110. I am grateful to the press for permission to reprint this material.

J. Ellis (✉)
University of Calgary, Calgary, Canada
e-mail: jellis@ucalgary.ca

© The Author(s), under exclusive license to Springer Nature Switzerland AG 2023
J. Kingsley-Smith and W. R. Rampone Jr. (eds.), *Shakespeare's Global Sonnets*, Global Shakespeares, https://doi.org/10.1007/978-3-031-09472-9_13

of the New Queer Cinema. Jarman's attraction to the Renaissance was multi-faceted, including a straightforward fascination with the arcane knowledges of the alchemists, botanists, and Neoplatonists; an interest in artists and writers with whom he identified and whom he considered as gay forerunners; and a life-long loathing for the more reverential forms of the British period film, which he saw as celebrating and perpetuating a nostalgic, conservative version of England.[1] We can see all of these features of his engagements with the Renaissance at work in his adaptation of Shakespeare's Sonnets, *The Angelic Conversation* (1985).

The Angelic Conversation falls into the broad category of the experimental or non-narrative feature film. Although he started his film career as a set designer for Ken Russell, whose exuberantly anachronistic approaches to the period film were a clear influence, Jarman very quickly left studio filmmaking and took up a super-8 camera to make short, experimental films, at first simply documenting the various countercultural circles in which he moved. Very soon, however, Jarman began playing with time and the texture of the film image: filming at high speed and then re-filming the results, projecting at low speed to create a dreamy, stuttering effect, or projecting films onto images and re-photographing them, to layer up images. The super-8s were, for the most part, made to be shown at parties at Jarman's studio flat, in random order, with changing soundtracks; these spectatorial conditions, which made the films into an occasion for the formation of new communities and new relationships, are important to consider when thinking about Jarman's understanding of the purpose of cinema and its relation to the community.

Two of Jarman's early feature films that invoked Renaissance themes were clearly influenced by the punk movement of the mid-seventies, which had a substantial queer element. *Jubilee* (1978) is a punk apocalypse filmed during Elizabeth II's jubilee year, occasionally shuttling back to the first Elizabeth, whom we see walking in the Mortlake gardens of the alchemist John Dee (played by Richard O'Brien of *Rocky Horror* fame). This film would be followed fairly shortly after by Jarman's punk adaptation of *The Tempest*, employing a cut-up and rearranged script, with its action set in a decaying manor house. For Jarman, the stately home was symbolic both of the stifling nostalgia of the period film and

---

[1] For a more extended investigation of Jarman's interest in the renaissance, see Jim Ellis, "Queer Period: Derek Jarman's Renaissance," 288–315.

the stagnation of the English state. In one of his trademark anachronistic gestures, he replaces the goddesses of the masque in act four with the Black diva Elisabeth Welch singing "Stormy Weather" to an entranced Miranda and Ferdinand. Making a cabaret number by a Black singer the intensely joyful, emotional core of the film is one way of answering back to the racial dynamics of the play and its original moment, as well as to the generally all-white version of the past that the period film typically offers.[2]

The Angelic Conversation combines the formal experimentation of the early short films with Jarman's later interest in disrupting the period film's nostalgic reproduction of the past. In this film, Jarman uses the more intimate gauge of super-8 to explore the terrain of gay desire, using the sonnets as the occasion for reflection and expansion.[3] The film was made with a technique similar to that of his early home movies: he shot most of *The Angelic Conversation* at very high speed, projected it slow, and re-filmed the result, using a video camera connected to a U-matic deck (Jarman 1987, 145). The result, as Jarman said of his short film "*Sebastiane* Wrap" (1975), is that the films "work rather like a slide show, you're always pulled back to the image."[4] The images in the film trace out a very loose narrative of desire held together by the soundtrack, on which Judi Dench reads fourteen of Shakespeare's Sonnets; we also hear music by Coil and Benjamin Britten, and other occasional sounds like the crashing of waves or the heavy ticking of a clock.

It is useful to begin a consideration of *The Angelic Conversation* by reflecting on the choice of the sonnets themselves. The most obvious reason to use Shakespeare's *Sonnets* as the backbone of the film is that they are the most famous of the Renaissance sonnet sequences, written by the central icon of the age. They represent cultural capital and can act, therefore, as a site of cultural contestation. Moreover, given the homo-erotic nature of the first part of the sequence—the sonnets addressed to the young man—the choice makes sense for a film that is, to some degree,

---

[2] For a more extended treatment of this topic, see Jim Ellis, "Conjuring *The Tempest*: Derek Jarman and the Spectacle of Redemption," 265–284. For a classic account of the heritage film that is roughly contemporaneous with Jarman, see Andrew Higson, "Re-presenting the National Past: Nostalgia and Pastiche in the Heritage Film," 109–29.

[3] I am using "gay" rather than "queer" here and elsewhere in this essay to specify the historical moment of the film, which predates queer politics.

[4] Commentary accompanying a program of super-8 shorts shown at Berkeley.

concerned with building or asserting a gay tradition. Indeed, it is largely on the basis of these sonnets, rather than other literary works or historical evidence, that Shakespeare has been claimed by a succession of gay artists, in spite of the fact that the final sonnets in the sequence address the poet's love for the duplicitous dark lady, who simultaneously disgusts him and incites his lust. While the film is by no means a simplistic claiming of Shakespeare for a gay tradition, using the *Sonnets* as the backbone of a reverie on gay desire is, nonetheless, a provocative political gesture, one which resists a long history of heterosexualizing the crown jewel of the English literary tradition.

A related, but less remarked upon, reason for choosing the sonnets is the particular portrait of desire that they offer. Unlike Edmund Spenser's *Amoretti*, which traces out a Neoplatonic exaltation of the poet's beloved, or Philip Sidney's *Astrophel and Stella*, which idealizes the cruel Petrarchan mistress, Stella, Shakespeare's *Sonnets* offers a more complex and less idealizing examination of what can be seen as heterodox desires. In her commentaries on the sequence, Helen Vendler remarks that "the sonnets show the cycle of idealization, infatuation, and inevitable disillusion twice over, once with a male love-object and once with a female"(638). Shakespeare's sequence is both a development of and a break from the earlier traditions of sonneteering; in spite of the dreamy quality of the film, Jarman's use of these sonnets might similarly be seen as a break with, or at least a distancing from, an earlier utopian strain in gay discourse.

It is significant that in selecting the fourteen sonnets he includes in the film, Jarman does not simply take those from the first part of the sequence that addresses the attractive young man, which would have made the film a more straightforward celebration of gay romance. Instead, he ignores for the most part the early sonnets (which, in any case, frequently urge the young man to marry and reproduce), and ranges over the entire sequence, using as an epigraph for the film lines from one of the final sonnets (151), which reflects on the inevitability but also the value of romantic disillusionment. Isolated by themselves, however, the lines register differently: "Love is too young to know what conscience is, /Yet who knows not conscience is born of love?" (151.1–2). These lines suggest that desire is itself amoral (and thus object-choice is not a matter of morality), but the experience of love (any experience of love) is the foundation of morality. In this poem, argues Vendler, Shakespeare "admits the libidinal base of adult consciousness itself" (639). This is not the same as the Neoplatonic insistence on the essentially moral nature of desire, which lifts us up out of carnality and moves us toward heavenly understanding. In these poems, disgust as much as delight is what breaks us out of egoism and leads us to both self-consciousness and a recognition of the other (the foundation of ethics), and this is a desire that is always solidly rooted in the flesh. This is a highly appropriate sentiment for a film whose politics are grounded upon an insistence on the centrality of sexual expression in human experience, and also, of course, on an insistence that certain sexual practices traditionally regarded as degraded are equally an avenue to greater self-consciousness and indeed, to ethical being.

Both the *Sonnets* and *The Angelic Conversation* can thus be seen as charting new ground in their different historical moments. Joel Fineman famously argues that by shifting away from the idealizing poetry of praise previously associated with sonnets, Shakespeare moves from a poetics of homogeneity to a poetics of heterogeneity. In so doing, argues Fineman, "Shakespeare in his sonnets invents the poetics of heterosexuality" (17). Jarman can be seen in this film to be exploring new psychic terrain, a post-Stonewall gay consciousness, while at the same time inventing a filmic poetics that would allow for such an exploration. The inclusion of the *Sonnets* in the film is thus something of a strategic reclamation. The homoeroticism of the early sonnets is underlined, and the poet's despair at the heterodox nature of his heterosexual desire for the Dark Lady in the latter part of the sequence is redeployed for other purposes.

The film selects a group of sonnets from across the sequence (57, 90, 43, 53, 148, 126, 29, 94, 30, 55, 27, 61, 56, and 104), and rearranges them to construct (or suggest) a new narrative. Jarman himself described the film thus: "A series of slow-moving sequences through a landscape seen from the windows of an Elizabethan house. Two young men find and lose each other. The film ends in a garden" (1984, 133). This sketchy outline is very similar to what one gets when one tries to sum up the narrative in a sonnet sequence ("A poet is infatuated with a narcissistic young man, who disappoints him. He winds up infatuated with an unfaithful woman."). The interest of a sonnet sequence lies not in its narrative complexity, but rather in the way it registers a series of lyrical moments of consciousness that are related to or that arise from the implied story. This is the most productive way of viewing the film as well. The slight narrative that it offers does not bear (or indeed, reward) as much examination as what might be called the experience of the film: the series of images, sounds, and textures that act as meditations (or prompts for meditations) on certain themes.

Jarman starts with a poem of cheerily masochistic longing: "Being your slave, what should I do but tend/Upon the hours and times of your desire?" (57.1–2). The poems that follow trace out an arc that is suggestive of a particularly gay experience of desire. We move from poems of longing and anxiety (57, 90, 43), to a poem marveling at the beauty of the beloved (Sonnet 53), which is juxtaposed with another (Sonnet 148) about finding something beautiful that the rest of the world deems inappropriate: "If that be fair whereon my false eyes dote, / What means the world to say it is not so?" (148.5–6). The central poem of this new sequence, from which came the title of a pioneering gay play and film,[5] meditates on what it means to be an outcast, and how love compensates for the world's scorn: "When in disgrace with Fortune and men's eyes... Haply I think on thee... For thy sweet love rememb'red such wealth brings / That then I scorn to change my state with kings" (29.1, 10, 13–4). Sonnet 94 thinks about the power of the beautiful man; Sonnet 30 returns to the contrast between worldly disappointment and the private joy taken in contemplation of the beloved; and Sonnet 55 continues this thought by contrasting worldly monuments with this more intimate tribute to the beloved: "Not marble nor the gilded monuments / Of princes shall outlive this pow'rful rhyme" (55.1–2). Two poems originally about sleeplessness caused by thinking on the beloved (27, 61) become, via the imagery, poems about staying awake after sex, looking in wonder at the beloved sleeping. This is followed by a sonnet of parting (56), in which, argues Vendler, "the yearning of a heterodox form of attachment to be a socially sanctioned one is visible" (272). Finally, the sequence ends with an elegiac tone, offering reassurances that the beloved's beauty will not fade, at least not in memory: "To me, fair friend, you never can be old" (104.1). This sentiment is reminiscent of the poet C. F. Cavafy's homoerotic elegies (and in particular, "Before Time Could Change Them"), memorably illustrated by David Hockney in a 1966 edition of prints that Jarman identified as groundbreaking.

---

[5] John Herbert, *Fortune and Men's Eyes* (New York: Grove Press, 1967). This highly successful pre-Stonewall prison drama featured a number of gay characters and in the climactic scene Sonnet 29 is recited by the queer character, Mona, to calm another prisoner down. The play was workshopped in 1967 by Dustin Hoffman at the Actors Studio, with Hoffman playing the lead role of Smitty and Jon Voigt co-starring. It had a year-long run in London in 1969, including three months in the West End, and was released as a film in 1971.

As can be seen even in this brief overview, the film is strategic in its use of the sonnets, neither completely faithful nor completely anachronistic. Some of the dominant themes are retained (erotic obsession, longing, heterodox desires, alienation); others from the sonnets do not show up (sexual disgust, misogyny, reproduction); while others, as we have seen, are to some degree reconfigured by the imagery that accompanies them or by their placement in the new sequence. Other elements of the sound-track work in a similarly multivalent way: the music is a mix of occasionally jarring, discordant themes written for the film by the queer experimental music group *Coil* (along with music from their appropriately named EP, *How to Destroy Angels*), interspersed with the more romantic "Sea Inter-ludes" from Benjamin Britten's modernist opera *Peter Grimes*. The choice of this latter music is significant both for its content and its author. The opera concerns itself with a tormented outsider, and Britten's homosexu-ality was an open secret that was the barely concealed subject of a number of his works.

If the soundtrack constructs a few different gay lineages for the film via the voice-over and the music, the image track constructs yet more. The Renaissance imagery of the film is an obvious match for the sonnets, and it connects with Jarman's earlier films of the past. A number of impor-tant images recur. We start with a young man looking wistfully out of the diamond-paned windows of a country house, evoking both the Eliz-abethan period and the conventions of the period film, which this film will resist. In discussing his setting of *The Tempest*, Jarman said the stately home is "the indispensable prop for the English way of life... Any film or TV series that has one is half-way to success" (*Dancing Ledge*, 172). Later, a young man in a vaguely Elizabethan outfit uses a circular mirror to flashlight into a camera, much like the character Ariel in *Jubilee*. Other images are reminiscent of Jarman's version of *The Tempest*: a young man on a beach performs a variety of enigmatic tasks, including carrying a barrel, while elsewhere another man carries a log on his shoulders, sugges-tive of both Caliban and Ferdinand. In a series of images that appear to be shot directly on video, a young man ceremonially washes and then kisses a tattooed man who is installed on a throne, while a third figure, holding a pair of torches, looks on. The tattooed man is evocative of the hierophantic figures that show up both in Aleister Crowley's occultism and in the films of Kenneth Anger, and can be related back to Jarman's interest in Renaissance *magi* and arcana (we see similar connections in Jarman's *Tempest* through the figure of Prospero). More generally, we get the recurrent images of flowers and gardens, which Jarman persistently associates with the Renaissance.

The Renaissance imagery does not allow us the unproblematic access to the past that the heritage film typically offers. We are not meant to believe that we are looking at characters from the past. For one thing, the young man looking out through the diamond-paned window is wearing a black dinner jacket and has a recognizably 1980s haircut. Nor does the juxtaposition of past and present function in the same way as the aggressively anachronistic props in Jarman's *Caravaggio*, where the art critic, Baglione, uses a manual typewriter and another character a gold pocket calculator. Here, the historical imagery and references work to suggest or to forge a continuity with the time of the *Sonnets*, in order to claim a cultural inheritance. What the film is doing, in a sense, is reading these poems in the present, or at least, from the present of a gay British filmmaker in the 1980s.

Steven Dillon places *The Angelic Conversation* in the genre of the poetic film, a genre that frequently explores themes of sexuality and subjectivity. The film locates itself more narrowly in a tradition of gay filmmakers working within this genre, which includes Cocteau's Orpheus trilogy (especially *The Blood of a Poet* [1930–32]), Kenneth Anger's *Fireworks* (1947), and Jean Genet's *Un Chant D'Amour* (1950). In particular, *The Angelic Conversation* recalls Cocteau in its suggestion of an Orphic journey to the underworld (the scenes with the tattooed man) and it draws on some of Anger's favorite biker imagery in its underworld sequence. Genet's film can be seen as a reaction to the earlier films by Cocteau and Anger,[6] and Jarman's film as a development of Genet's.

Un Chant d'amour is a tightly structured film about a literally clos-eted desire. Set in a prison, it juxtaposes actual attempts at metaphoric intercourse (prisoners swinging a garland of flowers between two barred windows, one prisoner blowing smoke through a straw into another prisoner's mouth, a guard forcing a gun into a prisoner's mouth) with sequences of a prisoner and a guard's fantasies of sexual intercourse. Desire in the film can only be consummated metaphorically, or via displacement. Genet more or less disowned the film later in life, and

---

[6] "Cocteau was one of the early key practitioners of film poetry and Jean Cau was certain that *Un Chant d'Amour* was heavily influenced by—if not derivative of—Cocteau's *Blood of a Poet*" Genet certainly viewed Kenneth Anger's short film *Fireworks* (1947) in 1949, and the two bear comparison in their visions of homoerotic desire." Jane Giles, 81.

its producer dismissed it as a romantic, immature work (Giles, *Criminal Desires*,135). It is certainly true that the tightly schematic imagery leaves little room for complexity or depth, and the fantasy sequences are highly (but no doubt purposefully) pastoral. It is at least partly by virtue of the intervening years that Jarman's film can be seen as a response to and further development of Genet's and, of course, as an advance on his own film *Sebastiane*, which can be seen as an intermediate point between the two. *Sebastiane* is set in a similar terrain as *Un Chant d'Amour*[7] (isolated army encampment vs. prison) and offers similarly lyrical, pastoral treatments of gay desire set against brutal violence. *Sebastiane*'s treatment of homosexual desire, however, is indebted to Gay Liberation discourse, attempting to disengage it from pathology and criminality by inventing what amounts to a gay spirituality, or at the very least, by insisting on the utopian possibilities of a liberated sexuality.

What, in turn, distinguishes *The Angelic Conversation* from Jarman's earlier film is a retreat from (or advance beyond) the idealism of the Gay Liberation years. The film still offers lyric portrayals of gay desire, but it does this within the context of an exploration of gay psychology. It is one of the functions of the sonnets Jarman chooses to offer a complex, non-idealized portrait of desire. What distinguishes the film from others in the genre of poetic or lyric film, gay or otherwise, is its insistence on placing this exploration of subjectivity in relation to the outside world. Here is where we might see the influence of another, earlier, gay film-maker working in a much different tradition: Eisenstein, the subject of Jarman's *Imagining October* (1984). Echoes of Eisenstein occur visually in a couple of places, most notably in a repeated side-angle shot of a young man kneeling on a beach, holding up a shell, looking much like a statue. More crucially, however, Jarman uses Eisensteinian montage to place the psychological exploration within a political context. The most obvious examples of this are the repeated images of a chain link fence and a radar tower, as well as images of a burning car, turned on its side. As Jarman writes, "Destruction hovers in the background of *The Angelic Conversation*; the radar, the surveillance, the feeling one is under psychic attack; of course, we are under attack at the moment" (Jarman, *The Last of England*, 133). The first time we see the radar tower it is cross-cut with

---

[7] Jarman himself draws attention to the shared "obsession with the language of closed structures, the ritual of the closet and the sanctuary... the prison cells of Genet's *Un Chant D'Amour*, the desert encampment of *Sebastiane*"; *The Last of England*, 60.

images of the young man with the flashing mirror, which in earlier films is associated with alternative desire. The cross-cut echoes the juxtaposition in the sonnets of the private, heterodox desire with the hostile outside world. What is notable here, and what is largely absent from earlier gay films, is the clear emphasis placed on the interconnections of sexuality, subjectivity, and history.

The development of themes and images from his earlier films is matched by the film's reinvestigation of certain formal techniques he used in the 1970s. *The Angelic Conversation* returns to the experimental super-8 format of the earlier "home movies," only now combined with video, which was emerging at this point as the next home movie format. Jarman says of *Sebastiane* that, "The home movie is the bedrock, it records the landscape of leisure: the beach, the garden, the swimming pool" (Jarman, *The Last of England*, 54). The super-8s of the 1970s documented a newly emergent social terrain, alongside their more formal experiments with filmic space. Both of these pursuits are taken up again in *The Angelic Conversation*; Jarman notes that "All the things that happen in that film were things that happen in 'home movies', like down on the beach swimming, walking through the landscape, going to the stately home"(Field and O'Pray, 55). The home movie as a form is particularly suitable for Jarman's version of the Renaissance, or, at least, for this particular Renaissance exploration.

If the home movie records the "landscape of leisure," *The Angelic Conversation* alerts us to the fact that the landscape of leisure is, not surprisingly, also the landscape of desire. This is often effaced in the home movie, which is almost by definition a chaste genre, its chastity underscored by its demonic doubles: the stag film and the amateur sex video. Desire is banished from the home movie, and homoerotic desire, in particular, is the true serpent lurking in the grass, given that the familial ideology that the home movie reproduces is specifically premised on its exclusion. But, at the same time that they attempt to banish desire, home movies are nonetheless strongly marked by it: as Jarman notes, "In all home movies is a longing for paradise" (*The Last of England*, 54). They record real gardens, in other words, but long for ideal ones. In both the sonnets and Jarman's film, this longing is connected in the first instance to homoerotic desire: it is a longing both for its immediate object, the beautiful young man, but more importantly for the time and space of that desire. This, for Jarman, is always connected with the garden, or, as he says elsewhere, "our corner of Paradise, the part of the garden the

Lord forgot to mention" (*Modern Nature*, 23). This is one reason why the film ends in the space of the Elizabethan garden.

Daniel O'Quinn argues in his essay on *Modern Nature* that Jarman associated what O'Quinn calls the sacred, "sodomitical" space of the garden with a different apprehension of time. Time in the garden is opposed to what might be called monumental time; O'Quinn locates in Jarman's work a critique of "an imperial allegory in which time and knowledge colonize history such that access to paradise has become prohibited" (118). Imperial time or monumental time is linked both to the experience of time that Benedict Anderson argues characterizes the modern nation and also, of course, to our modern sense of narrative, which both the home movie and *The Angelic Conversation* eschew.

The home movie format is well suited formally to the sonnet sequence, particularly Shakespeare's, which is so centrally concerned with time and with longing. As we've seen, the first lines of the film are from Sonnet 57: "Being your slave, what should I do but tend / Upon the hours and times of your desire." On the soundtrack, we hear the heavy tick of an old clock, which accentuates the stuttering pace of the images. The rhythm of the images, says Jarman, is like that of a heartbeat; we might note as well it comes close to the beat of iambic pentameter, the meter of the sonnet. What we get is a different experience of temporality: a series of discrete moments in which the texture of time becomes evident. Like the sonnet sequence itself, the film becomes a concatenation of individual moments of apprehension, taking place in an eternal present: in lyric time, in other words, rather than monumental time. This different experience of time is connected to a different experience of space. The graininess of the image draws attention to its texture (particularly in those moments when we see either flames or water), and while they are not entirely dispelled, we become aware of how the illusions of depth and motion are created on the screen. Like the super-8s of the 1970s, the film's re-processing of the images draws attention to the screen as a space: as with the garden in *The Garden of Luxor* (1973), the space of *The Angelic Conversation* is a purely cinematic one, its constructed nature visible to the eye. Moreover, the experience of watching the film lulls us into a particular mental space, a dreamy receptivity, where the succession of images works on our imagination and where the boundary between self and film becomes blurred. This apprehension of a different kind of time and a different experience of space is crucial to the project; the film, we might say, inhabits the space of the garden in order to resist the monumental time of the nation.

The return to this particular space and time in the Renaissance is a way of returning to the point where this particular version of nationhood was being newly consolidated, and most importantly, the film resists a particular construction of time, narrative, and nationhood in the present.

To what extent, we might wonder, is the home movie a Renaissance genre? Social historians argue that the Renaissance was marked by the establishment of a clear separation between the public and private spheres, which accompanied both the emergence of what would become the middle class, and the invention of the nuclear family. It is in very real ways, then, the ideological home of the home movie. But the Renaissance is also a prime site for the contestation of ownership of England. Shakespeare, Elizabeth, and the English Renaissance were, and of course still are, potent sources of meaning for nationalist ideologies; as Jarman notes, "Elizabethan England is our cultural Arcadia, as Shakespeare is the essential pivot of our culture"(Field and O'Pray, "Interview," 49). For English nationalist ideologies, then, the Renaissance *is* home, and a cursory glance at the production of the British film industry from its origins to the present would suggest that the Renaissance period film is the nationalist equivalent of the home movie. Each new example is an attempt to capture, or perhaps inhabit anew, the cultural Arcadia. By returning to this Arcadia, these films re-imagine the national home and family. How this cultural home is pictured, then, and who makes it into the frame, have an obvious importance.

When questioned about the politics of *The Angelic Conversation*, Jarman immediately remarked upon the effort "to reclaim Shakespeare for a homoerotic tradition" (Field and O'Pray, "Interview," 56). One need only reflect on the complete effacement of the sonnets' homoerotic themes in John Madden's film *Shakespeare in Love* (UK, 1996) to see that this is not some quaint project from the early days of Gay Liberation. The heteronormative conceit of *Shakespeare in Love* is that, as the character of Viola de Lesseps puts it, "stage love will never be true love while the law of the land has our heroines being played by pipsqueak boys in petticoats." Consequently, the sonnets that were originally addressed to the young man now turn out to be written to a young woman. In essence, the film suggests that the only authentic desire is heterosexual; everything else is just dressing up. This film, which is only one example of a centuries-long tradition of heterosexualizing Shakespeare, is a particularly apt demonstration of Jarman's claims about the politics and the problems of period films. Costume drama, he wrote, is "a delusion based on a collective amnesia, ignorance and furnishing fabrics. (Lurex for an Oscar)" (Jarman, *Queer Edward II*, 86). It is something of an irony that Sandy Powell, Jarman's longtime costume designer from *Caravaggio* onward, won an Academy Award for *Shakespeare in Love*.

The problem is not just the familiar one of under- or mis-representation, of writing Blacks or gays or women out of history. *Shakespeare in Love* would not have been a more historically accurate film had the Gwyneth Paltrow role been played by Leonardo DiCaprio. It has to do as well with the texture of that representation itself, and with an understanding of the psychic dimensions of cultural memory. Here is where *The Angelic Conversation* differs from some of Jarman's other Renaissance films, like *Caravaggio* or *Edward II*, in spite of the historical self-reflexivity that is signaled in their use of creative anachronism. *The Angelic Conversation* uses the resources and especially the affective pull of the home movie in order to intervene at one of the key sites of English nationalist fantasy. It is not enough, in other words, to rewrite or correct history, which might imply that history was stable, knowable, and real. *The Angelic Conversation* understands that the history involved in nation-alist imaginings offers itself as an answer to the longing for home, which is often literalized in the period drama's obsession with stately homes. The strategy the film employs is not to critique the longing, but to shift the grounds; what Jarman offers is not so much a corrective as an alternative mythology. Through the dream-like time and texture of the film, Jarman offers a counter-memory, a memory of homoerotic desire. What makes this peculiarly effective is precisely the choice of form: by invading the grounds of the home movie, which records the alternative time of leisure, and the alternative space of the garden, Jarman challenges the production of the nationalist present by intervening in the representation of its past.

The anniversary of Jarman's death in 1994 was marked in 2014 by a series of events, including a symposium on "Early Modern Jarman," at King's College, London, on February 1, in which I participated. The evening prior to the symposium featured a 24-hour screening of *The Angelic Conversation* in the King's College chapel. Appropriately enough, the design of the chapel is Renaissance Revival—a nineteenth-century interpretation of this foundational moment of England's glory. The film was projected onto what appeared to be a bedsheet that had been strung up near the front of the chapel, with the images visible from both sides. The mode of the projection and the mood of attendees evoked the super-8 screening parties from Jarman's early career, and indeed, the

234   J. ELLIS

atmosphere was convivial and even festive, with at least one couple making out in a darker corner of the room. Jarman would surely have approved. Sitting in this nineteenth-century version of the Renaissance, watching the super-8s of a much-loved figure in gay history, and enjoying the community of a diverse assortment of friends and potential friends, I felt that I was, for the first time, experiencing the film as it was intended to be viewed. If the home movie functions to manufacture home, then Jarman's home movies of Shakespeare are uniquely successful, working to reclaim the English Renaissance as a home for queer desire.

REFERENCES

Anderson, Benedict. 1991. *Imagined Communities: Reflections on the Origin and Spread of Nationalism*. London: Verso.
Dillon, Steven. 2004. *Derek Jarman and Lyric Film*. Austin: University of Texas Press.
Ellis, Jim. 1999. "Queer Period: Derek Jarman's Renaissance." *Out Takes: Essays on Queer Theory and Film*, ed. by Ellis Hanson. 288–315. Durham, NC: Duke University Press.
———. 2001. "Conjuring The Tempest: Derek Jarman and the Spectacle of Redemption." *GLQ: A Journal of Lesbian and Gay Studies* 7.2: 265–284.
———. 2009. *Derek Jarman's Angelic Conversations*. Minneapolis, MN: Minnesota University Press.
Field, Simon and Michael O'Pray. 1985. "On Imagining October, Dr. Dee and Other Matters: An Interview with Derek Jarman." *Afterimage* 12 (Autumn 1985): 40–59.
Fineman, Joel. 1986. *Shakespeare's Perjured Eye: The Invention of Poetic Subjectivity in the Sonnets*. Berkeley: University of California Press.
Giles, Jane. 2002. *Criminal Desires: Jean Genet and Cinema Persistence of Vision*. Vol. 2. Creation Books.
Herbert, John. 1967. *Fortune and Men's Eyes*. New York: Grove Press.
Higson, Andrew. 1993. "Re-presenting the National Past: Nostalgia and Pastiche in the Heritage Film." In *Fires Were Started: British Cinema and Thatcherism*, ed. Lester Friedman. 109–29. Minneapolis, MN: University of Minnesota Press.
Hockney, David. 1966. "Illustrations for Fourteen Poems by C. F. Cavafy."
Jarman, Derek. 1984. *Dancing Ledge*, ed. by Shaun Allen. London: Quartet Books. Print.
———. 1987. *Last of England*, ed. by D. L. Hirst. London: Constable.
———. 1991. *Queer Edward II*. London: BFI Publishing.
———. 1992. *Modern Nature*. London: Vintage.

———. Super-8 roll #1, #2, #3. Pacific Film Archive, Berkeley, CA. Video.
Jarman, Derek, director. 1979. *The Tempest*. Produced by Guy Ford and Mordecai Schreiber. Kendon Films.
———. 1985. *The Angelic Conversation*. Produced by James Mackay.
———. 1986. *Caravaggio*. Produced by Sarah Radclyffe. British Film Institute.
———. 1991. *Edward II*. Produced by Steve Clark-Hall and Antony Root. Working Title.
O'Quinn, Daniel. 1999. "Gardening, History, and the Escape from Time: Derek Jarman's *Modern Nature*." *October* 89: 113–26. Print.
Rich, B. Ruby. 2004. "New Queer Cinema." *Sight and Sound* 2.5 (September 1993). Reprinted in *New Queer Cinema: A Critical Reader*, ed. by Michele Aaron. 15–22. Edinburgh: Edinburgh University Press.
Vendler, Helen. 1997. *The Art of Shakespeare's Sonnets*. Cambridge, Mass: Belknap Press.

CHAPTER 14

Institutions of Love and Death: Shakespeare's Sonnets in Elderly Care Facilities

Nely Keinänen and Jussi Lehtonen

While Shakespeare's sonnets have been analysed at length, and are a staple of English literature curricula across Europe, it seems that professional theatrical performances of the sonnets are not very common. In the English-speaking world, a rare exception is Peter Brook's *Love is My Sin*, a duet of 31 sonnets, which was first performed in 2007 at the Theatre Des Bouffes du Nord, with Natasha Parry and Bruce Myers.[1]

[1] In 2010, it was performed at the Duke Theatre in New York (Isherwood 2010) and in 2011 at the Rose Theatre in Kingston (Billington 2011), with Parry and Michael Pennington, but has not been extensively revived.

N. Keinänen
University of Helsinki, Helsinki, Finland
e-mail: nely.keinanen@helsinki.fi

J. Lehtonen (✉)
Finnish National Theatre, University of the Arts Helsinki, Helsinki, Finland
e-mail: jussi.lehtonen@kansallisteatteri.fi

© The Author(s), under exclusive license to Springer Nature
Switzerland AG 2023
J. Kingsley-Smith and W. R. Rampone Jr. (eds.), *Shakespeare's Global Sonnets*,
Global Shakespeares, https://doi.org/10.1007/978-3-031-09472-9_14

In 2014, the Berliner Ensemble joined with the director Robert Wilson to perform "Shakespeare's Sonnets", a musical pageant with music by Rufus Wainwright, but this also seems to have been an isolated production (Isherwood 2014a, b). Since 2013, the New York Shakespeare Exchange's "Sonnet Project" has been commissioning films of individual sonnets and has since expanded to three series: New York City, the United States, and International. In addition to these direct performances of Shakespeare's sonnets, in 1998 the Acting Company commissioned one-act plays inspired by various sonnets, *Love's Fire*, but this has rarely been revived (Isherwood 1998; Toomer 1998). In a foreign language context, questions of translation and cultural identification also figure in the rare performances of Shakespeare's sonnets. In the Portuguese Tiago Rodrigues' *By Heart* (2013), for example, ten members of the audience were invited onstage to learn Shakespeare's Sonnet 30 "by heart and not by brain", which Francesca Rayner describes as a "way of individually and collectively maintaining Shakespeare at the heart of European cultural memory" (Rayner 2017, 27, 39). In this chapter, we are less interested in questions of cultural transmission, but rather in the emotional and psychological significance of Shakespeare—and the arts more generally— in closed institutions where people are being held or cared for, so their abilities to seek out cultural experiences are limited.

Here, a Shakespeare scholar (Keinänen) and actor/theatre researcher (Lehtonen) team up to analyse *Rakkaus ei ole ajan narri* [*Love's Not Time's Fool*], a monologue based on Shakespeare's sonnets. In 2006– 2011 Lehtonen toured the piece around various care institutions in Finland (and occasionally Sweden): assisted living centres for the elderly, dementia units, homeless shelters, drug rehabilitation facilities, psychiatric hospitals, and prisons. The tour was the starting point of Lehtonen's artistic doctoral thesis at the University of Arts in Finland. His research strategy was that of *artistic action research* (Lehtonen 2015), which combines two disciplines: (1) *Artistic research*, i.e. research done by an artist about their subjective artistic process, whose results can be a piece of art, written report, or a new method. At the same time, for example, the piece of art provides material for research (Hallnäs 2017; Hannula et al. 2014, 15–16); and (2) *Action research*, a qualitative research strategy where information is produced in cycles of action and reflection, where the aim is to improve the practices of a community (McNiff 2017).

Lehtonen analysed his experiences of the tour in two Finnish-language publications. In *Samassa Valossa: Näyttelijäntyö hoitolaitoskiertueella*

[*Under the Same Lights: An Actor on Tour in Care Facilities*, 2010], he focuses on the ways that Shakespeare's sonnets take on different meanings in different acting spaces and especially with different audiences, as their different life situations shape what they respond to in the Shakespeare text, and their responses in turn shape the actor's connection with the audience. These themes are developed further in Lehtonen's doctoral dissertation, which analyses a course at the Theatre Academy he developed to help train actors to work in close contact with audiences living in different institutions (Lehtonen 2015). Now returning to this material a decade later, we turn the focus to Shakespeare, examining in more detail how it was precisely Shakespeare's sonnets which enabled Lehtonen to deepen his exploration of actor/audience contact, and the significance of theatre and the arts especially for people living on the fringes of society.

As he toured care homes, Lehtonen paid attention to the negative features of the welfare society. While it is important to take care of individuals who are in a vulnerable position, unfortunately this often leads to isolation. The walls between institutions of care and institutions of art, like the National Theatre, are thick and made of concrete. There is very little exchange. The problem has been around for a long time, and indeed sixty years ago sociologist Erving Goffman wrote about the effect of "total institutions" on their residents.[2] This kind of institutionalization is often linked to stigmatization. Goffman divides stigmas into three categories: bodily, social, and ethnic (Goffman 1961). Basically, any human quality can become a stigma depending on the values of society. Ageing, sadly, can also be seen as a social stigma (Nussbaum and Levmore 2017).

In this chapter, we examine the responses of elderly viewers to two broad themes raised in Shakespeare's sonnets that have been seen as taboo subjects for the elderly: love, sexuality and loss, and ageing and death. In Lehtonen's experience, elderly audience members reacted strongly to these issues, and seemed to enjoy discussing them after the performance. In a third section, we take up issues connected to memory loss and cognitive decline and the ability to "take in" poetry, demonstrating that Shakespeare's sonnets (in Finnish and Swedish translation) provided a

---

[2] A total institution is an isolated unit where people in similar life situations live a longer period of time in a routine-like and hierarchical setting. Life in a total institution leads to institutionalization of an individual. In Goffman's typology (1961, 4), total institutions are divided into 5 subgroups. Of these, "institutions established to care for people felt to be both harmless and incapable" include nursing homes.

point of contact even for patients with severe dementia. Shakespeare's sonnets became a means of integrating Finnish institutions of theatre and care, while providing elderly viewers with what they seemed to regard as a meaningful artistic experience, in some sense allowing them to resist the stigmatization of ageing.

We approach our topic from two different perspectives: Nely represents Shakespeare studies and brings an outside view to Jussi's work with the sonnets. For Jussi, this chapter is a re-reflection on action that took place more than ten years ago. Our main research material is Jussi's performance diary from the tour in 2006–2011 (introduced more fully below). With the passage of time, experiences already lived can get new significances. The paragraphs where Jussi is remembering his tour in the present of writing this chapter are in italics. The analytical sections have been jointly written.

INSPIRATION—A NEW TRANSLATION OF SHAKESPEARE'S SONNETS

Jussi: *Reading Kirsti Simonsuuri's Finnish translations of Shakespeare sonnets changed the way I thought about them. Earlier, I had seen the sonnets more as songs, probably because the rhymes were so dominating, at least in the old Finnish translations. Now I saw them as thematically open, beautiful, multi-layered texts in a modernized poetic form talking about very basic human conditions: love, loss, jealousy, the passage of time. I understood that these translations could work as an excellent base for a monologue performance.*

Although it is difficult to convey to foreign readers the literary qualities of Simonsuuri's Finnish-language sonnet translations, a few general comments can be made about her translation choices. When the translations were published in 2005, Simonsuuri's controversial choice not to reproduce the sonnet form was widely discussed in the Finnish press, though their literary qualities were praised.[3] In terms of form, the poems are 14 lines, with varying line lengths, usually more than 10 syllables.

---

[3] Writing for the leading Helsinki newspaper, Tomi Kontio (2005) roundly criticized the decision not to follow the sonnet form. For a much more measured response, highlighting the translation's strengths as well as weaknesses, see Salenius (2005).

Except for closing couplets, traditional sonnet rhyme schemes are not followed, though there are occasional rhymes or half-rhymes, as marked in the following example. The language is rhythmic, modern, visceral, and evocative.

73

Tuo vuodenaika jonka näet minussa a
kun **keltaisia lehtiä**, ei ainutta, tai muutama,
riippuu oksilta jotka vapisevat kylmän tullessa, a
kuorin paljaat rauniot, joissa **linnut vasta lauloivat.**
Minussa näet tuon päivän iltahämärän.
Auringon laskettua **hohde hiipuu** länteen
ja musta yö vie sen pian mukanaan
kuoleman veli, joka solmii kaiken lepoon.
Minussa näet tuon tulen **hehkuvan.**
Se lepää nuoruutensa tuhkan päällä,
kuolinvuoteella jolle viimein **sammuu,**
kun aika joka ruokki, söi sen **loppuun.**
Tämän näet. Se rakkautesi vahvistaa, b
rakastat sitä mistä pitää kohta luopua. b

That time of year thou mayst in me behold
When yellow leaves, or none, or few, do hang
Upon those boughs which shake against the cold,
Bare ruin'd choirs, where late the sweet birds sang.
In me thou seest the twilight of such day
As after sunset fadeth in the west,
Which by and by black night doth take away,
Death's second self, that seals up all in rest.
In me thou see'st the glowing of such fire
That on the ashes of his youth doth lie,
As the death-bed whereon it must expire
Consumed with that which it was nourish'd by.
This thou perceivest, which makes thy love more strong,
To love that well which thou must leave ere long.

Simonsuuri's translations gain their poetic qualities mainly from the use of sound devices, such as alliteration and internal rhyme. Particularly effective examples of the former include the /l/ and /v/ sounds of *linnut vasta lauloivat* ["birds were just singing"] (4) and the /h/ sounds in *hohde hiipuu* ["brightness fades"] (6), picked up a few lines later in the keyword *hehkuvan* ["glowing"] (9), which Helen Vendler (1999, 336) sees as a positive, erotic offering of the self after the ruined and faded objects of the first two quatrains, a theme we return to below. Assonance is also used, such as /u/ in *sammuu* ["go out"] (11) and *loppuun* ["to the end"] (12). Internal rhyme or near-rhyme can be seen in *keltaisia lehtiä* ["yellow leaves"] (2). Very clear and strong trochaic rhythms, which are natural to Finnish, also lend poetic weight, such as the string of trochees in mainly two-syllable words in *kuorin paljaat rauniot* ["**bark**'s bare ruins"] (4). These texts are rhythmic and sonoric, with much of the wordplay and imagery of the originals.

Inspired by Simonsuuri's new sonnet translations, Lehtonen invited director Pauliina Hulkko and composer Sanna Salmenkallio to work with him on a monologue based on Shakespeare sonnets. The premiere was held at the Finnish National Theatre, but from the very beginning the idea was to tour in different institutions. A literary and theatrical institution (Shakespeare) being brought to others. Three versions with different dramaturgies[4] and different durations (15, 35, and 60 minutes) were made. As he began performing the piece, Lehtonen began to think that the only way to find out what sorts of issues were "in the air" at the different venues, and what the inhabitants thought of Shakespeare and the production, was to get in touch with them as directly as possible, and therefore he gradually developed a three-part structure for his visits. He tried to arrive early enough to spend time getting to know the inhabitants and constructing a theatre space in their living rooms; then he would perform; and afterwards viewers were invited to speak about the thoughts and feelings the performance raised.

As this three-part performance model developed, Lehtonen found himself paying increasing attention to the first and third phases and began keeping a performance diary. The diary is his subjective memories of his feelings and observations before, during, and after performances, and what he afterwards remembered about what people said and how they reacted. As he wrote his diary, Lehtonen anonymized every comment. Neither the identity of any person nor the institutions where he performed can be deduced from these examples. Lehtonen did not formally interview anyone, nor record any conversations. It is very possible that he might have misunderstood what people said or remembered it wrong. At the time he began keeping the diary, Lehtonen did not know he would later use this material for research purposes, and so he did not seek permission from any individuals to use this material. In 2010, he published *Samassa valossa*, a handbook for artists wishing to perform in closed institutions, and was granted permission to use this material from institutions named in the book. In this article, we are quoting directly from his diaries (which have been translated into English by Keinänen for this chapter).

---

[4] The dramaturgies consisted of the choice and order of the sonnets that formed a dramatic plot. No other texts were used in the performance. There was an introduction where Lehtonen presented himself and the performance and invited people to discuss with him after the performance. In the longest version, the sonnets included were: 113, 74, 12, 104, 64, 3, 110, 57, 46, 58, 75, 129, 116, 73, 61, 12, 147, 97, 8.

Institutions of Love and Loss

One stigma of being old is that younger people assume that the elderly are somehow outside of the paradigms of love, sexuality, and desire (Nussbaum and Levmore 2017; Gewirtz-Meydan et al. 2018). But in speaking to the elderly after the performances, it was clear they responded to the many-sided views of love in Shakespeare's sonnets, not the least of which was the one expressed in the play's title, *Love's Not Time's Fool*. In his diary, Lehtonen recalls a viewer saying, "The performance asks whether love lasts a day, a week, a month or your whole life. I think your whole life". Another thought the performance addressed "a person's whole life and sexuality", clearly indicating that sexuality does not entirely fade in old age. The theme of youth and age sometimes brought out humorous responses. Once, when Jussi told an old woman that the performance was called *Love's Not Time's Fool*, she replied "No, it isn't".

Sometimes, however, viewers insisted that love *is* time's fool. Elderly women, in particular, reacted to Jussi's presence as a young male in the room. One explained: "You're a young man. Love, it only lasts a moment. They fall one at a time like rose petals. In the end you have nothing. You end up having to sit by yourself. There's nobody closer". Others echoed the theme that love is fleeting and only for the young. One resident commented, "Fortunately, the time of young love is over, all those times I fell unhappily in love". In commenting on what the performance made them think about, another contrasted their lost youth with the realities of their present day: "I thought about my youth. Back then I had the energy to come and go. Now we just sit here and someone spoons food into our mouths twice a day. Now we have neither love nor riches". Recalling one's youth, even in the context of a negative comparison with the present, nevertheless emphasizes that the elderly have a wealth of life experiences. In some cases, the performance triggered very powerful memories of love and marriage. Lehtonen records in his diary an incident where after a performance, a woman exclaimed, "Now I'm free! Now everything is ok", and started to cry. He writes:

> The situation was shocking but also very touching. When I recovered from my shock, I said that sometimes love can feel like a prison. Then the woman said: 'I got the man! The pain fades, but love... love remains'. Afterwards the caregivers told me that the woman had been married several times, both happily and clearly unhappily. Apparently the performance brought these different experiences to the surface.

Connected to these comments about the strong passions of youth, a few viewers noted the links between love and madness, the obsessive qualities of love and passion, another clear theme in Shakespeare's sonnets. Jussi recalls that the elderly responded powerfully to Sonnet 75, for example, with lines like "Possessing or pursuing no delight, / Save what is had or must from you be took" (11–12), which in the Finnish translation is emphasized with powerful rhythms and strong alliteration on /s/: *ei valloitus, ei saalistus tuo iloa, / vain saaminen ja pakko saada sinulta.* One viewer said, "That's what love is, the madness of life", while another said, "It took me a while to figure out that this was about the mental health problems caused by love". Viewers wondered about the male speaker who is rendered so distraught by unrequited love. One perceptively asked, "What's the difference between infatuation and love?", while others felt what was depicted in the sonnets was not love but pathology. In his performance diary, Lehtonen writes: "Interesting. The spectators might very well know better than me what love is". And one viewer concluded: "Love is complicated, I've accepted that".

One type of "madness" that came up is jealousy, a main theme of Shakespeare's sonnets. One woman, for example, said that the theme of jealousy hits a little too close to home. The performance evoked guilt she had experienced during World War Two when she'd gone to a dance while her husband was at the front. In his performance diary, Jussi recalls that the woman said that the way that he moved during the performance awakened these memories, showing that viewers respond to much more than just language. For at least one viewer, the performance evoked fears of whether she is loved right now. Jussi heard a woman who talked to her husband during the performance ask him:

> Do you love me?
> Do you love me now?
> Do you still love me?

After the performance, another woman beckoned Jussi to come over and planted a kiss on his cheek. These comments show that ideas about love, sexuality, passion, and even jealousy were all very important to elderly viewers, if only to be recalled by their absence, the theme we turn to next.

Jussi: *In* Rakkaus ei ole ajan narri, *my role was to play a man who goes crazy from the loss of love. Performing this for the elderly was really touching. There was an exchange. My duty was to embody love and loss the way I sensed them in the sonnets, in the audience, and in me. There's something special about Shakespeare's sonnets; all the ages come together. I was 32 when I started the tour and found different ages in my body: the old man I will become, the baby I once was, past and future generations, the corpse of death, and new life growing in the womb. The fact that I was performing this poetry to spectators who were in the last days of their lives made these associations especially strong.*

The performance empowered residents to speak about the loss of loved ones they had experienced in their own lives, and how lonely they felt as a result. In his diary, Jussi remembers many elderly women who spoke about the deaths of their husbands: "My life ended when my husband died". Another said the play was about love, adding, "my husband died ten years ago. Diabetes". During one performance, Lehtonen noticed that a woman who had initially said she did not want to attend had cried almost the whole time. Afterwards he asked her what she thought of the performance, and she replied: "It was nice. My husband is dead. I'm alone. We'll meet again in heaven".

A few female viewers had experienced the deaths of husbands as well as a child. A 100-year-old woman said:

I found this performance touching. Loss has always been a part of my life. My daughter, who was living in this same facility, died just a little while ago.

Lehtonen wrote in his performance diary: "I wondered about how these sonnets on death, loss and the passage of time might speak to a person whose agemates and close relatives were dying while her own life went on and on. A woman whose daughter has died of old age". The loss of a child evoked very powerful feelings, as in this response from another woman:

I ask why? Why was my eldest taken from me? Why would God do that? I wouldn't do this to my worst enemy. In terms of love, I'm [too] late. My husband is dead and one of my sons. You can never accept such a loss.

Not everyone appreciated seeing a performance which triggered such sad thoughts. One person asked, "Didn't Shakespeare write anything a bit more cheerful?" while another said she "cried the whole time". One concluded, "A comedy would have been better". Laughter and humour indeed functioned in unpredictable ways in the different settings Lehtonen performed in. Prisoners, for example, sometimes laughed hysterically at the sight of the forlorn lover. One old woman commented similarly: "We laughed when you writhed in despair. This was my life".

While many viewers commented on their losses with sadness, the performance gave others the chance to explain how they had learned to move forward. For example, one woman said that she liked the performance and spoke of her husband's death ten years previously, as well as her son's death two months prior. When asked whether the performance had brought these losses to mind, she replied, "Not at all. I've processed my losses". The performance and post-performance discussions perhaps also gave residents a chance to process their losses or at least articulate their feelings about love and loss and try to find happiness in the present. The monologue ended with Sonnet 8, whose last line in the Finnish translation is "You are nothing alone". Perhaps in response to this, after a performance, a resident said, "I found myself thinking how alone people are", but then another countered: "That last comment, about being alone. We're not. Here we have each other and love too. For each other and for the staff". An old woman had an equally uplifting take on love and loss, showing how important these themes were for nursing home residents: "Love, let it blaze! I had two husbands. My legs don't work, but I can still talk. Yes, this performance was about life, all of life. You remember the nice things, but the painful ones you forget".

INSTITUTIONS OF OLD AGE AND DEATH

Jussi: *During the* Rakkaus ei ole ajan narri *tour I visited nearly 100 care facilities in Finland and Sweden. I saw very different places. I saw a society where death is enclosed in institutions and thus made invisible. In some places people were brought to the performance in their beds as they were no longer able to walk. Sometimes there was a candle and photo on a table marking that a member of the community had recently passed away.*

The presence of death didn't shock me. Shakespeare's sonnets are real power poetry: with them, and through them, I could enter these institutions of death.

The sonnets are of course an institution in themselves, but I think they are also anti-institution. They go directly and frankly towards fundamental aspects of human life that are not always easy to talk about, such as death, the different sides of sexuality or jealousy. The sonnets resist labelling people. Life and death are in and on and around each other and cannot be separated. But I believe that no matter how much loss and death there was in the air during the performances, the sonnets spoke to the life in us. With the approach of death, a person might seem different, like a part of him/her has already gone away. But there is still a sense of life left that can be celebrated. Theatre and poetry could be a part of this celebration.

We have seen that the residents of old people's homes responded deeply to the themes of youth and age, love and loss in Shakespeare's sonnets. In the sonnets, love and procreation are presented as a means of defeating the passage of time, old age, and death: a theme which not surprisingly resonated deeply in elderly care settings. Sonnet 104 raises the issue of old age, "To me, fair friend, you never can be old" (1), and here the "process of the seasons" becomes a metaphor for the passage of time. When performing this sonnet Lehtonen sometimes found himself thinking of the many summers and winters his audience had seen. Sonnet 3 also includes references to ageing and death: "So thou through windows of thine age shall see / Despite of wrinkles this thy golden time" and the threat of dying "single". Sometimes these themes were enhanced in Simonsuuri's translation. In Sonnet 12, for example, the translation of the closing couplet ("And nothing 'gainst Time's scythe can make defence / Save breed, to brave him when he takes thee hence") ends in the word "death", which then gets extra weight from a half-rhyme in the closing couplet.

Sometimes it wasn't talk of death as such which provoked comments, but something in the stage business of the performance. For example, during Sonnet 61, where the speaker thinks about being kept awake by his love, Lehtonen spoke some of the sonnet lying down with his hands on his chest, which made a viewer think about how he would be laid out in his coffin:

> When you put your hands on your chest, I began to think about what position I'd be in in my coffin. How they'd put my hands.

This example also alerts us to the ways that it is not just the interpretation of words of a play that can trigger the audience, but also the actor's physical performance, voice, emotion, and contact with the audience. The living body of a much younger actor might even encourage older viewers to think more deeply about these themes. At times there was palpable relief expressed about being allowed to discuss difficult topics such as death, which seems not to be discussed very much in institutions serving the elderly. In response to the Finnish translation of the second line of Sonnet 64, which refers to a "grave" rather than Shakespeare's more metaphorical "outworn buried age", a viewer said: "You said something about a grave. Good. We should talk about death". In the same sonnet, in the Finnish version the closing couplet is more direct, saying "This thought is death", a small but perhaps significant change from Shakespeare's couching the idea as simile, "This thought is as a death". During one of the discussions, the department head at a long-term care hospital said: "It makes things easier when someone dares to speak about death directly. It would be good if we would speak about it more" (qtd in Lehtonen 2010, 93). Speaking more broadly, a resident commented: "Around here we mainly talk about the weather and food and Marevan,[5] but not usually about anything deeper. I found myself thinking that in my own life happiness has passed me by, so the performance made me sad".

Above we discussed the ways viewing and especially discussing Lehtonen's performance of Shakespeare's sonnets allowed residents and staff of elderly care institutions to discuss the themes of love and loss, ageing and death, and perhaps to challenge taboos connected to them. In the next section, we discuss a third stigma associated with ageing: the loss of memory and cognitive function and the ability to take in poetry Fig. 14.1.

"Understanding" vs "Experiencing" Shakespeare

Jussi: *For me as a performer of poetry the biggest enemy is a spectator who especially wants to understand what I mean by the words I speak. Poetry is not to be understood by reason. It is all about senses, associations, and rhythm. I find performing poetry for people with dementia very rewarding. They grasp emotions and atmospheres, are quick to make associations and let them out; they fly with the rhythmic elements and all kinds of changes in the performance. They are not afraid of showing how they feel; they might comment audibly, cry or scream during the performance. They might stand*

---

[5] This is an anti-coagulant medication.

Fig. 14.1 Jussi Lehtonen performing *Love's Not Time's Fool* monologue at an elderly care institution in Helsinki, Finland. Photo credit: Hanna Weselius

up and come touch you. For me, all of this is "understanding" poetry in a most elementary way.

Lehtonen believes the responsibility of the artist is to challenge the audience, whether that audience is in a theatre, prison, or elderly care facility. When he played in different types of elderly care facilities—assisted living centres, long-term care hospitals, dementia wards—his audiences had different levels of cognitive and/or physical abilities, and it was in these contexts where he most clearly came across ideas about whether Shakespeare was appropriate or accessible to the elderly. During one of the first performances of *Rakkaus ei ole ajan narri* to which staff from various care institutions had been invited in order to encourage them to book the show, Lehtonen encountered the kinds of stigma about the elderly which made him think about how institutions define the artistic taste of their residents.

> Jussi: *One nurse gave very worrying feedback. She said the performance is not suitable for old people's homes. "Because the residents prefer very traditional art". She had already booked the show but decided to cancel. I was shocked. It's true that the performance was not a traditional poetry reading. The style of acting was very expressive and included statements about basic human emotions and drives. I realized that acting them could break a potential taboo. I had already organized several shows in old people's homes and now felt very unsure. Was I doing something wrong?*

Lehtonen was disconcerted to realize that his performance would be perceived as inappropriate or even threatening by the arbiters of good taste, which, in the case of elderly care institutions, is usually the head nurse.

> Jussi: *The cultural program in care facilities seems to consist mostly of watching television. The priest will come regularly for religious activities. There is music and singing, and sometimes a children's choir will come and perform. The nurse's comment made me understand that somebody can see it as a risk to take a Shakespeare performance to an old people's home. And that somebody has taken a risk if I've been invited to come. I have always thought that one of the aims of art is to fight against stigmatization and institutionalization. The nurse's comment taught me that art can, paradoxically, also reinforce them.*

But while this nurse and others expressed reservations about the suit-ability of Shakespeare as entertainment for residents of care facilities, Lehtonen's experience was quite the opposite. Shakespeare's sonnets are demanding in terms of comprehension, yet their sounds, rhythms, and imagery provide elderly viewers with a point of contact. The responses of the elderly show a wide range of attitudes towards the difficulty of Shakespeare, and in some of them we can see institutional stigmatiza-tion at work, along with the lowering of self-esteem that can accom-pany cognitive decline, loss of physical strength, health issues, and the growing isolation typical of old age (Lehtonen 2010, 81). In his diary, Lehtonen remembers that after a performance, a patient in a dementia ward commented, "I didn't understand a thing you said" and another, "Nobody here will understand any of this", though someone responded to the previous, saying "There might be some who do". Among the elderly, some seemed to blame themselves for not understanding Shake-speare, as this resident: "Great performance but I didn't understand it. I'm too stupid".

By contrast, several commented that while Shakespeare is difficult, with a little effort it is possible to understand his texts and that such effort is worthwhile. One resident commented, "I really had to work at it, to understand Shakespeare". A few commented that Shakespeare becomes easier to understand if you do not try too hard: "When I didn't try to understand, it went very well". A nurse in a dementia ward commented that "This was good for people with dementia as they don't even try to understand".

In his diary Lehtonen writes how patients with severe dementia could connect to Shakespeare's poetry, as seen for example in the way they repeated words:

Lehtonen: Seems seeing, but effectually is out [Sonnet 113]
Viewer: Sees, sees!

Or this dementia patient, who the nurse said often fakes sleep, who suddenly opened her eyes and replied ironically:

Lehtonen: On purpose laid to make the taker mad [Sonnet 129]
Viewer: Mad!

In his performance diary, Lehtonen recorded many examples of viewers responding to lines of poetry, and the context—art in one's own living room or dining hall—perhaps helped to enable a kind of participation:

> Lehtonen: ...mine eye is in my mind. [Sonnet 113]
> Woman: I see.
> Lehtonen: ...you never can be old. [Sonnet 104]
> Woman: Thank you!
> Lehtonen: Or gluttoning on all, or all away. [Sonnet 75]
> Woman: Oh poor you!

> Lehtonen: For I have sworn thee fair and thought thee bright,
> Who art black as hell, as dark as night. [Sonnet 147]
> A woman sitting in the back row: Oh she'll get lighter.

A sonnet-play asks its audience both to concentrate and to not concentrate, to simply experience the poetry. Despite the stigmatization in society of people with dementia, Lehtonen found that in some ways they were an ideal audience for a performance of Shakespeare's sonnets. This is not to idealize them, however. Many elderly people are all too aware of cognitive decline and loss of memory. When Jussi asked an older man what he thought of the performance, he answered "Not bad. I had some thoughts, but they're already gone".

CONCLUSION

After the *Rakkaus ei ole ajan narri* tour in 2006–2011, Lehtonen became Artistic Director of the Touring Stage of the Finnish National Theatre, which aims to bring performances and workshops to different institutions, e.g. social and healthcare, prisons, and reception centres for asylum seekers.[6] Bringing art to closed institutions became a part of the national art institution, a historical change which in part got its start through the Shakespeare sonnet project. Art in closed institutions raises the question of possible therapeutic effects of arts (Fancourt and Finn 2019). This debate is problematic, however. The connection between a work of art

---

[6] The Touring Stage also develops socially oriented documentary theatre, where performances are made with differently marginalized communities in order to make their voices heard in society (Lehtonen 2021b, 45–46). https://kansallisteatteri.fi/kiertuenayttamo/.

and its effect is associative: you cannot guarantee an outcome. In an era where everything is given an instrumental value, the value of the sonnets seems holistic, rich, deeply human, and timeless. In Lehtonen's experience, the sonnets enabled a special kind of contact, connection, and communication between actor and audience (Lehtonen 2010). This is not something which can be measured. It is art in action.

> Jussi: *In addition to Shakespeare I have performed many other kinds of poetry and drama in old people's homes. In this practice, and in my academic research, I have investigated how the performance changes in the presence of different audiences and with the special characteristics of the venue. When theatre is played in people's homes, their presence and lives become part of the performance, and they shape the performance and the performer's conception of what it is about* (Lehtonen 2015). *In care facilities,* Rakkaus ei ole ajan narri *was often about love and loss, and the presence of fragile old people affected the way I embodied these themes. In prisons, the same monologue tended to talk about jealousy, isolation, and waiting. The muscular and tattooed men in the audience might have changed my presence onstage and my conception of the poems. In drug addiction units, we started to hear and see different forms of addiction in the sonnets and in the performance. Shakespeare's sonnets contain vast spheres of life, and in a way have an answer to many questions. For me, they opened doors to explore hidden realities of the welfare society. They showed me how identification in theatre is two-fold: the spectators identify themselves with the performer and what is being performed, and at the same time, to a surprisingly high extent, the performer identifies himself with the audiences and sees the meaningfulness of his/her work through their presence and reactions. And ultimately, the sonnets showed me the power of art in conditions where there is a big call for it.*

Lehtonen's sonnet monologue *Rakkaus ei ole ajan narri* shows that the boundaries between different institutions can be made more permeable: Shakespeare, a global institution if ever there was one, can become a tool to break down boundaries between the National Theatre, a theatrical institution which needs to continuously re-legitimize itself, and care institutions, which seek to develop their practices to enable their inhabitants to live as full and meaningful lives as possible within the confines of their institutionalization. Goffman's ideas about stigma are also a kind of institution. While the concept is useful and can be used to make visible social inequalities, there is also the risk that it becomes too fixed and deterministic, as though a stigma, or an individual's stigmatization, were inevitable and unchanging, stigma or no stigma, black or white. In order to solve challenging social problems, however, we need the ability to distinguish various shades of grey, to understand the dynamic mechanisms affecting the fates of individuals (and institutions). We need to understand that any one of us might one day be subject to some stigma, or knowingly or unknowingly stigmatize somebody else, and that these roles can shift in an instant depending on a society's values and attitudes.

Rakkaus ei ole ajan narri highlighted the fluidity of roles, the two-way nature of theatre, so it seems appropriate to give the last word to a resident in an old people's home who asked: "Were we a good audience?".

Acknowledgement This work has been partly supported by the Academy of Finland research project ArtsEqual (grant number: 293199).

References

Acting Company. 1998. *Love's Fire: Seven New Plays Inspired by Seven Shakespearean Sonnets*. New York: HarperCollins.

Billington, Michael. 2011. "Love Is My Sin—Review". *The Guardian*, January 17.

Fancourt, Daisy and Saoirse Finn. 2019. *What Is the Evidence on the Role of the Arts in Improving Health and Well-Being? A Scoping Review*. Copenhagen: WHO Regional Office for Europe (Health Evidence Network (HEN) Synthesis Report 67).

Gewirtz-Meydan, Ateret, Trish Hafford-Letchfield, Yael Benyamini, Amanda Phelan, Jeanne Jackson, and Liat Ayalon. 2018. 'Ageism and Sexuality. Contemporary Perspectives on Ageism'. In *International Perspectives on Aging 19*, eds. Liat Ayalon and Clemens Tesch-Römer. Springer Open, 149–62. https://doi.org/10.1007/978-3-319-73820-8_10.

Goffman, Erving. 1961. *Asylums: Essays on the Social Situation of Mental Patients and Other Inmates*. New York: Doubleday.

Goffman, Erving. 1986 (1963). *Stigma: Notes on the Management of Spoiled Identity*. New York: Simon & Schuster.

Hallnäs, Lars. 2017. "Once Again... What Is Artistic Research? (Questions: The Situation of the Field and Concepts)". In *Futures of Artistic Research. At the Intersection of Utopia, Academia and Power*, eds. Jan Kaila, Anita Seppä, and Henk Slager (Hrsg.). Helsinki: Academy of Fine Arts, Uniarts. https://helda.helsinki.fi/bitstream/handle/10138/246117/Futures_of_artistic_research_kirja.pdf?sequence=1&isAllowed=y%20.

Hannula, Mika, Juha Suoranta, and Tero Vadén. 2014. "Artistic Research Methodology: Narrative, Power, and the Public". *Critical Qualitative Research* 15. New York: Peter Lang.

Isherwood, Charles. 1998. "Love's Fire". *Variety*, June 23.

Isherwood, Christopher. 2010. "Shakespeare's Sonnets Get a Turn on the Stage". *New York Times*, April 2 [Rev. of Peter Brook's *Love Is My Sin*].

Isherwood, Christopher. 2014a. "His Majesty the Queen". *New York Times*, October 1 [Preview of Berliner Ensemble's *Shakespeare's Sonnets* at the Brooklyn Academy of Music, music by Rufus Wainwright, dir. Richard Wilson].

Isherwood, Christopher. 2014b. "Words Felt, If Not Quite Fathomed". *New York Times*, October 8 [Review of Berliner Ensemble's 'Shakespeare's Sonnets'].

Kontio, Tomi. 2005. "Shakespearen ikuiset sonetit tulevat taas". *Helsingin Sanomat*, April 9.

Lehtonen, Jussi. 2010. *Samassa valossa: näyttelijäntyö hoitolaitoskiertueella.* Helsinki: Avain.

Lehtonen, Jussi. 2015. *Elämäntunto: näyttelijä kohtaa hoitolaitosyleisön.* Acta Scenica 43. Helsinki: Taideyliopiston Teatterikorkeakoulu. https://helda.hel sinki.fi/bitstream/handle/10138/156950/Acta_Acenica_42.pdf?sequence=1&isAllowed=y.

Lehtonen, Jussi. 2021a. "Ilmaisuyhteisö Kansallisteatterissa: eettisiä haasteita yhteisöllisesti suuntautuneessa dokumenttiteatterissa". In *Yhteisötaiteen etiikka*, eds. Lea Kantonen and Sari Karttunen. Helsinki: Taideyliopiston Teatterikorkeakoulu, 97–128.

Lehtonen, Jussi. 2021b. "Touring Stage of The Finnish National Theatre". In *Love in a Cold Climate: Creative Ageing in Finland*, eds. David Cutler, Raisa Karttunen, and Jenni Räsänen. London: The Baring Foundation, 45–46. https://cdn.baringfoundation.org.uk/wp-content/uploads/BF_Creative-ageing-Finland_WEB.pdf.

McElroy, Steven. 2013. "Taking Shakespeare's Sonnets to the Streets of New York". *New York Times*, April 3.

McNiff, Jean. 2017. *Action Research: All You Need to Know*. Sage: London.

New York Shakespeare Exchange. The Sonnet Project. https://nysx.org/pro grams-2/sonnet-project/. Accessed 10 September 2021.

Nussbaum, Martha C. and Saul Levmore. 2017. *Aging Thoughtfully: Conversations About Retirement, Romance, Wrinkles, & Regret*. New York: Oxford University Press.

Rayner, Francesca. 2017. "Dehierarchizing Space: Performer-Audience Collaborations in Two Portuguese Performances of Shakespeare". *Multicultural Shakespeare* Vol 15 (30): 27–41. http://doi.org/10-1515/mstap-2017-0003.

Salenius, Maria. 2005. "Kesäklassikko: Shakespearea nautinnollisesti". *Kiiltomato*, August 10. https://kiiltomato.net/critic/william-shakespeare-nautin
tojen-ajan-aarre-william-shakespearen-sonetit/.

Toomer, Jeanette. 1998. "The Acting Company Fires Up Shakespeare's
Sonnets". New York: *Amsterdam News*, July 2. https://search-ebscohost-
com.libproxy.helsinki.fi/login.aspx?direct=true&db=a9h&AN=844503&site=
ehost-live&scope=site. Accessed 10 September 2021.

Vendler, Helen. 1999. *The Art of Shakespeare's Sonnets*. Cambridge, Mass.:
Harvard University Press.

CHAPTER 15

"Music to Hear…" from Shakespeare to Stravinsky

Manfred Pfister

For Marta with love and admiration

As much as its Italianate name suggests singing and song, the sonnet in Shakespeare's times hardly ever found its way into music or song. Of the literally thousands of sonnets written at the time only a handful of musical settings survive, and of Shakespeare's 154 sonnets, first published in 1609, not a single one was set to music by a contemporary composer—at least not to our knowledge (Kerrigan 2000, 442f).[1] We can only surmise why this should have been the case. One reason might be that most of Shakespeare's sonnets in particular are semantically too complex and compact to be readily accessible and comprehensible in musical settings; another likely reason is that its structure of three strictly rhymed quatrains

---

[1] There is one musical version of Shakespeare's Sonnet 116 by Henry Lawes, but what he set to music, probably in the 1630s, was not Shakespeare's original text but an adaptation into three six-lines stanzas (Duncan-Jones 1997, 458–460).

M. Pfister (✉)
Freie Universität, Berlin, Germany
e-mail: manfred.pfister@fu-berlin.de

© The Author(s), under exclusive license to Springer Nature
Switzerland AG 2023
J. Kingsley-Smith and W. R. Rampone Jr. (eds.), *Shakespeare's Global Sonnets*,
Global Shakespeares, https://doi.org/10.1007/978-3-031-09472-9_15

and a concluding couplet cuts across the two major Elizabethan forms of secular vocal music: the choral madrigal composed to stanzaic texts and the soloist "air" based on irregularly rhymed or unrhymed verses of varying lengths (Rupp 2005). So even if in Elizabethan English "sonnet" and "song" were frequently used as synonyms—most famously in John Donne's verse collection *Songs and Sonnets*, which does not contain a single sonnet in the strict sense of the word—it was only three centuries later that the marriage of sonnet and song in the musical setting of a Shakespearean sonnet was actually celebrated. In the first two of these three centuries, the sonnets had fallen into oblivion or disregard, and after their (re-) discovery and rise to the canonical heights of *Weltliteratur* in the early nineteenth century they continued to be ignored by all the notable composers of *Lieder* for another century,[2] before modern composers began to take up the challenge.[3] And that occurred in Russia, of all places, almost as early as in England or any other European culture closer to England.[4] Among the very first, to our knowledge, was Alexander Glasunov, who in 1916 set the timely sonnet 66, "Tired with all these, for restful death I cry," with its lament over political oppression and abuses to music, and other Russian composers were to follow suit: Dmitry Shostakovich in 1946, again with a version of sonnet 66; Dmitry Kabalevsky with a mini-cycle of *Ten Shakespeare Sonnets* (1953–1955); and Igor Stravinsky, working in America on the original English text, with his sonnet 8 first performed in 1954.

---

[2] B.N.S. Gooch and D. Thatcher in their five-volume *Shakespeare Musical Catalogue* (1991) enumerate some 40, almost exclusively English or American, composers of the nineteenth century engaging with Shakespearean sonnets, but all of them are virtually unknown and none of their settings have had any impact. Among them is the Roman Catholic journalist and Shakespeare scholar Richard Simpson, who apparently set the entire cycle to music in the mid-nineteenth century; only thirteen of them, however, were published in his *Sonnets of Shakespeare selected from a complete setting, and miscellaneous songs* (1878). See Gabler (2000, 770), and http://www.recmusic.org/lieder/s/simpson.html.

[3] For a more detailed history of the international reception of Shakespeare's sonnet see my "Introduction— Shakespeare's Sonnets Global 'in states unborn and accents yet unknown'" in Pfister and Gutsch, *Shakespeare's Sonnets Global* (2009), 9–29. Our survey of the global impact of Shakespeare's sonnets comes with a CDarchive containing, among other things, the recitations of all the translations in the nearly 80 different languages, visual material (book covers, illustrations), excerpts of films and other performances relating to the sonnets and some 220 musical setting, among them also Stravinsky's of sonnet 8.

[4] Only Ralph Vaughan Williams' setting of sonnet 71 (1896), antedates Glasunov's sonnet 66.

In its own times, the Elizabethan and Shakespearean sonnet, however, remained enclosed in its tightly knit and self-contained literariness, though opening itself up with its own literary means and aspiring to the conditions of its sister-arts of painting, music and theatre, in the visually suggestive description, in the musicality of its "soundscape" of assonance, alliteration and rhyme and in the theatricality of impassioned speech and gestures (Pfister 2005). More rarely, but then more emphatically, Shakespearean sonnets reached out for the other arts by making drawing or painting, song or instrumental music and acting or stagecraft part of their erotic scenario and, by doing this, turning them into a theme. Such inter-art moments punctuate Shakespeare's sonnet cycle, among them two striking instances show-casing the sister-art of music, two sonnets dedicated to the subject of music and revolving around musical performances: sonnet 8 and sonnet 128.[5]

8
Music to hear, why hear'st thou music sadly?
Sweets with sweets war not, joy delights in joy.
Why lov'st thou that which thou receiv'st not gladly,
Or else receiv'st with pleasure thine annoy?
If the true concord of well-tunèd sounds,
By unions married, do offend thine ear,
They do but sweetly chide thee, who confounds
In singleness the parts that thou should'st bear.
Mark how one string, sweet husband to another,
Strikes each in each by mutual ordering;
Resembling sire, and child, and happy mother,
Who, all in one, one pleasing note do sing;
Whose speechless song, being many, seeming one,
Sings this to thee: 'Thou single wilt prove none.'

128
How oft, when thou, my music, music play'st
Upon that blessèd wood whose motion sounds
With thy sweet fingers when thou gently sway'st
The wiry concord that mine ear confounds,
Do I envy those jacks that nimble leap
To kiss the tender inward of thy hand,
Whilst my poor lips, which should that harvest reap,
At the wood's boldness by thee blushing stand.
To be so tickled, they would change their state
And situation with those dancing chips
O'er whom thy fingers walk with gentle gait,
Making dead wood more blest than living lips.
Since saucy jacks so happy are in this,
Give them thy fingers, me thy lips to kiss.
(Shakespeare 2000, 80, 140)

The first, "Music to hear, why hear'st thou music sadly," is part of the introductory sequence of 17 sonnets—the so-called "procreation

---

[5] For an earlier musicological comparison of these two sonnets, see Blick (1999).

sonnets"—persuading a young and charming aristocrat to marry and beget a child. The second, "How oft when thou, my music, music play'st," comes right after the great thematic turn from the sonnets addressing the Fair Young Man, which make up the greater part of the entire cycle, to the second, shorter part, sonnets 127–154, which speak of a rival object of desire, a lady—the "Dark Lady" of Victorian sonnet criticism—soliciting not Platonic worship but offering sensuous pleasures. The two music sonnets do not only occupy structurally similar positions within the cycle, but their close interrelationship is also highlighted by a whole set of pointed correspondences and contrasts. To begin with, both open with the word "music" echoing in their first lines in striking and attention-catching rhetorical repetition: the chiasm of "*Music* to *hear*, why *hear'st* thou *music* sadly" in sonnet 8 and the *geminatio* or *antistasis* of "How oft, when thou, my *music, music* play'st." What re-enforces this echo across the two parts of the cycle is that in both sonnets the word "music" refers first to the beloved addressee: he, the sound of his voice, is "music to hear," and she, "my music," is music incarnate. Only then do both sonnets turn to music itself, both using instrumental, not vocal music, as their main model: the music of the lute or a consort of viols in sonnet 8 and the keyboard music of a virginal in sonnet 128.

Beyond these significant similarities, the two sonnets deal with music in quite different ways and to quite different purposes. Sonnet 128 stages a lively genre scene in which the lover watches his lady perform on her virginal. This romantic scenario revolves around a time-honoured *topos* of erotic poetry: the lover's jealous empathy and identification with an object close to erogenous parts of the beloved's body—the sparrow picking at her lips and nestling in her bosom in the *Carmina* of Catullus, the flea in John Donne's eponymous poem, Juliet's glove in *Romeo and Juliet* (2.1.67f) or, with a musical turn closer to Shakespeare's sonnet, the viol embraced by the mistress and its strings tickled by her in act III, scene iii of Ben Jonson's comedy *Every Man Out of His Humour* (1600).[6] Shakespeare gives this traditional conceit or *concetto* a witty new turn, envying the keys of the virginal, these nimble and saucy "jacks," their tender contact with the erotically receptive and eroticizing inward of the

---

[6] "You see the subject of her sweet fingers there – Oh, she tickles it so; that – She makes it laugh most divinely;—I'll tell you a good jest now, and yourself shall say it's a good one: I have wished myself to be that instrument, I think, a thousand times, and not so few, by heaven!" (Jonson 1910, 1.111).

lady's hand, and he elaborates it with ingenious playfulness across the three quatrains and the concluding couplet. It is less the music itself than its performer and her performance that are being eroticized here. Accordingly, there is no serious engagement with the philosophy of music here, its power to move or express emotions or to symbolize larger harmonies, but a light-heartedly Catullian or Ovidian celebration of music as a stimulant of sensuous pleasure and part of the erotic game of wooing and winning (Edmondson and Wells 2004; Trillini 2008).

Sonnet 8 is quite different. It does not tell a story nor set up a scene, but unfolds an argument intending to persuade the addressee, the fair young man, to abandon his bachelor state, get married and beget a child. In this, it is in line with the preceding seven sonnets, indeed with all the procreation sonnets. They all sing to the same tune, varying only the reasons adduced to support their argument: time, that will all too soon destroy his beauty, unless he passes it on to an heir; the law of nature which calls for creative reproduction; his perfection as a Platonic ideal which needs to be manifested in ever new materializations; familial and social responsibility which urges the young man blessed with status, wealth and beauty to turn away from sterile narcissism to generous sharing and procreation; finally, the need to leave an image of his perfections to authenticate the poet's praise of his beauty beyond his own life span. Sonnet 8 chimes in with this, yet is different in adopting an elaborate allegorical model for the argument: music and its "true concord of well-tunèd sounds" (verse 5). This also, like the motif of the eroticized performance of virginal music in sonnet 128, draws upon a topos, in this case a *concetto* most recently employed in Sir Philip Sidney's *Arcadia* (1590). In book III, chapter v of this courtly prose romance, the wicked Cecropia tries to persuade Philoclea to marry her son. Her long speech provides Shakespeare with a number of images and arguments for his procreation sonnets, among them, with particular relevance to sonnet 8, consort music as a persuasive metaphor for the superiority of married life over lonely bachelordom: "And is a solitary life as good as this? Then can one string make as good music as a consort" (Sidney 1987, 333).

Why should Stravinsky have turned to Shakespeare's sonnets at all and why to this particular sonnet? After all, his *Three Songs from William Shakespeare*, composed in 1953 and first performed on 8 March 1954 in Los Angeles at one of the "Concert Evenings on the Roof" and opening with sonnet 8, were his first songs ever since his *Four Russian Songs* of 1919, and it was only with *The Rake's Progress* to an English libretto by W. H. Auden and Chester Kallman in 1951, and with his *Cantata* (1951–1952), that the Russian expatriate (and, since 1946, American citizen) turned to English texts (Kirchmeyer 2002, 464–67). To continue this new English strain in the *Three Songs from William Shakespeare*, the figurehead of English poetry, may be regarded as a gesture of homage to his new host culture, as part of his *rite de passage* to naturalization in an Anglo-Saxon world, as building a bridge between the Russian tradition of setting Shakespearean sonnets to music, which, as we have seen, goes back to Glasunov in the early twentieth century, and his new American cultural contexts. No wonder Stravinsky dedicated both the *Cantata* and the *Three Songs* to American musical institutions: the "Los Angeles (Chamber) Symphony Society" and Peter Yates' and Robert Craft's concert society "Evenings on the Roof." What is beyond doubt, however, is that it was W. H. Auden who had guided him to Shakespeare's poetry. All three songs—the sonnet and two songs from the plays, "Full fadom five" from *The Tempest* (1.2) and "When Dasies pied" from *Love's Labour's Lost* (5.2), all three of them with references to music, song and sound—are contained in the second volume of W. H. Auden's and Norman Holmes Pearson's five volume anthology of *Poets of the English Language* (1950). Sonnet 8 opens the Shakespeare section here, which begins with a mini-cycle of twenty-five of the sonnets. And that Stravinsky found his texts here is made more than probable by the fact that he follows the old-spelling versions adopted in Auden's anthology—and becomes a certainty once one realizes that he even reproduces a misprint from his source, "Sings this *for* thee" instead of the much stronger "Sings this *to* thee" in the original final verse.[7]

* * *

Sonnet 8 is by no means an easy or readily accessible poem. The difficulties begin already with the first half-verse, which Stravinsky uses as his incipit title: "Musick to heare." How easily it can be misunderstood is instanced in the paraphrase offered in Kirchmeyer's *Kommentiertem Verzeichnis der Werke und Werkausgaben Igor Strawinskys bis 1971*. Here we read: "Das inhaltlich schwer nachzuerzählende Liebesgedicht [...]

---

[7] Auden and Pearson (1950, 2.154). The English edition of the anthology (London: Eyre & Spottiswoode, 1952) has corrected the mistake and Stravinsky meant to correct it, but it has survived into the printed scores; see Stravinsky (1955, 5).

wird mit der rhetorischen Frage eröffnet, wie eine dem Ohr zugeneigte Musik schmerzen könne." ("This poem of love, the content of which is difficult to paraphrase [...] opens with the rhetorical question how music friendly to the ear might cause pain").[8] Nothing could be further off the mark, and one can only hope that composers understand the texts they set to music better than the musicologists commenting upon their work. No: "music to hear" is a vocative invoking the beloved friend as a person whose voice and personal charms are beautiful and harmonious as music. As in sonnet 128, the addressee is equated with music in the very first line. And the question is by no means a rhetorical one that would presuppose its answer. It is a real question, which confronts us immediately with a paradox: how can someone so musical in himself be made sad by music or listen to it with a heavy mind, regretfully or even unwillingly? This paradox dominates the whole first quatrain and will be followed by related paradoxes in the following parts of the sonnet, down to the final paradox of the concluding couplet juggling with the oppositions of "many" and "one," of "single" and "none." The paradox is a form of ingenious and witty more than of impassioned speech, and what passion there is here manifests itself as much in the direct, dramatic and emotionally charged appeal to the young man as in the "hammering out"—to use the King's expression in *Richard II* (5.5.5)—with passionate intensity its paradoxical metaphors or allegories to serve a particular argument. All the four lines of the first quatrain take us through a see-saw rhythm of oppositions: "Music to hear,—why hear'st thou music sadly"; "Sweets with sweets war not,— joy delights in joy"; "Why lov'st thou that—which thou receiv'st not gladly"; "Or else receiv'st with pleasure— thine annoy" (Vendler 1997, 79–82). These initial paradoxes relate to the attitude of the listener to music and adumbrate a musical aesthetics of reception which links music to melancholy. Robert Burton was to dedicate an entire chapter to this in his *Anatomy of Melancholy* of 1621, "Music as Remedy" (IV, v, ii, 3). But, as he argues towards the end of the chapter, music is not only a remedy for melancholy but also a stimulant of melancholy pleasures: "Many men are melancholy by hearing music, but it is a pleasing melancholy that it causeth" (Burton 1932, 2.118). Shakespeare knew about such melancholy pleasure of music and has Jaques in *As You Like It* call for a song because he "can suck melancholy out of a song, as a weasel sucks

---

[8] Kirchmeyer (2002, 464) (my translation).

eggs" (2.5.12), and Jessica in *The Merchant of Venice* comment upon the consort music drifting through the moon-lit night: "I am never merry when I hear sweet music" (5.1.69). This sets up the sonnet's addressee as one of those fashionably melancholy dandies that walked the Elizabethan social and theatrical stages and were immortalized in the visual arts in Nicholas Hilliard's miniature portrait of a "Young Man Amongst Roses" (ca. 1588)—beautiful, elegant and refined, self-enamoured, a bit blasé and cultivating his "annoy" or *ennui* (verse 4) as a higher kind of pleasure.

This pleasurable melancholy is, however, not everything music has to communicate to him. There is more to it, and this more is disclosed in the following two quatrains, which now turn from the paradoxes of the recipient's attitude to music to the paradoxes of music in itself. Music with its "true concord of well-tunèd sounds" (verse 5) has a lesson to teach him. The harmony emerging from the interplay of the various instruments of a consort of viols and the resonances and chords between the strings of a single lute or viol (verses 9–10) are held up to him in reprimand of his monadic, self-centred and self-enamoured life. This aesthetic *e pluribus unum* draws upon a long tradition of Platonic music theory, in which the "mutual ordering" (10) of sounds in musical compositions is based upon, and in turn provides a model for, the wider harmonies of mathematics, ethics, familial and social life, nature, politics, metaphysics, astronomy, and the entire cosmos. Sir John Davies' *Orchestra, or a Poem of Dancing* had recently, in 1596, summed up this musical micro- and macrocosmos analogy as a central part of what critics have called the "Elizabethan World Picture" (Tillyard 1943) and Shakespeare himself, in the last scene of *Merchant of Venice* (5.1.53–88), extends the musical "touches of sweet harmony" (57) drifting across the lagoon to comprise both the internal and social order of man, the order of nature and the translunary music of the spheres. In this Platonic vision, music and dance become allegories of love conjoined in marriage and, at the same time, matrimony is turned into an allegory of music. Accordingly, in our sonnet the *laus musicae* by way of allegory praises love and incites to it, and simultaneously music takes on allegorically the "unions married" (6) of "sweet husband to another" (9) in the "mutual ordering" (10) of love in marriage.

This allegory revolves around the "one string" highlighted by the speaker at the beginning of the third quatrain with his explicit "Mark!". The exact musical or musicological reference of this wilfully ingenious *concetto* is, however far from unambiguously clear—one recent editor of *The Sonnets*, John Kerrigan, called it downright "obscure" (183). Does it refer to the resonance one string engenders in neighbouring strings? This is the reading suggested by G. Blakemore Evans in his New Cambridge edition, who offers the following paraphrase: "Observe how one (lute?) string, performing as a kind ('sweet'; musically, 'well-tunèd') husband (compare 'sire' (11)) in relation to another string (compare 'mother' (11)), when struck produces each through the other a reciprocally ('mutually') harmonious resonance, which, spreading to a third string (a 'child' (11), reduces all three to one harmony." And he supports his reading with a quotation from *The Virtuous Octavia*, a contemporary play by Samuel Brandon:

> When anyone doth strike a tuned string,
> The rest, which with the same in concord be,
> Will shew a motion to that senseless thing;
> When all the other neither stirre nor play. (Shakespeare 1996, 122)

Or does the "one chord" actually refer to a "monochord," that one-string instrument used ever since Pythagoras and Euclid and Guido d'Arezzo to demonstrate the mathematical order and proportions—"the mutual ordering," in the language of our sonnet—underlying musical intervals or to determine as a rule, as the "canon," the consonance of the strings employed in the performance of the musical piece?[9] We need not decide between the two readings. They can very well exist side by side here, as they contain the same lesson to the young man: "Du mußt Dein Leben ändern!"—you have to renounce singleness and integrate yourself into the wider orders and harmonies of family, society and the cosmos suggested by the musical metaphors. What the young man has to learn here is "the parts that [he] should [...] bear" (8)—*nota bene* not the *single* part of self-enamoured bachelor he has played so far, but "parts" in the *plural*.[10] And "parts" is a word that in the context of the two-way allegory of love and music straddles both domains: both the "parts" a musician performs and the "parts" or talents given to him by nature and heredity to be

---

[9] I owe the reference to the monochord to Albrecht Riethmüller, my musicological colleague at the Freie Universität Berlin, who, by inviting me to a Stravinsky conference ("Between Emotion and Objectivity: Igor Stravinsky," Berlin, 26–27 January 2012), triggered my interest in the composer's engagements with Shakespearean texts.

[10] The text in Stravinsky's score misprints "part" for "parts".

passed on to his child, as well as his sexual "parts" and the "parts" he has to play in social life—that of man, aristocrat, husband and father. It is at this juncture that sonnet 8 joins the argument of the other procreation sonnets. Where, however, their persuasions only aim at exhorting him to sire an heir, here the appeal to procreation is preceded by the appeal to enter a loving union and is withheld until the last quatrain and the final couplet. This new departure is marked by the striking change from indicative to imperative and the emphatic deictic gesture of "Mark" at the beginning of the third quatrain, and it is in this quatrain that the duo of loving man and woman is extended to a trio that includes "sire, and child, and happy mother" (11). The sonnet ends on a crescendo of paradoxes: the *unisono* of their three voices joined in one melody (12), their "speechless song" sung by many as if they were one, and finally the most pointed of the paradoxes, the message of the music to him: "Thou single wilt prove none" wittily turns a proverb derived from an Aristotelian axiom against him: "One is no number." This last half-verse, which warns the young man that he will remain a nonentity if he fails to enter the bond of married love and transmit his gifts to his progeny, sums up and concludes the argument with epigrammatic concision, and this sense of closure is further re-enforced by conjoining two lexical leitmotifs that resound as near-homophones throughout the whole sonnet: "sing," "song" and "single"; "not" and "note"; "one" and "none."

* * *

Let me return to Stravinsky at this point to consider how he responded in his musical setting to Shakespeare's sonnet 8.[11] Being no musicologist, my observations will, of course, be rather limited and in fairly untechnical terms. And, of course, I do not take it for granted that a composer like Stravinsky would—or even should—feel called upon to interpret the sonnet with, and in, his music the way I as a literary scholar and critic have tried to do it hermeneutically. To begin with, I know next to nothing about Stravinsky's textual sensibility, his attention to the text and its subtle and often ambiguous or ambivalent details. In this respect, I am

---

[11] Recordings of Stravinsky's setting can be found on the CD of *Shakespeare's Sonnets Global* and on YouTube (directed by Pierre Boulez and sung by Anne Murray); another version, directed by Stravinsky and sung by Cathy Berberian, can be found on disk 15, track 30 of the *Works of Igor Stravinsky* (22 CDs, Sony).

in the position of W. H. Auden, who did not only feel honoured, but also alarmed when Stravinsky invited him to write the libretto for *The Rake's Progress*, "having heard [...] that Stravinsky had said more than once that, in setting words to music, not the words but only the numbers of syllables mattered" and that, having so little English, Stravinsky "might distort the language to the point of unintelligibility" (Qtd Carpenter 1983, 352). Moreover, why should the modern composer not have felt like wilfully distorting the poem and composing his music against its grain, downtoning its exalted emotions and flights of fancy in a spirit of "New Sobriety" or "New Objectivity" (*Neue Sachlichkeit*)?

What, for instance, do we make of the surprising change of voice he introduces in his song? In Shakespeare's text, as the context of the immediately preceding and following sonnets makes quite clear, the speaker's voice is a male voice, a man speaking to a man, a friend more mature than the young friend he is exhorting. Stravinsky, in contrast, writes his "Musick to heare" for a mezzo soprano, a female voice accompanied by flute, clarinet and viola. Does Stravinsky use the human voice like an instrument here and neutralize the gender divide? Or is this the kind of cross-casting which was the norm in Shakespeare's theatre, albeit there all female roles were performed by male actors? Or is it rather the kind of cross-casting which we encounter so frequently in modern Shakespeare productions playing with gender and exhibiting its social constructedness by having actresses perform male roles or vice versa? Taken this way, Stravinsky's setting might aim at pointedly re-casting Shakespeare's scenario, turning the elder man's reproach of the younger man's narcissism into a wooing female voice, his lady's, "sweetly chiding" and gently pleading with him. This might also account for the emotional charge of the song, which is—to my ear—not that of an argument hammered out forcefully but one of tender, plaintive and insistent persuasion.

The tone for this is set in the song's eight-bar instrumental prelude, which prepares the stage, as it were, for the speaker to watch the addressee listening to a trio of flute, clarinet and viol, the latter recalling the consort of viols Shakespeare's sonnet suggests. The mood of this introduction is, however, dominated by the flute which, singing sweetly in *dolce cantabile*, as the score has it, anticipates the sonnet's emphasis on the sweetness of music. The words "sweet" or "sweetly" will resound four times in the three quatrains of the sonnet, invoking in a synesthetic metaphor widely diffused in medieval and early modern music theory an emotional charge that links music not with exalted passions but with softer, feminine affects, with religious devotion and with sadness and melancholy.

The sweetness of the melody and harmony reaches its greatest intensity in the last bar of the instrumental introduction with the perfect harmony of c and c' in the flute and g" in the viola. Together they form an octave (c—c') and a fifth (c'—g"), the most perfect consonances and most pleasing to the ear in their "confusion,"[12] their fusion of difference and similarity. The mathematical proportions are 1:2 for the octave and 2:3 for the fifth, which precisely divides the octave into the two consonances of the fifth and the fourth. As in Pythagorean musical theory odd numbers stand for the male and even numbers for the female, the sequence of 1–2–3 may suggest the gender relations between father–mother–boy child. And indeed, when we reach in the song itself Shakespeare's "sire, and child, and happy mother," the centre of the musical analogy, we find the notes of g,' a,' bb,' d" in the singing voice. They constitute the most consistent development of the harmonies in bar 8. Where in the introduction the absolutely best consonance, the octave, is divided into two consonances, here the second-best consonance, the fifth, is harmoniously divided. The fifth relating to father and mother frames the child's bb', which complements the "empty" fifth into a minor triad and forms with the father's note a minor third and with the mother's a major third. We see—or rather, hear—that Stravinsky might hardly have done more to assimilate the harmonic side of his setting to Shakespeare's words. This beautifully harmonious sequence of intervals in the sung melody is, however, wilfully broken up almost beyond recognition in the a-tonal instrumental accompaniment with its unsingable melodic leaps, erasing, as it were, the vision of harmony and perfect proportion evoked in Shakespeare's words, as sung by the mezzo soprano voice.[13] Thus, Stravinsky appears to be working *with*, and *against*, Shakespeare's poem at the same time, marking historical distance and difference while attempting to bridge it in his subtle inter-art negotiations between Renaissance and present, between poetry and chamber music.

[12] Shakespeare uses this term, harking back to ancient musical theory, in the famous passage about music in *A Midsummer Night's Dream* (4.1.109) to create a pun that conjoins its double meaning of "disorder" and "perfect fusion"; see Maier (2002).

[13] I thank my musicological colleague Franz Michael Maier for having opened my ear to such subtleties.

In contrast to other musical settings of Shakespearean sonnets, Stravinsky does not highlight the structural division of the sonnet into three quatrains and a concluding couplet by pauses or instrumental intermezzi. They follow uninterruptedly one upon the other, though with a marked change in the melodic line and the rhythmic *gestus* at the turn from the second to the third quatrain, where the singing voice returns to the series of six semiquavers on one note with which the song began. The music thus divides Shakespeare's sonnet into two major parts at the very point where a Petrarchan sonnet also changes its argument, together with the prosodic change from the initial two quatrains of its octave to the two tercets of its sestet, and where Shakespeare also, in spite of the different structure of his sonnet form, often initiates a *volta* in the argument; in the case of sonnet 8 this is marked by the change from the declarative sentences of the first part to the emphatically deictic imperative of "Mark" extending across the final six verses.

When the end is reached, Stravinsky defeats the audience's expectation of closing of the instrumental frame and pointedly withholds the solace of a balancing counterpart to the instrumental prelude.[14] His musical rendering ends on the last word of the sonnet; the sense of closure he creates rests on an abrupt silence which enacts ominously the sterile negativity of "none." To my lay ear, this final gesture reverberates with a music that, while it lasts, increasingly and wilfully dissociates itself from music's "true concord," its "well-tuned sounds," "unions married" and "mutual ordering," which Shakespeare's music sonnet evokes so eloquently throughout. Such harmonies do not seem to be available any longer, neither in love nor in music nor any other art, so what is left for the modern composer confronted with them is what Karl Heinz Bohrer recently called "Ästhetische Negativität."[15]

References

Auden, W. H., and Norman Holmes Pearson. 1950. *Poets of the English Language*. New York: Viking Press.

---

[14] In the overall structure of the *Three Songs from Shakespeare*, the seven-bar instrumental postlude to the last of the three songs, "When Daisies pied," the spring and cuckoo song from *Love's Labour's Lost*, does, however, close the frame and create a strong sense of closure (private communication by Albrecht Riethmüller).

[15] Karl Heinz Bohrer, *Ästhetische Negativität* (München: Hanser, 2002).

Blick, Fred. 1999. "Shakespeare's Musical Sonnets Numbers 8, 128 and Pythagoras". *Upstart Crow: A Shakespeare Journal* 19: 1–17.

Bohrer, Karl Heinz. 2002. *Ästhetische Negativität*. München: Hanser.

Burton, Robert. 1932. *The Anatomy of Melancholy* [1621]. Intro. Holbrook Jackson. London: Everyman's Library. 2 vols.

Carpenter, Humphrey. 1983. *W. H. Auden. A Biography*. London: George Allen and Unwin.

Edmondson, Paul, and Stanley Wells. 2004. *Shakespeare's Sonnets*. Oxford: Oxford University Press.

Gabler, Hans Walter. 2000. "Shakespeare in der Musik". In *Shakespeare-Handbuch*, 4th edition. Ed. Ina Schabert. Stuttgart: Kröner.

Gooch, B.N.S. and D. Thatcher. 1991. *Shakespeare Musical Catalogue*. Oxford: Oxford University Press.

Jonson, Ben. 1910. *Every Man Out of His Humour* [1600] in *Ben Jonson's Plays*. Ed. Felix E. Schelling. London: Everyman's Library.

Kirchmeyer, Helmut. 2002. *Kommentiertes Verzeichnis der Werke und Werkausgaben Igor Strawinskys bis 1971*. Abhandlungen der Sächsischen Akademie der Wissenschaften zu Leipzig, Philologisch-historische Klasse, 79. Stuttgart/Leipzig: S. Hirzel.

Maier, Franz Michael. 2002. "'Mine Ear Is Much Enamoured of thy Note'. Musikalische Grundbegriffe in Shakespeare's *A Midsummer Night's Dream*". *Archiv für Musikwissenschaft* 59: 33–50.

Pfister, Manfred. 2005. "'As an Unperfect Actor on the Stage': Notes Towards a Definition of Performance and Performativity in Shakespeare's *Sonnets*". In *Theory Into Poetry: New Approaches to the Lyric*. Ed. Eva Müller-Zettelmann and Margarete Rubik. Amsterdam: Rodopi, 207–228.

Pfister, Manfred. 2009. "Introduction—Shakespeare's Sonnets Global 'in States Unborn and Accents Yet Unknown'". In *Shakespeare's Sonnets Global*. Ed. Manfred Pfister and Jürgen Gutsch. Dozwil: Edition SIGNAThUR, 9–29.

Pfister, Manfred, and Jürgen Gutsch. 2009. *Shakespeare's Sonnets Global*. Dozwil: Edition SIGNAThUR.

Rupp, Susanne. 2005. *Die Macht der Lieder: Kulturwissenschaftliche Studien zur Performativität weltlicher Vokalmusik der Tudorzeit*. Studies in English Literary and Cultural History, 15. Trier: Wissenschaftlicher Verlag Trier..

Shakespeare, William. 1996. *The Sonnets*. Ed. G. Blakemore Evans. The New Cambridge Shakespeare. Cambridge: Cambridge University Press.

Shakespeare, William, 1997. *Shakespeare's Sonnets*. Ed. Katherine Duncan-Jones. The Arden Shakespeare. London: Thomas Nelson.

Shakespeare, William. 2000. *The Sonnets and A Lover's Complaint*. Ed. John Kerrigan. London: Penguin.

Sidney, Sir Philip. 1987. *The Countess of Pembroke's Arcadia (The Old Arcadia)* [1590]. Ed. Victor J. Stretkowicz. Oxford: Oxford University Press.

Simpson, Richard. 1878. *Sonnets of Shakespeare Selected from a Complete Setting, and Miscellaneous Songs*. London.

Stravinsky, Igor. 1955. *Three Songs from William Shakespeare*. Hawkes Pocket Scores. New York: Boosey & Hawkes.

Stravinsky, Igor. 2007. *Works of Igor Stravinsky*. 22 CDs. Sony.

Tillyard, E. M. W. 1943. *The Elizabethan World Picture*. London: Chatto & Windus.

Trillini, Regula Hohl. 2008. "The Gaze of the Listener: Shakespeare's Sonnet 128 and Early Modern Discourses of Music and Gender". *Music and Letters*, 89.1: 1–17.

Vendler, Helen. 1997. *The Art of Shakespeare's Sonnets*. Cambridge, Mass.: Harvard University Press.

CHAPTER 16

William Shakespeare's Sonnets in Russian Music: Traditions—Genres—Forms

Stefan Weiss

Anyone investigating the role of the sonnet form in Russian vocal music will inevitably come to two conclusions. The first concerns the choice of poems: Russian composers past and present have turned only rarely

For manifold help in the preparation of this study, and for a lively exchange of ideas, the author is indebted to numerous persons, especially Lidia Ader, Maria Bychkova, David Fanning, Anna Fortunova, Levon Hakopian, Tamara Levaja, Arnt Nitschke, Jan Philip Schulze, Sara Springfeld and Henrieke Stahl. This essay was originally published in German in the volume *Das Sonett und die Musik; Poetiken, Konjunkturen, Transformationen, Reflexionen*, ed. by Sara Springfeld, Norbert Greiner and Silke Leopold, Heidelberg: Universitätsverlag Winter, 2016. The translation came about with the invaluable help of Maria Lehmann and Ferran Planas Pla.

S. Weiss (✉)
Hochschule für Musik, Theater und Medien, Hannover, Germany
e-mail: Stefan.Weiss@hmtm-hannover.de

© The Author(s), under exclusive license to Springer Nature Switzerland AG 2023
J. Kingsley-Smith and W. R. Rampone Jr. (eds.), *Shakespeare's Global Sonnets*, Global Shakespeares, https://doi.org/10.1007/978-3-031-09472-9_16

273

to original Russian sonnets; instead, they prefer translated world literature, with William Shakespeare, so it seems, being the most frequently
musicalized sonneteer in Russian musical culture. The second conclusion,
however, concerns the term "musical culture" itself which, with respect
to Russian Shakespeare adaptations in music, should be set in the plural
form to do justice to the actual circumstances. Since the 1970s at least,
Shakespeare's sonnets have had a firm place not only in the highbrow art
song (*Lied*) but also in popular musical contexts of Soviet and post-Soviet
Russia. Examples of this development can be found in abundance on the
Internet platform YouTube if one knows how to enter the search words
"Shakespeare" (Шекспир) and "sonnet" (сонет) in Cyrillic script.[1] Two
examples may give just a small impression of the stylistic breadth with
which the 154 sonnets have been set to music in the Russian-speaking
world.

The first example takes us to Barnaul, the capital of the Altai region
south of Novosibirsk. In November 2009, the Theatre of Musical
Comedy of that city is hosting a concert by *Sibir*, the local orchestra
of folk instruments. The video[2] shows that at the end of a rendition
of Henry Mancini's *Pink Panther Theme*, a guest star enters the stage:
the international opera soloist Vladimir Ognev. Here Ognev, known for
his occasional forays into popular genres, croons into the microphone a
musical setting of Sonnet 130, "Eë glaza na zvëzdy ne pochoži" ("My
Mistress' Eyes are Nothing Like the Sun"). The song was composed by
the conductor of that evening, Igor Novikov, as part of a *Malen'kaja
simfonija sonetov* (*Little Sonnet Symphony*) that also includes settings of
Sonnets 5 and 126. More challenging than the question of genre—song
or symphony?—is the style of this setting, which could best be described
as "light entertainment", a big-band-type sound based on folk instruments like balalaika and bayan. How much of the spirit of Shakespeare's
words, one may wonder, has survived the long journey to South Siberia?
(Fig. 16.1).

---

[1] On the handling of transcriptions from Cyrillic: In this paper, Russian proper
names are generally romanized according to the reader-friendly BGN/PCGN transcription
("Shostakovich"). In the case of bibliographical information, titles of works and quotations, however, where unambiguity has priority over legibility, the decision was made in
favour of the ISO transliteration ("Šostakovič").

[2] The video described here can be found at http://www.youtube.com/watch?v=pK3
979-Bgus, last accessed on November 26, 2021.

Fig. 16.1 Vladimir Ognev and the orchestra *Sibir* performing Igor Novikov's setting of Sonnet 130

Some years earlier, in March 2005, from the large stage of the Palace of the Republic in Minsk, Belarusian television is broadcasting a concert devoted to the oeuvre of composer Valery Golovko.[3] Among the performers is the youthful-looking singer Ruslan Alekhno (Fig. 16.2), who has won the talent show *Narodnyj artist* (*People's Artist*) on Russian television the year before; later he would go on to represent Belarus at the *Eurovision Song Contest*. Accompanied by the Belarusian Presidential Orchestra—a symphony orchestra with an integrated rock band that dominates the sound on this occasion—he sings "Priznajus' ja, čto dvoe my s toboj", Golovko's setting of Shakespeare's Sonnet 36 ("Let Me Confess That We Two Must be Twain"). This is mainstream pop, starting with a soulful ballad-like introduction and continuing with an up-tempo main section, which may not be strikingly original but is catchy, nonetheless. For the composer Golovko, as for Novikov, this song did not remain the only Shakespeare sonnet setting. His 1998 album *Ispoved'* (*Confession*) contains this one and Sonnets 66 and 128. Within the large-scale form of the album, dedicated to the memory of his wife, Tamara, who had died in an accident the year before, Golovko assigned the three sonnets

[3] The video can be found at http://www.youtube.com/watch?v=Qt8R5vCM2AA&feature=related, last accessed on November 26, 2021.

Fig. 16.2 Ruslan Alekhno and the Belarusian Presidential Orchestra performing Valery Golovko's setting of Sonnet 36

the function of "overcoming the tragedy of life step by step through the theme of love" (Golovko, n.d. [1998]).

That Shakespeare's sonnets might serve as lyrics for popular songs may be disturbing to those for whom the setting to music of "classical" poetry goes hand in hand with the idea of "classical music". In the Russian-speaking world, however, a Shakespearean sonnet set in the guise of a popular style apparently arouses no more surprise than a setting of the same poem in a high culture idiom. Based on this observation, my paper attempts to trace the path of this poetry in the various genres of Russian music. Of particular interest along this path is the aspect of form. For a composer interested in setting a Shakespearean sonnet with its three four-line quatrains and the concluding two-line couplet, a readily available musical form that goes with it simply does not exist. Although the Shakespearean sonnet seems to present fewer obstacles to a strophic realization than the Petrarchan sonnet, which is divided into two quatrains and two tercets, its conception as a strophic song inevitably leads to the problem that the concluding couplet cannot be reconciled with the laws of the musical form.

In the academic *Lied* tradition, composers usually solve such a problem by following the strategy of through-composition, which, in extreme cases, dispenses a priori with any relic of a strophic structure and continuously presents new musical ideas to fit with the poem's semantic progress.

Table 16.1   Igor Novikov, "Eë glaza na zvëzdy ne pochoži" (Sonnet 130, "My Mistress' Eyes are Nothing Like the Sun"; Translation: Samuil Marshak), from *Malen'kaja simfonija sonetov*

Poem sections[4]	Textless sections of setting	Music	Comments
	Ritornello	B (short)	
1Q		A	First strophe
	Ritornello	B (short)	
2Q		A	Second strophe
3Q		B (full)	Contrasting section
	Interlude	B (twice)	Scat singing
Cp		A'	Accompaniment reduced

It is in popular genres that the problem of finding a musical dramaturgy for the Shakespearean sonnet takes on greater urgency because here academic through-composition is not an option. Thus, especially in the context of popular musical cultures, the decision to set a sonnet to music is likely to lead to unusual interpretations of form based on a strophic conception. In this respect, Russian musical settings of Shakespeare's sonnets offer a wealth of material that is worth studying (Table 16.1).

Novikov's setting of Sonnet 130, for example (Table 16.1), shapes two musically identical strophes (A) from the first two quatrains. This material makes its reappearance only with the couplet, but in lower dynamics and a new, somewhat restrained orchestration that musically underlines the point of the poetic *volta*. The musical motifs of section A return in a new, reflective mood at the very moment the speaker of the poem professes that all the ugly things that could be said of his mistress will not change his love for her. For the intervening third quatrain, Novikov invents a contrasting musical section (B) that elaborates on the short motif of the instrumental *ritornello*. This section—a "bridge" or "middle eight", in the terminology of popular song—is then prolonged by a textless vocal interlude on the same musical material, now performed in "scat" style by the singer. The concluding couplet is thus highlighted as quintessential in two respects: on the one hand, through the preceding temporary suspension of the textual level, which the wordless interlude entails, and, on

---

[4] The abbreviations apply to this and all following form schemes: 1Q, 2Q, 3Q = first quatrain, etc.; Cp = couplet, rep. = repeat.

Table 16.2   Valery Golovko, "Priznajus' ja, čto dvoe my s toboj" (Sonnet 36, "Let Me Confess That We Two Must be Twain"; Translation: Samuil Marshak), from the album *Ispoved'*[5]

Poem sections	Textless sections of setting	Music	Comments
	Introduction		Introduction and 1Q in slow tempo
1Q		A	First strophe
2Q		B	Chorus
	[rep. 2Q]	B'	
3Q		A'	Second strophe
	[rep. 2Q]	B	Chorus
	[rep. 2Q]	B'	
Cp		C	Climax
	Solos (piano, electric guitar)	C' + C'	
	[rep. Cp]	C''	

the other, through the long-expected return of the initial idea (A) with a simultaneous, significant transformation of musical gesture into the realm of the pensive and dreamy (Table 16.2).

Valery Golovko's setting of Sonnet 36 also emphasizes the couplet as a climax, but formally in a quite different way (Table 16.2). It assigns new and apotheotic material (C) to the last two lines, the impetus of which is so great that it virtually enforces its own multiple repetition: first in the form of instrumental solos, then via a final recapitulation by the singer. Up to that point, however, the setting unfolds according to the scheme of a strophic song with a chorus.

The fact that in Golovko's setting, the second quatrain (B) is heard four times—twice after the first quatrain and twice after the third one—is not unusual for the chorus of a pop song, but it is likely to annoy Shakespeare enthusiasts as much as purists of the academic *Lied*, even if this particular sonnet—and this particular translation—are not semantically at odds with this musical solution. Thus, a possible uneasiness regarding the appropriate style may extend to the form as well. But scepticism may also arise on the side of pop musicians. Do these poems, with their high level

---

[5] The form scheme corresponds to the version that was played live at the Minsk concert in 2005. The album version is longer because it contains another run-through of form sections A (guitar solo) and B (chorus) before the couplet. This version is also accessible via golovkoworld.com (last accessed on November 26, 2021).

of complexity, even fulfil the prerequisite for attracting the interest of a mass audience, as is expected of popular songs? It may be reasonable to assume that not only Shakespeare's language and imagery are problematic from the point of view of pop culture, but also the logic of the sonnet form itself. When it comes to that, however, the composers of the *Lied* tradition also had their problems.

SHAKESPEARE SONNETS IN RUSSIAN AND SOVIET ART SONG TRADITIONS (1900–1970)

According to all available data, César Cui was the first Russian composer ever to publish any settings of poems in sonnet form. His *Four Sonnets by Adam Mickiewicz for a Solo Voice with Piano Accompaniment* op. 48 were printed in 1892 by the Berlin editor Simrock in three languages (German, Polish and Russian). At this earliest point in the history of composing sonnets in Russian music, the decision itself to create an entire collection of sonnets is remarkable. It was anything but obvious in the context of the European *Lied*, and, in retrospect, appears daring in view of the difficulties that confronted its realization by composers. At the time Cui published his opus 48, only the *Tre sonetti di Petrarca*, which Franz Liszt had composed in its first version in the years 1842–1846, could have served as models. Franz Schubert's three sonnets by Petrarca D 628–630, composed as early as 1818, were still unpublished. Among Russian composers, however, this strategy soon found a follower in Mikhail Ippolitov-Ivanov, who in 1907 transferred the principle of the musicalized sonnet collection to Shakespeare's poetry. His *Ten Shakespeare Sonnets* op. 45 represent the first known musical settings of Shakespeare's sonnets in Russia.[6] To the best of my knowledge, between the collections of Cui and Ippolitov-Ivanov no other Russian composer had published another setting of a sonnet by any given poet.

To achieve his ten-piece-collection, Ippolitov-Ivanov, a student of Nikolay Rimsky-Korsakov, adapted to his needs the first complete Russian translation of the sonnets published by Nikolay Gerbel in 1880. Of the

---

[6] A letter by the composer to the work's dedicatee, Nazari Rayski, shows that the ten songs were written in summer 1907 (Sokolov 1986, 150–51). On the basis of the publisher's plate number, the edition may also be dated 1907. See the entry on the publisher P. Jurgenson in: *IMSLP Petrucci Music Library*, https://imslp.org/wiki/P._Jurgenson, last accessed on November 26, 2021. The plate number of the edition is 32357.

ten sonnets, the composer adheres closely to Gerbel's wording in only one; it is the famous Sonnet 18 ("Shall I compare thee to a summer's day") that concludes Ippolitov-Ivanov's collection. While in this case there are only minor changes of words and word order, the liberties taken with the translations in the remaining nine songs are many. At least one line in each poem is omitted or thoroughly rephrased for the settings. The edition itself does not indicate these deviations from the original.

An example of such an irreverent procedure—which appears to be entirely absent from later Russian Shakespeare sonnet settings—is Ippolitov-Ivanov's setting of Sonnet 98 ("From You I Have Been Absent in the Spring"). There, the last four lines of the original say of the flowers:

> They were but sweet, but figures of delight,
> Drawn after you, you pattern of all those.
> Yet seemed it winter still, and, you away,
> As with your shadow I with these did play.

Gerbel's translation reads:

> Zatem čto prelest' ich – krasa vesny i leta –
> Liš' kopiej tvoej javljalas' vsjudu mne.
> No vsë že sneg krugom ležavšim mne kazalsja
> I imi, kak tvoej ja ten'ju, zabavljalsja.

> [Because their beauty – the adornment of spring and summer – / Appeared to me everywhere only as a copy of yours. / But still the snow seemed to lie all around me / And so I was amused by them, as by your shadow.]

Instead of these four lines, Ippolitov-Ivanov sets to music only two, which he possibly wrote himself. Only one part of the Gerbel translation remains: namely, the passage about "the adornment of spring and summer":

> Ved' dlja menja odna, krasa vesny i leta
> Ljubov' moja, moja Anneta!

> [For to me the adornment of spring and summer alone / Is my love, my Annette!]

One day, perhaps, biographical research on the composer will establish the identity of the lady in question. With regard to the mutilation of the sonnet form in his song collection, this is only the bizarre tip of the iceberg. In three sonnets (73, 92 and 149), for example, even the couplet is deleted without replacement, and Sonnet 33 is set to music in the form of a mere eight-line version that leaves not a single verse of the original intact. The reason for this literary massacre is not known. Gerbel's translation in iambic hexameters was considered weak in Russian literary circles, and as the translator himself had died in 1883, Ippolitov-Ivanov probably took these liberties without causing much offence. In the context of the history of sonnets in Russian music, however, the incident draws our attention to the specific problems with which composers are faced when setting these poems. These problems arise not only from the absence of a regular strophic structure, but also from the particular combination of length and complexity so characteristic of these poems.

Stylistically, Ippolitov-Ivanov's collection seems old-fashioned in the context of turn-of-the-century *Lied* conventions. Moreover, it did not make too high a demand on the performers, even though its dedicatee, Nazari Rayski, was a celebrated tenor of his day. The piano part, in particular, is conspicuous for its adherence to stereotyped patterns, which often characterize the pieces throughout. In the tenth song, the aforementioned "Shall I Compare Thee to a Summer's Day" (see Table 16.3), the pattern is an octave pendulum repeated in flowing triplet motion. During the entire song, it is suspended only once during the couplet, thereby emphasizing its function as a punchline. Dynamically, too, the couplet stands out, with the indication "forte" found only at this place in the song. The song is through-composed although an A-B-A' form shines through in the way the three quatrains are set.

In my attempt to give a reliable overview of Russian musical settings of Shakespeare's sonnets in the framework of the art song tradition, I am greatly indebted to the meticulous research that has gone into the *Shakespeare Music Catalogue* by Bryan Gooch and David Thatcher. The Gooch/Thatcher catalogue contains a list of internationally verifiable musical settings of the sonnets prior to 1991 (Gooch and Thatcher 1991, 1965–2087). Although the list is certainly not complete, it provides us with a relatively safe guarantee that Ippolitov-Ivanov's 1907 collection initially found few successors in Russia (see Table 16.4). There is evidence of three individual sonnet settings from the Shakespearean jubilee year of 1916, but afterwards, Russian and later Soviet composers continued to

Table 16.3 Mikhail Ippolitov-Ivanov, "Kak ja sravnju tebja s roskošnym letnim dněm" (Sonnet 18, "Shall I Compare Thee to a Summer's Day"; Translation: Nikolai Gerbel), No. 10 of the *Shakespeare Sonnets op. 45*

Poem sections	Textless sections of setting	Music	Comments
	Prelude		Brief establishment of the accompanying octave pendulum
1Q		A	
2Q		B	
3Q		A'	Similarity to A only in the first two lines
Cp		C	Highlighted dynamically, as well as by suspension of pattern
	Postlude		Resumes music of prelude

carelessly pass by this body of poetry for another 25 years. Thus, it is all the more surprising that an upward trend began in the 1940s and gained full force in the 1950s.

It is certainly no coincidence that the turning point occurred during World War II, when the Soviet alliance with the United Kingdom gave rise to an increased mutual interest in the culture of the allies. The 1940s also brought two poetic impulses that did much to endear Shakespeare's sonnets to Soviet composers. In 1942 and 1944, Boris Pasternak's celebrated translations of selected sonnets received their first, albeit isolated, musical settings, of which the one of no. 73 by the little-known Igor Belza certainly had less impact on successors than Dmitri Shostakovich's setting of no. 66.[7] At the end of the decade, a new translation of all sonnets by Samuil Marshak appeared in print (Maršak 1949), which was awarded a Stalin Prize (second degree) in 1948 and experienced phenomenal success in the years to follow. Numerous editions and, in particular, musical settings attest to the status of this translation as the canonized one for the Russian-speaking world. Boris Budnitskiy's setting of Sonnet 30, supposedly the first of the Marshak translations, was reputedly composed in 1948, the year Marshak received the Stalin Prize. However, it remained

[7] On Shostakovich's composition see Redepenning (2016).

Table 16.4 Russian musical settings of Shakespeare's sonnets from 1907 to 1950 (all for voice and piano)

Year	Composer and work, year of first printing, voice range as indicated [or inferred]	Sonnet number (place in collection given in Roman numerals)	Translator
1907	Mikhail Ippolitov-Ivanov: *Shakespeare Sonnets* op. 45, 1907 [high]	18 (X), 33 (VII), 71 (I), 73 (VI), 92 (V), 98 (III), 99 (IV), 106 (IX), 109 (VIII), 149 (II)	Nikolay Gerbel
1916	Sergey Trailin: *Shakespeare's Sonnet 30*, 1916 [high]	30	Vladimir Shuf
1916	Alexander Glazunov: *Two Shakespeare Sonnets*, 1966 (in Šnitke 1966, 286–95) [high]	66, 147 (the latter unfinished)	Anatoli Kremlev
1942	Dmitry Shostakovich: *Sonnet LXVI* / Nr. 5 of *Six Romances* op. 62, 1943 (consulted edition: Šostakovič 2012), bass	66	Boris Pasternak
1944	Igor Belza: *Shakespeare's Sonnet 73* op. 34 No. 2, 1945[8] [middle]	73	Boris Pasternak
1946	Mieczysław Weinberg: *Six Shakespeare Sonnets* op. 33, 2017,[9] bass	55 (I), 63 (II), 64 (III), 66 (VI), 71 (V), 154 (IV)	Nikolay Gerbel
1948	Boris Budnitskiy: *Romance* (Ms.)[10]	30	Samuil Marshak
1949	Felix Glonti: *Two Sonnets* (Ms.)[11]	unknown	unknown

unpublished and could not be perused for the present study (see Table 16.4).

It wasn't until 1955 that Marshak's translation yielded a milestone for the musical reception of Shakespeare's sonnets in the Soviet Union.

[8] Composition date 1944 according to Gooch and Thatcher (1991, 2038).

[9] Arnt Nitschke (Peermusic, Hamburg) kindly provided me with a copy of the manuscript, dated 1946.

[10] Not perused. My only source is Gooch and Thatcher (1991, 2004): "MS n. d. [*ca.* 1948]".

[11] Not perused. My only source is Gooch and Thatcher (1991, 2085).

The effect of Dmitry Kabalevsky's *Ten Shakespeare Sonnets* op. 52 on other composers can be deduced from the fact that immediately after their first publication, a veritable flood of further settings appeared. If the ten *Shakespeare Sonnets* by Ippolitov-Ivanov had remained without a successor, with only three more individual sonnet settings following in the ensuing 35 years, then the first six years alone after the publication of Kabalevsky's work would have already seen 24 more sonnet settings from the pens of five composers, all of them being part of collections consisting exclusively of Shakespeare sonnets (see Table 16.5). At the beginning of the 1960s, the phenomenon spread to composers from other Soviet republics; when they appeared in print, the Lithuanian (Gooch and Thatcher 1991, 2084) and Ukrainian (ibid., 2077) settings received an alternative Russian textual underlay, using Marshak's translation. Further settings of Marshak's translations followed, with reduced intensity, and have continued until today. A striking number of these are conceived for low male voices, baritone or bass, the register chosen by both Shostakovich in his setting of Sonnet 66 and Kabalevsky in his 1955 collection. Earlier composers had preferred high voices (see Tables 16.4 and 16.5).[12]

Since then, other translations have hardly played a role for Russian composers—those of Pasternak were occasionally used; their impact was, of course, limited because he only translated three individual Shakespeare sonnets into Russian, and not, like Marshak, all 154. It was only through Marshak's translation that Shakespeare's sonnets became familiar reading in Russia in a comprehensive sense. Since the 1960s, however, critical voices have accused the translator of having given a one-sided impression of Shakespeare. In 1969, Mikhail Gasparov and N. S. Avtonomova wrote about Marshak's Shakespeare from the perspective of literary criticism: "The serene, sublime, balanced and wise poet of the Russian sonnets [i.e. Marshak's translation] differs from the frenzied, inexhaustible, brilliant and passionate poet of the English sonnets. The English Shakespeare wrote sonnets for his friend and his lady; the Russian Shakespeare wrote

---

[12] In addition to the composers named in the tables, the following ones made their Shakespeare sonnet settings explicitly for bass or baritone: Boris Buevskiy (Ukrainian/Russian) 1966, Mikhail Glukh 1967, Alexander Lokshin 1969, Oleg Barskov 1973, Alexander Pirumov 1979, Boris Getselev 1982, Jekaterina Prichodovskaja 2008. In contrast, Zigmas Aleksandravičius (Lithuanian/Russian) 1960, Maria Zavalishyna (Ukrainian/Russian) 1961, Nikolay Dremljuga (Ukrainian/Russian) 1977, Mikael Tariverdiev 1980 and Viktor Agranovich 2007 demand higher voices.

Table 16.5 Russian settings of Shakespeare sonnets between 1950 and 1959 (all of them for voice and piano)

Year	Composer and work, year of first printing, voice range as indicated [or inferred]	Sonnet Number (place in collection given in Roman numerals)	Translator
1955	Dmitry Kabalevsky: *Ten Shakespeare Sonnets op. 52*, 1955 (consulted edition: Kabalevskij 1969), bass	8 (VII), 13 (VI), 27 (II), 30 (IV), 71 (VIII), 76 (X), 81 (I), 90 (IX), 102 (III), 153 (V)	Samuil Marshak
1955	Vera Krasnoglyadova: *Three Sonnets by William Shakespeare*, Sonnet 7 printed in 1955, the rest: Ms.,[13] high or middle	7, the rest unknown	Samuil Marshak
1955	Anatoly Bogatyrev: [Eight] *Romances on Words by William Shakespeare op. 29 and op. 30*, 1959/1975,[14] soprano or tenor	43 (op. 29/1), 56 (op. 29/2), 61 (op. 29/3), 81 (op. 29/4), 90 (op. 29/5), 97 (op. 30/1), 98 (op. 30/3), 142 (op. 30/2)	Samuil Marshak
1956	Mikael Tariverdiev: *Three Shakespeare Sonnets* (Ms.)[15]	27, 39, 55	Samuil Marshak
1958	David Pritsker: *Five Shakespeare Sonnets*, 1968/69,[16] baritone	61, 70, 96, 97, 99	Samuil Marshak
1959	Grigori Frid, [Five] *Shakespeare Sonnets op. 34*, 1964,[17] baritone	12 (I), 27 (IV), 29 (V), 50 (II), 153 (III)	Samuil Marshak

sonnets for us and eternity" (Gasparov and Avtonomova 2001, 406). This may give an idea of the reservations which are typical of the way the Soviet 1960s came to a reckoning with the culture of the early 1950s, with the monumental classicism of the late Stalin period as a chief target. Elements of this classicism also characterize the external appearance of Marshak's publication (see Fig. 16.3) as well as the style of Kabalevsky's settings.

[13] Not perused. See Gooch and Thatcher (1991, 1971 and 2085).

[14] Not perused. See Gooch and Thatcher (1991, 2014 and 2022).

[15] Not perused. See the list of works in Cuker (1985, 285).

[16] Sonnets 97 and 99 are contained in Pricker (1968, 38–45). The others are contained in Pricker (1969, 28–39). Dates of composition are given in the editions.

[17] The edition has an additional English text underlay.

Fig. 16.3   Shakespeare's sonnets in the translation by Marshak; book cover of the 1949 edition

An example of this is Sonnet 30 ("When to the Sessions of Sweet Silent Thought"), which makes use of the vocabulary of law and bookkeeping to add up the speaker's past sufferings and losses. In the concluding couplet, the added losses are contrasted with the love for the friend; in the balance, it turns out that love outweighs all past suffering. Kabalevsky sets this poem as a crescendo from pianissimo to fortissimo. The song is through-composed; each of the three quatrains as well as the couplet start from new musical ideas (Table 16.6). Immediately before the couplet, however, Kabalevsky places a piano interlude consisting of a monumentally amplified recapitulation of the first quatrain's central motivic idea. Dramaturgically, this interlude functions as an instrumental climax as

Table 16.6 Dmitri Kabalevsky, "Kogda na sud bezmolvnych, tajnych dum" (Sonnet 30, "When to the Sessions of Sweet Silent Thought"; Translation: Samuil Marshak), No. 4 from *Ten Shakespeare Sonnets* op. 52

Poem sections	Textless sections of setting	Music	Comments
	Prelude		
1Q		A	pianissimo
2Q		B	piano, poco a poco più agitato
3Q		C	piano, crescendo, forte
	Interlude	A'	fortissimo
Cp		D	fortissimo

Fig. 16.4 Bassist Leonid Kharitonov performing Kabalevsky's setting of Sonnet 30 in 1974

well as a reminder of the initial problem, before the couplet—as vocal climax—brings the solution.

The scoring of the vocal part with a bass is undoubtedly adequate to the profound seriousness that characterizes the approach of Soviet composers to this poetry. A filmed rendition of this Kabalevsky sonnet with bass Leonid Kharitonov (Fig. 16.4)[18] documents the performative

---

[18] http://www.youtube.com/watch?v=RlgpiyHeF9Q&feature=related, last accessed on November 29, 2021.

approach that goes with it. Set against a gloomy backdrop of a forest in evening, Kharitonov resolutely directs his gaze either towards the floor or into the depths of the room, while the pianist abides, as it were, in anonymity, her face remaining invisible in the film. The monumentality of the composition finds its counterpart in the narrowly confined facial expressions and gestures of the two performers.

SHAKESPEARE SONNETS IN SOVIET POPULAR MUSIC (1970–1990)

Kharitonov's rendition of Kabalevsky's Sonnet 30 was filmed in 1974, at a time when Shakespeare's sonnets were already gaining a foothold in Soviet music in a way far removed from late-Stalinist classicism. As far as can be determined, it was around 1970 that Soviet popular music cultures first made contact with this poetry, a contact which continues in post-Soviet Russia to this day. Interestingly, the popular adaptations also fall back on Marshak's translations even though these had been accused by literary critics like Gasparov and Avtonomova of stressing the sublime and wise aspects of the sonnets too much and of marginalizing their passionate sides. Apparently, musicians saw it quite differently. Lack of passion could hardly explain the appeal of this poetry in popular music and the appearance of new settings almost year after year.

If one wanted to name only one aspect of Marshak's translation that may have favoured its reception in popular culture, a likely candidate would be the reduction of the originals' linguistic complexity. The translation of Sonnet 130, "My Mistress' Eyes are Nothing Like the Sun", whose composition by Igor Novikov in easy-listening style for baritone and folk instrument orchestra was mentioned at the beginning of this paper, may serve as an example. In their quite complex syntax, lines 7–8 from Shakespeare's original—"And in some perfumes is there more delight/ Than in the breath that from my mistress reeks"—appear hardly recommendable for use as the lyrics of a popular song of the 1970s. Marshak's translation,

> A telo pachnet tak, kak pachnet telo, / Ne kak fialki nežnyj lepestok
> [And her body smells like a body smells, / Not like the violet's delicate petal]

uses very direct language in the first line, almost coarse in content and sound, while the artificial inversion in the second one vividly evokes all those stilted comparisons which the speaker of the poem ridicules. In the language of these two lines, the finely voiced irony of Shakespeare's period joins forces with brutal mid-twentieth-century realism. This may serve as an example of how Marshak made this poetry accessible to popular consumption like no Russian translator before him.

When it comes to the reception of Shakespeare in popular music, the *Shakespeare Music Catalogue* is no longer of any help, as it completely excludes this segment of musical life. Based on research on the Internet, I would tentatively date the beginning of a Russian history of popular Shakespeare sonnet settings with Sergey Nikitin. Nikitin was a member of the "bard culture" that emerged as an expression of alternative life and thought in the universities of the Soviet Union from the 1960s onwards. The performance of self-penned popular songs to the guitar is called "bardovskaja pesnja" ("bard song") in Russian, but also "avtorskaja pesnja", which means "self-composed song" and indicates that here no pop starlet is performing other people's products, but that the performer himself or herself is the creator of the song. From the 1960s onwards, the Russian "bard" is the equivalent of the "singer-songwriter" in Anglo-phone popular culture. Nikitin, too, performed his own music, but mostly used existing poetry for the lyrics. In 1973, he set Shakespeare to music for the first time: namely, Sonnet 90 ("Then Hate Me When Thou Wilt, if Ever, Now"), which he conceived for solo performance with his own guitar accompaniment, in accordance with the conventions of the bard scene (Fig. 16.5).[19] The speaker of this poem recognizes his beloved's intention to leave him and only asks her not to inflict this as a final blow, but to do it immediately so that he has the worst behind him.

It is striking that in the Russian popular music of the 1970s, it was precisely Sonnet 90 that was set to music at least two more times, and there is reason to suppose that the chain of popular successes related to these settings was an initial spark in the reception of Shakespeare in that culture. One of these settings reached an audience of millions by virtue of its performance by Alla Pugacheva, the shooting star of Soviet pop music at the time. Sergey Nikitin's wife, Tatyana, later described this duplication

[19] From an undated video, http://www.youtube.com/watch?v=X7y7FFX7ODo, last accessed on November 29, 2021.

Fig. 16.5   Sergey Nikitin performing his setting of Sonnet 90

as the result of calculated market research: "At the time of Alla Borisov-na's [i. e. Pugacheva's] first successes, serious managers did a 'screening' of the songs that had been a success with the public before her. And Alla Borisovna then took some lyrics that had already been sung by Sergey, for example Shakespeare's sonnet no. 90".[20] A somewhat friendlier inter-pretation sees Pugacheva's taking on of this sonnet as the artist's first momentous attempt to set a literary text herself, thereby bringing move-ment into the fixed system of categories that dominated Soviet "estrada" (pop) culture at the time, and to place greater value on the "lyrical" song type as opposed to the "social" one (MacFadyen 2001, 210; 228–231). In any case, probably no setting of a Shakespeare sonnet ever achieved wider circulation in Russia than Pugacheva's Sonnet 90. Both as part of her double album *Zerkalo duši* (*Mirror of the Soul*) and as part of the film *Ženščina, kotoraja poët* (*The Woman Who Sings*), the song reached an audience of millions in 1978. *The Woman Who Sings* turned out to

[20] Quoted from *'Citaty o Šekspire i Ne Tol'ko [Quotes Not Just about Shakespeare]'*, in *Russkij Šekspir. Informacionno-issledovatel'skaja baza dannych [Russian Shakespeare. Database for information and science]*, https://rus-shake.ru/original/citations/, last accessed November 29, 2021.

Fig. 16.6 Alla Pugacheva performing her setting of Sonnet 90 in the film *Ženščina, kotoraja poët* (*The Woman Who Sings*)

be one of the most successful Soviet films in terms of audience appeal; Pugacheva basically plays herself in it (Fig. 16.6).[21]

Even though Nikitin's setting of Sonnet 90 is indebted to the singer-songwriter idiom and Pugacheva's version to the conventions of mainstream pop, a formal comparison is worthwhile as it suggests that Pugacheva took over from Nikitin not only the text but also his specific strategy of setting the sonnet (see Table 16.7). On the highest formal level, both settings are of a two-part nature, a repeated binary sequence of thoughts (in Nikitin AB-AB, in Pugacheva AAB-AB). Before, between and after these pairs, both composers place an instrumental or textless *ritornello* with vocalises. Although the second idea, marked as "B", is introduced at different points in the respective settings—Nikitin uses it for the second quatrain and Pugacheva only for a partial repetition of this section—both recapitulate this musically contrasting material for the couplet. Of all the compositions considered for this study, this particular attempt to link the couplet musically to the overall dramaturgy is encountered only in these two settings (see Appendix, Table 16.9). Thus, the impression of a strophic structure is created in both. Nikitin's version, however, seems to consist of just two strophes while in Pugacheva's there appear to be three. By means of a partial repetition of the second quatrain,

---

[21] Source: http://www.youtube.com/watch?v=dJlsgeQuhWQ, last accessed on November 29, 2021.

she derives two additional lines of text, which she uses for the contrasting idea B.

Shakespeare's path into Soviet popular music can in part be explained by the success of Sonnet 90. In the 1970s, it made its way through both the "bard"/singer-songwriter scene and mainstream pop; in addition, there was at least one more setting of that poem by the Soviet hard rock band VIA *Samocvety*. However, the discovery of the sonnets by musicians from outside the academy was also favoured by the fact that in the Soviet Union (and later Russia), the boundaries between popular and high culture have never been as hard as in Western Europe.

Table 16.7 "Už esli ty razljubiš', – tak teper'" (Sonnet 90, "Then Hate Me When Thou Wilt; if Ever, Now"; Translation: Samuil Marshak) in the settings by Sergey Nikitin and Alla Pugacheva

	Nikitin		*Pugacheva*	
Poem sections	Textless sections of setting	Music	Textless sections of setting	Music
	Ritornello with vocalises		Ritornello with vocalises	
1Q		A		A (l. 4 repeated)
2Q		B		A' (without rep.)
[Repeat of lines 7–8]	–	–		B
	Ritornello with vocalises, shortened		Ritornello with vocalises, shortened	
3Q		A		A'
	Transition with vocalises		–	–
Cp		B' (only 2nd half of B)		B'
	Ritornello with vocalises, shortened		Ritornello with vocalises and text repetition, fadeout	

For Western composers of the "high culture" camp, it would have been hardly conceivable to set a Shakespeare sonnet in a popular style, so as to fit the idiom of a pop singer. Yet in the Soviet Union, exactly such a case is documented for the composer Tikhon Khrennikov, who in the West is probably better known for his official functions as secretary of the Soviet Composers' Union than for his music. Khrennikov's setting of Sonnet 40, in translation by Marshak, was created in 1983 for a TV production of his Shakespeare ballet *Lyubov'ju za lyubov'* (*Love for Love*), based on the comedy *Much Ado about Nothing*. The sonnet setting was written with Pugacheva in mind, who embodied the role of the singer in that production, and with obvious reference to her earlier, by then well-known, rendition of Sonnet 90.[22] Obviously, circumstances surrounding music in the Soviet Union were such that, for a composer of art music, the occasional foray into a popular idiom was anything but disreputable. Musicians of the Soviet pop scene, in contrast, had been taught by the accessibility of Marshak's translation not to be afraid of using Shakespeare's sonnets as lyrics. As a result, the poems incited a great variety of stylistic border crossings.

The *Eight Sonnets by William Shakespeare* by the Armenian composer Mikael Tariverdiev, who is hardly known in the West but popular in Russia, above all for his film music are an example of such a crossing of borders. In 1956, when still a student of composer Aram Khachaturian, Tariverdiev had already written a collection of three Shakespeare sonnets. These early attempts that possibly followed the model set by Kabalevsky (see Table 16.5) remained in manuscript form and could not be perused for the present study. In 1980, Tariverdiev turned again to Shakespeare and his sonnets, setting nine more of Marshak's translations in a chanson-like idiom. As the title page of the manuscript indicates, the songs relate to the narrative film *Adam ženitsja na Eve* (*Adam Gets Married to Eve*), in which they are sung by the composer himself.[23] Two years later, and

---

[22] Pugacheva's guest appearance in the TV ballet production is available on https://www.youtube.com/watch?v=hzxS5p72CRs, last accessed December 2, 2021.

[23] As well as the corresponding orchestral score, the piano version (Tariverdiev, n. d. [1980]) can be viewed at http://notes.tarakanov.net/composers/t.htm (last accessed December 1, 2021). Regardless of the title, the work actually contains nine sonnets because Tariverdiev combined the thematically related Sonnets 7 and 13 into a single,

independently of the movie, a TV production was dedicated to these songs, *Mikaèl Tariverdiev—Sonety Šekspira*. This is essentially a filmed concert with Tariverdiev as singer and pianist accompanied by a chamber orchestra, interspersed with shots of nature in springtime and softly drawn sequences of young women skipping through green groves in slow motion. Both productions are currently (2021) available on YouTube, as are excerpts of a documentary uploaded in 2010 of a Russian school lesson in which a teacher attempts to introduce an 8th or 9th grade class to Shakespeare's sonnets by way of Tariverdiev's settings.[24] In any case, these compositions appear to have reached a certain degree of popularity.

That Tariverdiev's sonnet settings have received so much attention in Russia may be due to their curious placement in the intermediate realm between popular and high culture—a circumstance that might make it correspondingly difficult for a comparable work to be taken seriously in the West. If, on the one hand, the gesture of the *chanson* guarantees an emotional accessibility that is indispensable for popular music cultures, on the other hand, the settings are characterized by a wealth of musical ideas and a formal complexity that meet high-cultural expectations. The performance situations in which one encounters the work are correspondingly diverse. The concert filmed in 1982 for the Russian TV production, for example, stages the composer as an exponent of academic musical culture (Fig. 16.7) in front of a large organ case in a philharmonic setting. Yet, in a performance by the guitar-and-vocal-trio *Meridian* at the Soviet pop festival *Pesnja 81* (*Song 81*) on New Year's Day 1982, Tariverdiev's setting of Sonnet 102 firmly belongs to the glittering world of the estrada (Fig. 16.8).

Regardless of its stylistic features, Tariverdiev's setting of Sonnet 102 provides an independent and original answer to the question of how the poetic form of the sonnet can be interpreted musically. Its structure A-B-A-C-D-A-E-A, superficially reminiscent of the form of a *rondo*, is owed

---

extensive setting. The remaining songs are based on Sonnets 76, 93, 102, 116, 117, 137 and 143.

[24] Movie *Adam Gets Married to Eve*: https://www.youtube.com/watch?v=DUs R4z1BVhk; TV concert: https://www.youtube.com/watch?v=5WE2bywtZxs; School lesson: http://www.youtube.com/watch?v=X-6RVcYQ07E and http://www.youtube.com/watch?v=kgDMoM7-qek&NR=1, all last accessed December 1, 2021.

Fig. 16.7 Mikael Tariverdiev (piano) performs his Shakespeare Sonnets on Russian television with the Chamber Ensemble of the Soviet Ministry of Culture Symphony Orchestra

Fig. 16.8 The Trio *Meridian* performs Tariverdiev's Sonnet 102 in the television show *Pesnja 81*

in part to the decision to divide the first two quatrains of the poem into two verses each and to recapitulate the beginning of the poem at the end (see Table 16.8). With this gambit, Tariverdiev not only creates smaller formal units than in the settings discussed earlier, but also the possibility of combining two formal strategies. In the wealth of musical ideas that are spread out in following the thoughts of the poem (A-B-...C-D-...E-...), he obeys the academic principle of through-composition; at the same time, however, the permanent recourse to the initial idea (A-...A-...A-...A) links the song to the refrain forms so common in popular music. Thus, even in its formal layout, the song reflects its peculiar place between the two realms of academia and pop.

In this respect, Tariverdiev's setting makes one aware of an added interest in the topic as a whole. Shakespeare's sonnets are a phenomenon that continues to thrive in numerous segments of Russian musical culture, a challenge in terms of content and form that musicians from the most diverse milieus and scenes feel called upon to take up. The results—views on the same material from various perspectives—are an eloquent testimony not only to the diversity of the manifold "worlds" but also to the unity of the "one world" of music, a unity that is usually easier to deny than to propagate. No one would deny that high and popular culture are separated by many, perhaps even decisive, features. The case of Shakespeare's sonnets in Russia, however, gives an idea of how much common ground continues to exist.

Table 16.8 Mikael Tariverdiev, "Ljublju, – no reže govorju ob ètom" (Sonnet 102, "My Love is Strengthened, Though More Weak in Seeming"; Translation: Samuil Marshak) from *Eight Sonnets by William Shakespeare*

Poem sections	Textless sections of setting	Music
1Q, lines 1–2		A
1Q, lines 3–4		B
2Q, lines 1–2		A
2Q, lines 3–4		C
3Q		D
Cp		A
	Textless contrasting section	E
[rep. 1Q, lines 1–2]		A

Appendix

Table 16.9   A formal comparison of the sonnet settings mentioned in the text

Text	Ippolitov-Ivanov 18	Kabalevsky 30	Nikitin 90	Pugacheva 90	Tariverdiev 102	Golovko 36	Novikov 130
i							B
1Q	A	A	A	A	A	A	A
					B		
i							B
2Q	B	B	B	A	A	B	A
					C		
*2Q			B			B	
3Q	A	C	A	A	D	A	B
*2Q						B	
*2Q						B	
i		A					B
Cp	C	D	B	B	A	C	A
i					E	C	
*Cp						C	
*1Q					A		

1Q–3Q: first to third quatrains; Cp: Couplet
*indicates the recapitulation of a section of text that has already been put to music earlier in the same setting
i: textless pre- or interlude (only shown here if the corresponding passage takes on the character of an independent formal section due to its extension or the significance of its material)
The marking of variants by the apostrophe (A versus A') has been omitted in this table

References

Texts

Cuker, A. 1985. *Mikaèl Tariverdiev*. Moscow: Sovetskij kompozitor.

Gasparov, Michail, and N. S. Avtonomova. 2001. "Sonety Šekspira – perevody Maršaka [Shakespeare's Sonnets – Marshak's Translations]". In Michail Gasparov, *O russkoj poèzii. Analizy, interpretacii, charakteristiki [On Russian Poetry. Analyzes, Interpretations, Character Traits]*, 389–409. Saint Petersburg: Azbuka.

Golovko, Valerij. n.d. [1998]. "Valerij Golovko ob al'bome *Ispoved'* (avtorskaja annotacija) [Valeri Golovko About his Album *Confession* (Commentary by the Composer)]". CD booklet notes, digitized on https://tunnel.ru/post-valerijj-golovko-kompozitor-poeht-s-otlichiem-zakonchil-ehstradnoe, last accessed on November 26, 2021.

Gooch, Bryan N. S., and David Thatcher. 1991. *A Shakespeare Music Catalogue*. Vol. 3. Oxford: Clarendon Press.

MacFadyen, David. 2001. *Red Stars: Personality and the Soviet Popular Song, 1955-1991*. Montreal: McGill-Queen's University Press.

Maršak, Samuil. 1949. *Sonety Šekspira v perevodach S. Maršaka [Shakespeare's Sonnets in S. Marshak's Translations]*. Moscow: Sovetskij pisatel'.

Redepenning, Dorothea. 2016. "Boris Pasternak, Dmitrij Schostakowitsch und William Shakespeares Sonett Nr. 66". In *Das Sonett und die Musik: Poetiken, Konjunkturen, Transformationen, Reflexionen*. Ed. Sara Springfeld, Norbert Greiner, and Silke Leopold, 275–93. Heidelberg: Universitätsverlag Winter.

Šnitke, B. 1966. "A. Glazunov. Dva Soneta Šekspira [A. Glasunov. Two Shakespeare Sonnets]". In *Russkaja muzyka na rubeže XX veka. Stat'i, soobščenia, publikacii [Russian Music on the Threshold of the 20th Century. Articles, Communications, Editions]*. Ed. M. K. Michajlov and E. M. Orlova, 283–95. Moscow: Muzyka.

Sokolov, N[ikolaj] N[ikolaevič], ed. 1986. *M. M. Ippolitov-Ivanov. Pis'ma, Stat'i, Vospominanija [Letters, Essays, Reminiscences]*. Moscow: Sovetskij kompozitor.

Scores

Belza, Igor'. 1945. *Semdesjat tretij sonet Šekspira dlja golosa i fortepiano [Shakespeare's Sonnet No. 73 for Voice and Piano] Op. 34 Nr. 2*. Moscow: Muzfond.

Cui, César. n.d. [1892]. *Vier Sonette von A. Mickiewicz für eine Singstimme mit Begleitung des Pianoforte Op. 48*. Berlin: Simrock.

Frid, Gr[igorij]. 1964. *Sonety Šekspira/Sonnets by Shakespeare Op. 34 dlja baritona v soprovoždenii fortepiano/for Baritone with Piano Accompaniment.* Moscow: Muzyka.

Ippolitov-Ivanov, M[ichail]. n.d. [1907]. *Sonety V. Šekspira soč. 45.* Moscow: Jurgenson.

Kabalevskij, D[mitrij]. 1969. *Desjat' sonetov Šekspira v perevodach S. Maršaka soč. 52 dlja basa v soprovoždenii fortepiano, Tret'e izdanie [Ten Shakespeare Sonnets in the Translation by S. Marshak Op. 52 for Bass with Piano Accompaniment, Third Edition].* Moscow: Muzyka [first edition 1955].

Pricker, D[avid]. 1968. *Izbrannye romansy i pesni. Tetrad' 1 [Selected Romances and Songs. Book 1].* Leningrad: Muzyka.

———. 1969. *Izbrannye romansy i pesni. Tetrad' 2 [Selected Romances and Songs. Book 2].* Leningrad: Muzyka.

Šostakovič, Dmitrij. 2012. "Šest' romancov na slova U. Raleja, R. Bёrnsa i U. Šekspira dlja basa i fortepiano soč. 62/Six Romances on Verses by W. Raleigh, R. Burns and W. Shakespeare for Bass Soloist and Piano Op. 62" (1942). In *Kamernye vokal'nye sočinenija i pesni/Chamber Compositions for Voice and Song.* Ed. Manašir Jakubov. Novoe sobranie sočinenij/New Collected Works 95. Moscow: DSCH.

Tariverdiev, M[ikaėl]. n.d. [1980]. *Vosem' sonetov V. Šekspira. Iz muzyki k kinofil'mu 'Adam i Eva'. Klavir [Eight Sonnets by William Shakespeare. From the Music for the Film 'Adam and Eve'. Vocal Score].* Ms.

Trailin, S[ergej] A[leksandrovič]. 1916. "Sonet Šekspira XXX". *Russkaja muzykal'naja gazeta,* no. 15–16 (April): 365–68.

Weinberg, Mieczysław. 2017. *Six Shakespeare Sonnets, Op. 33. Song Cycle for Bass and Piano.* Hamburg: Peermusic.

CHAPTER 17

"Moody Food of Us that Trade in Love": Re-Mediations of Shakespeare's *Sonnets* in Popular Music

Mike Ingham

The word "sonnet", being derived from the Italian *sonetto* (literally "little song"), suggests a strong affinity with acoustic reproduction and reception, as opposed to the contemplation of the printed word alone. In the pirated collection of sonnets entitled *The Passionate Pilgrim*, published by William Jaggard in 1599, the eighth sonnet begins: "If music and sweet poetry agree/ As they must needs, the sister and the brother ...". The sonnet writer—almost certainly Richard Barnfield, and not Shakespeare, as Jaggard's title implied—invoked the popular music of Dowland and the popular poetry of Spenser to exemplify what he saw as the

---

"Give me some music; music, moody food/ Of us that trade in love."
Shakespeare, *Antony and Cleopatra*, Act 2, scene 5, 1–2.

M. Ingham (✉)
Chinese University, Ma Liu Shui, Hong Kong
e-mail: mikeingham@gmail.com

© The Author(s), under exclusive license to Springer Nature Switzerland AG 2023
J. Kingsley-Smith and W. R. Rampone Jr. (eds.), *Shakespeare's Global Sonnets*, Global Shakespeares, https://doi.org/10.1007/978-3-031-09472-9_17

close correspondence and concord between the "sibling" arts. Dowland is also commonly thought to have set some of Spenser's poetry, and to have been influenced by it in some of his extremely popular compositions. We can trace the reciprocity between poetic lyrics and popular songs, as Dowland's undoubtedly were in the early modern era, while we can equally discern the relationship between popular culture and commerce, then, as now. Nonetheless, despite what Jane Kingsley-Smith has aptly referred to as Shakespeare's Sonnets' "stimulus to invention" (Kingsley-Smith 2019: 1), there have been relatively few significant art-song settings.[1] As regards other musical genres, whereas the jazz idiom developed a small, but significant, tradition for sonnet adaptation—as exemplified by Duke Ellington's 1957 instrumental suite, "Such Sweet Thunder" and the jazz song settings of Johnny Dankworth and Cleo Laine, and more recently those of Belgian jazz performer, Carroll Vanwelden—pop song composers have tended to avoid the *Sonnets* until relatively recently.

Shakespeare's *Sonnets* are often appreciated for the musicality of their sound when they are euphoniously recited by actors such as Patrick Stewart, John Gielgud and Helena Bonham Carter, to name but a few. Music regularly intersects with dramatic verse in Shakespeare's work and is featured in the plays more concretely through the inclusion of songs and/or musicians diegetically, as a theatrical component in the play's plot, or elsewhere by analogy, as in Sonnets 8, 128 and 129 where music is a central metaphor, and represents a joyful or melancholy mood, or has sexual connotations of touch and intimate play. The sonnets' regular rhythmic pattern and four-line quatrains with alternating rhymes, together with their use of assonance, alliteration, consonance and internal rhymes, makes them conducive to musical setting. That said, the conventional closing couplet and 14-line form are harder to assimilate into a standard 4/4 song-verse structure. Conversely, the *volta*, or turn, at the end of the eighth line provides the songwriter with an opportunity to introduce a bridge-type section for the sake of variation. While there is an intrinsic musicality in poetic terms, the sonnets lack the verbally repetitive features of song lyrics and their default iambic pentameter, rather than tetrameter, also poses a challenge to the adapter in relation to the typical four-beat, four-bar construct common to popular song. The stress-timed

---

[1] Those by Hubert Parry, Benjamin Britten, Igor Stravinsky and Einojuhani Rautavaara are the most notable, but only Parry and Rautavaara set more than a single sonnet.

nature of the English language, in both spoken voice recitation and sung delivery, enhances natural, meaning-based stress and phrasing, although note duration and pitch features in song rely on musical, rather than poetic speech conventions. Thus, translating a sonnet to song form represents a formidable, though not insuperable, task. A further consideration is an extent to which the song-composer impersonates the voice of the source text—i.e. the sonnet author talking to himself (as in Sonnet 146) or to a single addressee, whether "the fair youth" or "the dark lady"— or opts to appropriate it and thus personalize the target text, at least in his/her own head.

The simple question that arises when considering the translation and remediation of the sonnet, and by extension of poetry in general, to a popular music form, is this: is it viable both commercially and artistically? As Roy Shuker has pointed out in his section on Lyric Analysis in *Popular Music, The Key Concepts*, there is a perceived dichotomy between so-called "art rock" lyrics—"those akin to romantic poetry with lots of covert and obscure allusions" (Shuker 2005: 157)—and mainstream commercial rock/pop lyrics which are seen by some commentators and music listeners as "banal" and "worthless", despite the fact that the latter "do in some sense matter to their listeners" (ibid., 157). The corollary of this critical class and taste issue, as Shuker notes, is clarified by popular music writer Simon Frith's pertinent question: "how do words and voices work differently for different types of pop and audience?" (ibid., 157) This sociological approach often presupposes a ready-made audience according to age group, socio-economic class, gender, etc., for particular types of popular music. While it is tempting for critics to pigeonhole Shakespeare settings in popular music stylings as belonging to a loose category of adult contemporary rock/pop or progressive folk, idiosyncratic song interpreters who defy generic boundaries are capable of bridging what they regard as an artificial and preconceived divide. In the case of Shakespearean sonnet settings, as we shall explore here, much depends on the singer-songwriter's ability to create a song whose whole transcends the sum of those parts discussed in the previous paragraph. This definition also offers us a paradigm of the classic popular song—as well as the artist—that cuts across the typically rigid and tightly policed borderline between high culture and popular culture. Paul McCartney has expressed—Hamlet-like, in a nutshell—the meaning of genuinely popular songwriting: "When you think about it, when you're writing a song, you're always trying to write something that you love and the people will love" (see Meredith 2015).

On his 1985 solo album "The Dream of the Blue Turtles", the British singer, Sting, formerly of the rock band, *The Police*, borrowed phrases from the opening quatrain of Sonnet 35, "No more be grieved at that which thou hast done", some of which were paraphrased and absorbed into a verse of the song "Consider Me Gone". He duly acknowledged the source text in the sleeve notes. On his next album, he borrowed the second half of the opening line of Sonnet 130, "My mistress' eyes are nothing like the sun", for his song "Sister Moon", as well as for his album title. Sting's later interpretations of Dowland songs with lutenist Edin Karamazov on the 2006 album "Songs From the Labyrinth" may have raised expectations that he would compose a setting of the Shakespeare sonnets he evidently admired. However, no modern pop settings in English of an entire sonnet were commercially recorded by any artist until the millennium. Perhaps there was a residual perception among many popular singer-songwriters that they were unsuitable as song lyrics, or even sacrosanct as potential source texts. "Shakespeare's cultural authority" (Lanier 2002: 53), to use Douglas Lanier's phrase, proved both attractive and prohibitive to pop composers: they liked to allude to characters from his plays, or deliberately misquote him[2], but setting his words offered a greater challenge.

This was to change with the advent of the new century and especially the Shakespeare quatercentenary year of 2016. Suddenly, the juxtaposition of Shakespeare and pop culture became a little more fashionable,[3] and the sonnets found themselves translated into hip-hop rhythms and styles, but typically only in the context of educational workshops. However, a few intrepid singer-songwriters took on the challenge of releasing their sonnet-based songs commercially. Among the small number of popular musical recordings of settings, anticipating or celebrating the quatercentenary, those by eclectic, American-Canadian artist,

[2] As Morrissey, of British indie band The Smiths, did in the 1986 song "Cemetery Gates", deliberately misquoting a line from *Richard III* for effect related to the song's meaning.

[3] So-called "pop sonnets", pop song lyrics skillfully reworded as sonnets, posted in 2014 by Erik Didriksen, are adaptations of pop songs in Shakespearean sonnet form. While they are certainly amusing and ingenious parodies of the Shakespearean sonnet, they should not be confused with the converse practice of literary adaptations into the popular song genre. See https://www.folger.edu/shakespeare-unlimited/pop-sonnets/.

Rufus Wainwright (*All Days Are Nights: Songs for Lulu*, 2010) and veteran Australian singer-songwriter Paul Kelly (*Seven Sonnets and a Song*, 2016) created the most harmonious "concord of well-tunèd sounds" of music and poetry.

My essay focuses on the independent compositions of Wainwright and Kelly, respectively, and argues that, despite the longstanding perception of some critics (see, for example, Wilson 1922: 158), Shakespeare's Sonnets and contemporary popular songs should not be wedded, certain versions reflect the propitious agreement of "music and sweet poetry". It explores the intertextual and intermedial relations between the respective singer-songwriters' settings and their hypotexts, as well as focusing on the intrinsic qualities that lend themselves to musical adaptation found in the sources. Thematic, harmonic and affective elements of the musical setting, while obviously deriving inspiration from the composer's original imagination, need also to reflect the sonnet's poetic structure and emotional trajectory, even if the setting emphasizes other nuances of meaning. Two case-study settings by Wainwright and Kelly, respectively (Sonnets 20 and 29 by Wainwright and Sonnets 18 and 138 by Kelly) will be analysed for their overall interpretation and musical elements—sonority, tonality, melody, tempo, timbre—as well as their felicitous treatment of the versification, rhythm, stress patterns, phrasing, prosodic features and tropes of the source texts. It is important to contextualize this study within a growing, yet often under-acknowledged, field of inter-semiotic translations/adaptations of literary texts that have appeared in Anglophone popular music from the 1960s onwards, and not simply as homage to Shakespeare. As Mark Fortier has argued: "Expressing a text in a different semiotic system (images or music, for instance) or rewording a text in the same language can also be thought of as a form of translation ..." (Fortier 2016: 1047).

Earlier, in 2002, there had been several recordings and live performances of sonnet settings in popular style as part of Joy Gelardi's and Michael Kamen's *When Love Speaks* project, including separate performances of the much-loved Sonnet 18 by Bryan Ferry (Roxy Music) and David Gilmour (Pink Floyd), of Sonnet 29 by Wainwright, of Sonnet 35 by folk-blues singer, Keb' Mo', and Sonnet 8 by South African vocal group, Ladysmith Black Mambazo. Wainwright's contribution to this project was the only one not composed by Kamen himself, although the individual performers shaped the distinctive sonorities of their respective performances to a considerable extent. A number of reviewers and scholars commented favourably on Kamen's live performance and CD project, including Julie Sanders in her 2007 book *Shakespeare and Music: Afterlives and Borrowings* and Adam Hansen in his 2010 book *Shakespeare and Popular Music*. By way of an example of how a sonnet adaptation remediates and augments Shakespeare's text, Hansen discusses the R'n'B version of Sonnet 35 by American Blues artist Keb' Mo' "whose processed vocal textures both sustain and supplant Shakespeare's words" (Hansen 2010: 43) a definition that is useful in considering the adaptation process. While Ferry's version of Sonnet 18, "Shall I Compare Thee", was included on the *When Love Speaks* album, Gilmour's vocal interpretation, accompanied by Kamen on piano, is arguably a more moving and mellifluous rendition. His judicious phrasing, articulation and pitching of a composition with a challenging vocal range emphasizes the interplay between the home major key and passing minor chords and the sonnet's corresponding contrasts of mood. The octave leap between "I" and "compare" and "winds" and "do" in the odd lines of the opening quatrain, subsequently repeated in lines 7 and 11, also helps endow the setting with a distinctive melodic contour. Academic, Stephen Buhler, who has produced his own sonnet adaptations in popular song style for teaching purposes, has described the through-sung composition structure as hymn-like:

> [T]he first quatrain serves as a verse, but the second quatrain serves as a responsorial, before the third quatrain introduces a bridge. The couplet ("So long as men can breathe") repeats elements from the bridge section, with a lengthy rest after the clause, "So long lives this…" (Buhler 2016: 234)

Gavin Bryars' mixed-mode sonnet project in 2009, *Nothing Like the Sun*, featured American folk and rock vocalist Natalie Merchant's exquisite minor-key version of Sonnet 73, "That time of year thou may'st in me behold"; her setting was written for it, and is also included on her 2017 anthology album *Rarities*. Merchant's vocal interpretation of the sonnet is predominately pensive and introspective, conveying the sonnet's underlying themes of transience and evanescence to a moody strings, acoustic guitar and piano accompaniment, and the setting showcases her crystalline voice in the higher vocal range as well as her more melancholy timbre in the lower range. In 2012, another ambitious crossover project was released as a commercial recording, namely the album, *Shakespeare*

Sonnets, consisting of settings by Robert Hollingsworth, in collaboration with his traditional instrument ensemble, I Fagiolini. The album was intended to represent an intersection between the popular music sound of Shakespeare's time and modern interpretations and recording techniques, but only Sonnet 18, "Shall I Compare Thee to a Summer's Day", in a limpid vocal rendition by Irish folk singer, Cara Dillon, accompanied by husband and fellow folk artist, Sam Lakeman, worked as a song that transcended the rather formulaic early modern pastiche. This latter album illustrated many of the pitfalls of attempting to merge Shakespearean language and musical instruments with a contemporary popular song style, without the interpretive mediation of a distinctive popular vocalist. Only Dillon's voice stood out from the blandness and merely competent craftsmanship, in place of inspiration, that permeated most of the recording. By contrast, although only a minority of the sonnets covered in Kamen's project were musical settings, they were all interpreted in a vocal style that was familiar to fans of performers like Keb' Mo', Ladysmith Black Mambazo and Annie Lennox (performing Marlowe's "Come Live With Me and Be My Love" from *The Passionate Pilgrim*).

Kamen's star-studded collective of sonnet reciters and musical interpreters on the album may well have inspired Wainwright's three subsequent sonnet settings on the 2010 album, *All Days are Nights: Songs for Lulu*, as well as his more ambitious fusion of classical and pop arrangements on *"Take All My Loves": 9 Shakespeare Sonnets* (2016). His sonnet versions are better known than Kelly's, which do not appear to have been prompted by *When Love Speaks*—unsurprising given the fact that the Australian singer was not involved. Kelly and Wainwright worked independently, unaware of each other's forthcoming Shakespeare sonnet project, but subsequently linked up long-distance to express mutual appreciation of their respective albums (see Zuel 2016). While Kelly is less fêted than Wainwright outside his native country, both sets of transpositions, employing different genres, styles and musical arrangements, engage in a creative and satisfying dialogue with the source poems. The original lyrics of both singer-songwriters tend towards the confessional, a song mode that coheres neatly with the confessional Shakespearean sonnet, and both employ appropriately contrastive, tonal harmony, more often than modal. Both performers are respected and accomplished songsmiths, and their respective settings break new ground, and reflect the new century's rapport between Shakespeare and popular music culture. In many respects, they represent an evolutionary process following on from earlier fusions of the Shakespeare sonnet and popular musical forms, including the Kamen project and Wainwright's collaboration with Robert Wilson for a rather grandiose 2009 Berliner Ensemble stage production based on Shakespeare's Sonnets.

I propose that the selected sonnet settings, together with another written especially by Kamen for his 2002 project, namely his setting of Sonnet 18, not only occupy a liminal position between high culture and popular culture, but exemplify best practices in the art of popular song transposition. Moreover, I argue that they can be considered effective, free-standing song compositions, independent of the projects from which they originated. In this respect, they are analogous to a hit song such as The Who's "Pinball Wizard", which succeeded as a pop song beyond the context of the 1969 rock opera, *Tommy*, in which it first featured. Wainwright's *Take All My Loves* project reprised two pop music settings from *All Days are Nights*, and added a fresh version of Wainwright's setting of Sonnet 29, sensitively interpreted by vocalist Florence Welch of the indie band Florence and the Machine. Apart from these, the project resembled a Kamen-style homage of sonnet recitations and avant-garde classical settings. Kelly's was also a concept album comprising mainly Shakespeare sonnet settings, but including his setting of a Sidney sonnet and Shakespearean song from *Twelfth Night*. As is the case with Wainwright's remediations, only a few work as melodically, harmonically and rhythmically strong songs, independent of the concept album context in which they feature. I suggest this "top tracks" phenomenon parallels the standard practice of popular music artists who release the catchiest songs from a new album as chart singles.

TWO RUFUS WAINWRIGHT SETTINGS

Listening to Wainwright's Shakespeare settings, we detect a sense of reciprocity between the contemporary songwriter's taste and aesthetics and those of his illustrious lyricist. The homoerotic implication of these particular sonnets and the songwriter's own homosexual orientation constitute only the most obvious parallel, but others are more related to form and style. The wistful, sometimes self-ironizing tone of both source text and song adaptation suggests Wainwright's empathy with Shakespeare's motifs and expressive deployment of the sonnet as vehicle. Wainwright's piano and vocal rendition of Sonnet 29 ("When, in disgrace with fortune and men's eyes") for Kamen's project proved "a marriage of true minds", inaugurating what has proved an enduring relationship between Shakespeare's Sonnets and Wainwright's songwriting and performance practices. Sanders praises this, his first adaptation effort, for its "beautiful congruence between poem and performance style" (Sanders 2007: 186). The version on the 2016 album performed by Florence Welch is more typical of standard pop music accompaniment and production; Welch's accomplished rendition showcases her wide vocal range supported by Wainwright's backing vocals and is fascinating in its transformation of the gender implications of the latter's original. The redemption of life's anxieties and inevitable self-doubt is presumed to be represented by a male lover in the source sonnet and Wainwright's setting, but with Welch's version the gender implications are more opaque and ambivalent.

Wainwright's modified, strophic setting of Sonnet 29 is based on a simple diatonic chord progression, but features a wide-ranging melody and a subtle counter-melody in the accompanying cello part. As with many pop ballads, the opening instrumental bars prefigure the mood and impulses of the song, especially in the descending *glissando* grace-note figure played on the banjo, subtly contrasting with the rising and falling melodic contours of the opening lines: "When in disgrace with fortune and men's eyes/I all alone beweep my outcast state"; the musical contour here echoes the falling and subsequent lifting of the spirits that is the poem's central theme. The conjunct (step) motion in the configuration of the second and third quatrains conveys the analogy of the irrepressible song of the "lark at heaven's gate" perfectly, while the slow coda with its elongated notes emphasizes the elation of the closing couplet. Unlike many contrastive final couplets in Shakespeare's Sonnets that represent a rebuttal, or "sting in the tail", this one gloriously caps the poem's mood and meaning, which Wainwright's exultant coda fittingly reflects. The initially melancholic melody line, with its ascending and descending figures in the first two quatrains, parallels the volatility of the persona's shifting emotions; then the voice rises inexorably in the third quatrain to soar an octave above on the same melodic notation as the opening quatrain, evoking the mind and spirit, "like to the lark at break of day arising", to sing "hymns at heaven's gate". The clarity of Wainwright's cracked but mellow voice, and the felicitous "word-painting" of the melodic and harmonic components, succeed in conveying the sonnet's emotional and mental trajectory on both emotional and intellectual planes. His distinctively extended coda on the closing couplet, in which note values are drawn out and vowel sounds thereby sustained, creates a free-floating effect. Indeed, the tempo and meaning of the song seem somehow suspended in space, as though mind has truly risen above matter, before the speaker's triumph over self-doubt in the final line, "I scorn to change my state with kings".

Florence Welch's measured and confident rendition fourteen years later on the *Take All My Loves* album reconfigures the song with a tight combination of drums, bass, acoustic guitar, keyboard and backing vocals (by Wainwright and Ben de Vries) and showcases the singer's mellifluent and soaring mezzo-soprano voice. Indeed, the critical consensus was that Welch's performance on "When in Disgrace with Fortune and Men's Eyes" represented one of the clear highlights of Wainwright's uneven pop-classical fusion work. The cover version showcases her wide vocal range and control and her, by turns, airy and powerful voice, starting in the lower register and rising step-like to the purity of her upper-register "head voice"; it also features her vibrato technique to great effect, as Wainwright's version did likewise, both in the line cadences and in the sustained notes of the mainly monosyllabic "For thy sweet love remembered such wealth brings / That then I scorn to change my state with kings". The musical arrangement of the final quatrain and couplet, with added synthesizer and prominent keyboards, together with the male backing vocals, thickens the texture of the song, but such is Welch's exquisite poise and vocal timbre her voice soars lark-like above the mix. Another characteristic of this version is the accentuation of the second and third beats of the introduction and first quatrain, which imparts a curious waltz feel that lightens and colours the song's steady backbeat rhythm.

Wainwright's simple strophic setting of Sonnet 20, "A woman's face", also ranks with the best melodic interpretations of the sonnet form as a classic contemporary love song. While some poem settings for the popular song genre, including some of Wainwright's on *Take All My Loves*, are arguably too complex, and thus encroach on the semantic content of the text by over-emphasizing its affective properties or obscuring its theme and figures of speech, in his setting for *All Days are Nights* the singer-songwriter keeps the musical arrangement simple. Against a slow-tempo piano backing of block chords, in which the major home key is nuanced by use of suspension and the relative minor, he weaves a sublime melody that allows the sonnet's perfect compound of thought and emotion to speak for itself; the melodic line employs repetition, but also features a soaring lift in the third line of each strophe, as well as the subtly effective, melismatic delivery on the word "amazeth" immediately preceding the *volta*. Overall, Wainwright's sultry vocal timbre, judicious accentuation and elegant *legato* phrasing highlight the prosody and phrasal contours of the poem with a sequence of harmonic shifts and resolutions that match the dichotomous master/mistress conceit of the text to perfection. The closing couplet features a reprise of the melody, but no corresponding lift, as it aptly concludes on a mood of ambivalence and mystery, seemingly half-way through the verse.

In the context of this performance, the "congruence" to which Sanders alludes arises from the vocalist's skillful fusion of prosodic features, vocal phrasing and melodic contour with the text's semantic units of thought, both at the individual line and quatrain levels. Wainwright's structural and melodic sensibility in Sonnet 20 is impeccable, and his *sostenuto* delivery works well in exploiting Shakespeare's strategy of employing repeated feminine line endings to play up the theme of the sonnet; his setting highlights and extends the final weak syllable of the line to convey a melancholic "dying fall" in the cadences of each musical and vocal phrase. As with Sonnet 29, the musical arrangement of the same sonnet differs considerably on Wainwright's more grandiose 2016 concept album, in contrast to the stripped-back version on *All Days are Nights*. Nonetheless, the vocal line is similarly rich and clearly enunciated, even if the song's introduction and finale are more lushly produced, as can be discerned from the over-elaborate string and synthesizer arrangement. On a more positive note, the modified 2016 version features a descending chord pattern in the introduction that is recapitulated, with the bass echoing the descent, thereby enhancing the sonnet's intimate musicality. Ultimately, though, it was the unembellished original solo version that particularly appealed to Wainwright and Shakespeare aficionados alike.

Two Paul Kelly Settings

The veteran Australian troubadour set six Shakespeare Sonnets, including Sonnets 44 and 45 as a diptych, as well as the song "O Mistress Mine", on his 2016 Shakespeare album, but two of his sonnet settings stand out and were included on subsequent albums for that reason. Kelly's version of Sonnet 138 is also featured on his 2019 *Live at Sidney Opera House* album, while his Sonnet 18 setting is included in the *Songs From the South, Greatest Hits* collection, released the same year. The latter is an up-tempo modified strophic composition, starting with Kelly singing the opening strophe *a capella* against warm but subdued minor-to-major harmony; in the second and third quatrains the melodic figure begins a fifth higher, and foregrounds the major key, providing a suitably bright contrast that connotes the "eye of heaven". Kelly adds subtly scored strings into the mix at this point following a simple, finger-picked accompaniment in the second strophe. The song's characteristic interplay between major and minor harmony not only underscores the light and shade that is central to the poem's meaning, but also informs its binary imagery. Equally felic- itous, the notation of Kelly's setting is in tune with the poem's emotional trajectory, as exemplified by the descending figure on line 8 following the word "declines" and preceding the bright, assertive major key of "But thy eternal summer" at the turn. After a short instrumental break, featuring Alice Keath on banjo backed by guitar and string section, Kelly reprises the text in an identical melodic and harmonic fashion. Here the setting adds female backing vocals and retains the restrained sound of strings; it ends effectively with a *rallentando* that serves to bring its infectious, up-tempo rhythm to a halt in the final cadence.

As the imaginative animated music video for the official release of the song suggests, Kelly's "Sonnet 18" excels, like Wainwright's Sonnets 20 and 29, in the idiom of sophisticated pop with a fairly broad appeal. Kelly, who is sometimes unfairly portrayed as Australia's equivalent to Bob Dylan, employs a rather nasal delivery, with a twang reminiscent of more earthy Australian and American popular singers. At the same time, his delivery and timing are flawless, as illustrated in performance by his smooth interpretation of the feminine rhyming pair "ow'st" and "grow'st" in Shakespeare's third quatrain. Kamen's version of the same sonnet, with its ethereal melody, ably interpreted by the breathy croon of Brian Ferry and the serene vocal chords of David Gilmour—both inter- pretations classy and assured—may be considered among the very best of popular music settings, but Kelly's has a folksy wisdom and down-to- earth quality that does full justice to the poem's thematic emphasis on mutability and permanence. Once the listener accepts the song's distri- bution of words into a four-beat musical phrase that is at odds with the more even phrasing of the typical sonnet recitation, it is an inter- pretation that works extremely well, one that maximizes the sometimes overlooked device of the caesura to promote lyrical cohesion. Listening without prejudice or preconception, this setting turns out to be as effec- tive and pleasurable as the more smooth-flowing Kamen setting, despite its major stylistic differences.

Whereas Sonnet 18 is adapted into a folk-rock style that is familiar to fans from Kelly's substantial back catalogue, his bluesy R'n'B setting of Dark Lady Sonnet 138, "When my love swears that she is made of truth", is more unpredictable as a choice, but equally effective as a popular song. In his setting of "When I compare thee", Kelly takes a degree of poetic licence with the natural prosody and iambic rhythm by placing strong beats on the normally unstressed words "I" and "do" in lines 1 and 3 in order to fit his mellifluous melody. However, in Sonnet 138 his jazzy accentuation, sometimes across the beat and sometimes slightly behind it, strongly supports the syncopated delivery, and works to the advantage of an interpretation that has something in common with earlier R'n'B legends, such as Ray Charles and Dr John (Mac Rebennack). Here, Kelly takes greater licence to spectacular effect. His coup in this setting is to adapt the sonnet's closing couplet, with its paronomasia of sexual congress and mutual deception, into an extremely catchy refrain, which is sung twice in the middle of the song before the melodic lift of the third strophe, and repeated four times as an outro; he thus transforms Shakespeare's penultimate line: "Therefore I lie with her, and she with me" into the lyrically felicitous, "Yes, I lie with her, and she lies with me", heavily accentuating the encoded ambiguity of "lie" and employing the caesura to powerful effect.

The song accompaniment of slinky piano, acoustic bass and light jazzy drumming on the original recorded version underscores all of the dark irony and paradox of the sonnet text, while downplaying its misogynistic associations, thanks to Kelly's wry delivery. In a subsequently released YouTube version of the song Kelly is accompanied only by pianist Paul Grabowsky, giving equal prominence to the latter's jazzy piano intro-duction and continuity; their collaboration showcases the remarkable synergy between the two performers, and demonstrates how effectively the regular, light ictic stress of the sonnet metre can be translated into the heavier, if less frequent, stresses in the stretched and syncopated vocal phrasing of the R'n'B groove. The result is one of the boldest and most radical transpositions of a Shakespeare sonnet in terms of genre, far from the winsome love-song idiom of Wainwright, Ferry and Gilmour. It is akin in some respects to Keb' Mo's version of Sonnet 35 or Ladysmith Black Mambazo's Sonnet 8, but Kelly's adaptation conveys the nuances and subtext of the original poem more luminously than either of the above, despite their undoubted song qualities.

CONCLUSION

Aesthetic and artistic reciprocity is often underestimated as a factor in motivating sonnet setting and performance when presumed Shakespeare "tributes" are considered in the popular press, even if adaptation scholars are keenly aware of its significance. I have, therefore, intentionally focused more closely on the target product, as opposed to the source, in this necessarily limited analysis. My study suggests that, despite the acoustic evidence that most popular song settings of Shakespeare's verse represent no more than thoughtfully crafted remediations, a few, including the two each by Wainwright and Kelly discussed above, are viable as stand-alone popular songs in their own right, unmitigated by homage to the Bard.

Astutely paraphrasing the closing phrase of Sonnet 18, "and this gives life to thee", and translating it as "this *performance* gives life to what these words express", Adam Hansen indicates the importance of reciprocity between translations, adaptations and variations and their sonnet sources (Hansen, 2010: 34). Similarly, Kingsley-Smith highlights the importance of renewal and "re-voicing": "[f]or the Sonnets to continue finding readers in the twenty-first century, they need to be dispersed, fragmented and re-voiced" (Kingsley-Smith 2019: 250). In other words, the future reception of the sonnets depends to a great extent on the kind of re-imagining for a popular music audience that the more melodic and characterful transpositions of Wainwright and Kelly epitomize. Michael Kamen's melodious setting of Sonnet 18, particularly in David Gilmour's interpretation, likewise stands out from other more workmanlike compositions. Much depends, naturally, on the thorny question of defining a popular music audience, since pop music caters for a very diverse range of subjective tastes, each with its own distinct channel for access to preferred genres and categories of music.

That said, the likelihood of a sonnet being "re-voiced" in a mainstream pop style is probably remote, and for many pop music aficionados the compositions of singer-songwriters like Wainwright and Kelly can sound alienating or pretentious because they are unfamiliar. The most likely genre in which new approaches to sonnet setting can be explored may, therefore, be in hip-hop, since rap vocal styles are closer to spoken-word delivery than most other genres. This would be a logical development of the above-mentioned workshopping experimentation with hip-hop sonnets, but it remains to be seen whether hip-hop artists can build on the pioneering work of the Hip Hop Shakespeare Company, and begin to set complete sonnet texts. Without the stimulus of another Shakespeare centenary or anniversary, such a project might seem commercially unsound, even if considered artistically viable. In any case, Kamen's project and Wainwright's and Kelly's respective settings have pointed the way, and demonstrated the potential for reciprocity between the sonnets and popular music, as those of Dankworth and Laine did in an earlier period. It is likely they will, in their turn, be recycled and re-heard in the context of popular culture as love songs, for which a certain W.S. happens to be the lyricist. In this respect he joins the impressive company of Ira Gershwin, Jerry Leiber, Hal David, Gerry Goffin, Eddie Holland, Bernie Taupin and many other latter-day pure wordsmiths whose lyrics were wont to "trade in love".

References: Printed

Buhler, Stephen. 2016. 'Palpable Hits: Popular Music Forms and Teaching Early Modern Poetry.' Faculty Publications, Department of English, University of Nebraska, Lincoln, pp. 228–241. https://digitalcommons.unl.edu/cgi/viewcontent.cgi?article=1171&context=englishfacpubs

Fortier, Mark. 2016. 'Translation, Adaptation, "Tradaptation".' In K. Rowe, T. Hoenselaars, A. Kusunoki, A. Murphy, & A. Da Cunha Resende (Authors) & B. Smith (Ed.), *The Cambridge Guide to the Worlds of Shakespeare* (pp. 1046–1050). Cambridge: Cambridge University Press. https://doi.org/10.1017/9781316137

Hansen, Adam. 2010. *Shakespeare and Popular Music*. London and New York: Continuum Books.

Kingsley-Smith, Jane. 2019. *The Afterlife of Shakespeare's Sonnets*. Cambridge: Cambridge University Press. 978-1-009-06006-6

Lanier, Douglas, 2002. *Shakespeare and Modern Popular Culture*. Oxford and New York: Oxford University Press.

Sanders, Julie. 2007. *Shakespeare and Music: Afterlives and Borrowings*. Cambridge: Polity Press.

Shuker, Roy. 2005. *Popular Music, The Key Concepts*. Oxford: Routledge. 2nd edition.

Wilson, Christopher. *Shakespeare and Music*. 1922. Re-issued as an e-book 30 March 2011b. http://www.gutenberg.org/ebooks/35721

References: Online

Meredith, Kyle. Paul McCartney interview with *Paste Magazine*, 9 January 2015. https://www.pastemagazine.com/music/paul-mccartney/paul-mccartney-on-songwriting-the-beatles-and-revi/

Zuel, Bernard. "Paul Kelly, Rufus Wainwright and William Shakespeare, together at last", *Sydney Morning Herald*, 19 April 2016. https://www.smh.com.au/entertainment/music/paul-kelly-rufus-wainwright-and-william-shakespeare-together-at-last-20160413-go5cxq.html

References: Recordings

Gilmour, David. 2002. "Sonnet 18, "Shall I Compare Thee to a Summer's Day". On DVD *David Gilmour in Concert*, directed by David Mallett. EMI (U.K.)/Capitol (U.S.)

Hollingsworth, Robert & I Fagiolini. 2012. *Shakespeare: The Sonnets*. Abbey Records.

Kamen, Michael and Various Artists. 2002. *When Love Speaks*. Compilation. RADA and EMI Classics.

Kelly, Paul. 2016. *Seven Sonnets and a Song*. Gawdaggie/Universal.

Kelly, Paul. 2019a. *Live at Sydney Opera House*. Australian Broadcasting Corp. ABC.

Kelly, Paul. 2019. *Songs From the South, Greatest Hits*. Gawdaggie/Universal.

Wainwright, Rufus. 2010. *"All Days Are Nights": Songs for Lulu*. Verve Records.

Wainwright, Rufus. 2016. *"Take All My Loves": 9 Shakespeare Sonnets*. Deutsche Grammophon.

YouTube Links

David Gilmour Sonnet 18. https://youtu.be/Y5Q03kUMCf0.

Paul Kelly Sonnet 18. https://vimeo.com/156341497.

Paul Kelly Sonnet 138. https://youtu.be/8lOh3trTo-0 and https://garyware.me/2021/04/26/sonnet-138-by-paul-kelly-and-paul-grabowsky/.

Rufus Wainwright, Sonnet 20. https://youtu.be/6aEp7ErHXgE and https://youtu.be/57IFBqViNOI.

Rufus Wainwright Sonnet 29. https://youtu.be/ngk4sRQ2C-Y.

Florence Welch Sonnet 29. https://youtu.be/NOx-nypnHwo.

PART III

Global Issues in the Sonnets

CHAPTER 18

"O'er-Green My Bad" (Sonnet 112): Nature Writing in the *Sonnets*

Sophie Chiari

The *Sonnets* are fraught with references to nature, and much has already been said of the tropes related to flowers and the seasonal cycle in connection with love and the passing of time.[1] Yet Shakespeare's green world remains to be explored from a different perspective. Far from being equated with wilderness, his poetic environment is fashioned by man: gardening and agriculture are part and parcel of his vision of nature, mainly seen in terms of cultivation. Nonetheless, if the sonnets written between 1595 and 1597 abound with references to good husbandry,[2] the

---

[1] References to the *Sonnets* come from Duncan-Jones 1997. Other references to Shakespeare are drawn from Wells and Taylor (2005).

[2] For a chronology of the *Sonnets*, see Edmonson and Wells (2020, 24).

S. Chiari (✉)
Université Clermont Auvergne, Clermont-Ferrand, France
e-mail: sophie.chiari@orange.fr

© The Author(s), under exclusive license to Springer Nature Switzerland AG 2023
J. Kingsley-Smith and W. R. Rampone Jr. (eds.), *Shakespeare's Global Sonnets*, Global Shakespeares, https://doi.org/10.1007/978-3-031-09472-9_18

poet also deploys a black-pastoral approach to nature,[3] depicted as imperfect, corrupt and malign. What is green is not simply nice and fresh, it is also unripe and immature, and it appears that only the 'black lines' of the poet can appropriately render the young man's fairness (Sonnet 63, l. 13). Compellingly, throughout his *Sonnets*, Shakespeare goes well beyond the traditional opposition between the human and the non-human. Lovers groan and moan like beasts, mountains take the shape of the absent beloved. These collapsing boundaries allow the poet to give unprecedented agency to a peculiarly hostile environment. Just like the dark lady, the 'cold valley-fountain' (Sonnet 153, l. 4), turned into a 'seething bath' (l.7), has the capacity to cure and contaminate at the same time. The 'canker in the fragrant rose' (Sonnet 95, l.2) dangerously threatens life's beauty, while 'worms' (Sonnet 146, l.7) survive men by feeding on them.

Given that the 1609 *Sonnets* 'never before imprinted' are not a continuous sequence but an anthology of poems, composed over 'an almost thirty-year period',[4] it is not possible to ascribe to them what might be called a 'green narrative'. My point, therefore, is neither to turn them into an environmental sequence nor to give Shakespeare the purposes of a naturalist. I want, instead, to explore the poet's unsettling mode of engaging with the natural world.[5] Does he involve his readers in an anthropocentric mode of reading, or does he prompt them, on the contrary, to adopt an ecocentric perspective on the multiple facets of the human and physical environments he depicts in his verse? In trying to set out tentative and nuanced answers, what I ultimately hope to show in this ecocritical reading of Shakespeare's poems is the way the amorous ordeal of the poet is conveyed in terms of ecological crisis.

GOOD HUSBANDRY

'From fairest creatures we desire increase, / That thereby beauty's rose might never die' (Sonnet 1, l. 1–2): the first two lines of *Shakespeare's Sonnets*, by beginning with a reference to nature's unsurpassable, yet

---

[3] I define 'black pastoralism' as a type of literature that refashions traditional pastoral conventions in order to fit a nature in crisis rather than an idyllic green world.

[4] Ibid., p. 25.

[5] I am therefore making mine Robert Kern's statement that 'ecocriticism becomes most interesting and useful [...] when it aims to recover the environmental [...] orientation of works whose conscious or foregrounded interests lie elsewhere' (Kern 2000, 11).

evanescent, beauty, set the tone of the anthology, poised between an idealised green world and a productive nature. Indeed, through seasonal imagery on the one hand, and botanical, agricultural and (sometimes jarring) pastoral references on the other, the natural sphere is given pride of place in the poems.

If blackness is mostly regarded as a female feature, greenery is presented as one of the remarkable attributes of the fair youth. The word 'green', which appears six times in Thorpe's edition (Sonnets 12, 33, 63, 68, 104, 112), typically refers either to an authentic and vivid beauty or to youth and innocence ('he in them still green', Sonnet 63, l. 14), with sometimes a hint at bitterness and immaturity. On a connotative (or metaphorical) level, the 'green' youth needs to be tended, like a plant, by a competent gardener in order to grow and prosper. On a denotative (or pragmatic) level, nature needs to be sustained and nutrified in order not to dry up prematurely. Sonnet 75 alludes to 'sweet seasoned showers' (l. 2) nourishing 'the ground' (l. 2), which are paralleled with 'food to life' (l. 1).[6] Springtime rain is here seen as a source of renewal, announcing the possibility of fruitful crops. Shakespeare's nature is, thus, a practical one, first and foremost regarded as man's habitat and principal means of sustenance.

We have seen that the *Sonnets* start with a reference to nature and 'increase' (Sonnet 1, l. 1), a word which also crops up in three other poems (Sonnets 11, 15 and 97), and whose manifold resonances are worth noting here (Herman 1999, 266). While the term points to procreation, it also refers to '[t]hat which grows or is produced from the earth; vegetable produce, crops' (*OED* 7.a). This now archaic sense is clearly at work in Sonnet 97, where the poet, contrasting winter's 'bareness' (l. 4) with the fecundity of the previous season, evokes 'The teeming autumn big with rich increase / Bearing the wanton burden of the prime' (l. 6–7). With Autumn being likened to a pregnant woman ready to give birth, the sexual imagery elsewhere associated with spring finds here fruition in images of pregnancy and birth.

Because of its association with ripeness and the autumnal season, pregnancy is also conveyed through the use of agrarian tropes. In *Shakespeare's*

---

[6] Shakespeare probably had in mind one of the litanies of the 1559 *Book of Common Prayer* which emphasised the fertilising power of rain: 'Sende us [...] such moderate raine and showers, that we may receive the fruytes of the earthe to our comforte'. See Cummings (2011, 122).

Nature, Charlotte Scott argues that, in the *Sonnets*, the ethnocentric, nature-culture binary is challenged and reworked by a focus on cultivation (Scott 2014).Indeed, the poems put forward a cultivated nature where husbandry makes the earth fecund and exploitable by men. At the same time, they replicate and complicate the traditional nature/woman binary. This is obvious in Sonnet 3, where the theme of husbandry is explicitly dealt with in connection with the begetting of children: 'For where is she so fair whose uneared womb / Disdains the tillage of thy husbandry?' (l. 5–6). If the simile between not having children and letting fertile land go to waste was not new (Hermann 1999, 267), the sonnets betray a particular angst which emerges in the poet's misogynistic clichés. Indeed, 'womb' significantly rhymes with 'tomb' (l. 7), which denotes the speaker's anxiety when it comes to reproduction, for the fact is that, in order to reproduce himself, the fair youth must deceive his friend and have sex with a female rival. In another procreation sonnet, Shakespeare repeats the same theme, still in the interrogative mode: 'Who lets so fair a house fall to decay, / Which husbandry in honour might uphold / Against the stormy gusts of winter's day?' (Sonnet 13, l. 9–11)? Once again, these lines supply a rather utilitarian view of nature, as the management of earth's natural resources seems to be the only way of countering 'decay' (l. 9).

In this firmly agricultural perspective, harvest time, when nature's products are ripe, appears to be the most desirable season.[7] Early on in the anthology, the speaker addresses his beloved male friend as 'the world's fresh ornament / And only herald to the gaudy spring' (Sonnet 1, l. 9–10). In these pivotal lines, spring is not well-apparelled yet: fruition is deferred to some unspecified future time. The youth is 'now' (l. 9) pre-eminent, but the adjective 'fresh' suggests that his supremacy will be short-lived and that competition may soon appear in the form of a new crop of desirable young men. Similarly, in Sonnet 98, April is a young man wearing magnificent clothes, 'proud pied April, dressed in all his trim' (l. 2). Yet, the green of early spring is merely ornamental because, once again, this early growth cannot yet be harvested. As a result, nature in the *Sonnets* seems to be 'inseparable from the mindset of agriculture' (Clark 2019, 35), and its worth is narrowly dependent upon its domestication. Shakespeare's poetic environment is for the most part fashioned

[7] The following development is indebted to Dympna Callaghan's paper, 'Shakespeare's Gaudy', at the Strange Habits' Conference (January 2021, Clermont-Ferrand).

by man and resorts to what Timothy Morton calls 'agrilogistics' (Morton 2016, 38): gardening and agriculture are inherent in his vision of nature, mainly seen in terms of cultivation.

Early modern gardening implied planting and grafting, occupations that suggest order and improvement—two necessary qualities for an ideal commonwealth. Shakespeare generally uses the language of grafting within the discourse of perfect friendship (Shannon 2002); yet in the sonnets, it promotes a more sensuous male–male relationship. As Vin Nardizzi observes, the last line of Sonnet 15, 'I engraft you new' (l. 14), 'links procreation to poetry-making through an image of plant grafting' (Nardizzi 2009, 83). The process of engrafting is not a purely natural one as it requires human intervention to join the stem of a plant to the stock of another plant. Nature must, therefore, be improved by human intervention in order to display its full potential. In Sonnet 37, the same image crops up: 'I make my love engrafted to this store' (1.8). Interestingly, the Greek root of the word 'graph' (*grapheíon*) refers to a pencil. Shakespeare may thus, through the use of the verb 'engraft', allude both to a semi-natural, semi-artificial form of reproduction, and to a literary means of procreation (Matz 2008, 83). Sonnet 53 corroborates this idea, bringing forward the 'spring and foison of the year' (l. 9)—'foison' designating both an abundant harvest and a prolific literary production. The poet's reference to his own writings is here expressed in agricultural rather than in gardening terms, but the logic is the same: reproduction ultimately becomes a matter of poetry rather than a matter of sex in the *Sonnets*.[8]

As previously seen, the onus placed on 'agrilogistics' also implies that the language of nature is intertwined with that of commerce. Just like 'love', which is 'merchandised' (Sonnet 102, l. 3), nature, which supplies a myriad of metaphors to describe the passion and amorous feelings, is sometimes 'reduced to the value of a saleable commodity' (Duncan-Jones 1997, 314). As Charlotte Scott has shown, the logic of cultivation in the procreation sonnets generally determines the speaker's attitude to (re)production and profit (Scott 2014). While Sonnet 21, for example, alludes to the conceits that sonneteers usually associate with the beloved (1. 6–7), the last line rejects these compliments by alluding to the threats posed by an increasingly commercial society: 'I will not praise, that purpose not to sell' (1. 14). The traditional opposition between nature

---

[8] See also Matz (2010, 480).

and market is thus challenged early on in the poems: natural beauties are undermined by self-interested relationships and monetary ambitions.

BLACK PASTORALISM

Harvested crops, however, do not simply pave the way for profit and exchange. They also announce the 'white and bristly beard' of winter (Sonnet 12, l. 8): nature is, therefore, regarded both as a provider and as an enemy. While there is no such thing as ecophobia in the Sonnets (the speaker nowhere expresses a pathological aversion towards nature), Shakespeare tries to de-poeticise the natural elements traditionally used by sonneteers in order to endow them with new creative potentialities. Doing so, he acknowledges that, if the natural world sustains man, it can also emphasise his own degradation, subjected as it is to 'the wastes of time' (Sonnet 12, l. 10): the violet can indeed be 'past prime' (l. 3) and the 'lofty trees' 'barren of leaves' (l. 5), even though they rarely appear as such in the conventional verse of the period. Occasionally, rather than an addition of riches, nature is reduced to a catalogue of losses by the speaker who dismisses the flowers of rhetoric to promote, instead, an aesthetics of waste, ruins and stains. '[E]ternity', he observes, paradoxically 'proves more short than waste or ruining' (Sonnet 125, l. 3–4). Challenging the values of the early modern *copia*, the *Sonnets* rely on sharpness and brevity so as to convey authentic feelings, including envy, despair, disgust and helplessness. Traditional comparisons with the natural elements are ironically questioned ('Shall I compare thee to a summer's day?', Sonnet 18, l. 1), at best, and radically dismissed ('My mistress' eyes are nothing like the sun', Sonnet 130, l. 1), at worst. Rather than 'false compare' (Sonnet 130, l. 14), the *Sonnets* highlight a sometimes crude realism in order to delineate the complexities—and the cruelties—of love.

Nature's 'changing course' (Sonnet 18, l. 1) means that the natural beauties generally praised by poets are bound to wither and die. In Sonnet 129 ('Th' expense of spirit in a waste of shame / Is lust in action', l. 1–2), the poet exploits the effects of both sexual and natural disenchantment. Indeed, waste hints at loss, squandering and decay, both spiritual and environmental: in quest of intense pleasure, the human being, in this context, is both hunter and hunted, predator and prey. Borrowing some of Timothy Clark's observations, we may say that he 'becomes [himself] a kind of threshold object, a natural/cultural hybrid able to register the dislocations and derangements of this fluid boundary' (Clark 2019, 71).

Man is but one component of the natural world and is subject to the same losses as trees, plants and flowers.

Even worse, in Sonnet 94, 'sweetest things turn sourest by their deeds; / Lilies that fester smell far worse than weeds' (l. 13–14): the natural world is submitted to 'base infection' (l. 11) and, as a result, is threatened by an apparently irreversible corruption. In the only 15-line sonnet of the anthology, Sonnet 99, the poet establishes 'a potentially unlimited catalogue of flowers' (Duncan-Jones 1997, 308). The flowers of rhetoric are here materialised by magnificent spring flowers which all steal the beauty of the beloved. Yet they are all threatened to be eaten up by 'A vengeful canker' (l. 13) which will slowly destroy them.

Decay is not limited to flowers. Elsewhere in the anthology, the earth is 'sullen' (Sonnet 29, l. 12) and 'silver fountains' are soiled with 'mud' (Sonnet 35, l. 2). By the same token, the poems also shed light on stains (Sonnet 33, l. 14; Sonnet 35, l. 3; Sonnet 109, l. 8 and 11) and impure things and creatures. While the night (the lovers' refuge *par excellence*) could be regarded as starry by budding poets, Shakespeare prefers to see it as 'sullied' (Sonnet 15, l. 12) and as foreshadowing the young man's corruption. All in all, he showcases a poetics of impurity which successfully turns dirt, stains and mud into literary objects.[9]

In this debasing environment, nature may still provide mediocre poets—those deprived of a 'well-refined pen' (Sonnet 85, l. 8)—with its usual share of worn-out images. In some of his tongue-in-cheek lines, Shakespeare asserts that genuine love cannot be shaken by tempests; that it does not vary and can be defined, so to speak, as 'a navigational *fixèd mark*' (Sonnet 116, l. 5–6) (Vendler 1998, 489). In the volta of Sonnet 116, however, the speaker debunks this pseudo-Petrarchan vision of love and bitterly remarks that nature imposes the rule of time on every living (human and non-human) creature: the third quatrain makes clear that physical beauty is, in the end, altered by time and that love is dissolved by death. 'The earth devour[s] her own sweet brood', the poet declares in Sonnet 19—a line echoed in Sonnet 74, where he asserts that 'The earth can have but earth' (l. 7). He hammers the point home later in the anthology: 'The earth can yield me but a common grave' (Sonnet 81, l. 7). Yet, contrary to the human world, the natural one can turn corruption into generation: life, as a result, is likely to emerge from putrefaction.

---

[9] On this, see also Chiari (2018).

So, as nature reclaims the bodies of the dead (corpses become 'the prey of worms', Sonnet 74, l. 10), it ultimately transforms them into organic matter—a fact acknowledged by the speaker who anticipates his being 'rotten' 'in earth' in Sonnet 81 (l. 2). This natural, recycling operation finds its equivalent in the poetic process put forward by the poet: like the worm, his pen can transform mortality into eternal life and make the beloved remembered and celebrated after his death.

No wonder if time is one of the sonnets' obsessions. However, the speaker seems to ignore nature's cyclical time, obsessed as he is with (de)generation and finitude. Reacting to the predominant conventions of Petrarchan poetry, he asserts, for instance, that the very orbs can no longer be seen as an expression of radiance and longevity. Even the radiant sun is seen declining (Sonnet 18, l. 7) (Fineman 1986, 147). The sky, in particular, becomes a site of tension between embellishing and creative forces, on the one hand, and poisonous exhalations, on the other. Significantly, while the word 'sky' itself appears only once (Sonnet 15, l. 6), it is materialised through 'clouds' that are said to 'blot the heaven' (Sonnet 28, l. 10).

Through the pathetic fallacy, weather imagery is thus made to convey deceit and woe in some of the lines aimed at a male addressee: the poet's tears are like 'rain' on his 'storm-beaten face' (Sonnet 34, l. 6); the atmosphere, full of 'rotten smoke' (l. 4), is hardly breathable—a reality familiar to most Londoners subject to the city's appetite for coal and, as such, to its growing pollution. The 'ugly rack' (Sonnet 33, l. 6) in the sky conceals the sun, ruining the world's beauty, and the same image is at work in Sonnet 34, where 'base clouds o'ertake' the poet 'in his way' (l. 3). Clouds obfuscate the poet's horizon both literally and metaphorically, and they contribute to making the sky much less insubstantial than in most traditional sonnets: they give shape to emptiness—in other words, they 'giv[e] to airy nothing / A local habitation and a name' (*A Midsummer Night's Dream*, 5.1.16–17).

So, if nature, in the *Sonnets*, seems in crisis, it is mainly because the poet refuses to see it as a mere reservoir of Petrarchan metaphors. Indeed, Shakespeare no longer supplies the meliorative references one can expect in traditional sonnet sequences. In Sonnet 130, the coral (l.2), the snow (l.3) and the roses (l.5), i.e. all these ethereal objects which are the archetypal ornaments of sonneteering, are dismissed in favour of more elemental forces: as the black mistress 'treads on the ground' (l. 12), the earth gains in complexity and is regarded as a powerful incentive to life.

The mistress is herself a potent telluric black force, a star shedding no light (Sonnet 132, l. 7), a morning/mourning sun shining but weakly (l. 5).

Nature's Agency

Because, in the sonnets, the natural world is not reduced to the Petrarchan imagery of lack and excess which characterised the poetic production of Elizabethan England, it becomes part and parcel of man's everyday world and, even more than that, it is bestowed with a capacity to exert power on human beings. This means that nature cannot be easily comprehended or apprehended: endowed with an agency of its own, it turns out to be fairly unpredictable. Logically, then, the speaker refuses to read what will happen next in the shifting sky (Sonnet 14, l. 1–6). It is impossible, he concludes in Sonnet 14, to predict the future: 'the more control we seem to have over the natural environment, the less we actually have', he even seems to imply (Estok 2009, 208). However, man's behaviour and misdemeanours can, to a certain extent, be anticipated, according to the tenets of the humoral theory which subtly underpins the *Sonnets* as a whole.[10]

Humoral theory, in the early modern period, relied on the belief in the agency of nature. The human body was thought to be composed of the four elements, each with distinct properties (Sonnet 45, l. 7). The balance of these elements, called 'life's composition' by the speaker (Sonnet 45, l.9), made for a harmonious existence. However, the sonnets precisely stage the contrary, by putting forward a battle of the elements: while a fiery desire burns the lover, the cold heart of the beloved makes him/her turn to other conquests. Life is therefore chaotic in essence and transforms the lover into a malcontent. In Sonnet 44, the enamoured speaker acknowledges, for example, that he is only made of dull elements, i.e. earth and water (l. 11), which makes him depressed, while his beloved is characterised by 'slight air, and purging fire' (Sonnet 45, l. 1), which makes the young man confident and full of energy.[11]

---

[10] Its presence is made obvious in Sonnet 91, in which the poet asserts that 'every humour hath his adjunct pleasure' (l. 5).

[11] The early modern construction of gender also partly relied on the theory of humours. Sixteenth-century medical epistemology, shaped by humoral theory, ascribed a cold and wet disposition to the female body in contrast with the hotter and drier male.

This early modern conception of humanity as heavily dependent on natural properties tended to blur the line separating the human from the non-human. No wonder if the speaker frequently attributes human features to the natural world. According to Joshua Rottman, this 'tendency toward anthropomorphization' suggests a moral concern for nature, non-humans being 'conceptualized as possessing more humanlike minds, thus having a heightened capacity to be harmed' (Rottman 2014, n.p.). This concern emerges in a variety of poems like Sonnet 113, where 'The mountain, or the sea, the day, or night' (l. 11) are shaped to the 'feature' of the beloved (l. 12). While nature is traditionally represented as female in most poems of the period, the *Sonnets* supply a more subtle vision of the natural world: nature is gendered according to the lover's desire. It can, therefore, be male or female, depending on the speaker's fluctuating sexuality. Of course, clichés die hard: in Sonnet 137, an idealised female beloved is compared to a *locus amoenus* or 'a several plot' (l. 9)[12] and, in a reverse movement, nature is personified as a 'sovereign mistress' (l. 5) in Sonnet 136. In his 'botanical' sonnets, Shakespeare also echoes the traditional representation of female genitals 'covered with a flower', indicative of menstruation (called 'flowers' by Shakespeare's contemporaries) and the sexual act ('defloration') altogether.[13] However, he gives a new twist to this nature/woman binary by adumbrating the vision of a triumphant femininity reconciling reproduction and 'pleasure' (Sonnet 97, l. 11). Remarkable for their pregnant 'seasonal and horticultural imagery', Sonnets 97, 98 and 99 manage to convey 'through colour, scent, and emotional valence the intimacy of the body's inner psychic and imaginative life' (Harvey 2010, 320–321). Indeed, as Shakespeare alludes to 'the lily's white' (Sonnet 98, l. 9) and the 'deep vermilion' (l. 10), he does not simply hint at the delights of spring, he also adumbrates the pleasures of carnal (and fecund) love.

The speaker of the sonnets thus de-centres the traditional anthropocentric perspective on which most early modern poets relied. Whereas they usually compared plants to humans, he compares humans to plants. In Sonnet 15, for instance, the process of human growth (and decay) is described in horticultural terms—'men as plants increase' (l. 5)—and in

[12] Cf. Sonnet 16, in which gardens are seen as 'maiden gardens' (l. 6) ready to receive the seeds of male gardeners.

[13] The 'proud lap' of Sonnet 98 is an allusion to the female pudendum. See Harvey (2010, 320).

Sonnet 25, the 'Great princes' favourites' are given plant-like attributes since they are said to 'spread' 'their fair leaves' (l. 5). Similarly, instead of animals endowed with human features, the poet presents humans behaving like beasts: his unhappy lovers groan (Sonnet 50, l. 11 and 13; Sonnet 131, l. 6 and 10; Sonnet 133, l. 1) and their sexual drives make them look like animals. The analogy between the speaker and the horse, in Sonnet 50, shows how much the weary poet can identify with the wounded beast. In that sense, the *Sonnets* partake of what Charles T. Wolfe calls 'the materialist blurring of the human/animal divide' (Wolfe 2017, 148) in the early modern period—a blurring that would result, in the late seventeenth century, in the 'humiliation of human sovereignty and uniqueness' (Wolfe 2017, 151). The most blatant instance of this eco-centred perspective is to be found in the only openly religious sonnet of the anthology, Sonnet 146, where the microcosmic human body is depicted as a 'sinful earth' having the 'soul' at its core (l. 1). One can choose to read in the sonnet's opening line a biblical reminiscence that human life began as earth, dust or clay or a strong assertion of the ambivalent power of the earth—or soil—both as a locus of regeneration and as a place of degradation.

Compellingly, throughout Thorpe's anthology as a whole, Shakespeare goes well beyond the traditional opposition between culture and nature (or the human and the non-human). Indeed, the *Sonnets* 'becom[e] a space in which the non-human world can loosen itself from the weight of human perceptions' (Clark 2019, 68). This space displaces the anthropocentric modes of reading induced by the procreation sonnets. Sonnet 20, for instance, famously propounds that nature personified has 'painted' (l. 1) the feminine face of the young man and has 'pricked [him] out for women's pleasure' (l. 13). Nature is no longer traditionally depicted as a beloved female here. Proposing a refined interplay between art and nature, Shakespeare portrays it as an artist, a Pygmalion-like sculptor endowed with creative powers and able to fashion a creature fitting its tastes and answering its desires.

Man, as a result, looks much less potent than his natural surroundings: in the universe he lives in, wood and stones can have some disconcerting agency. In Sonnet 128, the poet watches his mistress play the virginal, and he acknowledges that 'dead wood' is 'more blessed than living lips' (l. 12). Nature's agency, however, is perhaps most impressive when the speaker resorts to maritime tropes, for the ocean imagery, present in several sonnets, gives the poems an unprecedented scope. The ocean of

Sonnet 56 ('Let this sad interim like the ocean be', l. 9), which reflects a shift from time ('today', 'tomorrow', 'interim') to space (Vendler 1998, 271), is a frighteningly vast space keeping the lovers apart. The 'hungry ocean', in Sonnet 64 (l. 5), echoed by the 'boundless sea' of Sonnet 65, is said to 'gain / Advantage on the kingdom of the shore' (Sonnet 64, l. 5–6). As sheer elemental forces, land and sea are in competition against one another, while man is but a diminutive presence in such a grandiose environment. In Sonnet 80, the poet alludes to his 'saucy bark' (l. 7) which navigates on his beloved's 'broad main' (l. 8). His rival, by contrast, is identified with a much larger boat ('your worth, wide as the ocean is, / The humble as the proudest sail doth bear', l. 5–6), not unlike the 'heavily armed Spanish galleons' of the Spanish Armada (Duncan-Jones 1997, 270). Once again, in Sonnet 86, the speaker points to 'the proud full sail of [the rival poet's] great verse' (l. 1), that is to say, to the vessel of the rival poet. Sea life and poetic life actually merge here: the sea, like poetry, happens to be a transformative force. It is, therefore, a fitting metaphor to comment on the artistic process of the sonneteer, made of emulation and rivalry, creation and imitation, inspiration and influence (from the Latin *influere*, 'to flow into').

As already seen above, the poet repeatedly sees himself as a bark on the vast sea—a space which offers no relief and which, in the end, threatens to dissolve his love. In Sonnet 117, he finally acknowledges that he has 'hoisted sail to all the wind / Which should transport [him] farthest from [his beloved's] sight' (l. 7–8). Interestingly, this metaphoric vision reworks the usual symbolism of the (female) sailboat violently tossed by the rough sea. In the poem, the ship becomes a masculine entity, a trope debunking traditional clichés about feminine sailing boats engulfed by the waves.

Shakespeare goes even further. The sexual promiscuity of the dark lady is repeatedly seen in maritime terms as she is, in Sonnet 137, 'the bay where all men ride' (l. 6). By the same token, the 'large and spacious will' (l. 5) of Sonnet 135, in which Will wants to hide his will, is strongly reminiscent of that 'worth, wide as the ocean' (l. 5), on which Will's 'saucy bark' (l. 7) in Sonnet 80 'doth wilfully appear' (l. 8). Strikingly enough, whereas the speaker generally points to loss and absence, the maritime world is a world of depth and surfeit which never overflows its shores.[14] As such, it aptly symbolises the lovers' unsatiable desire (Sonnet 135, l. 9–10).

---

[14] Cf. Juliet's statement in *Romeo and Juliet*: 'My bounty is as boundless as the sea, / My love as deep' (2.1.175–76).

Conclusion: Overgreening the Sonnets

Shakespeare's *Sonnets* do reveal a changing dynamic between the Elizabethans and their environment. We have seen that the natural habitat presented by the poet, marked by the advent of the Anthropocene, is in no way a space untouched by humans: on the contrary, it is a productive world, yielding crops, flowers and fruits when properly tilled and tended. However, the green and blue worlds of the sonnets cannot be seen as an idealised agrarian (or maritime) space, for they also prompt us to reflect upon a natural environment apparently in crisis, where loss, decay and overpowering elemental forces predominate. Yet this crisis happens to be a mode of being to the world. While the early procreation sonnets seemingly set out landscapes of pastoral fantasy, Shakespeare also provides us with a dark landscape of weeds and cankerous plants that invites a reassessment of the role of nature. By putting forward the roles of plants and flowers, he probes the variety of the biosphere and searches for natural properties likely to inspire the human world.

Significantly, the poet willingly evokes his own art in environmental terms: his words are flows, his lines are flowers. And if poetry is a mirror up to nature, by a similar process, nature can be regarded as an open book, gathering feelings, impressions, intuitions, thereby containing the whole gamut of emotions which most budding poets generally depend upon.

The green leaves mentioned in Sonnet 97 (l. 14), as a result, could well be leaves of paper—the same leaves on which the sonnets might have been composed separately to be later bound together (Edmonson and Wells 2020, 20). Even more obviously, in Sonnet 73, the conjunction of 'choirs', spelled 'quires' in the Quarto (and therefore reminiscent of unbound sheets), and 'leaves', implies an allusion to the leaves of paper on which Shakespeare wrote his sonnets.[15]

Shakespeare thus aimed at 'overgreening' his poems in order to collapse the human/non-human boundary and to promote instead an organic vision of the world where the mineral, the vegetal, the animal and the human spheres are made to overlap.[16] In Sonnet 112, the speaker asks: 'For what care I who calls me well or ill / So you o'er-green my bad,

---

[15] See also Callaghan (2008, 127).

[16] It is this pioneering vision which was to triumph in the animist island of *The Tempest*.

my good allow?' (l. 3–4). While this has traditionally been seen as an allusion to Robert Greene's 1592 attack on Shakespeare, other meanings may be ascribed to these lines. Greenery being indicative of rejuvenation and of improvement, the poet seems to say that the presence of his beloved makes him a better man. However, 'over-green' may also hint at green vitriol,[17] which was one of the ingredients of ink—and it is worth noting here that Sonnet 112 refers to printing (or making an 'impression', l. 1) as the poet alludes to a 'vulgar scandal stamped upon [his] brow' (l. 2)—and which could also be used by gardeners to prevent the spreading of moss. Once again here, greenery provides the poet with palimpsestic meanings and helps him bring to life a complex and nuanced reality which, in the sonnets, is as much organic as it is intellectual. Obsessed with the transformative power of nature (as Ovid before him), inspired by its cyclical decaying and regenerating processes, Shakespeare sought to represent the non-human in fresh and vibrant ways; not as a discrete sphere pole apart from men and women's preoccupations, but as a green world of multiple voices endowed with an agency of its own, a hardly perceptible universe worth representing and celebrating along with the fair youth and the dark lady.[18]

REFERENCES

Callaghan, Dympna. 2008. *Shakespeare's Sonnets*. Malden, MA: Blackwell Publishing.

Chiari, Sophie. 2018. "Shakespeare's Poetics of Impurity: Spots, Stains, and Slime". In *Etudes Epistémè. Profane Shakespeare – Perfection, Pollution and the Truth of Performance*, No. 33, 2018. https://doi.org/10.4000/episteme.2164

Clark, Timothy. 2019. *The Value of Ecocriticism*. Cambridge: Cambridge University Press.

Cummings, Brian. 2011. *The Book of Common Prayer. The Texts of 1549, 1559, and 1662*. Oxford: Oxford University Press.

---

[17] *OED*, 'green vitriol': '*n*. now chiefly *historical* crystalline ferrous sulphate, a pale blue-green salt formed by the action of sulphuric acid on iron or certain of its compounds'.

[18] This universe faded into obscurity after the publication of the 1609 quarto and, even after its rehabilitation, its particular approach to nature still went undetected; we only start to rediscover it now as brimming with life in all its forms. For further details on the reception of the sonnets, see Kingsley-Smith (2019).

Duncan-Jones, Katherine (ed.). 1997. *Shakespeare's Sonnets*. London: Thomas Nelson, The Arden Shakespeare.

Edmonson, Paul, and Stanley Wells (eds.). 2020. *All the Sonnets of Shakespeare*. Cambridge: Cambridge University Press.

Estok, Simon C. 2009. "Theorizing in a Space of Ambivalent Openness: Ecocriticism and Ecophobia", *Interdisciplinary Studies in Literature and Environment*, No. 2 (Spring 2009): 203–25.

Fineman, Joel. 1986. *Shakespeare's Perjured Eye. The Invention of Poetic Subjectivity in the Sonnets*. Berkeley: University of California Press.

Harvey, Elizabeth D. 2010. "Flesh Colors and Shakespeare's Sonnets". In *A Companion to Shakespeare's Sonnets*, ed. Michael Schoenfeldt. 314-28. Chichester: Wiley-Blackwell.

Herman, Peter C. 1999. "What's the Use? Or, The Problematic Economy in Shakespeare's Procreation Sonnets", In *Shakespeare's Sonnets*, ed. James Schiffer. 263-84. New York: Garland Publishing.

Kern, Robert. 2000. "Ecocriticism—What Is It Good For?", *Interdisciplinary Studies in Literature and Environment*, Vol. 7, No. 1 (Winter 2000): 9–32.

Kingsley-Smith, Jane. 2019. *The Afterlife of Shakespeare's Sonnets*. Cambridge: Cambridge University Press.

Matz, Robert. 2010. "The Scandals of Shakespeare's Sonnets", *English Literary History*, Summer 2010, Vol. 77, No. 2: 477–508.

Matz, Robert. 2008. *The World of Shakespeare's Sonnets: An Introduction*. Jefferson, NC, and London: McFarland.

Morton, Timothy. 2016. *Dark Ecology: For a Logic of Coexistence*. New York: Columbia University Press.

Nardizzi, Vin. 2009. "Shakespeare's Penknife: Grafting and Seedless Generation in the Procreation Sonnets", *Renaissance and Reformation / Renaissance et Réforme*, Vol. 32, No. 1 (Winter/Hiver 2009): 83–106.

Rottman, Joshua. 2014. "Breaking Down Biocentrism: Two Distinct Forms of Moral Concern for Nature", *Frontiers in Psychology*, vol. 5, 2014. https://www.ncbi.nlm.nih.gov/pmc/articles/PMC4138930/ (https://doi.org/10.3389/fpsyg.2014.00905).

Scott, Charlotte. 2014. *Shakespeare's Nature: From Cultivation to Culture*. Oxford: Oxford University Press.

Shannon, Laurie. 2002. *Sovereign Amity: Figures of Friendship in Shakespearean Contexts*. Chicago and London: University of Chicago Press.

Vendler, Helen. 1998. *The Art of Shakespeare's Sonnets*. Cambridge, MA: The Belknap Press of Harvard University Press.

Wells, Stanley, and Gary Taylor. 2005. *The Oxford Shakespeare. The Complete Works*. Oxford: Clarendon Press, 2nd ed.

Wolfe, Charles T. 2017. "Boundary Crossings. The Blurring of the Human/Animal Divide as Naturalization of the Soul in Early Modern

Philosophy". In *Human and Animal Cognition in Early Modern Philosophy and Medicine*, ed. by Stefanie Buchenau and Roberto Lo Presti. 147–72. Pittsburgh: University of Pittsburgh Press, 2017.

CHAPTER 19

Black Luce and Sonnets 127–54

Duncan Salkeld

In the bustle of London, Shakespeare seems to have noticed an extraordinary gem in the ear of an African woman, its glint lodging in his memory. The image first appears in his dramatic writing when Romeo espies Juliet and compares her to a "a rich jewel in an Ethiope's ear" (1.5.43). A similar moment occurs again in Sonnet 27 where the speaker imagines his beloved "like a jewel hung in ghastly night", making "black night, beauteous, and her old face new" (27: 10–12). In Sonnet 28, the night is associated directly with a dark skintone ("swart-complexion'd"), while the lover's image "gild'st" the evening (28: 11–12). This cluster of ideas—jewellery, night-time and skin-shade—occurs also in Sonnets 127–54. In this sub-sequence, a black woman (the so-called "dark lady") is described as "the fairest and most precious jewel" (131: 4) and "dark as night" (147: 13–14). Dazzling and enthralling as this woman is, she is also described in the language of prostitution. According to Francis Meres's *Palladis Tamia* (1598), Shakespeare circulated his sonnets "among his private friends". Although the identity of this woman remains unknown,

D. Salkeld (✉)
University of Chichester, London, UK
e-mail: D.Salkeld@chi.ac.uk

documentary sources can shed some light on the London world of these "private friends". It is worth asking whether we know of any woman associated with the Elizabethan sex trade, possibly brown-skinned, who might have had connections to Shakespeare's circle. This chapter argues that there was one woman in Shakespeare's world who seems to have fitted that description or met those criteria. Her married name was Lucy Baynam, but she was more popularly known in London as Black Luce and in literary texts as Lucy Negro or Negra.

In 1588, Elizabeth I presented Sir Francis Drake with a jewel showing the head of an African man, carved in ivory and superimposed over the profile of a white woman. As David Olusoga has written, "the black African, perhaps in this case a black emperor, had become part of the visual culture of the age, a figure in the English imagination" (Olusoga 2016, p. 17). Through the work of critics and historians such as Imtiaz Habib (2008), Miranda Kaufmann (2017), Onyeka Nubia (2019), Sathnam Sanghera (2021) and Olusoga, we have come to understand more fully that black history and British history have been inseparable for centuries. Images of Africa were dotted all around early modern London in tavern and shop signs: "The Black Boy" in Canwick (Candlewick, now Cannon) Street, in Eastcheap, and in St. Paul's; "The Tiger's Head" in St. Paul's; "The Oliphant" (Elephant) in Smithfield; "The White Lion" taverns in Lombard Street and East Smithfield; and "The Red Lion" at Cloth Fair in Smithfield, and on London Bridge (BCB 2.76^v, 3.199^v-200^v, 273^v). As Olusoga reminds us in a discussion of world trade, for the late Tudors "[t]he real lure of Africa was gold" (p. 42: pp. 43–50). Perhaps it should not be surprising that also amid the bustle of London, we find a black man living and working as a goldsmith in Cheapside in 1576.

Cheapside housed a number of ornate goldsmith's shops.[1] According to John Stow, this central London thoroughfare was notable for "the most beautiful frame of fair houses and shops, that be within the walls of London, or elsewhere in England, commonly called Goldsmiths Row, betwixt Bread Street end and the Cross in Cheap" (Kingsford 1908, I, p. 345). In 1578, Thomasine Breame, a high-class prostitute who charged expensive fees, confessed at Bridewell that she had slept with "a goldsmith in Cheapside, one Pinder she taketh his name to be" at The White

---

[1] Thomas Middleton's *A Chaste Maid in Cheapside* (*c.*1613) centrally concerns the gulling of Master Yellowhammer, a Cheapside goldsmith.

Lion in Lombard Street. A shadowy figure named East had taken him to her. In Breame's words, "the goldsmith was a tall man with a great beard reddish uncut; he went in a gown citizen-like; his face is of a black swart colour". According to another deponent, "one Mr Pendar, a goldsmith, a black swart man with a grim visage" slept on separate occasions with prostitutes Jane Trosse and Breame (BCB 3.21^r: 28 June 1576). We learn from testimony at Bridewell that Trosse occasionally worked from East's house (BCB, 3. 266^r), that among Breame's customers was "one Courtney, Lord Hunsdon's man", and that although East arranged various assignations for her (including at the French ambassador's residence), Breame sought to have him "beaten" for getting her poor money (BCB 3.13^v, 28^r). Pinder (or "Pendar") was evidently a man of striking appearance and some wealth. At the White Lion in Lombard Street, he paid Breame 10 shillings (BCB, 3. 298^v).[2]

Between 1594 and 1596, Carey, Lord Hunsdon, was the patron of Shakespeare's company, The Lord Chamberlain's Men. This was not a world from which Shakespeare was detached. He and Pinder had more than an interest in jewellery in common: they shared London acquaintances too.

Gilbert East and Black Luce

Looking for historical identities in Shakespeare's sonnets—the fair youth, the rival poet or friend and the so-called "dark lady—is sometimes regarded as a futile or even unhelpful endeavour" (Schalkwyk 1994, p. 398; Jacobson 2010).[3] Paul Edmondson and Stanley Wells write, "It is time for readings and studies of the Sonnets to leave behind these biographical tropes" (Edmondson and Wells 2020, p. 23). At the same time, they accept that Sonnets 22, 57, 89, 134, 135 and 143 pun on Shakespeare's first name "Will" (p. 33); that 145 appears to play on Anne Hathaway's name (p. 4); and that many of the sonnets are "deeply

---

[2] The will of goldsmith Nicholas Pinder, made on 6 October 1595 (PROB 11/85/414), states that he was born in Milk Street, close to Cheapside. If Pinder was "Pendar", he was born a citizen, perhaps a second or third generation Black man.

[3] Schalkwyk's purpose was to challenge what he termed a prevailing "revulsion against biography" (p. 398).

[4] Other collections dedicated to her included Richard Barnfield's *The Affectionate Shepherd* (1594), songs by Charles Tessier, and Bartholomew Young's 1598 translation of Montemayor's *Diana*.

personal poems, written out of Shakespeare's own experience" (p. 32). They point out that many of the sonnets "contain what might be regarded as personal allusions" and "refer to actual individuals" (34). They also print the so-called "dark lady" poems (127–52) as a distinct series or subsequence (pp. 55–81). If, as Edmondson and Wells argue, Shakespeare's *Sonnets* are "likely to encompass many different occasions and people in his life" (p. 37), then the search for further details can be neither futile nor unhelpful.

Other sonneteers scattered hints in their poems alluding to historical figures. Penelope Rich, sister to the Earl of Essex, Robert Devereaux, had several collections dedicated to her, including Sir Philip Sidney's *Astrophil and Stella* which was printed posthumously in 1591 (Wall 2004).[4] Sidney puns on her name: "Rich fools there be" (No. 24). He may prove her "slave", but he hopes to "grow rich, naming my Stella's name" (No. 35). Michael Drayton took Warwickshire resident Anne Goodere as his model of femininity in *Idea in Sixtie Three Sonnets,* which was first printed as *Ideas Mirrour Amours in quatorzains* in 1594 (No. 13, sig. C3^r). When Samuel Daniel revised his collection *Delia* (first printed in 1592), he filtered out some autobiographical details, but left a clue that "Delia" lived near him beside the river Avon (No. 48). Henry Constable's *Diana* contains at least one sonnet dedicated to Penelope Rich's daughter (Sullivan 2004). Little may be known about these women but without them, the poems would lose an important part of their rationale.

Shakespeare's sonnets sometimes seem epistolary in nature (for example, 26, 38 and 44) yet they can be frustratingly shy about their addressees. We learn that Shakespeare found a young man absorbingly beautiful, androgynous, socially superior and deserving of respect but, beyond these hints, the youth's character remains relatively colourless. Similarly, the rival poet and/or friend are little more than shadows. By contrast, the "mistress" of 127–54 cuts a striking figure. She appears to have been musical (128), real (130), controlling (131), compellingly attractive (132), dominating (133), sexually available to other men (135), given to lying (138), cruel or proud (140) and likely to pass on a venereal infection (144). She possesses qualities akin to Shakespeare's dramatic characters—the commanding presence of Queen Margaret, Tamora and Cleopatra, but also the venality of Doll Tearsheet and Kate Keepdown. It is not far-fetched to think her portrayed as a kind of Renaissance dominatrix: "Thou art as tyrannous, so as thou art" (131: 1).

Sonnets 127–54 come close to portraiture in delineating her appearance and character. They explicitly state that she has dark eyes (132: 1–3), hair like "black wires" (130: 4) and dark skin (130: 3, 132: 14). With breasts that are "dun" (grey-brown or chestnut-brown), she has an appearance some regard as "coloured ill" (144: 4). Her poor reputation seems in part to have been earned. She is a temptress, a "heaven" that leads men to "hell" (129: 13–14), and "black" (Shakespeare's word) in her deeds (131: 13). She makes men become her "slave", imprisoned in her "jail" (133: 4, 13). She demands money, has men "mortgaged" to her "will" (134: 2), and those who beg for liberty must "pay the whole" (134: 14) yet remain "fast" bound (134: 8). Her sexual parts are her "will". The speaker would hide his "will" in hers (135: 6): "Ay, fill it full with wills, and my will one" (136: 6). Those parts are, however, available to all, as "[t]hings of great receipt" (136: 7). The speaker knows he is one of many: "Though in thy store's account I one must be" (136: 10). "Among a number", he counts himself almost "nothing", yet he cannot escape her control (136: 7–11).

The poems develop these disreputable implications in detail. Beautiful but available, she is a "bay where all men ride" (137: 6); her glances are "hooks" to which his "heart is tied" (137: 8). She may be a private space ("a several plot") but she is also "the wide world's common place" (137: 8–10). She "lies" in every sense of the word (138: 2, 13) and commits "foul faults" (148: 14). Sonnet 144 ends with an allusion to her passing on a venereal infection: "Till my bad angel fire my good one out" (144: 14).[4] Her actions result in "refuse" or leavings:

> Whence hast thou this becoming of things ill,
> That in the very refuse of thy deeds
> There is such strength and warrantise of skill,
> That, in my mind, thy worst all best exceeds? (150: 5–8).

Shakespeare's use of the noun "refuse" here adds a sense of squalid or sordid waste. The same sonnet continues,

> O! though I love what others do abhor,
> With others thou shouldst not abhor my state: (150: 11–12)

---

[4] On the sexual implications of these lines, see annotations in the editions by Kerrigan (1986), Duncan-Jones (1997), and Burrow (2002).

Colin Burrow's editorial annotation of these lines concurs with that by
Katherine Duncan-Jones: "a play on 'whore' or 'turn into a whore' seems
likely, as in the name 'Abhorson' (the executioner and son of a whore in
Measure) and in Desdemona's 'I cannot say "whore", / It does abhor me
now I speak the word', *Othello* 4.2.165–6. This sense may be picked out
by *with others* (by sleeping with others) in the next line" (Burrow 2002,
p. 680). Duncan-Jones adds a comment on the bawdy implications of the
word "raised" in the poem's penultimate line, especially when considered with the sonnet that follows it (Duncan-Jones 1997, 416). So who
might this remarkable woman have been? We can only guess. The pimp
William Mekyns confessed in November 1576 that "Mistress Elizabeth
Kelsey with a pearl in her ear is an arrant whore ... she continues the
fashion with Dutch, French, Spanish, Italian and all". She would sometimes wear a silk gown and was once rewarded with a gold ring (BCB
3. 92^v and 3. 170^r). According to Henry Boyer, a painter and pimp,
Kelsey kept company with other women including Anne Levens, one of
the highest-earning prostitutes in Elizabethan London (BCB 3. 188^r).
These women were carried by Mekyns and Boyer between two brothels
in and around Turnmill (or "Turnbull") Street, Clerkenwell, which were
jointly run by Luce Baynam and Gilbert East. These two figures were
central to London prostitution in the 1570 s. East was almost certainly
the man who took Master Pendar to Thomasine Breame at The White
Lion in Lombard Street. He was eventually arrested and interrogated:
but though her house was raided at midnight, Baynam, otherwise known
as "Black Luce", always somehow managed to escape prosecution (BCB
3. 22^v-25^r, 92^r-92^v; Salkeld 2012, 136–7).

We can trace key stages in the life of Gilbert East from a variety
of archival sources. He first surfaces on 31 October 1576 when he is
described as "of Turnmylstrete" and discharged from Bridewell. We learn
from his serving-maid Jane Lewis that East and his wife Margaret had
lived in Great Bartholomew's, Smithfield, in 1574, working in conjunction with brothel owners Thomas and Dorothy Wise in Whitefriars.
Together, they gained a reputation as "notorious infamous bawds and
adulterous persons, very abominable". Lewis stood accused of commit-
ting "adulteries with many persons whereby East got much money" (BCB
3. 266^r). In her testimony, Anne Levens confessed that she lay in several
houses across London, including at Gilbert East's and Black Luce's in
Clerkenwell. On 21 January 1577, Elizabeth Kirkman testified that East
kept Mary Dornelly for "great" and "wealthy" guests, dressing her in

a silk gown or velvet gaskins (trousers)—"not for the common sort". East and Black Luce were in business together and shared the profits of their houses equally. East would force his wife upstairs to sleep with men when no other girls or women were available. He took goods as well as cash in payment and kept his earnings in a dish in a cupboard "where he had great store of money all by lewdness". East's landlord, William Breche, the high constable of Clerkenwell, slept with Dornelly. According to Kirkman, the "abominableness" at East's house "is not meet to be spoken" (BCB 3. 280^{r-v}). In her testimony, Dornelly confirmed Kirkman's confession: "East and his wife are two abominable and lewd persons, none worse in the world" (BCB 3. 280^r-281^r).

East next surfaces on Bankside in 1588 in the Southwark token books where he is listed as living at Boar's Head Alley, in a property owned by Philip Henslowe (Foakes 2002, p. 249). This building seems to have adjoined "The Porpentine", a tenement or victualling house mentioned in *The Comedy of Errors* as the Courtesan's abode: "Sir, he dined with her there, at the Porpentine" (*Errors*, 5.1.276). The token books give East as there through the 1590s until his move in 1605 to a nearby tenement called "The Cardinal's Hat". Around 1600, Henslowe took East into his employment. We learn from Henslowe's book of memoranda or "*Diary*", that in that year he enjoyed regular dinners (on at least 29 occasions) with East and Peter Street, the carpenter who built the Globe, Fortune and (partially) Blackfriars playhouses. By 1603, East was working as Henslowe's bailiff, probably as a rent collector and enforcer (Foakes, 192–3, 245).

In testimony at Bridewell, East's wife is named Margaret. An entry in the marriage registers of All Hallows Church, Lombard Street, reads "6 February 1568 Gilbert East and Margaret Yugle". Assuming East married at around the age of 21, we can estimate approximate dates for significant events in his life. His birth year would have been around 1547; he would have been close to 30 when prosecuted at Bridewell in 1576, around 40 when living on Bankside in 1588 and just over 50 when working for Henslowe in 1600. A burial register entry for St. Saviour's, Southwark reads, "28 April 1622 Gilbert East". We cannot be absolutely certain that these records refer to the same person, but the name Gilbert East is rare in this period and the likelihood is strong. By the end of the sixteenth century, East was living and working in London's theatrical centre, had a close working relationship with Henslowe and would have known residents on Bankside around Boar's Head Alley. Those neighbours included several actors (including, in 1607, Shakespeare's brother Edmund and the King's Men player Lawrence Fletcher).

We know that in the 1570 s Jane Trosse worked on occasions from East's house in Turnmill Street, Clerkenwell. We know also that Breame was close to at least one man in the circle of Shakespeare's patron. Trosse was sufficiently well-known for Thomas Nashe to make a joke at her expense near the start of *The Unfortunate Traveller* (1592). Nashe quipped that the French town of "Turwin" [Térouanne] opened up in surrender "to more than Jane Trosse did" (Steane 1971, 254). It is barely plausible that Shakespeare was not acquainted with East through his associations with Henslowe, the Rose theatre and Bankside. He undoubtedly would have known "Courtney" and knew well the London suburb of Clerkenwell, its reputation and associations with Gray's Inn. Other Clerkenwell residents included co-actor Christopher Beeston, Edmund Tilney (Master of the Revels) and George Wilkins, the writer with whom Shakespeare collaborated on *Pericles*. In the 1570s, Matthew Shakespeare lived there too, married to Isabel, in all likelihood the sister of George Peele, dramatist and co-author of *Titus Andronicus* (Salkeld 2012, 142–144).

What then of Black Luce? We do not know for certain that she was dark-skinned although the evidence points in that direction. She is twice referred to as "Negro" or "Negra", a term used consistently throughout the sixteenth century to denote people of African or Iberian heritage. We learn from the Bridewell prosecutions that her brothel in Clerkenwell was frequented in the 1570s by "great" and "wealthy" men. Luce had been running her business in Clerkenwell since at least 1573. There is no record of her being brought before a magistrate (there are gaps in the records), and it is probable that, given the high status of some of her customers, she enjoyed some protection from prosecution. After a brief reference to her in the Bridewell records in 1578 (BCB 3.318^r), Black Luce disappears until she surfaces again as "Lucy Negro" on 20 December 1594 at the lawyers' college, Gray's Inn.

Accommodating some 200 students, Gray's Inn lay just north of Holborn, within easy walking distance of the infamous brothels of Turnmill Street and Clerkenwell. A record of its 1594 Christmas revels, eventually printed in 1688 under the title *Gesta Grayorum*, provides an account of the coronation of a mock "Prince" of Gray's Inn, known as "the Prince of Purpoole" (Bland 1968, p. 5).[5] The *Gesta Grayorum* is filled with the kind of bawdy, ribald humour one might anticipate from a sixteenth-century college for young men. It includes a list of invited guests attending that evening. Third in this list of guests is "*Lucy Negro*, Abbess *de Clerkenwell*" who "holdeth the Nunnery of *Clerkenwell*, with the Lands and Privileges thereunto belonging, of the Prince of *Purpoole* by Night-Service in *Cauda*, and to find a Choir of Nuns, with burning Lamps, to chant *Placebo* to the Gentlemen of the Prince's Privy-Chamber, on the Day of his Excellency's Coronation" (Bland 1968, pp. 16–17). The announcement of her presence is deeply satirical: the priory of Clerkenwell had been dissolved in the reign of Henry VIII, and by 1594 it had a very different kind of "abbess" whose votaries were known for their "burning lamps" (infected sexual parts). These "Nuns" were willing to provide "Night-service" and "chant *Placebo*" (i.e. play at being servile). Lest the bawdy implications of these terms seem unclear, "*Cauda*" literally refers to the tail area of an animal.[6]

The Gray's Inn guest-list places Black Luce in the Great Hall on 20 December 1594, just eight days before Shakespeare's company played *The Comedy of Errors* there as part of the festivities. According to the *Gesta Grayorum* account, the performance ended in chaos, leading to the occasion being remembered thereafter as "the Night of Errors" (Bland 1968, 34). In the play, Dromio of Syracuse says of the Courtesan, "Nay, she is worse, she is the devil's dam; / and here she comes in the habit of a light wench: and thereof / comes that the wenches say 'God damn me'; that's as / much to say 'God make me a light wench'. It is / written, they appear to men like angels of light: / light is an effect of fire, and fire will burn; / ergo, light wenches will burn. Come not near her" (4.2.50–4). His words chime with the *Gesta Grayorum*'s reference to "burning lamps" and the last line of Sonnet 144: "Till my bad angel fire my good one out" (144: 13–14). Shakespeare's play includes its own Black Luce. Dromio puns on the name of the kitchen-maid Luce, whom he describes

[5] Portpool was the name of the "manor" in Holborn in London in which Gray's Inn was situated.

[6] In these references, *Gesta Grayorum* puns on the following terms: OED, "knight-service" n. †1 "The military service which a knight was bound to render as a condition of holding his lands"; "Placebo", n. †2, "to sing (a) placebo: to play the sycophant or flatterer; to be servile"; and "Cauda", n., "A tail-like appendage, as *cauda equina*, the bundle of nerves at the base of the spinal cord".

as "swart" (3.2.100). A Gray's Inn audience was likely to catch the name's Italian sense (i.e. "luce" or "light"), the moral implications of a "light" woman, and the way the word sounded in English (i.e. "loose"). Dromio of Syracuse quips, "If thy name be called Luce (i.e. 'loose'), Luce thou hast answered him well" (3.1.53–4). In the *Gesta Grayorum*, the word "Negarian" is consistently used throughout that text as a reference to dark-skinned strangers (see Andrea in Traub 2016, 77–92).

"Lucy Negro" seems to have been well-known and admired at Gray's Inn. We know she entertained "great company" at her house in Clerkenwell (BCB 3.104^r and 279^v-280^r).[7] The *Gesta Grayorum* records that less than a week after the "Night of Errors", on 3 January, the Earls of Cumberland, Essex and Southampton joined William and Robert Cecil and others at the revels. Henry Carey, his son George and William Herbert, 3rd Earl of Pembroke were all members of Gray's Inn (Foster 1889, pp. 56, 66; Bland 1968, 35). The Earl of Essex and other noblemen brought the lawyers' festivities to a close in a celebration before Elizabeth at Court on Shrove Tuesday (Bland 1968, 88). Edmund Tilney and his brother Robert (who had a track record of liaisons with prostitutes) were also members at Gray's and lived in Clerkenwell. Intriguingly, a Nicholas Pinder also belonged to Gray's Inn. The Inn's admissions book has an entry on 30 April 1638 for Samuel "son of Nicholas Pinder, late of this Society" (Foster 1889, p. 217).

Black Luce was known well beyond the Inns of Court. In Thomas Heywood's *Edward IV, Part One* (1600) Captain Spicing bids the audience farewell before going to the gallows: "Commend me to black Luce, bouncing Besse, and lusty Kate, and the other pretty morsels of man's flesh. Farewell, pink and pinnace, fly boat and carvel, Turnbull and Spittle; I die like a man" (10: 162–5). Barnabe Barnes, in *The Devil's Charter* (1606), alludes to her as a kind of enchantress: "I conjure thee by *Negra Luciaes* name" (de Somogyi 1999, p. 55). Playwrights, it seems, could induce audience laughter by invoking her name. Black Luce would have been familiar (through East, if none other) with the playhouses in Shoreditch on Bankside. One of her pimps, painter Henry Boyer, also worked for Rose Flower, a Shoreditch prostitute bawdily mentioned in the *Gesta Grayorum* (Bland, 66). On 23 September 1601, the Bridewell

---

[7] "When Black Luce had any great guest …this examinate or such other women as East had should go to them to Luce's house and wear Mary Dornelly's gown, and Luce Baynham should have the one half of the money and East the other half" (BCB 3.279^v).

court heard of a "Master Taylor's son" who lay with Helen Balson (alias Hudson) "at Black Lewces house" (BCB, 4.263^r). By this time, Luce had acquired a public reputation and early readers of Sonnets 127–54 were likely to bring her to mind.

Beyond the 1606 allusion to her in *The Devil's Charter*, Black Luce disappears from the historical record. She is thereafter remembered only in the title of a mid-seventeenth-century piece of doggerel (Brook, 1661, p. 30).[8] Traces begin to fade for East too. The register of St. Saviour's, Southwark, records on 17 April 1603 the burial of a Margaret East, almost certainly Gilbert East's spouse. Margaret seems to have died at around the age of 53 years. There is no subsequent re-marriage of Gilbert East in the registers but the following year, Henslowe enters a "Lewce East" into his list of tenants at The Boar's Head (Foakes 2002, p. 249). There the trail goes cold until East's burial at St. Saviour's on 28 April 1622. In sum, what we know of Black Luce surfaces through documentary fragments, scraps and literary sources. Unlike many of her associates, including Thomasine Breame and Gilbert East, there is no record of her testimony. She herself is silent. We encounter her mainly via her connections with men—with East, the rowdy young lawyers of Gray's Inn, the magistrates at Bridewell, and possibly with Shakespeare. None of these men made her famous or significant: an entrepreneur, she did that for herself.

"Beauty Herself Is Black"

Shakespeare's sonnets to his black "mistress" repeatedly dwell on her eyes. They are not, as Petrarchan versifiers would have it, like the sun (130:1). Dark in hue, they appear to pity or mourn for the poet. They can seem cruel or wounding but sometimes soothe and bathe the "fire" of his love. Sonnet 153 picks up the topic of the mistress's "eye" or "eyes" from 130, but now it is the speaker who has been burned or sexually infected. Continuing this line of thought, the final two sonnets portray him seeking a cure for an unwanted "love-kindling fire" and "lively heat". Aware of other "men diseased", he applies "a seething bath" to "strange maladies" (153:3–8), caught through a "heart-inflaming brand", "hot desire" and "love's fire" (154:7–12). It is not just the speaker's heart that has been

---

[8] The poem is mistaken in its conflation of Black Luce with Luce Morgan.

inflamed. He confesses he has sought out a sweating tub in hope of cure, "But found no cure, the bath for my help lies / Where Cupid got new fire: my mistress' eye" (153: 13–14). The last two sonnets adapt a six-line epigram by sixth-century Byzantine poet Marianus Scholasticus, a fact that leads Edmondson and Wells to regard them as early, school-boy academic exercises. But dwelling on venereal infection and echoing lines about a "mistress", they fit the series 127–52 and seem to cap it off with baleful, even painful self-reproach. Filled with innuendo, these are verses for the bookseller's top shelf.

The "mistress" of Sonnets 127–54 possesses such charisma that the speaker declares: "Then will I swear beauty herself is black, / And all they foul that thy complexion lack" (132: 13–14). The sonnet here addresses whiteness and deems it foul by comparison. Repeatedly, Shakespeare runs an argument for seeing pale skin as needing cosmetics or "painting" and so false, but black skin as authentic and naturally beautiful. Aaron, in *Titus Andronicus*, scorns Chiron and Demetrius as "white-limed walls", saying, "Coal-black is better than another hue,/ In that it scorns to bear another hue" (4.2.97–99). Biron, in *Love's Labour's Lost*, replies to King Ferdinand's racist sentiments, with a similar reasoning:

> O, if in black my lady's brows be deck'd,
> It mourns that painting and usurping hair.
> Should ravish doters with a false aspect;
> And therefore is she born to make black fair.
> Her favour turns the fashion of the days,
> For native blood is counted painting now;
> And therefore red, that would avoid dispraise,
> Paints itself black to imitate her brow. (4.3.254–61)

In the first sub-sequence (Sonnets 1–126), lilies and roses are white and red; but in the second, no such roses lie in this woman's cheeks (127: 6). Like the night made new (27: 12), she gleams like a gem: "Thou art the fairest and most precious jewel" (131: 4).

When Shakespeare wrote in 132 that "beauty herself is black", this was not an altogether original proposition. As Farah Karim-Cooper has shown, other writers including George Gascoigne and Richard Brome expressed a similar idea (2006: 145–6). In a sonnet written "In prayse of the browne beauty, compiled for the love of Mistresse E. P. as foloweth", Gascoigne wrote: "A lovely nutbrowne face is best of all". Richard Brome, in his play *The English Moor, or the Mock Marriage* (composed around 1636/7), has the character Quicksand argue that a black complexion bears more authenticity than a white one painted with cosmetics: "Is not an *Ethiope*'s face his [ie. God's] workmanship?". Sonnet 127 proposes a similar kind of argument: dark complexions have been "slandered" as illegitimate. Since white women's cosmetics ("Art's false borrowed face", 127: 6) have "profaned" natural beauty, blackness owns an authenticity or truthfulness whiteness lacks. These thoughts follow with simple inevitability to an idea fundamentally challenging to whiteness: "now is black beauty's successive heir" (127: 3). Beauty no longer steps golden-haired and pale-hued out of an oyster-shell, as in a painting. The "old age" that belied blackness has passed and now black is "counted fair": for "every tongue says beauty should look so" (127: 14). It is not simply a question of finding whiteness wanting or admiring blackness: in Sonnets 127–54 Shakespeare makes a statement about art, creating what Caroline Randall Williams has termed "a black aesthetic" (in conversation: see also Randall Williams 2015).

It would be simplistic to think that Shakespeare's connections with race are limited to approving or disapproving lines in his works. As Reuben Espinosa has shown, they are far more extensive and complex than that (Espinosa, 2021; also Macdonald 2021). There are, undeniably, racist sentiments expressed in Shakespeare's works. Julia would rather not look on black Thurio (*The Two Gentlemen of Verona*, 5.2.13–14), Lysander rejects Hermia as a "tawny tartar" (*A Midsummer Night's Dream*, 3.2.264) and Portia notoriously mislikes the Prince of Morocco for his "complexion" after being explicitly asked not to (*The Merchant of Venice*, 2.7.79; cf. 2.1.1). The more overt racists in Shakespeare, such as Iago, Roderigo, Brabantio in *Othello* and Gratiano in *The Merchant of Venice*, tend to be characters that audiences despise. But attitudes in Shakespeare are rarely one-dimensional. To speak or write of race in the sonnets is to address anxieties about domination, rejection, compulsion, shame, betrayal, sexual intimacy and health. The drama of race in these poems concerns not just the poet's inferiority but the woman's disruptive, female power. We cannot pretend that the emotional, cultural and sexual energies of these poems are simple, that their syntax is not often tortuous and that their intentions are quickly apprehended. It is perhaps their absorption in emotional and physical pain, and their honesty, that make these twenty-seven poems seem so compelling.

The Sonnets are a set of intimate, personal documents rooted in their own wider social moment. They identify whiteness and call it "foul", and regard blackness as compellingly desirable and valuable. In doing so, they chime with other contemporary voices (including Gascoigne and Brome) that condemned the prejudice and cruelty so often inflicted by early modern colonialists. Even in the mid-sixteenth century, more enlightened views about skin colour were possible. In 1553, Edward VI wrote a letter of goodwill addressed to "all Kings, Princes, Rulers, Judges, and governors of the earth", asking that English merchants trading in far places might be received with the same goodwill. The letter was printed in the collected "Decades" of Pietro Martire (or "Peter Martyr") d'Anghiera (1457–1526), a series of works translated into English by Richard Eden and printed in the shop of Edward Sutton in 1555. In a chapter on "The colour of the Indians", Martyr writes, "One of the marvellous things that God useth in the composition of man, is colour: which doubtless cannot be considered without great admiration in beholding one to be white and another black, being colours utterly contrary. Some likewise to be yellow which is between black and white: and other of other colours as it were of diverse liveries". He notes that these skin-tones can differ "by degrees" and that there are "diverse sorts of blackness". He concludes by observing that God has created these differences "to declare his omnipotence and wisdom in such diversities of colours as appear not only in the nature of man, God's wisdom & power is seen in his works, but the like also in beasts, birds, and flowers, where diverse and contrary colours are seen in one little feather, or the leaves growing out of one little stalk" (Martire d' Anghiera, 1555, sig. 310^v-311^r). For Martyr, at least, a different, more hopeful history was possible: one small feather or the petals on a single stem could tell as much.

There were other similar voices too that directly challenged the violence of colonial forces. Having witnessed massacres and atrocities at first hand (many of which he recorded), Spanish Dominican friar and bishop Bartolomé de las Casas spent most of his life urging that Spanish colonisers treat indigenous people of the Americas with kindness, respect and understanding. Las Casas's accounts of Spanish brutality, and his pleas for restraint and diplomacy were repeatedly published in late sixteenth- and early seventeenth-century English editions (Las Casas 1577). In 1542, he successfully persuaded Charles V to pass the "New Laws of the Indies for the Good Treatment and Preservation of the Indians". He later defended the rights of indigenous cultures in the Valladolid Debate of 1550–1551 (Clayton 2009; Castro 2009). Although these perspectives and laws would soon be eclipsed, forgotten or ignored, and used by the

English for anti-Spanish propaganda (Brook 1656), they were still circulating in print even in the mid-seventeenth century. To draw attention to voices such as those of Peter Martyr or Bartholomé de Las Casas in no way diminishes racism's long, insidious and murderous history. It is merely to highlight that there were choices to be made then as now.

CONCLUSION

In *Love's Labour's Lost*, we have another "dark lady", Rosaline. Shakespeare seems initially to have wavered over whether Rosaline should be pale or dark-skinned. Biron asks Costard to deliver a letter into her "white hand" (3.1.163), yet Ferdinand also observes, "By heaven, thy love is black as ebony" (4.3.243). Biron's reply includes a sonnet, much in the style of Sonnet 127, that has the following line: "All ignorant the soul that sees thee without wonder" (4.2.112). The line captures the poet's feeling for the brown-skinned woman in Sonnets 127–54, notwithstanding her many betrayals. For all her vices, there is virtue in her complexion—a potential to dazzle, captivate, create wonder and poetry. Those who lack her skin colour seem, by comparison, "foul". Shakespeare seems to have understood that whiteness could be "foul" and "ignorant". We know it often still is. A different future, these poems state, was possible. In the end, we do not know who the so-called "dark lady" of these poems was. Sonnets 127–54 do not tell us. They point not to an identity but to that hoped-for future: "now is black beauty's successive heir" (127: 3). If, after four hundred years, that third line still unsettles, so much more the need to address the reasons why.

REFERENCES

Bridewell Court of Governors' Minute Book (BCB), Bethlem Museum of the Mind, Beckenham, Kent, UK.

Bernadette Andrea, 2016. "Amazons, Turks, and Tartars in the Gesta Grayorum and The Comedy of Errors" in *The Oxford Handbook of Shakespeare and Embodiment: Gender, Sexuality and Race*, ed. by Valerie Traub, 77–92. Oxford and New York: Oxford University Press.

Bland, Desmond (ed.). 1968. *Gesta Grayorum; or, The History of the High and Mighty Prince Henry, Prince of Purpoole, Anno Domini 1594*. Liverpool: Liverpool University Press.

Brook, Nathanial (printer). 1661. *Wit and Drollery*. London.

Burrow, Colin (ed.). 2002. *William Shakespeare: The Complete Sonnets and Poems*. Oxford and New York: Oxford University Press.

Castro, Daniel. 2009. *Another Face of Empire*. Durham, NC and London: Duke University Press.

Clayton, Lawrence. 2009. "Bartolomé de las Casas and the African Slave Trade", *History Compass* 7, 6 (November 2009): 1526–1541.

de Somogyi, Nick (ed.). 1999. *Barnabe Barnes, The Devil's Charter*. London: Nick Hern Books.

Duncan-Jones, Katherine (ed.). 1997. *Shakespeare's Sonnets*. London: Thomson Learning.

Edmondson, Paul and Wells, Stanley (eds.). 2020. *All the Sonnets of Shakespeare*. Cambridge and New York: Cambridge University Press.

Espinosa, Reuben, 2021. *Shakespeare on the Shades of Racism*. London and New York: Routledge.

Foakes, R. A. (ed). 2002. *Henslowe's Diary*, 2nd ed. Cambridge and New York: Cambridge University Press.

Foster, Joseph, 1889. *The Register of Admissions to Gray's Inn, 1521-1889, Together with the Register of Marriages in Gray's Inn Chapel, 1695-1754*. London: Hansard.

Habib, Imtiaz. 2008. *Black Lives in the English Archives, 1500-1677: Imprints of the Invisible*. Farnham and Burlington, VT: Ashgate.

Jacobson, Howard. 2010. "'Call off the Search for the Real Dark Lady. Shakespeare wasn't Shakespeare. And I'm Not Me". *The Independent*, 11 January 2013, accessible at https://www.independent.co.uk/voices/comment/call-off-the-search-for-the-real-dark-ladyshakespeare-wasn-t-shakespeare-and-i-m-not-me-8448529.html.

Karim-Cooper, Farah. 2006. *Cosmetics in Shakespeare and Renaissance Drama*. Edinburgh: Edinburgh University Press.

Kaufmann, Miranda. 2017. *Black Tudors: The Untold Story*. London: Oneworld.

Kerrigan, John (ed.). 1986. *William Shakespeare: The Sonnets and A Lover's Complaint*. London: Penguin.

Kingsford, C. L. (ed.). 1908. *John Stow: A Survey of London*, 2 vols. Oxford: Clarendon Press.

Las Casas, Batholomé de. *The history of trauayle in the West and East Indies, and other countreys* (London, 1577); *The Spanish colonie, or Briefe chronicle of the acts and gestes of the Spaniardes in the West Indies* (London, 1583); and *The Tears of the Indians* (London, 1656).

MacDonald, Joyce Green. 2021. "The legend of Lucy Negro". In *The Routledge Companion to Black Women's Cultural Histories*, ed. by Janell Hobson. London and New York: Routledge.

Martire d' Anghiera, Pietro (Peter Martyr). 1555. *The Decades of the Newe Worlde or West India*. London.

Nelson Alan H., 1998. "George Buc, William Shakespeare, and the Folger *George a Greene*". *Shakespeare Quarterly*, 49, 1 (Spring, 1998): 74–83.

Nubia, Onyeka. 2019. *England's* Other *Countrymen: Black Tudor Society*. London: Zed Books.

Olusoga, David. 2016. *Black and British: A Forgotten History*. London: Macmillan.

Purchas, Samuel. 1626. *Purchas his pilgrimage. Or Relations of the world and the religions obserued in all ages and places discouered, from the Creation vnto this present*. London.

Sanghera, Sathnam, 2021. *Empireland: How Modern Britain is Shaped by its Imperial Past*. London: Penguin.

Salkeld, Duncan. 2012. *Shakespeare Among the Courtesans: Prostitution, Literature and Drama, 1500-1650*. Farnham and Burlington, VT: Ashgate.

Schalkwyk, David. 1994. "'She never told her love': Embodiment, Textuality and Silence in Shakespeare's Sonnets and Plays". *Shakespeare Quarterly*, 45 (1994): 381-407.

Steane, J. B. 1971. *Thomas Nashe: The Unfortunate Traveller and Other Works*. Harmondsworth: Penguin.

Sullivan, C. Constable, "Henry (1562–1613), Polemicist and Poet". *Oxford Dictionary of National Biography*, retrieved 5 January 2022, from https://www.oxforddnb.com/view/, https://doi.org/10.1093/ref:odnb/9780198614128.001.0001/odnb9780198614128-e-6103.

Traub, Valerie (ed.). 2016. *The Oxford Handbook of Shakespeare and Embodiment: Gender, Sexuality and Race*. Oxford and New York: Oxford University Press.

Wall, A. 2004. "Rich [née Devereux], Penelope, Lady Rich (1563–1607), Noblewoman". *Oxford Dictionary of National Biography*, retrieved 5 January. 2022, from https://www.oxforddnb.com/view/https://doi.org/10.1093/ref:odnb/9780198614128.001.0001/odnb9780198614128-e-23490.

Williams, Caroline Randall. 2015. *Lucy Negro, Redux*. Ampersand Books.

CHAPTER 20

Shakespeare's Sonnets in the ELT Classroom: The Paradox of Early Modern Beauty and Twenty-First Century Social Media

Simona Laghi

In recent years, the value of teaching literature in ELT classrooms has come in for renewed attention. The study of literary texts is seen not only to foster language skills, but also to generate insights into other cultures and histories which, in turn, promotes open-mindedness and self-reflection in ELT students. Due to their complexity, Shakespeare's works are seen as particularly suitable to boost advanced skills and to empower students to participate in the world beyond their classroom, exploring controversial topics that are closely interwoven with their lives but not easy to address and explicate (Thomson and Turchi 2016, 7–9). Indeed, as Greenblatt argues, the Renaissance appears to be the period

S. Laghi (✉)
University of Rome "Tor Vergata", Rome, Italy
e-mail: simona.laghi@uniroma2.it

in which our civilization originates (hence the term "early modern"), and it anticipates contemporary issues whose "traces" can be found in Shakespeare's works (Greenblatt 1980, 74; 1988, 7). But while this approach is commonly applied to the plays, little attention has been devoted to the Sonnets' potential. This essay shows how Sonnets 127–130, 131, and 132 might be the starting point to reflect on the impact that unrealistic digital images disseminated via social media have on identity formation as well as on mental health, and how these images become the basis of discrimination against people whose external appearance departs from accepted models. The ubiquity of social networking sites spurs us to investigate how digital images of the body influence users and what consequences this might have on psychological health, interpersonal relationships, education, and working environments. It has been shown that there is a connection between social media usage and body dissatisfaction, self-objectification, dieting, and cosmetic surgery (Faradouly and Vartanian 2016, 1; Di Gesto et al. 2021). The increase in self-exposure, especially the activity of posting selfies, seems to affect self-esteem (Veldhuis and Alleva 2020, 4). Indeed, social media users are creators of content and their aspiration to be represented according to an unrealistic ideal of beauty impels them to use the editing software offered by the photo-based media to modify body shape, complexion, and skin colour. It has been proved that this activity detaches users from reality and "can alter an individual's perception of one's appearance" with a consequent increase in the acceptance of cosmetic surgery with the hope of fitting the aesthetic canon (Di Gesto et al. 2021). The obsession with exterior appearance and its representation shows that human identity is still the result of a process of self-fashioning with similar features as those illustrated by Greenblatt analysing the Renaissance (Greenblatt 1980). Hence, a teaching activity on the impact of digital images of the body in forming identity might be meaningful for twenty-first-century students and exceptionally valuable if the springboard for such an investigation is offered by Shakespeare's Sonnets.

After an introductory section on how the Sonnets' reception has influenced their reading, understanding, and teaching, this essay gives an overview of beliefs concerning the representation of the self in early modern England with the aim of highlighting that these Sonnets disclose a criticism of stereotypes about external appearance and identity that were widespread in Shakespeare's time. The focus is on how the symbolism of colours, in particular the binarisms of black and white as well as blackness and fairness, defined human identity. Each Sonnet is then analysed in the form of an intercultural and interdisciplinary teaching proposal that aims to encourage reflection and debate on how the circulation of a stereotyped idea of beauty on social media might create bias that affects people's well-being and leads to discrimination.

THE SONNETS IN THE TWENTY-FIRST CENTURY

In ELT literature anthologies, the focus is generally on Shakespeare's Sonnets 18 and 130, which are seen as authentic material of great value to improve students' language skills and knowledge of the poems' structure, possibly with some insights into Petrarch's poetry (Bower et al. 2002; Moss 2017). Focussing on these two Sonnets enables readers to explore in parallel the themes of procreation and love through the figures of the "Fair Youth" and the "Dark Lady" (De Grazia 1993; Bell 2007).

Malone's editorial work, published in 1780, which divided the Sonnets into two sequences directed at two addressees, continues to have a significant influence (Shakespeare 2020, 22). Yet, as Jane Kingsley-Smith highlights, the idea that the Sonnets are ordered according to a narrative sequence appears baseless and misleading (Kingsley-Smith 2019, 37). The assumption that the first part is addressed to a mysterious "Fair Friend", possibly the Earl of Pembroke or Shakespeare's patron, the Earl of Southampton, and the second part, from Sonnet 127, to a "Dark Lady", possibly the Italian Emilia Lanier or Mary Fitton, although representing a fascinating detour into Shakespeare's biography, actually narrows the Sonnets' potential and their understanding. This can also be seen as a misreading, because the gender of the addressees appears "unstable and fluid" (Shakespeare 2020, 27). As far as Sonnets 127, 130, and 132 are concerned, they are likely to be addressed to a female character, while 131 might be addressed to either a male or a female (Shakespeare 2020, 28). Moreover, there is no description of a woman as a "dark lady" in the Sonnets, so this figure appears only to be an invention aimed at labelling the addressee (Kingsley-Smith 2019, 37). Furthermore, it seems that "other voices" are in the Sonnets, since they are likely to have resulted from collaboration with other writers, and there might be more than two addressees (Kingsley-Smith 2019, 10). Hence, as Edmondson and Wells argue, the biographical approach appears "simplistic and overrides the nuances and complexities" of the Sonnets (Shakespeare 2020,

23). Possibly, the attempt to consider the Sonnets as evidence of the poet's life story and the overall attempt to narrow the addressees to two people defined by gender in order to trace a narrative sequence lies in the need to make them "easier" not only to be critically discussed but mainly to be taught (Kingsley-Smith 2019, 3). This way of reading the Sonnets actually reduces their potential. Instead, by freeing them from this biographical approach and the sharp distinction into two sequences and genders, the perspective might be widened and enriched to include twenty-first-century readers' feelings, needs, and interests. Indeed, more than a narrative sequence, the Sonnets appear as a collection of poems, possibly of private reflections, where the poet's voice takes the shape of a unique Sonnet, or a pair of Sonnets or "mini-sequences" of Sonnets linked together (Shakespeare 2020, 17). Hence, the Sonnets might be seen "as a series of episodes, like snapshots taken at different times" on the feelings and suffering that love and passion can provoke (Edmondson and Wells 2004, 81). As Edmondson and Wells point out, their power lies in their "multi-layered subjectivities", in the plurality and fluidity of identities, so we can imagine reading them as if the poet's voice were addressed to us instead of trying to fix our attention on a specific, hypothetical person (Shakespeare 2020, 32). Attention should shift from the narrative sequence to the relationship between the poet's voice and the readers. Thus, in the education field, students might be spurred to be active readers to find in these poems what is meaningful for them in the contemporary scenario.

FASHIONING IDENTITY AND THE IDEAL OF BEAUTY: FROM EARLY MODERN TO POSTMODERN

In the Renaissance, the image of the human body was at the core of the ontological interpretation of the world encompassing the medical, political, legal, and religious domains. The human body functioned as a visual and literary metaphor that encapsulated the essence of the hierarchically structured Elizabethan society, which was theatrically represented. Rhetoric was the tool through which the individual was forged, since it "served to theatricalise culture, or rather it was the instrument of a society which was already deeply theatrical" (Greenblatt 1980, 162).

Clothes, countenance, and complexion were perceived as the visual representation of the individual's identity like costumes for actors on stage. During the Tudor dynasty, sumptuary laws were strengthened to classify and control people according to their external appearance and allow for their classification at first sight. At the end of the sixteenth century, there was already the awareness that dress was no longer a reliable mark of identity and rank; hence, the suspicion arose that an individual could perform a false public persona through a misleading outward appearance (Watt 2013, 52–53). It is no coincidence that the idea that human identity was a process of self-fashioning became widespread in this period (Greenblatt 1980, 2). The verb "fashion" started to be adopted by the poet Edmund Spenser with reference to the "forming of the self" and then circulated in other domains, implying an artful and creative process associated with the concept of transformation (Greenblatt 1980, 169; Jones and Stallybrass 2012, 1).

Complexion, like apparel, was perceived as a meaningful display of human identity. As Riehl points out, in the early modern period the face was "a site of power and means of empowerment: epistemological, political, and even divine" (Riehl 2010, 6). Interestingly, the word "face" comes from the Latin *facies*, which means form, appearance, figure, and it seems to have an intimate etymological interrelation with the word *facere*, which means to make, as well as being the root of the word "fashion". In Greek the word "face" is *prosopon*, which also stands for the actor's mask, which is called *persona* in Latin. Furthermore, the word "personality" derives from *persona*, a fact that reveals an intriguing link between this word and the actor's mask (Watt 2013, 79). As Watt points out, in order to be recognized by the law, human beings need to be represented by an abstract construction; hence, "the legal subject is said to have legal personality" as if concealed under the "mask of legal personality" (Watt 2013, 79). Therefore, the words "face", "person", "personality", and "fashion" seem to refer to the concept of human identity conceived as a creative process similar to that of an actor on stage.

In the Renaissance, the symbolism of colour was intertwined with medical as well as religious discourses and circulated through poetry, art, and material culture (Karim-Cooper 2021, 19; Hall 1995, 219). As Harvey points out, "colour is one of the most potent early modern discourses about the material person, about the relations between psychic life, gender, and the increasingly inscrutable, unreadable surface of the body"; indeed, bodily exterior appearance was also considered the display of the internal humours' interaction, the visual evidence of the "hidden interior" (Harvey 2007, 316–317) and "a reflection of the inner self" (Karim-Cooper 2021, 18). The process of fashioning one's own identity implied a reaction "to something perceived as alien, strange, or hostile" (Greenblatt 1980, 3–9). One of the most powerful rhetorical devices to self-fashion identity was the antinomy of black and white as well as blackness and fairness. As Hall points out, this binarism becomes "infused with concerns over skin colour, economics and gender politics" (Hall 1995, 2). Indeed, fairness and a pale complexion were perceived as natural, normal, and a dominant feature, while blackness not only had a wide range of negative associations, such as evil, death, and mourning, but was also associated with otherness (Karim-Cooper 2021, 19–21).

White and black as well as light and darkness expressed the two opposite poles of Good and Evil: the first was the epitome of God, life, the *civitate dei*; the latter was the epitome of Satan's power, death, and corruption, the *civitate hominum* (Caporicci 2014, 200). The aesthetic of fairness, far from being a trivial question of fashion, was an instrument to "circumscribe women" (Hall 1995, 8). Indeed, white was perceived as the colour of good and purity and the "component of the construction of womanhood" (Karim-Cooper 2021, 17–19), as opposed to black, which was associated with masculinity (Matthew-Grieco 1993, 62; Hall 1995, 8–9).

Beauty was conceived as harmony and balance of proportion, which were achieved by the "suppression of any distinctive, individuating marks" with a consequent "impersonality" (Greenblatt 2010, 22). Indeed, poetry and art celebrated "the smooth, unblemished, radiantly fair, and essentially featureless face and body" as the "cultural ideal" (Greenblatt 2010, 32). Consequently, an unconventional or marked body was seen with suspicion (Greenblatt 2010, 35). The belief in the close interrelation between outward appearance and inward nature led to identifying and judging people by relying on their exteriority also in the field of justice. Indeed, during trials, especially in witchcraft, the accused's body and face were scrutinized in search of the devil's marks or changes in countenance and complexion, because these were considered proof of guilt (Laghi 2021, 118).

At the core of the symbolism of colours was the monarch's image, whose countenance, complexion, and apparel contributed to creating a visual language that aimed to articulate and propagandize royal power. Painters purposely created the Tudor monarch's images "as icons of white privilege, divinity, and power" (Karim-Cooper 2021, 19) and Elizabeth I was represented as "the personification of divinely-ordained, imperial kingship" (Raffield 2010, 2). Her gorgeous dresses were an instrument to legitimize her royal authority (Carpi 2016), as was her expressionless face. It was an "empowering asset" because it was fashioned according to the early modern aesthetic canon and perceived as idealistically beautiful (Riehl 2010, 37). She was aware of this: "We princes are set on stage in the sight and view of all the world duly observed; the eyes of many behold our actions, a spot is soon spied in our garments, a blemish noted quickly in our doings" (quoted in Riehl 2010, 58). According to some reports, she used to wear a thick layer of makeup to emphasize her bright whiteness but also to disguise any marks of imperfection (Riehl 2010, 56). This process of beautification made her appear "a blank, expressionless mask" (Greenblatt 2010, 22–24). Her excessively and unrealistically white face reinforced the cult of fairness, as in the Ditchley portraits, to evoke the virtues of the female figure, such as purity and chastity, and to share them with her kingdom (Hall 1996, 466).

Given the importance of the symbolism of colour in fashioning identity, women tried to achieve radiant and fair skin according to this model. Thus, they tried to beautify their face with a thick layer of cosmetics, as if they were covering it with a mask. Yet, in doing so, they were subject to the accusation of deceiving onlookers artificially (Karim-Cooper 2006, 46). Indeed, as Karim-Cooper highlights, women were trapped in a paradox: "The mocking tone of condemnation of cosmetic embellishment places women in a paradoxical trap in which strict codes are set down, but the artificial pursuit of such codes is unacceptable" (Karim-Cooper 2006, 14). Many pamphlets and sermons circulated with criticisms of those women who tried to follow the aesthetic canon, who were apostrophized as "animals, witches, foreigners, prostitutes and even criminals ... idle, unnatural, sinful, hideous and monstrous" (Karim-Cooper 2006, 37), or accused of "altering" the face given by God (Matthews-Grieco 1993, 61). Philip Stubbes in *The Anatomy of Abuses* (1583) gave voice to this anti-cosmetic argument, stigmatizing cosmetics as the Devil's invention, an offence to God, and a sin (Stubbes 1877–1879, 67).

Shakespeare problematized the bias in conceptualizing beauty by representing striking female characters such as Rosaline in *Love's Labour's Lost*, whose black features are celebrated by Biron with a striking similarity to Sonnets 127 and 132 (Shakespeare 2020, 55–60). The Egyptian queen Cleopatra and Hermia in *A Midsummer Night's Dream* are also depicted as having dark complexions, yet they are attractive and beloved. With such "black beauties" Shakespeare was being highly innovative, since he created "forms of beauty that violate the prevailing cultural norms"

(Greenblatt 2010, 41). This challenging of beauty stereotypes highlights the fact that: "Beauty inheres in the beloved's identity, including those aspects of the identity—strange, idiosyncratic, imperfect—that do not fit normative expectation" (Greenblatt 2010, 44). Among these Shakespearean "black beauties" is the lady of the Sonnets who, although she does not fit into the aesthetic canon of fairness and lacks bodily perfection, is irresistibly seductive.

In fact, in this period, there was a vogue in poetry that prized black beauty (Schoenfeldt 2010, 99), as well as a fad for wearing cameos carved in onyx featuring black African figures. This jewellery could have a miniature portrait of an aristocrat locked inside it and was given as a gift. Interestingly, this habit was connected with the circulation of Sonnets (Hall 1995, 213). According to Hall, considering that art historians associate the increase in portraits with the "rise of individualism", the fad for exchanging cameos and miniature portraits also had a small role in the definition of aristocratic identity (Hall 1995, 213). In particular, the combination of onyx cameos with miniature jewellery reveals a rhetoric that "draws attention to skin colour in a way that may reinforce the value of whiteness" (Hall 1996, 464). This interrelation between visual culture and poetry in defining identity through the binarisms of black and white, blackness and fairness, darkness and light spurs us to analyse whether the Sonnets adhere to this rhetorical scheme or whether they challenge it.

Revealing Beauty Paradoxes and Bias Through the Sonnets

This discourse on beauty and identity that circulated in the Renaissance appears to be embedded in Sonnets 127, 130, 131, and 132. In this section, we will see that Shakespeare challenges the stereotypes by proposing a revolutionary concept of beauty and identity that is freed from the strict rules of the aesthetic canon and open to diversity. Such findings are potentially revealing for twenty-first-century students as social media users. As Hyman and Eklund argue, learning literature should be "the cultivation of a way of looking at the world" and literary sources like Shakespeare's works are "sites of contested meanings" that activate reflection on matters that directly concern students' lives (Hyman and Eklund 2019, 6–8). Therefore, through these Sonnets, students in advanced ELT classrooms may not only increase their language skills but also, by comparing early modern and postmodern ontological paradigms in interpreting exterior appearance, enhance their awareness of how unrealistic digital images of the body may affect one's self-esteem and health, as well as leading to the unequal and unfair treatment of those whose physical appearance departs from the models propagandized by social networks. Although the word "black" that recurs in these Sonnets has led scholars to reflect on the lady's ethnicity, this proposal aims to make students aware of discrimination based on outward appearance in a broader sense, so the debate might include the question of racial prejudice but not be limited to it.[1]

Considering that Shakespeare challenged stereotypes indirectly through metaphors, students might be involved in activities geared towards discovering the rhetorical strategies of his criticism. A close reading of each Sonnet enhances the learners' language skills and, as Thomson and Turchi point out, the OED might be helpful to explore the changes in the meaning and use of words (Thomson and Turchi 2016, 14–15–46). Prior knowledge of Renaissance material culture and the conception of the representation of the self might be helpful to activate students' interest, involving them more in the analysis (Thomson and Turchi 2016, 24). Indeed, Sonnets 127, 130, 131, and 132 challenge the rhetoric behind the binarism of black and white, echoing a revolutionary idea of light and darkness that was springing up in philosophy and in visual art in the Renaissance. As Caporicci highlights, Giordano Bruno in *De la Causa, Principio et Uno* (1584) conceives the universe as "a monism based on the non-hierarchical identity of spirit and matter" (Caporicci 2014, 202). Interestingly, in his philosophical treatise, Bruno explains this concept by quoting Psalm 139: "*Tenebrae non oscurabuntur a te. Nox sicut dies illuminabitur. Sicut Tenebrae eius, ita et lumen eius*' [Yea, the darkness hideth not from thee, but night shineth as the day: the darkness and the light are both alike to thee]" (Bruno 2004, 68). Moreover, in specifying that spirit and matter are unified in one principle, he points out: "two principles coincide into one, which is at the same time abyss and darkness, clarity and light, profound and impenetrate obscurity, and supernatural and inaccessible light" (Bruno 2004, 93). Finally, in an *Essay on Magic* concerning how to establish social bonds, he explains that things that appear to be opposite are actually complementary, adopting once more the metaphor of light and darkness: "we should especially

---

[1] On the reception and recent scholarship on the figure of the "Dark Lady", see Jane Kingsley Smith, *The Afterlife of Shakespeare's Sonnets* (Cambridge: Cambridge University Press, 2019), 229–242.

realize that a bright light extinguishes a bright light, and that without darkness, light does not shine, gleam, glitter and please" (Bruno 2004, 169). Hence, it seems that by using these metaphors Bruno overturns the idea that darkness and light are opposite poles and conceives them as complementary and equal in value in the infinite universe. This new sensibility is in visual art too. In Caravaggio's works human bodies are depicted with the clever use of dark colours so as to appear natural (Caporicci 2014, 205). Although it is unknown if Shakespeare was familiar with Bruno's theory and Caravaggio's paintings, he seems to share the same revolutionary perception: light and darkness, black and white, fairness and blackness coexist and are complementary in a non-hierarchical universe.

On the basis of this knowledge, the analysis might start from Sonnet 127, which seems to call abruptly for a change in fashion because it "signals its deliberate violation of literary and aesthetic conventions" (Schoenfeldt 2010, 98). With the words "In the old age black was not counted fair, /Or if it were, it bore not beauty's name; /But now is black beauty's successive heir", the poet seems to mark the passage between the past and present fashions, like those of prizing blackness in poetry and exchanging onyx cameos as gifts. Hence, Sonnet 127 appears to be conceived according to the same rhetoric of the binarism of black and white. Students might be guided to discuss whether this hyperbolic celebration of black, which appears to be an aspiration to be black, expresses the poet's adherence to fashion so as to strengthen the predominance of fairness as a mark of aristocratic identity, or whether it is a critique of the paradox hidden in the discourse on beauty. Indeed, Shakespeare mocks those who excessively rely on fairness and are deceived by a false appearance: "Fairing the foul with art's false borrowed face"; thus, he seems to adhere to the anti-cosmetic argument. It is worth pointing out that this Sonnet raises questions around exterior appearance that are still unresolved today. While in the Renaissance the model of female identity was propagandized through portraits, jewellery, and poetry, in the twenty-first century it is fashioned through digital images and amplified on social media. Paradoxes and bias still endure today. Indeed, those who self-fashion their body image according to aesthetic stereotypes with the aim of being positively assessed by their followers not only might suffer from social anxiety and eating disorders, but if they succeed in perfectly beautifying themselves according to aesthetic rules, they are often stigmatized for artificially shaping their body and face using cosmetics, surgery, or enhancement filters. Conversely, those who fail in this process of beautification or do not conform to the aesthetic canon but equally expose themselves are met with disapproval. Students' attention might be drawn to the fact that this method of comparing and assessing the body crosses the threshold between social networking and face-to-face relationships, becoming an insidious form of discrimination also in educational and working environments (Rhode 2010, 93).

Sonnets 130, 131, and 132 are linked to Sonnet 127 since they challenge the discourse on beauty by looking at black and white, darkness and light, from a new angle. Sonnet 130 might be compared to Petrarch's Sonnet "Erano i capei d'oro e l'aura sparsi", which is an example of the fusion between Provençal and classical elements (Kennedy 2011, 94). Petrarch prizes Laura's "earthly existence" with words that refer to light and brightness, and even compares her to an "angelic form" and a "celestial spirit" so as to emphasize her virtuous and fair interiority (Strier 2007, 79). Students might discuss whether Shakespeare abjures this model through parody or whether he recognizes its authority but overturns it to assert the singularity of his love and to highlight the equal value of diverse bodily features. The Sonnet is structured according to the Petrarchan tradition of the blazon, which is the celebration of the beloved by a "description that catalogues the parts of a woman's body" (Riehl 2010, 110). However, instead of emphasizing the canon of fairness, the poet proclaims his independence from it. Indeed, after the unconventional description of the lady, the reader is taken by surprise because the poet says: "I love to hear her speak", and she is "rare". As Strier highlights, "Shakespeare's speaker's point is not that his beloved is inferior; it is rather that she is quite special. He uses a word that comes close to asserting absolute value" (Strier 2007, 81). Interestingly, "rare" does not only mean "unusually good, fine, or worthy, splendid, excellent", but it also refers to something that is "uncommon, infrequent, unusual, exceptional" (OED). Hence, the poet seems to say that, although the lady departs from the aesthetic canon of fairness, she is attractive in his eyes; or rather, it is precisely because of her unconventional features, which mark her uniqueness and personality, that she appears lovable. One might notice that Sonnet 130 seems to be a cameo or a miniature portrait in words that could be compared to a digital snapshot that circulates on social networks today but, instead of being artificially manipulated with filters, it faithfully records the image of the lady as she really is, making her appear unique, different from all the others, and for this reason beloved.

Sonnets 131 and 132 highlight the bias according to which only those who fit the aesthetic canon of fairness can provoke the suffering of love. The discourse on the symbolism of colours and the interrelation between interior nature and exterior appearance are problematized with reference to conflicting feelings. In Sonnet 131, the poet expresses the suffering provoked by his passion through the use of the adjectives "tyrannous" and "cruel", which echo the Provençal and Petrarchan *topos* according to which the lady's attractive power hurts the lover. These expressions have been interpreted as directly addressing the lady's unfairness, both with reference to her exterior appearance and her inner nature, also due to the expression "In nothing art thou black save in thy deeds" (Duncan-Jones 1997, 376). Hence, students might discuss if these words echo Petrarch's *topos* or rather if they refer to the Renaissance symbolism of colours that associated black with negative connotations.

Sonnet 132 concludes this reflection on exterior appearance and its bias. The poet returns to expressing his suffering with the words "torment" and "pain" but ends with an eloquent couplet that challenges beauty stereotypes: "Then will I swear beauty herself is black /And all they foul that thy complexion lack". In order to prize his lover, he says that her black eyes, "those two mourning eyes", surpass in beauty "the morning sun of heaven", "the gray cheeks of East", and even the "full star", that is Venus the evening star (Shakespeare 2020, 60). The expression "gray cheeks of East" might be the personification of the "twilight of the early dawn" (Shakespeare 1997, 378) or of "the grey eastern clouds" (Shakespeare 2020, 237). According to Duncan-Jones, this expression is an ironic reference to the lady's face: "for in no scale of beauty can human cheeks be prised for being *grey*" (Shakespeare 1997, 378). However, students might observe that grey is only a shade resulting from the mix of black and white and that dawn, which is echoed in this Sonnet, is the moment when the darkness of night and the light of day merge. Moreover, even the most radiant skin might appear grey if it is scarcely illuminated, for example, at dawn. Hence, the poet looks at black and white as well as dark and light with a new perspective that breaks with the traditional rhetorical binarism. Thus, the expression "gray cheeks of East" does not necessarily have a negative connotation but it might contribute to giving in words a truthful snapshot of his lover's face, maybe at dawn.

Hence, conventional early modern symbolism is challenged in these Sonnets. White and black, light and dark, are not perceived as being opposite poles trapped in a rigid binarism but as both representing the shades of the infinite universe. There is not a unique type of beauty but an infinite range of beauties due to the combination of colours and bodily features. This reflection draws attention to the poet's awareness that the infinite variations of the shades of black and white, day and night, light and darkness mirror the diversity of human beings and their uniqueness in a variety of identities.

Although at first sight it seems that Shakespeare supports the anti-cosmetic argument, abjuring a fair complexion as the result of a process of beautification, or that he is referring to the fashion for prizing blackness in poetry or for exchanging cameos, further reflections reveal that his discourse gives voice to a criticism of the paradoxes and bias underlying exterior appearance in which early modern women were trapped and proposes a fluid, multifaceted, and inclusive concept of beauty and personal identity. It seems that these Sonnets are an attempt to break through the thick layer of cosmetics, which, like a theatrical mask, represented personal identity in the early modern period, so as to reveal beneath it the diversity of human beings. Therefore, these Sonnets could not only enhance students' language skills in facing a complex text but also empower them to discuss contemporary themes related to the representation of the self. As in the Renaissance, the twenty-first-century obsession with unrealistic physical perfection is a controversial question that concerns the self-fashioning of human identity, including the concept of "legal personality". Indeed, aesthetic stereotypes are still today like masks that represent the individual as a legal subject; however, if they are too strict and thick, they might conceal and suffocate the humanity behind them. Therefore, those who wear this mask to adhere to the stereotyped ideal of bodily perfection and identity are accused of deceiving onlookers, while those who do not fit it seem as if they are not wearing the mask of legal personality; they do not appear protected by the law, becoming targets of discrimination and exclusion from fair opportunities.

References

Bell, Ilona. 2007. "Rethinking Shakespeare's Dark Lady." In *A Companion to Shakespeare's Sonnets*, edited by Michael Schoenfeldt, 293–313. Oxford: Blackwell.

Bower, Chris, Walter H. Johnson, Lewis Cobbs, Jessica K. S. Wang, Deborah L. Beezley and Patricia M. Gantt. 2002. "Teacher to Teacher: Which of Shakespeare's Sonnets Do you Teach to Your Students?." *The English Journal*, No. 1 (September): 18–21.

Bruno, Giordano. 2004. *Cause, Principle and Unity. Essay on Magic*. Cambridge: Cambridge University Press [1998].

Caporicci, Camilla. 2014. "Dark is Light—From Italy to England: Challenging Tradition through Colors." In *Shakespeare and the Italian Renaissance. Appropriation, Transformation, Opposition*, edited by Michele Marrapodi, 199–214. Farnham: Ashgate.

Carpi, Daniela. 2016. "The Language of Clothing and the Law." *Pòlemos*, Vol. 10: 143–155.

De Grazia, Margreta. 1993. "The Scandal of Shakespeare's Sonnets." In *Shakespeare Survey 46*, edited by Stanley Wells, 35–49. Cambridge: Cambridge University Press.

Di Gesto, Cristian, Amanda Nerini, Giulia Rosa Policardo, Camilla Matera. 2021. "Predictors of Acceptance of Cosmetic Surgery: Instagram Images-Based Activities, Appearance Comparison and Body Dissatisfaction Among Woman." *Aesthetic Plastic Surgery*. https://link.springer.com/article/10.1007%2Fs00266-021-02546-3.

Edmondson, Paul, and Stanley Wells. 2004. *Shakespeare's Sonnets*. Oxford: Oxford University Press.

Faradouly, Jasmine and Lenny R. Vartanian. 2016. "Social Media and Body Image Concern: Current Research and Future Directions". *Science Direct*, Vol. 9: 1–5. www.sciencedirect.com.

Matthews-Grieco, Sara F. 1993. "The Body, Appearance, and Sexuality". In *A History of Women in the West. III Renaissance and Enlightenment Paradoxes*, edited by Natalie Zemon Davis and Arlette Farge, 46–84. Cambridge and London: The Belknap Press of Harvard University Press.

Greenblatt, Stephen. 1980. *Renaissance Self-Fashioning. From More to Shakespeare*. Chicago: The University of Chicago Press.

———. 2010. *Shakespeare's Freedom*. Chicago: The University of Chicago Press.

———. 1988. *Shakespearean Negotiation. The Circulation of Social Energy in Renaissance England*. Oxford: Clarendon Press.

Hall, F. Kim. 1995. *Things of Darkness. Economies of Race and Gender in Early Modern England*. Ithaca and London: Cornell University Press.

———. 1996. "Beauty and the Beast of Whiteness: Teaching Race and Gender". *Shakespeare Quarterly*, Vol. 47, No. 4: 461–475.

Hyman, Wendy Beth, and Hillary Eklund. 2019. *Teaching Social Justice Through Shakespeare. Why Renaissance Literature Matters Now*. Edinburgh: Edinburgh University Press.

Harvey, Elisabeth D. 2007. "Flesh Colors and Shakespeare's Sonnets." In *A Companion to Shakespeare's Sonnets,* edited by Michael Schoenfeldt, 314–326. Oxford: Blackwell.

Jones, Ann Rosalind and Peter Stallybrass. 2012. *Renaissance Clothing and the Material Memory.* Cambridge: Cambridge University Press.

Karim-Cooper, Farah. 2006. *Cosmetics in Shakespearean and Renaissance Drama.* Edinburg: Edinburgh University Press.

———. 2021. "The Materials of Race: Staging the Black and White Binary in the Early Modern Theatre". In *The Cambridge Companion to Shakespeare and Race,* edited by Ayanna Thomson, 17–29. Cambridge: Cambridge University Press.

Kennedy, William J., 2011. "European beginnings and transmission: Dante, Petrarch and the sonnet sequence". In *The Cambridge Companion to the Sonnets,* edited by A.D. Cousin and Peter Howarth, 84–104. Cambridge: Cambridge University Press.

Kingsley-Smith, Jane. 2019. *The Afterlife of Shakespeare's Sonnet.* Cambridge: Cambridge University Press.

Laghi, Simona. 2021. "Witchcraft, Demonic Possession and Exorcism: The Problem of Evidence in Two Shakespearean Plays". *Journal of Early Modern Studies,* Vol. 10 (March): 103–121. https://doi.org/10.13128/jems-2279-7149-12542.

Moss, Daniel. 2017. "Shakespeare Sonnets in the Undergraduate Classroom." In *The Sonnets: The State of the Play,* edited by Hannah Crawforth, Elizabeth Scott-Baumann and Claire Whitehead, 252–267. London and New York: Bloomsbury.

Raffield, Paul. 2010. *Shakespeare's Imaginary Constitution. Late – Elizabethan Politics and the Theatre of Law.* Oxford, Hart Publishing.

Riehl, Anna. 2010. *The Face of Queenship. Early Modern Representations of Elizabeth I.* New York: Palgrave Macmillan.

Rhode, Deborah L. 2010. *The Beauty Bias. The Injustice of appearance in Life and Law.* Oxford: Oxford University Press.

Schoenfeldt, Michael. 2010. *The Cambridge Introduction to Shakespeare's Poetry.* Cambridge: Cambridge University Press.

Shakespeare, William. 1997. *Shakespeare's Sonnets,* edited by Katherine Duncan-Jones. London: Arden Shakespeare.

Shakespeare, William. 2020. *All the Sonnets of Shakespeare,* edited by Paul Edmondson and Stanley Wells. Cambridge: Cambridge University Press.

Strier, Richard. 2007. "The Refusal to be Judged in Petrarch and Shakespeare". In *A Companion to Shakespeare's Sonnets,* edited by Michael Schoenfeldt, 73–89. Oxford: Blackwell.

Stubbes, Philip. 1877–1879. *The Anatomy of Abuses in England in Shakspeare's Youth* [1583], Part I, edited by F. J. Furnivall. London: The New Shakespeare Society.

Thomson, Ayanna, and Laura Turchi. 2016. *Teaching Shakespeare with a Purpose: A Student-Centred Approach*. London: Bloomsbury Arden Shakespeare.

Veldhuis, Jolanda and Alleva M. Jessica. 2020. "Me, My Selfie, and I: The Relations Between Selfie Behaviors, Body Image, Self-Objectification, and Self Esteem in Young Women". *Psychology in Popular Media*, Vol. 9, No 1: 3–13.

Watt, Gary. 2013. *Dress, Law and Naked Truth. A Cultural Study of Fashion and Form*. London and New York: Bloomsbury.

CHAPTER 21

Pop Sonnets: The Interplay Between Shakespeare's Sonnets and Popular Music in English Language Teaching

Katalin Schober

In his introduction to the collection, *Pop Sonnets. Shakespearean Spins on Your Favorite Songs*, software engineer, blogger, and self-proclaimed sonneteer, Erik Didriksen, humorously states that his sonnets are a selection of Shakespeare's "lesser-known" works, which "went largely unnoticed" by his contemporaries (Didriksen 2015, 11). Contrary to his claim to authenticity, the *Pop Sonnets* are popular songs of our times, skilfully rewritten as sonnets. First available on Tumblr, a blogging site, they were published as a collection by Quirk Books in 2015. The following sonnet, for example, refashions Idina Menzel's "Let It Go":

K. Schober (✉)
University of Konstanz, Konstanz, Germany
e-mail: katalin.schober@uni-konstanz.de

© The Author(s), under exclusive license to Springer Nature
Switzerland AG 2023
J. Kingsley-Smith and W. R. Rampone Jr. (eds.), *Shakespeare's Global Sonnets*,
Global Shakespeares, https://doi.org/10.1007/978-3-031-09472-9_21

> This mountainside, engulf'd in snow untouch'd,
> reveals the isolation I command;
> the icy storms that I once tightly clutch'd
> within my heart are blanketing the land.
> No longer could I heed my parents' will
> to hold my youthful hopes and fears at bay;
> so all have seen I've mastered winter's chill—
> my years of forced seclusion toss'd away.
> The page hath now been turn'd; I'll break the chains
> that kept restrain'd my true identity.
> This queen will rule, but o'er her own domain,
> without care for what they think of me.
> I'll not again the falling snow withhold,
> for I have ne'er been bothered by the cold. (70)

Didriksen's *Pop Sonnets* characteristically remodel popular songs, in that they adapt the Shakespearean Sonnet pattern of three quatrains and a rhyming couplet while adhering to the iambic pentameter most of the time. Similar to their early modern counterparts, the structure and the rhythm of the *Pop Sonnets* may vary slightly. Their poetic language creates a tone which may range from cheerful to passionate and tormented to irreverent, always depending on the specific popular songs they reference. In contrast to the Shakespearean tradition, however, the couplet does not usually contain a little turn in the line of argument, as developed by the previous three quatrains, but it mostly confirms the general idea of the poem. The above-mentioned song from Disney's feature film "Frozen" (2013), remodelled as a sonnet, concludes, for example, that the speaker has found her vocation and developed her identity in the process, thereby reinforcing the poem's general theme of self-empowerment: "I'll not again the falling snow withhold, / for I have ne'er been bothered by the cold".

Mainly modelled on the Shakespearean Sonnet form, Didriksen's sonnets creatively adapt and transform this pattern into a specific type of intermediality. Werner Wolf calls this transfer "intermedial transposition" (Wolf 2015, 462), in which "similar contents or formal aspects appear in works of different media and where, at the same time, a clear origin can be attributed to them in one of them" (460). In Didriken's case, the transformation is twofold in that the *Pop Sonnets* refer to two distinct sources: to the respective popular songs and to the Shakespearean Sonnet form. Not only do they reshape the popular songs, but also the early modern sonnet tradition. As a result, they add to the transhistorical relevance of Shakespeare's Sonnets, whose adaptations and transformations continue to reverberate in today's popular culture.

Thematically speaking, Didriksen's sonnets raise universal questions of love, morality, and authentic, poetic self-expression, thereby echoing some of the key themes of early modern sonnets. His versions of Spin Doctors' "Two Princes", Van Morrison's "Brown-Eyed Girl", or Soft Cell's "Tainted Love", for example, parallel Shakespeare's Sonnets 21, 116, and 147. They argue for a truthful rendering of one's passions; they cherish the constancy of true love; and they deplore deceit in love.

In all three cases, Didriksen's sonnets imitate Shakespeare's poetic language to convince the beloved of the intense passions experienced by the lyrical speaker. The opening lines of Spin Doctors' "Two Princes" are thus turned into the following verses: "Two noblemen before thee genuflect, / entreating thee in earnest for thy hand" (33). The speaker goes on to assure the addressee of the truthfulness of his love ("I'd be the truer love, if we should wed"), which he equates, in the closing lines, with an equally sincere depiction of his emotions: "By epithets, perhaps, or flow'ry prose, / I'll treasure all thy love how it's disclosed" (33). However, the couplet's description of "prose" as "flow'ry" raises questions about the relationship between the speaker's professed love and his claim to a truthful rendering thereof. It may either point to the overall futile endeavour to truly capture one's emotions in literature, or it may indicate a rather mocking tone, which, in turn, ridicules stock features of romantic love songs of our times, abounding in clichéd tropes. These themes parallel Shakespeare's Sonnet 21 in this respect. Didriksen's couplet, in particular, seems to echo the Shakespearean coda of "Let them say more that like of hearsay well, / I will not praise, that purpose not to sell"[1] (ll. 13–14) as these lines also advocate a natural style of writing and resist exaggerated images and comparisons of the beloved.

Other examples from Didriksen's collection explore the range of feelings commonly associated with deep love. His adaptation of Van Morrison's "Brown-Eyed Girl", for example, appreciates the constancy of true love which time cannot change. Even though "Father Time must always onward march" (32), the lyrical speaker only sees beauty in his beloved and does not cease to desire her: "I see the years endow'd thee

---

[1] The following edition is used: Shakespeare, William. [1609]/2010. *Shakespeare's Sonnets.* Ed. Katherine Duncan-Jones. London/New York: The Arden Shakespeare.

well with gifts / that do new passions in my breast ignite" (32). The theme of constant love resonates with Shakespeare's well-known Sonnet 116 and his idealised notion of unwavering love, which defeats even time: "Love's not Time's fool, though rosy lips and cheeks / Within his bending sickle's compass come; / Love alters not with his brief hours and weeks, / But bears it out even to the edge of doom" (ll. 9–12). Even if the time may leave traces and change the appearance, it cannot triumph over genuine emotions.

By contrast, Soft Cell's "Tainted Love" is turned into an example of the agonies of one-sided love, clearly imitating the Petrarchan idea of a disdainful mistress. In Didriksen's version of the popular song, the lyrical speaker opens his argument by lamenting the "torment [...] [he] endured", which "keeps [him] awake" (46). The beloved remains unavailable to the poet, who is left to deplore his cruel fate: "[F]or now thou drink'st the tears that do express / the ceaseless pain of courtship cruelly curs'd" (46). The exploration of love's torments parallels Shakespeare's idea of love as an illness beyond any cure, as expressed in Sonnet 147: "Past cure I am, now reason is past care" (l. 9). Both sonnets end with similar insights into the bitterness of unrequited love. Didriksen's couplet, for example, concludes with the unworthiness of this kind of disproportionate affection. It alludes to the title of the popular song "Tainted Love", thereby allowing its readership to decode its reference point: "Thou claim'st divinity's in am'rous pray'r, / and yet our love's been tainted past compare" (46). Hence, Didriksen's coda implies some immoral conduct on the part of the mistress and seems to reproduce Shakespeare's version, in which the speaker equally refers to his eye-opening disappointment: "For I have sworn thee fair, and thought thee bright, / Who art as black as hell, as dark as night" (ll. 13–14).

Interestingly, in some cases, Didriksen's appropriation of Shakespeare's Sonnets proves rather idealistic, which may add to the transhistorical attraction of the original. The sonnet modelled on One Direction's "What Makes You Beautiful", for example, echoes early modern Neoplatonic notions of a correlation between outer beauty and inner perfection:

> Thy confidence in Nature's gifts is strain'd;
> I know not why, for thine's a pleasing face.
> Pray, witness all the staring unconstrain'd
> by those who mark thine entrance to a place.
> Thy naked face is beauty unsurpass'd;
> thy countenance is not by rouge improv'd.

> Like Helen's, it could launch a navy vast,
> yet thy reflection leaves thee still unmov'd.
> My life, once dark, is bathed in brilliant light
> for thou hast graced it with thy presence sweet;
> yet thou'lt not see the passion thou'st ignite
> when thou hast fix'd thy gaze upon thy feet.
> Thy charms are temper'd with humility,
> and make thee still more beautiful to me. (17)

After praising the natural charm of his beloved ("Thy naked face is beauty unsurpass'd"), the lyrical speaker goes on to equate the joy he feels with heavenly light: "My life, once dark, is bathed in brilliant light / for thou hast graced it with thy presence sweet". The typically Neoplatonic metaphor of light is then linked to the idea of modesty, since the beloved seems to be oblivious of her influence over the poet: "[Y]et thou'lt not see the passion thou'st ignite / when thou hast fix'd thy gaze upon thy feet". The coda confirms the argument of the addressee's moral superiority once more.

Didriksen's idealised notion of love stands in stark contrast to those Shakespearean Sonnets which contain a criticism of the addressee, such as in the above-mentioned Sonnet 147 from the "Dark Lady" cycle. A disapproving tone is also to be witnessed in Sonnet 69 from the "Fair Youth" sequence, which explores the gap between a beautiful appearance and inner depravity as summed up in the couplet: "But why thy odour matcheth not thy show, / The soil is this, that thou dost common grow" (ll. 13–14). Mixing with anyone, the "Fair Youth" has obviously disgraced himself and is now too vulgar for the lyrical speaker's taste. Both poems— Didriksen's version of "What Makes You Beautiful" and Shakespeare's Sonnet 69—lend themselves to a comparative analysis, which focuses on the contrasting depictions of love and corruption.

A final comparative analysis highlights how the Petrarchan blazon is appropriated differently. Whereas Didriksen's version of "Just the Way You Are", performed by Bruno Mars, imitates the early modern convention of a blazon, Shakespeare's Sonnet 130 mocks and playfully converts it. As a result, "Just the Way You Are" may be termed a counter-poem to Shakespeare, while it may be seen as a continuation of the earlier Petrarchan tradition:

My mistress' eyes are nothing like the stars;
they've brighter shine than all those overhead.
Her hair's cascade her visage never mars
But effortlessly frames her face instead.
And yet, if I should tell her what I see—
that she hath been by Aphrodite bless'd—
she'd quietly demur and disagree
and I shall with these words sincere protest:
"When I observe thy countenance's grace,
I see no fault—no flaw one might repair;
and when a smile doth blossom 'cross thy face,
the world takes heed and stops to fondly stare.
No words could e'er sufficiently impart
all thy perfection, just the way thou art." (20)

The opening line clearly evokes Shakespeare's Sonnet 130 ("My mistress' eyes are nothing like the sun", l. 1), but the second verse breaks with the readers' expectations by overthrowing the original's argument. While Shakespeare's Sonnet mocks exaggerated tropes of the beloved's beauty, Didriksen's poem is well in line with the courtly blazon, cataloguing and boldly praising the addressee's manifold beautiful characteristics. It ends with the clichéd claim that words fail to capture "thy perfection" adequately, which, in turn, heightens the sense of an idealised version of love. Shakespeare's Sonnet, by contrast, seems to be more "modern" in that it makes fun of a worn-out tradition. Both sonnets encourage contrasting readings, which allow for a comparison of the various uses of the blazon, its continuations, and transformations.

INTERMEDIALITY IN THE CLASSROOM: BUILDING MULTILITERACIES

Recent developments in English Language Teaching (ELT) have drawn attention to changes in today's communication technologies and contexts, which have become increasingly interconnected and interdependent. Bill Cope and Mary Kalantzis, for example, link these radical shifts to the necessity of building, what they term, "multiliteracies" in the classroom, in order to equip learners with the skills needed to manage changing life experiences. They identify two distinct facets of "multiliteracies" as a process of meaning-making: on the one hand, the term comprises a sensibility to different cultures entailing a sense of empathy, that is the capacity to imaginatively put oneself in someone else's shoes in order to gain some understanding of his or her condition. On the other hand, the concept of multiliteracies refers to the ability to decode various modes of meaning-making, for example, verbal, but also visual, or acoustic ones: "The first is the variability of meaning-making in different cultural, social or professional contexts. [...] The second is the nature of new communication technologies. Meaning is made in ways that are increasingly multimodal – in which written-linguistic modes of meaning interface with visual, audio, gestural and spatial patterns of meaning" (Cope and Kalantzis 2006, 23).

When thinking about Didriksen's *Pop Sonnets,* these distinct aspects of multiliteracies overlap and complement one another. As discussed earlier, the sonnet collection modelled on popular songs of our times may be classified as a specific type of intermediality bearing at least two reference points which playfully interact with each other: select popular songs and Shakespeare's Sonnets. Hence, Didriksen's *Pop Sonnets* lend themselves to uses in ELT which aim at fostering multiliteracies, both with a focus on decoding inherently multimodal texts and on making sense of another culture, namely, the Elizabethan era. They may constitute, in this respect, low-threshold gateways to the original texts since the original popular songs may be used as accessible starting points for further explorations of the interplay between the sonnet tradition and popular music. By allowing for comparative close readings, Didriksen's *Pop Sonnets* may encourage their young readers to approach the more intricate early modern models as well (Rokison 2013). As a result, they may enhance the pupils' overall understanding of the Shakespearean Sonnet pattern and its early modern traditions, as well as its creative adaptations and transformations in the twenty-first century.

SUGGESTIONS FOR ENGLISH LANGUAGE LESSONS

Various analytical and creative approaches to multimodal texts (Lütge and Owczarek 2019; Rokison 2013) and to Shakespeare, in particular (Lange et al. 2015; Möller 2018; Pointner 2014), have been discussed in recent years by eminent ELT scholars. They all agree with Bill Cope and Mary Kalantzis that meaning-making is an inherently "dynamic process, a process of subjective self-interest and transformation" (Cope and Kalantzis 2006, 37), in which recipients actively recreate cultural products. Teachers will thus need to design tasks which encourage their pupils to relate to the texts, to the questions they raise, and the poetic worlds they construct. In ELT, Didriksen's *Pop Sonnets* are a true gem. By raising universal questions of love and immorality, they appeal to their adolescent readers, who have to tackle quite similar developmental milestones with regard to identity formation or the exploration of romantic relationships. Questions to be tackled in school might include: which paths should young adults choose in life, and which values should they take as some kind of orientation? Whom should they trust, and who might be there to share their experiences with them? What is important to them in friendships or in romantic relationships? These questions may be dealt with in learner-centred literature classes, in particular, since literary or poetic texts invite their readers to actively engage with the themes they set forth.

Learner-centred approaches to Shakespeare, as advocated by Ayanna Thompson and Laura Turchi (Thompson and Turchi 2016), or by Fiona Banks (Banks 2014), may contain more creative lesson designs, using drama techniques or creative writing tasks, for example, which offer opportunities to engage productively with the texts in question. Banks observes that creative approaches to teaching Shakespeare need to truly "value imaginative engagement and response" (5). She goes on to note that such teaching techniques invite learners "to suspend judgment, to ask 'what if?'" (5). Drama activities, in particular, "help teachers of [...] young readers step into fictional worlds that they have created with students, and engage in interpretations of literature that are social, innovative, critical and could transform classrooms into spaces where imagination fuels learning", as Thomas P. Crumpler and Linda Wedwick highlight when discussing literature classes for young adolescents (Crumpler and Wedwick 2011, 73). These activities may include dramatic readings, which ask pupils to embody select keywords taken from the sonnets. The learners may be encouraged to think of suitable nonverbal cues representing such keywords, for example, appropriate facial expressions, gestures, or other bodily movements. After presenting their readings to the other members of the group, the learners may then be asked to describe what they felt, and to what extent their sensations parallel the sonnet themes in question. As part of dramatic readings, the learners may equally experiment with their voice level, intonation, or pace of speech, and discuss to what extent these variations align with or alter the sonnets' main ideas.

Before we explore some sample lessons, which aim at building multiliteracies in the classroom, it is worth looking at more analytical approaches to teaching Shakespeare as well. Even if current reflections seem to prefer creative techniques, analytical tasks are also needed in order to enable the pupils to move from an initial appreciation of the texts to a more informed understanding of their poetic and structural complexity and of the cultural undercurrents with which they are imbued (Beach et al. 2016, 169–170). Laurenz Volkmann, for example, suggests close readings, which he regards as useful to decode the texts' "linguistic and thematic complexity, semantic density and structural interconnectivity" as tokens of their inherently poetic ambivalence (Volkmann 2014, 21).

These close readings may be complemented by intertextual arrangements, which allow the pupils to retrace the manifold adaptations and transformations of poetic themes and structures. Wolfgang Hallet advocates comparative approaches in ELT as a means of building contextualised knowledge in addition to single close readings (Hallet 2002). His approach is well in line with recent, transcultural tendencies in language education, which highlight notions of pluralistic, yet interconnected worldviews and thus advocate intertextual teachings of (multimodal) artefacts (Freitag-Hild 2019).

The following suggestions for lessons aim at building a cycle, which moves from an initial to a more differentiated knowledge of Shakespeare's Sonnets and their appropriation and transformation by Erik Didriksen. Therefore, analytical as well as creative tasks are combined, in order to enable the learners to connect new to prior knowledge and to deepen their overall understanding of Shakespeare's Sonnets.

Table: Lessons

Topic	Shakespeare's sonnets in transformation
Aims	To initiate and deepen the pupils' ability... • to compare Didriksen's *Pop Sonnets* with the popular songs they reference, and to articulate their first impressions • to compare Didriksen's *Pop Sonnets* with select Shakespeare's Sonnets, to recognise similarities and differences at thematic and structural levels, and to analyse aesthetic features in relation to the readers' responses they elicit • to understand Shakespeare's Sonnets in relation to their specific cultural context • to recreate Shakespeare's Sonnets, using drama and creative writing activities

(continued)

(continued)

Topic	Shakespeare's sonnets in transformation
Age	Secondary level, 15–18 years of age
Level	B 2 to C 1
Time	Eight to ten lessons (à 45 minutes)
Materials	• Didriksen's versions of Spin Doctors' "Two Princes", of Van Morrison's "Brown-Eyed Girl", and of Soft Cell's "Tainted Love" compared to Shakespeare's Sonnets 21, 116, and 147 • Didriksen's version of One Direction's "What Makes You Beautiful" compared to Shakespeare's Sonnet 69 • Didriksen's version of "Just the Way You Are" by Bruno Mars compared to Shakespeare's Sonnet 130
Lessons 1–2	Ask pupils to… • listen to select popular songs and to articulate their first impressions • to articulate their first ideas of "romantic love" • to read and compare select Pop Sonnets taken from Didriksen's collection with the popular songs they reference
Lessons 3–4	Ask pupils to… • work together in groups • compare Didriksen's Pop Sonnets with select Shakespeare's Sonnets, to recognise similarities and differences at thematic and structural levels, and to relate them to their prior knowledge of the Elizabethan era • to share their findings in class • to compare the concepts of "romantic love" as indicated by the sonnets to their previous notions thereof
Lessons 5–6	Ask pupils to… • work together in groups • to practise dramatic readings of select Shakespeare's Sonnets by connecting appropriate nonverbal cues to keywords, for example, facial expressions, gestures, and movements, as well as by experimenting with their voice level, intonation, and speed of speech • to present their dramatic readings to the class • to discuss the effects of their dramatic readings
Lessons 7–8	Ask pupils to… • work together in groups • to rewrite a Shakespearean Sonnet by transforming it into a sonnet using today's language and/or depicting their personal notions of "romantic love" • or to transform a Shakespearean Sonnet into a popular song • or to continue to read Didriksen's Pop Sonnets, to select one sonnet, to relate it to a Shakespearean Sonnet of their choice, and to devise another lesson for a comparative analysis

(continued)

(continued)

Topic	*Shakespeare's sonnets in transformation*
Follow-up lessons	Ask pupils to... • to present either their literary re-creations and to give feedback to their peers, • or to ask their peers to produce further comparative readings in form of a "book club"

Acknowledgements This work was supported by the "Qualitätsoffensive Lehrerbildung" in Germany, a joint initiative of the Federal Government and the Länder, funded by the Federal Ministry of Education and Research, which aims to improve the quality of teacher training. The author of this article is responsible for its content.

References

Banks, Fiona. 2014. *Creative Shakespeare. The Globe Education Guide to Practical Shakespeare.* London: The Arden Shakespeare.

Beach, Richard, Deborah Appleman, Bob Fecho, and Rob Simon. 2016. *Teaching Literature to Adolescents.* 3rd ed. London: Routledge.

Cope, Bill, and Mary Kalantzis. 2006. "From Literacy to 'Multiliteracies'. Learning to Mean in the New Communications Environment". *English Studies in Africa.* Vol. 49.1: 23–45.

Crumpler, Thomas P., and Linda Wedwick. 2011. "Readers, Texts, and Context in the Middle. Re-imagining Literature Education for Young Adolescents". In *Handbook of Research on Children's and Young Adult Literature.* Ed. Shelby A. Wolf et al., 63–75. New York: Routledge.

Didriksen, Erik. 2015. *Pop Sonnets. Shakespearean Spins on Your Favorite Songs.* Philadelphia: Quirk Books.

Freitag-Hild, Britta. 2019. "Interkulturelle Literaturdidaktik". In *Grundthemen der Literaturwissenschaft: Literaturdidaktik.* Ed. Christiane Lütge, 359–372. Berlin/Boston: De Gruyter.

Hallet, Wolfgang. 2002. *Fremdsprachenunterricht als Spiel der Texte und Kulturen. Intertextualität als Paradigma einer kulturwissenschaftlichen Didaktik.* Trier: WVT.

Lange, Joan, Connolly, Patrick, and Devin Lintzenich. 2015. "Connecting Students with Shakespeare's Poetry: Digital Creations of Close Readings". *The English Journal.* Vol. 104.4: 43–39.

Lütge, Christiane, and Claudia Owczarek. 2019. "Zur Rolle von Musik im kompetenzorientierten Fremdsprachenunterricht – audio literacy als Teil von multiliteracies". In: *Musik im Fremdsprachenunterricht*. Ed. Charlotte Falkenhagen and Laurenz Volkmann, 17–28. Tübingen: Narr Francke Attempto Verlag.

Möller, Stefan. 2018. "'Mine Be Thy Love.' Vom Text zur Musik: Shakespeares Sonette vertonen". In *Der Fremdsprachliche Unterricht Englisch*. Vol. 152: 40–45.

Pointner, Frank Erik. 2014. "'Two Loves I Have.' Teaching the Drama of Shakespeare's Sonnets". In *Shakespeare in the EFL Classroom*. Ed. Maria Eisenmann and Christiane Lütge, 35–60. Heidelberg: Universitätsverlag Winter.

Rokison, Abigail. 2013. *Shakespeare for Young People. Productions, Versions, and Adaptations*. London: The Arden Shakespeare.

Shakespeare, William. [1609]/2010. *Shakespeare's Sonnets*. Ed. Katherine Duncan-Jones. London/New York: The Arden Shakespeare.

Thompson, Ayanna, and Laura Turchi. 2016. *Teaching Shakespeare with Purpose. A Student-Centred Approach*. London: The Arden Shakespeare.

Volkmann, Laurenz. 2014. "Developing Symbolic Competence through Shakespeare's Sonnets". In *Shakespeare in the EFL Classroom*. Ed. Maria Eisenmann and Christiane Lütge, 15–34. Heidelberg: Universitätsverlag Winter.

Wolf, Werner. 2015. "Literature and Music: Theory". In *Handbook of Intermediality. Literature – Image – Sound – Music*. Ed. Gabriele Rippl, 459–474. Berlin/Boston: De Gruyter.

CHAPTER 22

Afterword: Around the World in 154 Poems, or, How to Do Things with Shakespeare's Sonnets

Walter Cohen

I

What does this volume seek to achieve? Not to provide a comprehensive overview of the English-language reception of Shakespeare's sonnets.[1] Not of their translation into almost 90 languages, including the usual suspects—Amharic, Basque, Esperanto, Farsi, Igbo, Korean, Kurdish, Malay, Maori, Romani, Sign Languages, Thai, Ukrainian, Vietnamese, and, of course, Klingon.[2] And not of the almost 1500 musical settings they had inspired by the late twentieth century, where the clear winner is #18 ("Shall I compare thee to a summer's day?") with 140 examples,

---

[1] For this matter, see Kingsley-Smith (2019).
[2] Pfister and Gutsch (2009, 2014).

W. Cohen (✉)
University of Michigan, Ann Arbor, MI, USA
e-mail: cowa@umich.edu

© The Author(s), under exclusive license to Springer Nature Switzerland AG 2023
J. Kingsley-Smith and W. R. Rampone Jr. (eds.), *Shakespeare's Global Sonnets*, Global Shakespeares, https://doi.org/10.1007/978-3-031-09472-9_22

occasionally from before 1850.[3] It might be helpful instead to think of the essays assembled here as a series of core drillings that as a group provides a meaningful, if not quite systematic, sample of both where and how the sonnets have been, and currently are being, appropriated. As the Table of Contents accurately indicates, the preceding chapters are concerned with two main issues—globality and performance. The claim here is not quite that these master categories amount to the same thing, or even that they are two sides of the same coin. It *is*, however, that every contribution crosses linguistic borders or at least deploys a multinational perspective, and that every chapter is also concerned to show the cultural work that the sonnets do. This means that each contribution goes beyond the standard, and crucial, practice of interpretation of the poems themselves.[4] To be sure, this collection includes a number of sensitive and thoughtful readings of individual sonnets. But those readings are consistently deployed in the service of the larger ends just mentioned.

2

The international and, often, polyglot character of the volume can be captured in part by the following chart, which, while excluding the editors' synthetic introductions, otherwise follows the volume's order of presentation.

The Global Sonnets

Author	Language	Location of Poems	Location of Author
Cottegnies	French	France	France
Steenson & Trissino	Italian	Italy	Italy; Switzerland
de Scarpis	Italian	Italy	Italy
Szele	Hungarian	Hungary	Hungary
Levi	Turkish	Turkey	Turkey
Refskou & Khair	Bangla, Malayalam, Hindi, Urdu	India, Bangladesh	Denmark
	Portuguese	Brazil	
	English	The Caribbean, Canada	

(continued)

[3] Gooch and Thatcher (1991) 3: 1965–2087.

[4] There are, of course, many distinguished volumes on the topic—prominent among them Booth (1969), Fineman (1987), and Vendler (1997), critics who often disagree with each other.

(continued)

Author	Language	Location of Poems	Location of Author
Oya	Japanese	Japan	Japan
Joubin	Chinese/Taiwanese	Taiwan	U.S
Krajník & Drozd	Czech	Czech Republic	Czech Republic
Minier	English	Wales	Wales
Keinänen & Lehtonen	Finnish	Finland	Finland
Pfister	Russian/English	U.S	Germany
Weiss	Russian	Russia	Germany
Ingham	English	Australia Canada/U.S	China
Ellis	English	U.K	Canada
Chiari	English	U.K	France
Salkeld	English	U.K	U.K
Laghi	English	Italy	Italy
Schober	English	Germany	Germany

What can be inferred from this table? First, five continents are represented, as well as over a dozen languages and nations. Nothing more needs now to be said on this score about the chapters concerning translation into foreign languages. Still, and this is the second and not surprising point, Shakespeare's sonnets themselves, in their original early modern English, are the focus in close to half of the essays. But in most of those cases, the location where the sonnets are in play, the institutional home of the essay's author, or both lie elsewhere—usually in a non-Anglophone nation. Thus, Sophie Refskou and Tabish Khair discuss the Anglophone Canadian writer, the remarkably named Sonnet L'Abbé, author of the equally remarkably entitled *Sonnet's Shakespeare* (2019). But L'Abbé is of mixed continental, racial, and linguistic ancestry; Refskou and Khair treat this work in the context of Shakespearean adaptation in Bangla, Malayalam, and Brazilian Portuguese; and they themselves lead their institutional lives in Denmark. Similarly, Manfred Pfister considers a musical adaptation of a Shakespearean sonnet in the U.S. in its original English; but that adaptation is the work of Igor Stravinsky, and Pfister is himself German. Mike Ingham writes from China about Anglophone—but not British—appropriations of the sonnets in popular music. Both Simona Laghi and Katalin Schober evaluate the possibilities of the sonnets in English-language teaching—in Italy and Germany, respectively. Sophie Chiari, situated in France, reviews the ecological implications of the sonnets, especially their emphasis on "a natural environment apparently in crisis, where loss, decay, and overpowering elemental forces predominate" (Chiari, **331**). Her line of argument might be extended by connecting these findings with the Little Ice Age, which was heading toward its most destructive phase at this time. Global in scope and a standard historiographical category,[5] it has yet to elicit much interest in literary study.

We move toward a more purely Anglophone environment with Márta Minier's account of an oppositional theatrical troupe. But that troupe was based in Wales, and part of the story involves its indebtedness to Antonin Artaud, as well as its travels and travails in Georgia, Armenia, and Azerbaijan. Similarly, Jim Ellis's essay, a Canadian "take," if you will, on Derek Jarman, attends to the international gay heritage—Eisenstein, Genet—of the British filmmaker. Finally, Duncan Salkeld undertakes what on first sight might seem a purely English inquiry into the identity of the Dark Mistress of the sonnets. But only at first sight. In a speculative but learned and plausible argument, he suggests that the historically attested prostitute Luce Baynam, known widely as "Black Luce," was in fact African, that she is the Dark Mistress described beginning in Sonnet 127, and that, whether or not the two preceding claims prove correct, this group of poems constitutes a sequence concerned with blackness. There's a suggestive parallel here to the lyrics of Shakespeare's older contemporary, Luís Vaz de Camões, the Portuguese national poet who, as a soldier, participated in his country's overseas imperial conquests. A striking instance of Camões's lyric response to empire is provided by "To a Captive Who Became His Lover in India, Called Barbara." There, the woman's name plays with the notion of barbarians, while the Petrarchan trope of the male lover as metaphorical captive of the imperious female beloved is uncomfortably played off against the historical reality of the female beloved as literal captive of her imperial male captor.[6] Finally, a striking and welcome feature of the institutional homes of the essayists, I might hypocritically add, is the almost total absence of representation from the centers of sonnet criticism, at least numerically: the U.K. and the U.S.

---

[5] E.g. Parker (2014)—one of many full-length accounts.

[6] Camões (1980) 3: 158–159; (2008), 152–153. Discussion: White (2008), 14–15.

3

But so what? How does any of this matter? What do we learn, beyond interesting details, that we didn't already know?

As both the table of contents and my second subtitle suggest, one way into the topic is through J. L. Austin's influential development of the category of performative utterances (e.g. "I do" in a wedding ceremony).[7] Performative utterances, performativity, and artistic performance are not the same thing. Still, there's an obvious family resemblance among the terms and the actions they seek to bring to light. The essays in this collection demonstrate that Shakespeare's poems can and do serve a considerable number, even a bewildering variety, of purposes—that translators, poets, actors, composers, and filmmakers do things with the sonnets. Nonetheless, much of this material may be organized under two rubrics—the formal and the social, with an inevitable blending of the two.

Formal, or literary, analyses possess bidirectional implications: both what they tell us about the target language or medium and what they tell us about Shakespeare's sonnets themselves. One way into these questions, at least as they pertain to international concerns, is through a comparison of the sonnets to the author's plays. As several of the essays point out, in language after language the reception of the plays precedes that of the sonnets. And that earlier reception of Shakespearean drama is not limited to the theater. Indeed, the tragedies lie directly behind some of the most celebrated novels of the late eighteenth and nineteenth centuries—Sterne's *Tristram Shandy* (1759–1767), Goethe's *Wilhelm Meister's Apprenticeship* (1795), Balzac's *Père Goriot* (1834), and Melville's *Moby-Dick* (1851), among many others.[8] The Shakespearean imprimatur seems to provide a rationale for the rising genre and often for a challenge to aesthetic norms in the target literary tradition. Although, as we have seen, instances also exist of musical adaptation of the sonnets prior to 1850, to which might be added occasional translation (Kingsley-Smith, **20.**; Cottegnies, **35**), it cannot be said that they serve anything like this function, at least until much later.

But eventually, they do. Before turning to the consequences of their reception *in* world literature, however, we might briefly flip the script and consider their reception *of* world literature—a line of argument that

---

[7] Austin (1962), esp. Lecture 1.
[8] Cohen (2017) 390–393.

could also be pursued with respect to Shakespeare's plays, though will not be here. Petrarch is of course the key and immediate predecessor of the English sonnet tradition. One of the backgrounds to Petrarch, though, and not by any means to Petrarch alone, is the medieval Latin lyric—itself indebted to Byzantine Greek poetry, behind which stand early Christian Syriac lyric and ultimately the Hebrew and Greek Bibles. A more proximate path into Petrarch runs back to the invention of the sonnet form in thirteenth-century Sicily, in a multilingual, multireligious milieu on which Arabic poetry probably exerted some influence. But the key predecessor to the Sicilian sonnet is the Occitan (formerly, Provençal) lyric of today's southern France. By the time it reaches Sicily, Occitan poetry has been influenced by the region's dualistic Catharism, an unintentionally sectarian belief system deemed heretical by the Church and traced back by many, but not all, scholars to—in reverse chronological order—the Bogomil heresy (tenth-century Bulgaria), the Paulician heresy (ninth-century Byzantium), late antique Manichaeism, and Zoroastrianism. Probably a more important influence on Occitan poetry, however, is the love lyric from al-Andalus, the Arabic-speaking, Muslim-ruled territory occupying much of what we now think of as medieval Spain. Certainly, the metrical schemes of early Occitan poetry are closer to those in Andalusi—Arabic than to the forms of any other possible predecessor. In short, Shakespeare's sonnets are likely to be the heirs and beneficiaries of poetic and intellectual traditions originating in multiple regions and languages extending to the east and south—to Continental Western and Eastern Europe, to Northwest Asia, and to North Africa.[9]

The poems are therefore both a product and a producer of world literature. Although, as my language suggests, some of these connections cannot quite be demonstrated beyond question, the overall point is not in doubt. Insistence on it need not imply any scaling back of Shakespeare's stature. Reviewing this background merely identifies one condition of possibility of that stature. The condition in question—indebtedness to a broad cultural heritage—is obviously not unique to Shakespeare. On the contrary, it is reasonably close to a universal truth. Emphasis on it here, then, might acquire a modest degree of force only because of Shakespeare's standing as the world's great original genius of literature and theater. If such is the case for Shakespeare, the generalization holds *a*

---

[9] Cohen (2017) 140–167, 201–211.

fortiori for all other poets and artists, including those who appropriate Shakespeare. Indeed, to return to the metaphor of flipping the script: we might speculate that the recourse to a range of prior traditions is a sign not of the lack but of the very ground of literary originality. This possibility is worth bearing in mind in what follows, particularly at the conclusion to these remarks.

This brief history of the sonnets' multicontinental inheritance, however, does not distinguish them from the plays, except at the level of detail. The Sinologist and comparatist Stephen Owen provides a useful framework for approaching the desired level of specificity. Owen distinguishes between fiction and poetry in contemporary discussions of world literature. Whereas fiction is often taken to be translatable without too much concern for the challenges of moving between languages, in poetry it is another story—especially if that poetry is lyric poetry and therefore does not itself tell a story.[10] Perhaps surprisingly, the same contrast holds between the sonnets and Shakespearean drama, even though three-quarters of the plays' lines are in verse. As a result,

> studying the reception of Shakespeare's *Sonnets*—rather than that of Shakespeare's plays—within the framework of the global South contributes an important critical perspective on Global Shakespeare both as a phenomenon and as a scholarly field. This is not only because Global Shakespeare tends almost exclusively to address afterlives of the plays, not the poems, but also because deploying the *Sonnets* as a case study in global reception requires first and foremost an unavoidable literary focus on the poetics of texts and their languages. . . . [D]ownplaying or downright dispensing with the Shakespearean text . . . may . . . have left Global Shakespeare with a critical paradox. That is, in leaving textual and linguistic poetics behind to focus on other media, scholarship might unintentionally overlook the rich literary and linguistic traditions of the global cultures that have engaged with the Shakespearean canon and continue to recreate it. (Refskou and Khair, **129–130**)

The problem is not limited to the Global South, of course—as many of the essays here attest. More generally, the larger audience for prose fiction or even for live theater, as well as the greater formal density of lyric poetry, leads to a systematic generic asymmetry in the availability of translated literature, to the disadvantage of lyric. Shakespeare's sonnets

---

[10] Owen (2003).

are therefore of interest in the context of world literature partly because their prestige makes them something of an exception to this rule. To be sure, they cannot stand in for all of their lyric predecessors and successors that—however distinguished—overwhelmingly fail to cross national or linguistic borders. But they can provide test cases for the place of poetry in conceptions of world culture, calling our attention to the international social function of literature beyond the level of plot, narrative, or even embodiment.

4

As this suggests, it is only a small step from the sonnets' global relationships to their social uses, even though one can approach the latter without recourse to the former. This is so because every "take" on Shakespeare is an "intervention" in the native poetic or other artistic tradition. Again, though the same holds for all translation, for all adaptation, it is more likely to be consequential with the sonnets partly because of Shakespeare's prestige, but partly because a number of the translators (or at least adapters of the sonnet form) were—or are—themselves outstanding poets and artists as well. The list, which boasts four Nobel laureates, includes Yves Bonnefoy and René Char in France, Giuseppe Ungaretti and Eugenio Montale in Italy, Lőrinc Szabó and Anna Szabó T. (or Anna T. Szabó) in Hungary, Talât Sait Halman in Turkey, Rabindranath Tagore and K. Satchidanandan in India, Derek Walcott in the Caribbean, and Boris Pasternak in the U.S.S.R. Significantly, many of these projects seem to entail a fusion of Shakespeare's and the poet-translator's voice.

Not surprisingly, the appropriation of the sonnets sometimes reinforces existing conventions or outlooks, while at others encouraging innovation and challenges to regnant norms. The frequent recourse to Sonnet 66 ("Tired with all these, for restful death I cry")[11] is an example of the latter (Kingsley-Smith, de Scarpis, Levi, Krajník and Drozd, Pfister, Weiss). But the poems can be used in either fashion or in ways that fall in between. We may even find a mix of these hypothetically opposed tendencies within a single translator, depending on which dimensions of the residual or the

---

[11] Shakespeare (2015) 2272: Sonnet 66, l. 1.

emergent are focused on.[12] Such differences among the articles are actually not a sign of disagreement. Rather, this is the way it has to be. To be
sure, the poems are more than blank slates. They may have had relatively
determinate meanings and effects in their own time, a supposition the
continuing scholarly disputes about these matters does not really undermine. But their subsequent use, regardless of whether or not the original
text is faithfully preserved, depends heavily on the context of reception.
And this remains the case regardless of the language, the medium, or the
social and political context into which they are inserted.

The reception abroad of, if not Shakespeare's sonnets in particular,
then certainly of their distinctively non-Petrarchan rhyme scheme, begins
early. The form is adopted by Joost von den Vondel, the leading poet
and dramatist of the Dutch Golden Age of the seventeenth century, as
well as by some of his contemporaries in the United Provinces. Why here
first? Why the borrowing of one of the features that usually distinguishes
the Shakespearean from the Continental sonnet? The explanation lies not
only in geographical proximity, commercial ties, and religious similarity
but also in linguistic affinity. By this time, Dutch has moved part of
the way down the path away from German already taken by English.
But only partly: the poetic adoption is also an adaptation. Dutch word
endings make the French Alexandrine a more congenial verse line than
the English iambic pentameter.[13] Awareness of the implications of such
differences is there from the start. Shakespeare's gender-bending Sonnet
20 relies exclusively on feminine rhyme, in a collection that relies almost
exclusively on masculine rhyme. And to return once again to Camões:
one of his sonnets breaks with the normative reliance on feminine rhyme
in Portuguese, Spanish, and Italian to produce a sonnet in which every
rhyme is masculine—though for less obvious thematic purposes. In any
case, Camões's move is replicated in contemporary Brazilian poetry.
Geraldo Carneiro's recourse to monosyllabic words and a ten-syllable
line similarly works against the grain of the Portuguese language and
Portuguese lyric, arguably with democratic ends in mind (Refskou and
Khair, 139).

As these examples suggest, the degree of structural similarity between
Shakespearean English and the language into which it is translated does

---

[12] For the terms, see Williams (1973) 121–127.

[13] Vondel (1870) 249; Shakespeare (1940) 395; Kooij (1990) 140–141.

not carry with it the force of inevitability. Again, we find different, even opposed, solutions not simply across, but also within, several individual languages, and even occasionally within an individual project. Do you preserve the structure (14 lines, iambic pentameter, distinctive rhyme scheme), thematic development, imagery, sound patterns, wit and irony, tone and feel? All? None? In France, the initial translations, from the early nineteenth century, are in one case in prose and in another in rhymed Alexandrines. These pioneering efforts set the rules of the ensuing debate. The first complete translation of the sonnets[14] and its immediate successors are in prose. This battle between verse and prose is a version of the quarrel between the Ancients and the Moderns, which also overlaps with the combat between high and natural style or between the native heritage of verse (sometimes augmented by partial adoption of Shakespeare's rhyme scheme) and the Romantic impatience with the dead hand of tradition and consequent recourse to prose translation as an alternative. This sometime-ideological conflict continues in the twentieth and twenty-first centuries, with the majority of translations still having recourse to Alexandrines (mostly rhymed), a persistence accompanied or contested, however, by increasing experimentation—for instance, with free verse. One sees here a variety of cultural and artistic issues. In addition, however, what stands out is the pressure exerted on translators by the monosyllabic, concise character of English, as in the early Dutch translations. Preservation of Shakespeare's meter and rhyme scheme, accordingly and ironically, may come at the expense of the feel of the original—of its language, wit, and irony—limitations sometimes exacerbated by archaism, poetic inversion, and the elision of articles (Cottegnies).

Variations on this theme can be found in Italian translations beginning in the 1940s. Here we find non-metrical renditions designed to accommodate the greater number of syllables needed in an Italian verse line. But also, on occasion, the recourse to hendecasyllables, chosen as the closest approximation to iambic pentameter and combined with the Shakespearean rhyme scheme. Strikingly, this latter strategy can be tied to an interest in returning to the Petrarchan tradition—the very tradition that Shakespeare both drew on and departed from. In a way, then, we witness here a process of retranslation back into the original Italian—a

---

[14] By Victor Hugo's son François-Victor Hugo (1865).

potentially disorienting perspective, though not necessarily a conservative one. For Eugenio Montale, the donning of Petrarchan garb proves
a means of evading censorship in the last days of Italian fascism. More
generally, easily visible differences in meter and rhyme are accompanied
by aural and semantic choices, as well as decisions on which sonnets to
translate, that collectively produce a variety of different, even opposing,
effects—for instance, the conflict between a romantic and a satirical view
of the sonnets and of the function of lyric more generally (de Scarpis,
Steenson, and Trissino).

The Dutch, Portuguese, French, and Italian versions just discussed all
suggest the challenges of translating the sonnets into languages that, from
a global perspective, are extremely close to English. Furthermore, they
share the Classical and, later, Western European heritage of poetry, as well
as a legacy of cross-fertilization. What happens when we move farther
from English—to Hungarian, Turkish, Bangla (the language of Bengali
culture), Malayalam, Japanese, and Chinese—only one of which (Bangla)
even belongs, with English, to the family of Indo-European languages?
In principle, the problems are similar, though in practice they are often
more acute. It will be convenient to organize the discussion around the
interplay between formal choices and social effects.

We can begin with what will prove a negative example. As an agglu-
tinating language, Hungarian cannot reproduce Shakespeare's monosyllabic effects, can only with difficulty be stuffed into a ten-syllable line, and,
more surprisingly, does not easily lend itself to appropriate rhymes—the
opposite of what we find in the polysyllabic languages of Western Europe.
Moreover, though the language has iambic tendencies, prosody turns not
on stress but on syllable length, as in Classical Greek and Latin, though
in this case on the alternation of long and short syllables. The problem
is exacerbated by a normative and often impossible commitment to strict
fidelity in Hungarian translation of the sonnets with respect to prosody,
metaphor, and content. The trade-off is evident in Lőrinc Szabó's postwar
re-translations of his earlier, interwar efforts—in a shift of emphasis in the
rendering of the opening quatrain of Sonnet 12, for instance, from the
poetic to the semantic. In the interim, Szabó seems to have been pro-
Nazi, though it is not clear to me that allegiance can be detected in either
version. It is otherwise with Anna Szabó T., where politics—in this case

a female perspective—is playfully prominent. Sonnet 135 begins, "Who-ever hath her wish, thou hast thy Will,/ And Will to boot,"[15] while her poem, back-translated into English, opens: "What does a woman want? She wants confessions,/ and wants lust" (Szele, **102**).

In Halman's Turkish translations, the recourse to syllabics plays a different role. Here, it represents a recovery of a dormant prosodic form—in the event with some success, given its subsequent resurgence. The rationale for recourse to a poetic mode associated nationalistically with popular culture in the wake of the triumph of the Young Turks is the recognition that Shakespeare's poems also draw heavily on the ordinary language of his time. In other words, the translation provides insight into the original, where the monosyllabic character of the diction arguably undercuts both the nominally iambic movement of the line and, in its verbal fireworks, the ostensible directness of the plain style (Levi). In South Asia, by contrast, translations of the sonnets seem to lack any comparable edge (Refskou and Khair, **136**). It is a different matter in East Asia. In postwar Japan, Ken'ichi Yoshida's translations into collo-quial Japanese may be understood as a contribution to the forging of a democratic society, albeit with a misogynistic slant on the Dark Mistress sonnets. They were also effective enough as poetry to influence leading poets of the late twentieth and early twenty-first centuries (Oya). Finally, with the establishment of the People's Republic of China (PRC) in 1949, Liang Shiqiu—previously attacked from the left for his anti-utilitarian, humanist view of literature—joins the Kuomintang emigration to Taiwan and the relocation of its seat of government there. Rather than pursuing the elitist strategy the above charges might imply, Liang breaks with the standard practice of deploying Classical Chinese for the translation of earlier literature, instead rendering the sonnets in modern vernacular Mandarin. But by retaining traditional characters, perhaps he implicitly distances himself from the age of the Red Terror under Mao on the Main-land, where simplified characters were gradually coming to prominence (Joubin). Does his occasional recourse to Taiwanese vocabulary also indi-cate an independence from the more limited White Terror under Chiang Kai-shek on Taiwan and from "the suppression of the local language and the native literary tradition" in his adopted home?[16]

---

[15] Shakespeare (2015) 2296: Sonnet 135, ll. 1–2.

[16] Yeh (2001) 458–60, quoted passage 460.

5

In many—perhaps most—of these cases, then, translations of the sonnets represent an effort to inflect the native poetic practice, to promote an ideological orientation, or both. That is, they are performances. This claim will seem self-evident when extended to the essays explicitly dedicated to performance and almost as much so when it comes to those grouped under "Global Issues in the Sonnets" in the Table of Contents. What has already been said about these chapters, under the rubric of globalism, need not be repeated here. Beyond that, four of the pieces concern dramatic performance—two in the theater, one in film, and one in elder care facilities. We might surmise that Shakespeare's other reputation as a playwright might have influenced some of these decisions. In the performances in Finnish elder care facilities, love and loss understandably take precedence as part of a therapeutic project (Keinänen and Lehtonen). Otherwise, gender and sexuality—aggressive sexuality (Minier), feminist critique (Krajník and Drozd; cf. Szabó T. above), and homosexuality (Krajník and Drozd, Ellis)—routinely come to the fore. Many of the articles on translation discuss the discomfort often provoked by the sonnets' unconventional, only rarely moralized sexuality. But of course these issues acquire far greater prominence when they take center stage.

Musical performance raises its own concerns—concerns, however, that overlap with both translation and dramatic adaptation. Just as prominent poets and a prominent filmmaker (Jarman) have engaged with the sonnets, so, too, have major composers tried their hand—Dmitry Shostakovich, Dmitry Kabalevsky, Stravinsky (Pfister, **258–259**; Weiss). Here, as well, we see both elite (Pfister, Weiss) and popular appropriations (Weiss, Ingham, Schober). And as in translation, formal problems loom large, albeit not the same ones. The sonnet's three quatrains can be interpreted as strophes, but the concluding couplet is harder to assimilate into any standard musical form. In Russian music, a semantically oriented solution, in which the music follows the ideas, is available in classical arrangements. But with popular appropriation, different strategies come to the fore. In the absence of an authoritative paradigm, one finds little or no structural standardization (Weiss). The other essays on the sonnets in popular music extend that perception, including via the interesting suggestion that, in today's musical landscape, the sonnets' "natural" home might be in rap (Ingham, **314**). Finally, as we have seen, the two pedagogical essays evaluate the utility of the sonnets in English-language instruction (Laghi, Schober). Both critics see in them a vehicle for students not only to develop analytical skills but also to reflect on their romantic aspirations as well as on constraining social stereotypes.

6

In the interest of synthesis, the forgoing account has deliberately ridden roughshod over disagreements among the various contributors—disagreements that often have a long history in sonnet studies. The same strategy will inform a final line of inquiry. This collection demonstrates not only the global reach of the sonnets but also the variety of cultural and social functions they may have. What, if anything, does this have to do with the question of Shakespearean universality? The issue has vexed criticism and performance on such grounds as race, gender and sexuality, language, and colonialism for at least fifty years, and really much longer. I think there is only one answer, and it will not be a popular one. Insofar as universality is taken to mean a granite-like unchanging view of Shakespeare, one that in addition places his works beyond reproach, then of course the prevailing concerns of recent generations and the discussions in each of the essays in this volume chip away at that image. But, to change metaphors, this is clearly a straw man. Shakespeare has been open to question from the start—by Ben Jonson for his lack of revision, Thomas Rymer on *Othello*, Nahum Tate in his rewriting of *King Lear*, Leo Tolstoy in his broad denunciation, and many others. Irreverent appropriations can be found in Henry Fielding, Laurence Sterne, and Mark Twain. *Othello* is appropriated to very different ends by Richard Wright and Tahib Salih, *The Tempest* by Aimé Césaire and Gloria Naylor.

But what all these "takes" on Shakespeare have in common with the present volume—including this Afterword—is that they reinforce Shakespeare's iconic status. It could not be otherwise. A hermeneutics of suspicion, even outright denunciation, only serves to remind us that Shakespeare is the touchstone. The sole means of decentering Shakespeare is through silence. That silence can be achieved in at least two ways. The first is through censorship (Kingsley-Smith, **19**), but this strategy, however effective at first, tends to be transitory. The second and more durable method is neglect. Some of Classical Latin and most of Classical Greek went into hibernation in the Western European Middle Ages. They of course returned to positions of remarkable prestige beginning in the

Renaissance and continuing through the nineteenth century. Since then, they have been in more-or-less continual decline—not, however, because of ideological opposition, as was the case with the medieval Church, but because they no longer seem to matter to many people. The positions of, say, Homer and Virgil today are noticeably shakier than they were when I entered college fifty-five years ago—among undergraduates, doctoral students, and faculty alike.

What about Shakespeare? It is safe to say that someday he will go the way of all flesh. But when? And has that process begun? Whatever the merits of Shakespeare himself, his international reputation coincides with the emergence of the U.K. as first a European and then a global power, beginning in the eighteenth century. It has been enhanced in the last seventy-five years by the U.S.'s inheritance (really, forcible wresting) of global dominance from the British Empire. And especially since the collapse of Communism as an economic and ideological force a little over a generation ago, it has benefited from the worldwide spread of English, for which there is no historical analogue. That spread is not only an effect of geopolitical, economic, technological, and military power; it is now also a cause and a quasi-independent variable—continuing its upward (or outward) trajectory even as the collective power of Anglophone nations begins, however modestly, to decline. As already suggested, the advance of English is unlikely to last forever. The history of the rise and fall of transregional languages tells us as much.[17] But it does not tell us when the reversal of fortune will begin, how long it will take, or what the end result will be. Insofar as Shakespeare's reputation is tied to the prestige and reach of English, as it surely is in part, it, too, will enter a period of relative diminution.

Has this process begun? Not in geopolitical terms. But if we look closer to home, we may see early signs. In violation of the global aspirations of this collection, my comments here will be limited to the U.S.—for reasons of competence and in the hope that these remarks will encourage comparable reflections on other countries and languages. In performance, both on stage and screen, Shakespeare's position remains secure, though the relative weight of Shakespearean production has obviously decreased in the age of streaming. If we look to our own line of work, we see (even) more of the same. Laments about the decline of the humanities in general

---

[17] Ostler (2010), esp. 267–286.

and of literature in particular are now centuries old. In higher education, however, the actual standing of these fields in the first six postwar decades remained pretty stable, with the exception of a dramatic, if temporary, upward blip in the 1960s. Since the financial crisis of 2008, however, the movement has been almost entirely downhill, whether we look at undergraduate enrollment, faculty openings, or publication. The decline may stop, but there is no reason to expect a recovery.

In this respect, Shakespeare's prominence has begun to wane, and the extent of that movement will become increasingly pronounced over the next two generations as it comes to characterize all age groups. In addition, literary study has witnessed a shift away from historical consciousness toward a relatively unconceptualized emphasis on the present—in this respect mimicking the antihistorical sensibility of American culture more generally. Further, the long-term shift from poetry to prose has worked in a limited way against Shakespeare's plays and to a greater extent against his sonnets. Nonetheless, Shakespeare has been more resistant to this trend than any other writer of his time or earlier, perhaps than any other author who died before the present century. To some extent, he has come to stand in for the old days, for the canon itself, so much so that his continued prominence has disguised the far-more-rapid eclipse of most, perhaps all, earlier writers.[18] In other words, while his relative importance as a representative of the literary past has increased, his relative importance as a representative of literature in general has diminished. In

---

[18] This conclusion is based on Google Ngram name-frequency graphs for roughly 20 well-known English-language writers, from Chaucer to Nabokov, between 1945 and 2008, drawing primarily on American publication. Many of these writers increased in frequency relative to Shakespeare in the early postwar decades, as U.S. academic institutions expanded rapidly. In the last generation, however, this trend has been reversed: nearly all these authors have shown a relative decline compared to Shakespeare. In other words, even before the prolonged crisis initiated in 2008, there was already evidence that Shakespeare was likely to be the last man, indeed the last person, standing. Similarly, the tendency for Shakespeare's relative prominence to mask the waning interest in earlier writers more generally can be gleaned from a 2007 attack by the conservative American Council of Trustees and Alumni on American English Departments for generally abandoning the Shakespeare requirement for English majors. The reply from the English Departments correctly pointed out that nearly all majors took a Shakespeare course anyway—to partly fulfill the requirement to take courses from earlier periods. In other words, the iconic status of Shakespeare encouraged both sides to ignore what was actually going on. See Google Books Ngram Viewer.

addition, the commitment to literary instruction of any kind has dramatically fallen off in English Departments, partly owing to expansion into the broader range of cultural studies, but mainly to the ever-increasing role of English composition in the curriculum, above all at community colleges. In themselves, these developments are neither good nor bad. They just are.

I have therefore emphasized recent developments not to warn of the coming cultural apocalypse but to suggest something close to the opposite—a modest reorientation in how we understand the appropriation of Shakespeare in general and of his sonnets in particular. Rather than worrying about how to get out from under the dead weight of an ideologically oppressive literary heritage, we should instead ask what an easily discardable tradition might have to offer us. We should ask what, if anything, is worth saving and turning to our own uses. Any fairminded reader of the twenty-one essays collected here, beginning with the two introductions by the editors, will come away with a sense of expanded possibilities, with a sense that "there are more things" you can do with Shakespeare's sonnets "than are dreamt of in your philosophy" of the English lyric.[19]

Acknowledgements I thank Asa Zhang, English Department, University of Michigan, for help with this essay. She is, of course, not responsible for any of the statements made in it.

References

Austin, J. L. 1962. *How To Do Things with Words*. Oxford: Clarendon Press.
Booth, Stephen. 1969. *An Essay on Shakespeare's Sonnets*. New Haven, CT: Yale University Press.
Camões, Luís de. 1980. *Lírica completa*. Ed. Maria de Lurdes Saraiva. 3 vols. Lisbon: Imprensa Naconal-Casa da moeda.
Camões, Luís de. 2008. *The Collected Lyric Poems of Luís de Camões*. Trans. Landeg White. Princeton, NJ: Princeton University Press.
Cohen, Walter. 2017. *A History of European Literature: The West and the World from Antiquity to the Present*. Oxford: Oxford University Press.

[19] Shakespeare (2015) 1784: *Hamlet* 1.5.168–169. As the reference to "philosophy" might imply, the "more things" include implications for translation theory—a topic, however, not pursued here.

Fineman, Joel. 1986. *Shakespeare's Perjured Eye*. Berkeley: University of California Press.

Gooch, Bryan N. S., and David Thatcher, eds. 1991. *A Shakespeare Music Catalogue*. 5 vols. Oxford: Clarendon Press. Vol. 3: *The Catalogue of Music: "The Tempest-The Two Noble Kinsmen, The Sonnets, The Poems, Commemorative Pieces, Anthologies*.

Google Books Ngram Viewer. https://books.google.com/ngrams.

Hugo, François-Victor, trans. 1865. *Oeuvres completes de W. Shakespeare*. 1859–1866. Vol. 15: *Sonnets—Poëmes—Testament*. Paris: Pagnerre, Libraire Éditeur.

Kingsley-Smith, Jane. 2019. *The Afterlife of Shakespeare's Sonnets*. Cambridge: Cambridge University Press.

Kooij, Jan G. 1990. "Dutch." *The World's Major Languages*. Ed. Bernard Comrie. New York: Oxford University Press. 139–156.

Ostler, Nicholas. 2010. *The Last Lingua Franca: English Until the Return of Babel*. New York: Walker and Co.

Owen, Stephen. 2003. "Stepping Forward and Back: Issues and Possibilities for "World" Poetry." *Modern Philology* 100: 532–548.

Parker, Geoffrey. 2014. *Global Crisis: War, Climate Change and Catastrophe in the Seventeenth Century*. New Haven, CT: Yale University Press.

Pfister, Manfred, and Jürgen Gutsch, eds. 2009; 2014.*William Shakespeare's Sonnets for the First Time Globally Reprinted: A Quatercentenary Anthology*. 2 vols. Dozwil TG, Switzerland: SIGNAThur. [SIGNAThur can't be divided as it currently appears. The correct possibilities are: SIG-NAThur or SIGNAThur.]

Shakespeare, William. 1940. *The Sonnets*. Pt. 2. *A New Variorum Edition of Shakespeare*. Ed. Joseph Quincy Adams. New York: Modern Language Association of America.

Shakespeare, William. 2015. *The Norton Shakespeare*. 3rd ed. New York: Norton.

Vendler, Helen. 1997. *The Art of Shakespeare's Sonnets*. Cambridge, MA: The Belknap Press of Harvard University Press.

Vondel, Joost van. 1870. *De Complete Werken*. Vol. 1. Foreword H. J. Allard. 'sHertogenbosch, H. Bogaerts.

White, Landeg. 2008. Introduction. *Collected Lyric Poems of Luís de Camões*. By Camões. 1–21.

Williams, Raymond. 1973. *Marxism and Literature*. Oxford: Oxford University Press.

Yeh, Michelle. 2001. "Modern Poetry." *The Columbia history of Chinese Literature*. Ed. Victor H. Mair. New York: Columbia University Press.

INDEX

© The Editor(s) (if applicable) and The Author(s), under exclusive
license to Springer Nature Switzerland AG 2023
J. Kingsley-Smith and W. R. Rampone Jr. (eds.), *Shakespeare's Global Sonnets*,
Global Shakespeares, https://doi.org/10.1007/978-3-031-09472-9

399

Printed in the USA
CPSIA information can be obtained
at www.ICGtesting.com
LVHW011642161123
764105LV00006B/382

9 783031 094712